D0797056

THE ZONDERVAN 2012 PASTOR'S ANNUAL

An Idea & Resource Book

T. T. CRABTREE

ZONDERVAN®

ZONDERVAN.com/
AUTHORTRACKER
follow your favorite authors

We want to hear from you. Please send your comments about this book to us in care of zreview@zondervan.com. Thank you.

ZONDERVAN

The Zondervan 2012 Pastor's Annual
Copyright © 1991, 2011 by Zondervan

Requests for information should be addressed to:
Zondervan, *Grand Rapids, Michigan 49530*

Much of the contents of this book was previously published in *Pastor's Annual 1992.*

ISBN 978-0-310-27591-6

All Scripture quotations, unless otherwise noted, are taken from the King James Version of the Bible.

Scripture quotations marked NIV are from The Holy Bible, *New International Version*®, *NIV*®. Copyright © 1973, 1978, 1984 by Biblica, Inc.™ Used by permission of Zondervan. All rights reserved worldwide.

Scripture quotations marked PHILLIPS are taken from *The New Testament in Modern English*, revised edition – J. B. Phillips, translator. Copyright © 1958, 1960, 1972 by J. B. Phillips. Used by permission of Macmillan Publishing Co., Inc.

Scripture quotations marked RSV are taken from the *Revised Standard Version of the Bible*, copyright © 1946, 1952, 1971 by the Division of Christian Education of the National Council of Churches of Christ in the USA. Used by permission.

Scripture quotations marked NEB are taken from *The New English Bible, New Testament*, copyright © 1961 by the Delegates of the Oxford University Press and the Syndics of the Cambridge University Press.

Scripture quotations marked AMP are taken from *The Amplified*® *Bible*, © 1954, 1958, 1962, 1964, 1965, 1987 by The Lockman Foundation. Used by permission.

Any Internet addresses (websites, blogs, etc.) and telephone numbers in this book are offered as a resource. They are not intended in any way to be or imply an endorsement by Zondervan, nor does Zondervan vouch for the content of these sites and numbers for the life of this book.

All rights reserved. The original purchaser of this product shall have the right to make one print-form copy here of, provided such copies are not resold or distributed to the general public. Otherwise, no part of this publication may be reproduced, stored in a retrieval system, or transmitted in any form or by any means—electronic, mechanical, photocopy, recording, or any other—except for brief quotations in printed reviews, without the prior permission of the publisher.

Printed in the United States of America

11 12 13 14 15 16 /DCI/ 27 26 25 24 23 22 21 20 19 18 17 16 15 14 13 12 11 10 9 8 7 6 5 4 3 2 1

CONTENTS

MISCELLANEOUS HELPS

Contributing Authors

H. C. Chiles	Wed.:	November 7, 14, 28
		December 5, 12
R. D. Culbreth	A.M.:	June 10
		September 9, 16, 23, 30
J. Ray Dobbins	P.M.:	December 9, 16, 23, 30
T. Hollis Epton	A.M.:	March 18
		April 15, 22
		May 6
	P.M.:	October 7, 14, 21, 28
		Funeral Meditations
William T. Flynt	P.M.:	May 6, 20, 27
		June 3, 10, 17, 24
James G. Harris	A.M.:	November 4
	P.M.:	November 11, 18, 25
		December 2
David G. Hause	A.M.:	February 5
		March 25
		April 1, 8
		September 2
R. Furman Kenney	A.M.:	December 9, 16, 23, 30
Howard S. Kolb	A.M.:	July 1, 8, 15, 22, 29
		August 5, 12, 19, 26
Leroy Koopman	Wed.:	November 21
Jerold R. McBride	Wed.:	January 4, 11, 18, 25
		February 1, 8, 15, 22, 29
Richard T. Moody	A.M.:	April 29
		October 7, 14, 21, 28
Roy D. Moody	Wed.:	March 7, 14, 21, 28
		April 4
R. Trevis Otey	P.M.:	September 2, 9, 16, 23, 30
Chester Smith	P.M.:	July 1, 8, 15, 22, 29
		August 5, 12, 19, 26
Bob W. Wood	P.M.:	January 1, 8, 15, 22, 29
		February 5, 12, 19, 26
		March 4, 11, 18, 25
		April 1, 8, 15, 22, 29
		Messages for Children and Young People

PREFACE

Favorable comments from ministers who serve in many different types of churches have encouraged me to believe that the *Pastor's Annual* provides valuable assistance to many busy pastors as they seek to improve the quality, freshness, and variety of their pulpit ministry. To be of service to fellow pastors in their continuing quest to obey our Lord's command to Peter, "Feed my sheep," is a privilege to which I respond with gratitude.

I pray that this issue of the *Pastor's Annual* can be blessed by our Lord in helping pastors to plan and produce a preaching program that will better meet the spiritual needs of the congregation to which they are called to minister.

This issue contains sermons by sixteen contributing authors who have been effective contemporary preachers and successful pastors. Each of these authors is listed with his sermons in Contributing Authors. I accept responsibility for those not listed there.

This issue of the *Pastor's Annual* is dedicated to the Lord with a prayer that he will bless these efforts to let the Holy Spirit lead us in preparing "A Planned Preaching Program for the Year."

JANUARY

▪ Sunday Mornings

John's primary purpose as he wrote the fourth gospel was to select events, actions, and the words of Jesus that would be most convincing in helping people to come to believe that Jesus was indeed the Christ, the Son of the living God (John 20:30–31). John was eager for people to experience abundant life through faith in Christ. "Finding the Abundant Life through Faith in Christ" is the theme for a series of messages based on passages from the gospel of John.

▪ Sunday Evenings

These are times that test our souls, when the very foundations of society are being threatened and our faith in Christ is being attacked. The inspired messages in the book of Hebrews can strengthen us and communicate to us the spiritual insight that we need for confident and courageous Christian living in the present. The book of Hebrews contains a message concerning "the supremacy of Christ" that is needed if we are to face the present and the future with the confidence and courage that we need for victorious Christian living during these critical times.

▪ Wednesday Evenings

The letter of James spoke to the problems that confronted the disciples of our Lord early in the first century of the Christian era. While circumstances may change, human needs do not change. Basically our problems today are the same as they were then. A series of expository messages based on the letter of James is suggested. The theme is "Personal Problems and the Practice of Pure Religion."

SUNDAY MORNING, JANUARY 1

Title: A Controlling Motive for the New Year

Text: "And many other signs truly did Jesus in the presence of his disciples, which are not written in this book: But these are written, that ye might believe that Jesus is the Christ, the Son of God; and that believing ye might have life through his name" (**John 20:30–31**).

Scripture Reading: John 1:35–50

Hymns: "God, Our Father, We Adore Thee," Frazer

"He Leadeth Me," Gilmore

"I Will Sing the Wondrous Story," Rowley

Offertory Prayer: Holy Father, we come to you on this first Lord's Day of the new year thankful that we are inclined to worship you and to seek your will in all of our ways. We come praying for your help that we might give ourselves completely to you as we walk through this year. Today we bring tithes and offerings as symbols of our desire to commit ourselves to you. Bless both the gifts and the dedication of our hearts to your honor and glory and to the proclamation of the good news of your love both in this community and to the ends of the earth. In Jesus' name we pray. Amen.

Introduction

The apostle John, writer of the fourth gospel, leaves his readers with no question concerning his motive for writing the gospel that bears his name. He sought to convince his readers that Jesus Christ is the Son of God. When a writer of Scripture specifically states his purpose, we must pay attention so that we can understand his primary and controlling objective.

John encouraged his readers to do something more than just give intellectual consent to the truth that Jesus Christ is uniquely the Son of God. He sought to persuade them to make Jesus Christ the Lord of their lives. John was vitally concerned that those who read his gospel come to experience life in its finest form and its richest quality.

Some say that the law of self-preservation is the first law of nature. John appeals to this motive in his presentation of the gospel. He affirms that God the Father is vitally interested in our eternal preservation (3:16). He affirms that Christ the Son came and gave his life that we might experience abundant life in the here and now (10:10). John desired that all people would come to experience abundant life through faith in Jesus Christ.

In John's statement of purpose, he affirms his use of the privilege of selectivity concerning the contents of his gospel. He did not tell the whole story that could have been told concerning the life, work, and teachings of the Lord. He omitted many things so that he might emphasize his controlling motive. He was eager to share the Good News so that people could come to know Jesus Christ as Lord and Savior. John, the beloved apostle, was an evangelist. As we face the new year, we should give serious consideration to letting John's controlling motive be the guiding principle for our lives as we walk through another year toward eternity.

John selected seven great signs, miracles, wonders, and illustrations under the guidance of the Holy Spirit to convince the minds and hearts of people that Jesus Christ is indeed the Son of God and worthy of all of the confidence they can place in him.

I. The turning of water into wine (John 2:1 – 11).

To understand the significance of this event, we need to get back into the historical situation. We find Christ, the Lord of life, attending a wedding in a simple home in Cana of Galilee.

    A. *Jesus prevented embarrassment to those who were not able to provide an abundance of wine for the crowd who came to the wedding.*

    B. *Jesus made possible increased joy on a festive and social occasion.*

    C. *Jesus demonstrated his unique power over nature.*

    D. *Jesus illustrated his availability, his ability, and his desire to make the last of life better than the first.*

Christ can make your life richer, fuller, and more joyful if you will trust him and obey him in love and gratitude.

II. The healing of the nobleman's son (John 4:46–54).

    A. *In this miracle Jesus revealed his power over disease.*

    B. *Jesus revealed his power over distance.* The nobleman's son was twenty miles away from where he and Jesus were having their conversation. Jesus said to the man, "Go thy way; thy son liveth."

    C. *This sign revealed Jesus' compassionate concern for people with heavy hearts.*

    D. *The nobleman and his household made a proper response to Jesus Christ.* He believed along with the rest of the members of his household. The nobleman now had a new Master.

III. The healing of the lame man (John 5:1–6).

    A. *Jesus healed a man who was helpless, lonely, and poor.*

    B. *The compassionate Savior genuinely cares for those who are helpless and worthless to others.*

    C. *This miracle took place on the Sabbath. By acting on the Sabbath, Jesus showed that the work of God is continuous and that it must not be limited by custom or tradition.*

    D. *Christ was also interested in the man's soul.* He was not content merely to render a medical ministry to the man. Jesus sought him out and encouraged him to forsake the way of sin (5:6–14).

IV. The feeding of the five thousand (John 6:1–14).

    A. *The compassionate Christ was concerned and continues to be concerned with those who suffer from physical hunger.*

    B. *With power Jesus was willing to meet the needs of those who suffered the pangs of hunger.*

    C. *Christ demonstrated his capacity and desire to use small things in a most significant manner to bless a great multitude.* He used this occasion of feeding people with bread to talk about the Bread of eternal life.

V. Walking on the sea (John 6:15–21).

    A. *The Creator Christ demonstrated his power over nature.*

    B. *The Creator Christ illustrated his power over the causes of human fear.* He said, "It is I; be not afraid" (v. 20).

C. *By coming to his disciples during the storm, Christ revealed his availability to aid the helpless and fearful in times of distress.*
   1. He sees us today and knows about our fears and our insecurity.
   2. He comes to us today walking across the sea of life to where we are.
   3. He comes to help us in our times of need.
   4. He saves us from the catastrophes we fear.

VI. The healing of the man born blind (John 9).

A. *Christ is the source of light and illumination concerning the mysteries of time and eternity.*
B. *Christ is the source of real life because he is the Son of God.* It is most interesting to note the progression in the man's understanding of Jesus. He knows Jesus simply as "a man" (v. 11), and then he speaks of him as "a prophet" (v. 17). He finally comes to believe in him as "the Son of God" (vv. 35–38).

VII. The raising of Lazarus (John 11:1–54).

A. *By this miracle we perceive the sincere sympathy of the Son of God for those who suffer grief and sorrow (vv. 17–35).*
B. *By this miracle Jesus revealed his lordship over life, death, and the grave (vv. 39–45).*

John the apostle was fully convinced that Jesus Christ had the power to resurrect. He can bring life to your heart and soul. He has the power to resurrect your family and to give you a new life and a new future.

Conclusion

We are not on the way to death. Instead, through Christ, we are on the way to eternal life, abundant life. Christ makes possible for us the life that grows and reproduces itself. During this year we must serve as those who do believe and live so as to persuade others to believe that Jesus Christ is indeed the Son of God who should also be the Lord of their lives.

SUNDAY EVENING, JANUARY 1

Title: Jesus: God's Last Word

Text: "God, who at sundry times and in divers manners spake in times past unto the fathers by the prophets, hath in these last days spoken unto us by his Son" (Heb. 1:1–2).

Scripture Reading: Hebrews 1:1–12

Introduction

The Bible is God's Word. Millions have had their lives changed by its message. Many attempts have been made to destroy the Bible, but all have failed. In AD 303 Diocletian, emperor of the Roman Empire, set out to destroy all of the

Bibles in the land together with the people who possessed them. He believed that Christians could not exist apart from the book they claimed as their rule of faith. Thousands of Christians were cruelly martyred in this bloody onslaught. Within a few years, Diocletian felt his drive had been so successful that he erected a column over a burned Bible and wrote on the column these words: *extincto nomine Christianorum* ("The name of Christian is extinguished"). Yet by AD 313, the new Roman emperor, Constantine, had declared himself a Christian and had adopted the symbol of the cross for the standards of his Roman army.

The Bible remains, not because of some magical power, but because of the risen Christ who stands behind it. He is the ultimate Word of God.

I. God's last word in communication (Heb. 1:1).

Ever since the garden of Eden, God has sought to communicate to people the message of life. The Bible is not only a record of God's communication, but is itself a part of God's communication. People can discover many things about the created universe, but only God can reveal to people the spiritual truths so necessary for life. In revealing himself to people, God had to take a barbaric, primitive people and lead them a step at a time, much like a father leads his child through the first faltering steps of walking. Sin had so blinded the minds of people that God could reveal only a small portion of truth at a time. God had to work slowly because people were slow to understand. The writer of Hebrews says it this way: "In the past God spoke to our forefathers through the prophets at many times and in various ways, but in these last days he has spoken to us by his Son, whom he appointed heir of all things, and through whom he made the universe" (1:1–2 NIV).

The Old Testament prophets were like people putting together a giant puzzle. Here and there God handed to them a piece of the picture. Each fragment was accurate but was only a part of the total picture.

The puzzle took final shape with the coming of Jesus Christ. Everything else remained in fragmentary form until Christ came to give unity to the picture and fullness to the prophecies. To look upon the Old Testament prophets is to look upon God's messengers, but to look upon Jesus is to look upon God in terms we can understand—God pictured in human terms. God began a communication to people thousands of years before he was to present his final communication—his last word—as Jesus Christ.

II. God's last word in salvation (Heb. 1:2–3).

Where salvation of the soul is concerned, Jesus Christ is God's last word. Prior to Jesus' coming, people experienced salvation through faith in God's promised Savior. Since Jesus' coming, people have experienced salvation through faith in the revealed Savior. Christ was truly God in the flesh! In "the radiance of God's glory" (v. 3 NIV), the word "radiance" depicts a beam of glorious light descending from the heavenly Father upon the earthly Christ in such a way that the same glory shines out from both. John also used the idea of light to speak of Christ: "The light shines in the darkness" (John 1:5 NIV).

Jesus Christ is divine, and for a brief moment during his earthly life, on the Mount of Transfiguration, the divine radiance shown through. The writer of Hebrews further describes Christ's divinity: "The Son is the ... exact representation of [God's] being" (1:3 NIV). This scriptural image denotes the imprint of a king's seal left when applied to warm wax. The image left on the wax is an exact reproduction of the royal seal. The writer of Hebrews is saying that Jesus Christ is the exact reproduction of God's essence—God's being.

Finally, Christ is pictured as being the Redeemer: "After he had provided purification for sins, he sat down at the right hand of the Majesty in heaven" (Heb. 1:3 NIV). Christ personally effected the removal of our guilt. He provided cleansing for our sins. Here the idea of his high priesthood is introduced. People need no other high priest, for Christ has provided the cleansing for sins. No one else can remove the stain of guilt from the souls of people. Christ is God's last word on what people can do about sin. Simon Peter realized this truth as he answered Jesus' question as to whether the disciples would also leave him: "Lord, to whom shall we go? You have the words of eternal life" (John 6:68 NIV).

III. God's last word in exaltation (Heb. 1:3).

When Jesus came in the flesh, the Jewish people were anticipating a conquering Messiah who would dispose of their Roman captors. Jesus tried to make clear to his disciples that his kingdom was not an earthly kingdom (John 18:36). Yet there would be a final triumph—a final exaltation—and again Jesus would be God's last word in it. The final exaltation will come when "the Lord himself shall descend from heaven with a shout" (1 Thess. 4:16).

The apostle Paul reminded the Philippians: "Wherefore God also hath highly exalted him, and given him a name which is above every name: That at the name of Jesus every knee should bow, of things in heaven, and things in earth, and things under the earth; and that every tongue should confess that Jesus Christ is Lord, to the glory of God the Father" (Phil. 2:9–11). Of course Christ was exalted following his resurrection when he "sat down at the right hand of the Majesty in heaven" (Heb. 1:3 NIV), but this final exaltation will not be fully manifested until his return.

The writer of Hebrews puts it like this: "In the beginning, O Lord, you laid the foundations of the earth, and the heavens are the work of your hands. They will perish, but you remain; they will all wear out like a garment. You will roll them up like a robe; like a garment they will be changed. But you remain the same, and your years will never end" (Heb. 1:10–12 NIV).

Heaven and earth, as we know them, will grow old. Christ will roll them up as one rolls up an old garment and lays it aside to be worn no more. Heaven and earth, as we know them, will be exchanged for new heavens and a new earth (Rev. 21:1). Scientists have set forth what is called the "second law of thermodynamics," the belief that the universe is gradually losing heat and is thus slowly running down. The Bible says it more poetically by describing the universe as an old garment that gradually is becoming worn out. In the face of such prospects,

God promises a final exaltation: "The kingdoms of this world are become the kingdoms of our Lord, and of his Christ; and he shall reign for ever and ever" (Rev. 11:15).

Conclusion

The prophets were great men, but they were only spokesmen for God. The Bible speaks of angelic beings, but they are only messengers of God to do his bidding. Only Jesus Christ is the Son of God.

James I of Scotland often traveled about his kingdom in disguise in order to acquaint himself with the real needs of his people. He disguised himself as a farmer and went under the name of "The Good Man of Ballengiech." Over the years, he developed close friendships with humble people who never dreamed that he was the king. During one of his disguised travels, the king was befriended by a poor countryman who risked his own life to become the king's friend. Later the same countryman was summoned to Stirling Castle where the king kept midwinter court. Naturally the poor fellow was horrified, because in those days to be summoned to the king's court usually was to be condemned for some crime. Little did the poor fellow know that the king before whom he was to appear was one and the same with "The Good Man of Ballengiech." Imagine the surprise on the face of the poor countryman when he looked up into the eyes of the one sitting on the throne fearing that he would hear a condemnation of death and seeing for the first time that the king was in reality an old friend. The summons to the king's court was not for condemnation but for reward (James Hastings, ed., "The Epistle to the Hebrews," in *The Speaker's Bible* [Grand Rapids: Baker, 1961], 13).

Jesus comes to us in much the same manner. He came among us as one of us to become both our Friend and Lord. He came as God's last word to us. The salvation that he offers is never obsolete or irrelevant. In these last times, God is speaking to us through his Son. We will do well to listen and to follow.

WEDNESDAY EVENING, JANUARY 4

Title: The Problem of Temptation

Text: "My brethren, count it all joy when ye fall into divers temptations; knowing this, that the trying of your faith worketh patience" (**James 1:2–3**).

Scripture Reading: James 1:2–18

Introduction

Most new Christians are shocked that temptations continue to come their way after their conversion experience. Many older and more mature Christians respond in utter disbelief when they fall into some sin to which they thought they were immune. To each of us comes that moment when we must face the fact that no one is beyond the influence of temptation. Once this truth is realized, we are in a position to understand temptation more clearly and to conquer it more effectively.

I. Proper attitude toward temptation.

"When all kinds of trials and temptations crowd into your lives, my brothers, don't resent them as intruders, but welcome them as friends" (James 1:2 PHILLIPS).

The proper attitude toward temptation is not defeatism; it is not an assumption that you are more sinful than others; rather, it is a realization that temptation is an opportunity for you to demonstrate what being a Christian really means.

II. Purpose of temptation (James 1:3–4, 12).

Five purposes of temptation are offered in these verses. The first is to test and strengthen your faith ("the trying of your faith," v. 3). Temptation is to the Christian what a football game is to the trained athlete—an opportunity to prove his ability (through Christ) to win. The second purpose is to increase your endurance ("patience," v. 3). The third purpose is to mature you ("perfect work," v. 4). The fourth is to develop independence ("wanting nothing," v. 4). Properly handled, temptation will lessen your dependence on others for moral encouragement. The fifth purpose is to bring rewards (v. 12). The rewards are happiness ("blessed") and real life ("the crown of life," v. 12).

III. Prayer during temptation (James 1:5–8).

The prayer for knowledge to handle our problems (v. 5) must be offered in absolute faith if we expect to receive anything from the Lord (vv. 6–7).

IV. Perspective that lessens temptation (James 1:9–11).

These verses call attention to a great help in conquering temptation—a proper perspective (sense of values) of the outward and inward, an awareness of the real values in life.

V. Person responsible for your temptation (James 1:13–18).

God is not the person responsible for your temptation (v. 13). Rather, he is the one responsible for all the good that comes your way (v. 17). We are inclined to lay the blame for crime on everyone except the criminal and sin on everyone except the sinner. The Bible refuses to do this.

You are the person responsible for your temptation (vv. 14–15). True, you cannot keep birds from flying over your head, but you can keep them from building nests in your hair.

Because of your own inward desires, you are responsible ("he is drawn away of his own lust," v. 14). Lust, which is the pull of your lower nature, begins as a fine thread of a spider's web and, if unchecked, becomes as strong as an iron chain.

Because you alone can put the sequence of sin into operation, you are responsible (v. 15). The sequence is thought, deed, penalty or lust, sin, death.

Because you alone can choose your moral pattern, you are responsible. You may choose to live by the standards set forth in God's Word, or you may choose to live by situation ethics.

Conclusion

The Ten Commandments have not been repealed. Although you may change your standards of morality, you cannot change the results of immorality, for "sin, when it is finished, bringeth forth death" (James 1:15).

SUNDAY MORNING, JANUARY 8

Title: The God Who Became Flesh

Text: "The Word became flesh and made his dwelling among us. We have seen his glory, the glory of the One and Only, who came from the Father, full of grace and truth" (**John 1:14 NIV**).

Scripture Reading: John 1:1–18

Hymns: "O Worship the King," Grand

"The Light of the World Is Jesus," Bliss

"My Redeemer," Bliss

Offertory Prayer: Holy heavenly Father, we come to give you the adoration of our hearts, the praise of our lips, and the gifts of our hands. Accept our tithes and offerings as an expression of our gratitude and as an indication of our recognition of your ownership and our trusteeship of all that we are and of all that we possess. Bless the use of these gifts toward the coming of your kingdom on the earth. We pray in Jesus' name. Amen.

Introduction

John, the beloved apostle, writer of the fourth gospel, was eager to convince and to persuade the people to believe fully that Jesus Christ was none other than the unique Son of God. He was persuaded that through faith in Jesus Christ, the "God-man," people could experience life in its richest quality.

John worshiped no insignificant Savior. He followed no weakling for a Lord. He was overwhelmed with amazement before the wonder and glory of his Lord.

Scholars believe John wrote his gospel in the great Greek city of Ephesus. He, like modern man, was faced with the problems of communication as he sought to proclaim and to publish the good news of God as he had discovered it in Jesus Christ. In attempting to communicate with his Gentile readers, he was led to use a concept that had both a Jewish and a Greek meaning. The Greeks used the word *logos*, translated "word," when they referred to the principle behind the universe and to the forces that exercised rational control over nature and the universe. *Logos* referred to "the order, the reason, the wisdom" that gave harmony to the universe. This word had been used by those who translated the Old Testament into Greek. John applied this term to Jesus Christ, declaring him to be the Word of God who came to reveal the truth of God.

I. Christ the Word clothed himself in human flesh (John 1:14).

In the first verses of his gospel, John declares that Christ, who is the Word, is eternal and is equal to God. John also says that Christ the Word was active in Creation, being the creative agent by whom all things came into being. Paul declares the same thought when writing to the Colossians (1:16–17).

John tells us that the Word of God clothed himself in human flesh and pitched his tent among people as God clothed in human flesh.

A. *The Word was made flesh in order that people might see God in a way that he had never been perceived before (John 1:18).*

B. *The Word was made flesh that he might destroy the devil (Heb. 2:14).*

C. *The Word was made flesh to deliver us from the fear of death (Heb. 2:15).*

D. *The Word was made flesh that we might have a compassionate and faithful High Priest (Heb. 2:17).*

II. Christ the Word came unto his own (John 1:11).

The Creator had come to visit his own creation.

A. *He came to his own home.*

B. *He came to his own town.*

C. *He came to his own community.*

D. *He came to his own creation. Some people rejected Jesus—some because they loved darkness and others because they did not understand.*

Some received Jesus as Savior and Lord, Teacher and Friend. Because they accepted him, we have been given the opportunity to accept him.

III. Christ the Word came to reveal the Father (John 1:18).

John had been present with two other apostles on the Mount of Transfiguration when Jesus had been transformed before them while in prayer. For a moment, his deity shined forth through the veil of human flesh, and the three apostles fell on their faces in fear and wonder. They were amazed by this manifestation of the glory of God on the face of their Lord and leader. John declares, "We beheld his glory, the glory as of the only begotten of the Father" (1:14).

A. *"He that hath seen me hath seen the Father."* On one occasion, Philip said, "Lord, show us the Father and that will be enough for us" (John 14:8 NIV). Jesus replied, "Anyone who has seen me has seen the Father" (v. 9 NIV). He wanted Philip to understand the relationship between himself and the Father (vv. 10–11).

B. *"I and my Father are one" (10:30).* When Jesus explained his relationship to God the Father to his disciples in the parable of the Good Shepherd and his sheep, he identified himself as being one with the Father. John was declaring that what Jesus was, the Father always had been and always will be.

C. *Jesus Christ is God's Word to us.* Jesus Christ, in his life and teachings, is a divine utterance of God. He is the inward and outward expression of the mind and heart of our Father God.

Jesus Christ, the Word, is the eternal God with a human body and with a human voice seeking to communicate with the minds and hearts of people.

Conclusion

Do you really believe that Jesus Christ is the Son of God? If so, you can believe what he tells us about the Father.

We are willing to trust a doctor on the testimony of those who have been his patients. We are willing to trust attorneys on the testimony of their former clients. We find it essential to put confidence in strangers on the testimony of others.

Let us put faith and trust in Jesus Christ on the testimony of John the apostle. Through faith in him as the Son of God, we can experience abundant life and can find the life that God wants to bestow on each of us as the gift of his loving heart.

SUNDAY EVENING, JANUARY 8

Title: Jesus: God's Answer to Despair

Text: " '[God] put everything under his feet.' ... Yet at present we do not see everything subject to him. But we see Jesus, who was made a little lower than the angels, now crowned with glory and honor because he suffered death, so that by the grace of God he might taste death for everyone" **(Heb. 2:8–9).**

Scripture Reading: Hebrews 2:1–15

Introduction

Years ago I learned that there is only one way to plow a straight furrow. The secret is to pick out some object at the other end of the field and to keep your eyes glued to that object every moment. If a rabbit popped out of a nearby thicket, you could not turn to watch him dash away. If you approached a little gully washed in the field by the last downpour of rain, you observed it, slowed the speed of the tractor accordingly, and after crossing it resumed full speed; but you had to do all of this while keeping your eye on the object at the end of the field. To plow a straight furrow, you had to see only what could be seen while fixing your eye on the object that had become your guide.

The writer of Hebrews has something of this in mind when he warns us against drifting away from the words of Christ. We all have our daily pressures and problems, but as long as we can see Jesus in the same picture, we are all right. It is when we begin to omit him from the total picture that we begin to drift from him. It is in this perilous course of action that we often succumb to despair and discouragement.

We can never escape the frustration and despair all about us if we treat with negligence the salvation we have experienced in Christ: "Therefore we ought to give the more earnest heed to the things which we have heard, lest at any time we should let them slip" (Heb. 2:1). The writer of Hebrews makes a contrast between the word spoken by angels (referring to the law given at Sinai), which carries with it a punishment when transgressed, and the word that came from Jesus himself, the gospel. If one cannot bypass the law without being punished, then how do Christians suppose they can live victorious Christian lives while neglecting the salvation they have in Christ? "How shall we escape, if we neglect so great salvation?" (v. 3).

To understand what is being said, we might look upon salvation as we would a garden. To be what it is meant to be, a garden must be weeded, watered, and looked after. If the weeds take over, it remains a garden, but it does not bear the fruit intended. The salvation that we have in Christ is indeed the gift of God, but we are responsible for the importance we give to it and for the fruit that comes from it. You cannot neglect the salvation in Christ and at the same time experience victory in your daily life. If every day does not include the living Christ, then you are inviting despair, for daily victory is found only in walking with the living Lord. We face the strong currents of life by fastening our gaze on Christ and anchoring our soul to his promises. Jesus is God's answer to life's problems.

I. Jesus is God's answer to sin's apparent triumph (Heb. 2:8–9).

God created humankind in his own image for the purpose of fellowship, yet on every hand this fellowship has been broken by sin. Since the Garden of Eden, God has graciously been seeking out sinful people: "Adam, Where art thou?" God asks this question, not because he cannot find the Adams of this world, but because he hopes by so asking to awaken the Adams to see themselves. God's divine creative plan as set forth in Genesis was that humans should have dominion over the earth. Yet on every hand we observe humans being mastered by the earthy. Man was formed from the dust of the ground and immediately rushed off to enslave himself to that same dust. Humans have been willing to scheme, lie, and kill to gain possession of a small plot of dust. In so doing, they have fled the fellowship of God to become a part of Satan's rebellion. They have followed the pattern of the bugs that run from the light when a stone is lifted to reveal their hiding place. "And this is the condemnation, that light is come into the world, and men loved darkness rather than light, because their deeds were evil" (John 3:19).

God created humans slightly lower in power than the angels, destined for glory and honor, intended to be master of all God's earthly creation (Heb. 2:7–8). Yet all about us we see sin's triumph: "But now we see not yet all things put under [man]" (v. 8). On every hand are sights to remind us that humankind is not occupying the place intended by God. Sin's triumph is apparent all around us. Yet when we add Jesus to the picture, everything changes: "We see Jesus, who was made a little lower than the angels, now crowned with glory and honor because he suffered death" (v. 9 NIV). Amid history's scattered ruins stands the changeless Christ: "Jesus Christ is the same yesterday and today and forever" (13:8 NIV).

Thoughtless, careless people wreck their own lives by ignoring Christ. They blur their destiny by living against the laws of God. Yet God's answer remains that through Jesus Christ people can still experience the crowning glory for which they were created.

II. Jesus is God's answer to suffering (Heb. 2:10).

Few things challenge our faith more than the sea of suffering in which we live. Especially is this true when suffering invades our own private lives and claims members of our own family. There are times when we stand helplessly by and watch tragedy invade our surroundings like a snarling wolf in a flock of sheep. The temptation of our heart at such moments is to cry out, "Why did this have to happen to me?" A minister tells of one of his flock whose son had just been killed in the war, who demanded of the minister, "Where was God when my son was killed?" The minister's answer was: "Just where he was when his own Son was killed" (George Buttrick, *God, Pain, and Evil* [Nashville: Abingdon, 1966], 166–67). Sickness and death are real happenings for which there is no easy philosophical answer. Buttrick reminds us that God's answer to these real happenings is another real happening—the ministry of the incarnate Christ, culminating in his death, burial, and resurrection.

When we behold suffering on every hand, we need to remember: "For it became him, for whom are all things, in bringing many sons unto glory, to make the captain of their salvation perfect through sufferings" (v. 10). This verse tells us that it was fitting for God to use suffering as a means of effecting Christ's victory over sin—a victory he shares with us. Christ, as the Captain of our salvation, fulfilled his ministry of vicarious death by means of much suffering. Jesus himself said, "For even the Son of man came not to be ministered unto, but to minister, and to give his life a ransom for many" (Mark 10:45). The word translated "captain" has in it the idea of a pioneer—of one who blazes the way. Jesus, our Leader and Savior, reached ethical and spiritual fullness through the route of suffering: "Who in the days of his flesh, when he had offered up prayers and supplications with strong crying and tears unto him that was able to save him from death, and was heard in that he feared; though he were a Son, yet learned he obedience by the things which he suffered; and being made perfect, he became the author of eternal salvation unto all them that obey him" (Heb. 5:7–9).

III. Jesus is God's answer to death (Heb. 2:14–15).

God's answer to the phantom of death is indeed another death—the death of Jesus Christ: "Forasmuch then as the children are partakers of flesh and blood, he also himself likewise took part of the same; that through death he might destroy him that had the power of death, that is, the devil; and deliver them who through fear of death were all their lifetime subject to bondage" (vv. 14–15). Jesus came in the flesh, was crucified on the cross, and was raised from the grave so that he might triumph over Satan as well as death. The Bible tells us that death entered the world because man succumbed to the temptation of Satan and sin. Satan's last blow to man was death, which cut off man's last opportunity to find forgiveness in God. The coming of Christ made apparent God's offer of salvation and victory, which extends beyond this mortal life. Jesus came to remove the fear of death and to bring an inner peace to those who live in anxious dread of death. Death stalks us quietly and follows us everywhere we go.

Into such a world came Jesus Christ to drink the dreaded death potion for us: "That he by the grace of God should taste death for every man" (Heb. 2:9). As Jesus revealed salvation, he removed the sting from death: "O death, where is thy sting? O grave, where is thy victory? The sting of death is sin; and the strength of sin is the law. But thanks be to God, which giveth us the victory through our Lord Jesus Christ" (1 Cor. 15:55–57). We find ourselves doomed, like Socrates, to drink the poisoned hemlock, and in that moment Christ comes to us and drinks it for us.

Conclusion

Helen Bagby Harrison, in writing the life story of her parents, who were pioneer missionaries to Brazil, tells in tender tones of the death of her aged mother. Helen and her mother were preparing to board a plane that would take them to a long-awaited family reunion when they noticed that the young man who was to pilot the plane was an old friend. Mrs. Bagby remarked in relief, "My, but it's good to know the pilot." Shortly after takeoff, Mrs. Bagby clutched at her heart in mortal pain. The daughter asked the pilot to turn back and land. He immediately did so, and Helen Bagby Harrison recalled that "it was good to know the pilot"! At the funeral service of her mother, Helen Bagby Harrison told those who gathered of this experience and went on to remark that it is even more important to know the Pilot when one sets out on this last journey, which her mother had just taken and from which there is no return (Helen Bagby Harrison, *The Bagbys of Brazil* [Nashville: Broadman, 1954], 154).

Jesus is our Pilot, and it is indeed good to know him.

WEDNESDAY EVENING, JANUARY 11

Title: The Problem of Living What You Learn

Text: "Do not merely listen to the word, and so deceive yourselves. Do what it says" (**James 1:22 NIV**).

Scripture Reading: James 1:19–27

Introduction

With your mind you may learn one lesson while with your life you teach quite a different lesson. "Taking God's name in vain" means far more than using God's name in a string of curse words. It also means to bear his name in vain—to accept the family name "Christian" yet not live the Christian life.

I. Caution.

"Be swift to hear, slow to speak, slow to wrath; for the wrath of man worketh not the righteousness of God" (James 1:19–20).

If you would live what you have learned about Christ, then you must practice caution in your language—be "slow to speak." Believing that the culture of highly bred horses would rub off on him, a common mule combed his hair, cut his mane, trimmed his ears, and managed to enter the local horse show. No one knew what he really was until in the excitement of the show he opened his mouth and "hee-hawed." Often our mouths reveal what kind of persons we are. Be careful what you say!

You must practice caution in your display of anger if you would live what you have learned—be "slow to wrath." No good ever comes from a display of anger, be it in the home, at the office, or in a church business meeting. The cause of Christ is harmed, and serious damage is inflicted on the testimony of the one displaying such anger.

II. "Get rid of all moral filth and the evil that is so prevalent" (James 1:21 NIV).

"Filth" literally means dirt and is used here as a symbol for moral defilement. "Evil" speaks of active hostility that finds pleasure in injuring others and disturbing friendships.

As cleansing is experienced, in the place of "filth" and "evil," the "word" is planted within (v. 21).

III. Correlation of hearing and doing.

James 1:22 is saying, "Don't just learn it—live it!" There must be a correlation between hearing and doing.

 A. *A plea.* Verses 22–24 contain a plea that if unheeded results in self-deception ("deceiving your own selves," v. 22). In your effort to appear more spiritual than others or to be some great Bible scholar when your life and attitude are inconsistent, you may deceive yourself, but you will never deceive others.

  If you do not heed this plea, you rob yourself of self-improvement (vv. 23–24). A man looks into a mirror, sees all of his blemishes, and resolves to correct them. But he soon forgets how disagreeable he appeared, and his resolutions go unkept.

 B. *A promise.* "But the man who looks intently into the perfect law that gives freedom, and continues to do this, not forgetting what he has heard, but doing it—he will be blessed in what he does" (v. 25 NIV) This promise is made to those who strive to do what they have heard (v. 25). This is a promise of happiness, for "this man shall be blessed" (v. 25).

C. *A practical demonstration (vv. 26–27).* In verse 26 we see a practical demonstration of an improper correlation. Here is a man who tries hard to appear pious and spiritually superior to others in the church. But he has one glaring fault: he cannot keep his mouth shut. He is always expressing his will (which he often confuses with "God's will"), cutting at others or passing on tidbits about others' past mistakes. James says this man's religion is invalid, it is "vain," and he serves as a practical demonstration of how not to live the Christian life.

A practical demonstration of a *proper* correlation of hearing and doing is offered in verse 27. "Pure religion" expresses itself in: (1) helping others in need ("to visit the fatherless and widows in their affliction") and (2) keeping your life free from sin ("to keep ... unspotted from the world").

Conclusion

"Being" comes before "doing." If you are what you ought to *be* in Christ, you will *do* what you ought to do for Christ. Live what you have learned.

SUNDAY MORNING, JANUARY 15

Title: How Have You Received Jesus Christ?

Text: "He came unto his own, and his own received him not. But as many as received him, to them gave he power to become the sons of God, even to them that believe on his name" **(John 1:11–12)**.

Scripture Reading: Matthew 21:33–41

Hymns: "Break Thou the Bread of Life," Lathbury

"He Included Me," Oatman

"Tell Me the Story of Jesus," Crosby

Offertory Prayer: Heavenly Father, you have given us your sinless Son, who came, lived, labored, and died that our sins might be forgiven and that we might receive the gift of eternal life. You have given to us your Spirit to be our Comforter, Guide, and Teacher. You have given us life with all of its opportunities and responsibilities. You have bestowed on us the power to get wealth. Today we thank you for your blessings on the labor of our hands. We bring a portion of the blessings that you have bestowed on us and return them to meet the expenses of the work of your kingdom both in this community and to the ends of the earth. Bless the use of these contributions to the spiritual welfare of those who are in need. In the name of our Savior we pray. Amen.

Introduction

The reception given to Jesus Christ forms one of the great tragedies of human history. Some have sympathized with the innkeeper of Bethlehem who rejected the plea of Joseph and Mary for a place to spend the night. Others have criticized the innkeeper for what appears to be a lack of sympathetic concern for a desperate couple. The only thing that Bethlehem had to offer was a stable. The reception that Bethlehem gave to the holy family was a foretaste of that which the Christ was to experience again and again.

Perhaps the innkeeper turned Joseph and Mary away because he was too busy to bother with them. Perhaps it would have been necessary for him to have turned other guests away if he had welcomed them. It is possible that he turned them away because they were poor. We can only speculate as to how Joseph and Mary would have been received had Joseph been carrying a bag of gold.

Our text speaks of how Jesus was rejected by some and welcomed by others. It is interesting to examine the biblical record of his rejection and also to see examples of the welcome that was extended to him. What is your attitude toward Jesus?

I. The record of Jesus' rejection.

Jesus came to his own world and to his own people. He came as a man would come to his own house. His world and his people should have recognized him and accepted him with a joyous welcome.

We cannot help but conclude that many were blind to Jesus' true nature. They had accepted attitudes and ambitions that created spiritual blindness. They did not see him as the Messiah who was promised by the prophets.

A. *Herod rejected Jesus as a rival for the throne of the kingdom (Matt. 2:16).* There are some who reject him today because they are unwilling to let him be the King of their empire.

B. *The Pharisees were blind because they had externalized religion.* They majored on legalistic outward performance of religious rites. They believed Jesus to be an impostor because he placed no emphasis on religious privileges based on ancestry or nationalism. They were in constant conflict with him because of his attitude toward the law and the traditions of their fathers. They emphasized a perfect observance of the 365 negative commands and the 248 positive commands of the Jewish law. They deeply resented Jesus and rejected him because of his all-inclusive spirit and his universal concern for sinners, outcasts, and Gentiles.

C. *The Sadducees had created a spiritual blindness that caused them to reject Jesus because they had secularized religion.* They were vitally concerned in the political situation and the economic conditions of the country. They were tremendously concerned at the point of how religious events in Jerusalem would affect their relationship with Rome. They discouraged any movement that would rock the boat or disturb the status quo.

D. *The scribes were blind and consequently rejected Jesus because they had professionalized religion.* They were the legalistic theologians who worked hand in glove with the Pharisees. There was no fire of God's love in their hearts. They were concerned only with keeping the laws of the past.

E. *The Zealots did not receive Jesus because they had nationalized religion and had identified their faith with anything that would contribute to the well-being of their country and that would point toward the defeat of the Roman Empire.* They were the extremists of their day. They were consumed with the idea of gaining their freedom from Rome. This was the consuming passion of their lives, and consequently they were unable to see or understand what Jesus was trying to communicate.

F. *The crowds rejected Jesus because he called for a revolutionary change in their attitudes and actions. He called for repentance and faith.* He encouraged them to alter their thoughts about God, self, life, and others. Because he did not fit into their concept and scheme of the way things should be, they rejected what he had to offer.

Have you rejected Jesus without really hearing what he has to say? Have you given serious consideration to what he is trying to communicate concerning God, humankind, life, and the future?

II. The record of Jesus' welcome.

A. *The welcome of Mary (Luke 1:34, 38).*
B. *The welcome of Joseph (Matt. 1:24–25).*
C. *The welcome of the shepherds (Luke 2:15–18).*
D. *The welcome of the wise men (Matt. 2:11).*
E. *The welcome of Simeon and Anna (Luke 2:25–32).*
F. *The welcome of John the Baptist (John 1:32–34).*

III. The receptions that are recommended (John 1:12).

A. *John the Baptist received him as the Lamb of God who came to take away the sin of the world (John 1:29, 32–34).*
B. *Nicodemus received him as a teacher come from God (John 3:2).*

> The Sermon on the Mount is a lecture of this divine Teacher who came from God. Our lives and our world would be different if we were to hear this Teacher and heed what he has to say today.

C. *Thomas received the risen living Christ as "My Lord and my God" (John 20:28).*

Conclusion

Do not treat Jesus as an intruder who would be an unwelcome guest in your life. Do not treat him as a thief who would steal something from you. Do not treat him as a policeman who is in search of a fugitive. Do not respond to him as a beggar who is in need of something from you. Do not avoid him as you would a funeral director who is waiting for you to die.

Trust Jesus as the Lamb of God who came to take away your sin. He was and is the Son of God who gives eternal life to those who receive him. Trust him as the Leader who leads through the night of the present into and through the perfect day of the future. Trust him as the only Lord who is worthy of your worship and ultimate loyalty. Trust him today and continue to trust him in all of your tomorrows.

SUNDAY EVENING, JANUARY 15

Title: Revolt against God

Text: "Take heed, brethren, lest there be in any of you an evil heart of unbelief, in departing from the living God" **(Heb. 3:12)**.

Scripture Reading: Hebrews 3:1 – 19

Introduction

There is something terribly final about revolt. Once open revolt is begun, anything short of victory is disastrous. For this reason, the American colonies were rather slow in taking the final action that would lead to open revolt against England. The chance for victory seemed slim, yet the chance did exist. In contrast, people often revolt against God when there is absolutely no chance of emerging victorious. It seems unimaginable that people made of dust formed in the image of God and made alive by the breath of God would ever openly revolt against God. Yet history is composed of one such incident after another.

I. The substance of revolt (Heb. 3:12).

Revolt is the exact opposite of faithful discipleship: "Take heed, brethren, lest there be in any of you an evil heart of unbelief, in departing from the living God" (v. 12). The main characteristic of an evil heart is unbelief. The unbelief spoken of here is the refusal to follow the leadership of Christ in the journey of faith: "in departing from the living God."

Revolt is brought about by a hesitant spirit that refuses to follow Christ. In Hebrews 3:12 the word translated "departing from" is a verb form of the word *apostasy.* The literal meaning of apostasy is "to stand off from." Rebellion is a standoffish relationship with God. There is much said about apostasy in the Bible. In Joshua 22:22 the word is used to speak of rebellion against God. Such rebellion amounts to a religious revolt against the authority of God.

Apostasy can be committed only by those who have identified themselves with Jesus Christ in a superficial way and then have gone on to live lives that are in utter revolt against the lordship of Christ. They are often described in terms of unregenerate church members. John describes such people as follows: "They went out from us, but they were not of us; for if they had been of us, they would no doubt have continued with us; but they went out, that they might be made manifest that they were not all of us" (1 John 2:19).

The writer of Hebrews is waving a red flag of warning concerning the possibility of one's professing Christ and yet possessing an evil heart of unbelief that manifests itself in a life that stands off from God and his leadership.

II. A case in point (Heb. 3:7 – 11).

The writer of Hebrews is not interested in vague generalities. He is quite willing to give us a "for instance": "So, as the Holy Spirit says: 'Today, if you hear his voice, do not harden your hearts as you did in the rebellion, during the time of

29

testing in the desert, where your fathers tested and tried me and for forty years saw what I did'" (vv. 7–9 NIV). The writer of Hebrews quotes from Psalm 95, which in turn describes two events in the history of Israel. The words translated "rebellion" and "testing" are translations from the Hebrew names of Massah and Meribah. In Exodus 17:1–7 the Israelites rebelled against Moses because of the lack of drinking water and expressed great regret at ever having left Egypt. God told Moses to strike the rock at Meribah, whereupon water came forth.

In Numbers 20:1–13 a similar instance again occurred, but this time Moses struck the rock in anger instead of speaking to it as God had specifically asked on that occasion. Although this was a rebellion also on the part of Moses, the main purpose of mentioning it here is to depict again the people's rebellion against the leadership of God. At every turn in the road, the people questioned God's leadership and sought to put him on the spot by certain demands: "where your fathers tested and tried me" (Heb. 3:9 NIV). There are times when it is an outright sin to require God to perform a miracle for your own satisfaction. This is to put God on trial by demanding signs. The incidents at Meribah and Massah revealed certain attitudes that would ultimately lead to outright revolt as the people refused to enter the Promised Land after having sent men to spy it out. God had told them that they would be able to overcome the tribes in the Promised Land, but they were determined to see for themselves; and having seen, they decided that God did not know what he was talking about. God's commentary reads as follows: "That is why I was angry with that generation, and I said, 'Their hearts are always going astray, and they have not know my ways.' So I declared on oath in my anger, 'They shall never enter my rest'" (vv. 10–11 NIV).

For the next forty years, the people would see God's work of judgment, having refused to yield to his work of grace. God's judgment was that the Israelites would wander in the wilderness until every person over twenty years of age had died (Num. 14:29). Someone has estimated that there may have been a million Israelites in that age range. If so, this would mean an average of sixty-eight deaths per day for forty years. If burial was made only during the daylight hours, this would mean an average of six funerals per hour for forty years. (However, we must note that when God poured out his wrath on the people [e.g., the snake plague], many more died at one time.) Each funeral procession was a mute reminder of the futile restlessness brought on when people revolt against God.

III. How to avoid revolt.

Revolt can best be avoided by a recognition of its nearness. Although the unregenerate alone are capable of complete apostasy from God, children of God are quite capable of taking part in minor revolts throughout their lifetimes for which they must suffer the chastening of God and the loss of Christian influence. The writer of Hebrews has purposely made a contrast between the Israelites' journey under Moses and the church's mission under Christ. The church is composed of God's "new Israel," and its mission is presented in terms of a "new exodus." The apostle Paul compared Christian baptism with the crossing of the Red Sea by the Israelites (1 Cor. 10:2ff.). Just as Israel crossed the Red Sea because of God's deliverance and set forth on a divine mission, so the Christian follows Christ in baptism and sets out on a divine pilgrimage.

Personal sin is capable of making us callous and less responsive to God: "Encourage one another daily, as long as it is called Today, so that none of you may be hardened by sin's deceitfulness" (Heb. 3:13 NIV). We are prone to fall for Satan's same old tricks time after time. A fox, having been caught in one trap, is forever wary of other traps. Yet even children of God seem never to learn the lesson about sin. Sin so easily deceives us. Our only hope of withstanding the temptation to revolt is to keep attuned to the voice of God: "Today, if you hear his voice, do not harden your hearts as you did in the rebellion" (v. 15 NIV).

The majestic stalagmites and stalactites seen in the beautiful Carlsbad Caverns were formed through the centuries by the constant dripping of water through the overlying limestone leaving deposits of crystalline calcium carbonate until at long last the hardened icicles were formed. Any one drop contains only a microscopic amount of sediment, yet the total accumulation is immense. Revolt against God begins with little things that are allowed to remain and stack up, one on top of the other, until God is hidden from our view, our hearts are hardened, and our ears are deaf.

God alone is able to set people free from the ravages of sin and the emptiness of a self-directed life. We remember Abraham Lincoln because he sought to set people free. Yet none of the great emancipation acts of history can compare to the freedom experienced in Jesus Christ. Revolt against Christ is revolt against the only freedom open to us. Otherwise sin becomes our master. If we choose to refuse to follow this Christ who speaks from heaven, then we have chosen a life of restlessness similar to that experienced by the Israelites during their forty years of wandering in the wilderness. Christ's voice is the voice of God. His authority is the authority of God. To profess him is to yield to that authority and thus to find life. The time to decide is today.

Conclusion

During his reign, the Syrian king Antiochus Epiphanes decided to stage an invasion of Egypt. Rome was displeased by the action and sent an envoy named Popillius to order Antiochus to forget his planned invasion. Popillius caught up with Antiochus just outside the border of Egypt. Since they had known each other previously, they spent a brief time in friendly conversation before Popillius quietly told Antiochus that he must abandon his invasion by order of the Roman Empire. Antiochus replied that he would think about it, but Popillius drew a circle in the dust around Antiochus. Popillius then told Antiochus to give thought to the matter but to make his decision before stepping from the circle. The picture is a vivid one. Antiochus had his army with him while Popillius was alone. Yet all the authority of the Roman Empire was behind Popillius. Recognizing this, Antiochus realized his only course of action was obedience.

Christ does not come to us in an overwhelming array of divine power. He comes in a quiet voice and bids us to follow him. Behind his invitation stands all the authority of the God who has given us life. Scripture warns against any other alternative: "See to it, brothers, that none of you has a sinful, unbelieving heart that turns away from the living God" (Heb. 3:12 NIV).

WEDNESDAY EVENING, JANUARY 18

Title: The Problem of Snobbery

Text: "My brothers, as believers in our glorious Lord Jesus Christ, don't show favoritism" **(James 2:1 NIV)**.

Scripture Reading: James 2:1–13

Introduction

Snobbery can invade even the church. For example, Christian young people on choir tours have been guilty of comparing notes on the kind of homes in which they were guests. Church members sometimes form opinions based on the clothes others wear to church. Those who visit in behalf of the church often are swayed by the part of town in which a newcomer lives. This is not a problem we outgrow. We must face it and in the light of sacred Scripture solve it.

I. Incompatibility of snobbery and Christianity.

"Don't ever attempt, my brethren, to combine snobbery with faith in our glorious Lord Jesus Christ" (James 2:1 PHILLIPS). Being a part of a snobbish clique (whether a social circle or a prayer cell) that whispers about others is incompatible with the Christian life. A snob cannot say, "I'm a Christian—I'm Christlike." When did Christ ever act snobbish?

II. Cruelty of snobbery (James 2:2–4).

How cruel can a person be? Here in our text we read of a poor man, shabbily clothed, who comes to worship service and is told to either stand or sit on the floor while a wealthy man comes to that same service and is received royally and offered a choice seat. James says that such cruelty comes from those who are inconsistent and are guilty of judging by false standards.

The poor and underprivileged suffer greatly, yet some Christians are cruel enough to act snobbish toward them and thus open wider the bleeding sore in their hearts!

III. Inconsistency of snobbery (James 2:5–7).

Snobbery is inconsistent with every choice God has made. "Hath not God chosen the poor of this world rich in faith?" (v. 5). It is further inconsistent with your avowed loyalty. You claim to be loyal to Christianity, yet you play up to the very ones who usually oppress you and speak evil of the name by which you are called (v. 7).

IV. Remedy for snobbery—the law of liberty, love (James 2:8–13).

James offers no "combination of ingredients" but rather offers one simple yet highly effective remedy: "Love your neighbor as yourself" (v. 8 NIV). How do you love yourself? Do you love yourself any less when you are out of cash or when honors have not come your way or when your clothes are not so new? The answer is no. You love yourself the same regardless of any external factors. So you ought to love others, regardless of money, status, clothes, or home.

The royal law, the law of liberty that is love, does five things.

A. *Love avoids false distinctions (v. 9).*

B. *Love protects you from sin (vv. 9–11).* To break God's law of love by snobbery is to be a "law breaker" regardless of how lily white you may be on all other accounts.

C. *Love colors what you say and characterizes what you do.* "Speak and act as those who are going to be judged by the law that gives freedom" (v. 12 NIV).

D. *Love makes allowances for others.* But "judgment without mercy will be shown to anyone who has not been merciful" (v. 13 NIV). Phillips says, "The man who makes no allowances for others will find none made for him."

Conclusion

Mercy triumphs over judgment!" (v. 13 NIV). A man who loves others as himself rejoices in opportunities of showing mercy rather than in sitting in judgment on another. Because he knows that he is saved by the grace of God and not by the human works, snobbery is one problem with which he is not bothered.

SUNDAY MORNING, JANUARY 22

Title: The Best Is Yet to Be

Text: "This beginning of miracles did Jesus in Cana of Galilee, and manifested forth his glory; and his disciples believed on him" (**John 2:11**).

Scripture Reading: John 2:1–11

Hymns: "All Hail the Power of Jesus' Name," Perronet

"He Is Able to Deliver Thee," Ogden

"O for a Thousand Tongues to Sing," Wesley

Offertory Prayer: Our Father, we come now to bring tithes and offerings to you. Help us to realize the importance of giving our total selves to you. Help us to place ourselves on the altar as an act of worship. We offer to you our hands and our hearts. We offer to you our tongues that they might tell the wondrous story of your love. Help us to be generous in our financial support of the ministries that proclaim your love and express your mercy to the needy. In Jesus' name we pray. Amen.

Introduction

Our Lord came to earth on a mission. To accomplish his purpose, it was necessary that people recognize him and respond to him as the Son of God.

Jesus refused to utilize the spectacular method of revealing himself that Satan suggested: "Then the devil taketh him up into the holy city, and setteth him on a pinnacle of the temple, and saith unto him, If thou be the Son of God, cast thyself down: for it is written, He shall give his angels charge concerning thee: and in their hands they shall bear thee up, lest at any time thou dash thy foot against a stone. Jesus said unto him, It is written again, Thou shalt not tempt the Lord thy God" (Matt. 4:5–7).

Jesus wanted to use a more effective method than a sensational display of divine power. He used signs to point to the truth of who he was. He taught and explained patiently and quietly the significance of these signs. By the sign of miracles, he revealed himself to be the divine Son of God. These miracles were never selfish; they were always for the benefit of someone in need.

The signs were actions and events that would say something. They were miracles with a significance, even as a parable is a story with a purpose.

If John the apostle lived today, he would make a good script writer for an ad agency (John 20:30–31). He probably would be able to prepare some excellent commercials for use on television. John used this approach in his attempt to convince his readers that they should accept Jesus Christ as the Son of God. He assured them that through a genuine confidence in Christ, they would find God, life, and joy.

Jesus' turning of the water into wine was the first of seven great signs that John the apostle selected for use in his gospel in order to try to win converts to Jesus Christ. He was an evangelist, and the fourth gospel was written from an evangelistic viewpoint.

Often we miss the whole point of this particular miracle because of our critical attitude toward the modern alcoholic beverage business that has helped to bring tragedy into the lives of many. Because of this attitude toward the highly advertised liquor industry, some of us have sought to explain this miracle away. Others have used this event as an endorsement for the use of alcoholic beverages. To take either of these viewpoints is to miss the point of what Christ was trying to impart concerning his nature and his purpose.

What does this sign tell us about Christ? Our text reveals that he "manifested forth his glory; and his disciples believed on him." In this event, the disciples discovered something wonderful about Jesus' character, his power, his purpose, and his activity. This revelation encouraged them to have faith in him. Let us look a bit more closely at this miracle.

I. Jesus revealed his concern for marriage, home life, and social joy.

A. *Jesus was invited to a wedding.* He should be invited to every wedding, for marriage has spiritual significance both for the present and for the future.

B. *Jesus acted generously and unexpectedly to prevent an embarrassing situation from developing*. Perhaps the crowd attending the wedding was much larger than had been anticipated, or perhaps the family was poor and unable to make adequate provisions.

C. *Jesus increased joy on a festive occasion by this miracle of turning the water into wine.* It is interesting to note how that Jesus seemingly was much at home in the midst of social fellowship around the table. Following his conversion, Levi, whom we know as Matthew, provided a great feast and invited many publicans and sinners to come that they might become better acquainted with his new Savior. It is interesting to note that our Lord describes the result of his entrance into one's life in terms of food, feasting, friendship, and fellowship (Rev. 3:20).

II. Jesus revealed his supernatural power over nature.

A. *"All things were made by him; and without him was not anything made that was made" (John 1:3).*

B. *He continues to be in control of his creation.* When Jesus turned the water into wine for this wedding reception, he was expressing the power that he continues to exercise over nature.

III. Jesus revealed his availability and ability to make the last better than the first.

A. *The water was turned into a wine that was far better than the wine that was served first.*

B. *Life with Christ is always better than life before Christ is permitted to enter one's heart.*

C. *A pastor had a couple approach him on Sunday morning with great smiles on their faces.* They called attention to the fact that this was their birthday — their spiritual birthday. It was their first anniversary as children of God. The wife spoke for both and said, "This year has been better than all of the rest put together." Christ had caused the last to be better than the first.

IV. Jesus revealed his policy of enriching everything that is placed at his disposal.

A. *Jesus turned the water into a superior wine.*

B. *The loaves and fishes from a boy's lunch were placed in the hands of Jesus.* He blessed them, the disciples distributed them, and five thousand men plus women and children dined sufficiently (John 6:9–13).

C. *Saul of Tarsus was a man with a great mind and with a great ambition.* Finally, he was stopped in his mad career of persecution by a unique experience with the living Christ. He fully yielded to the lordship of Jesus. Christ enriched, enlarged, and improved the heart, mind, and soul of this man.

D. *Jesus never robs, steals, or impoverishes.* He always returns to us something better than what we are able to present to him.

E. *Jesus gives his very best to the lowly and needy (Mark 10:45).*

V. Jesus revealed his ability and disposition to meet the deepest needs of his followers.

    A. *This miracle revealed his graciousness.*

    B. *This miracle revealed his sufficiency.*

    C. *This miracle revealed the security of those who trust and obey him.*

Conclusion

The disciples beheld Jesus' miracles and were so convinced that they were moved to put their trust in him. His way of life became their way of life. Does this event impart faith to you? Does this sign encourage you to trust Jesus more and to obey him more completely?

"Jesus Christ is the same yesterday, and today, and for ever" (Heb. 13:8). He is concerned about your total welfare. He has the power of God at his disposal and wants to make your future better than your past. He has a permanent policy of enriching and returning that which is placed at his disposal. He can meet the deepest needs of your life both now and in the future (John 14:1–3). The best is yet to be.

SUNDAY EVENING, JANUARY 22

Title: Resting in God

Text: "There remaineth therefore a rest to the people of God" (**Heb. 4:9**).

Scripture Reading: Hebrews 4:1–16

Introduction

The "rest" spoken of in the Bible has nothing to do with inactivity. It has nothing to do with a slow, rocking chair approach to life. My father helped me to understand the biblical concept of rest. For instance, if we were building a fence, we would dig the holes, place the posts, and stamp the dirt in tightly; then my father would say, "Now while we are resting, let's stretch the barbed wire and staple it to the posts."

When the Bible invites us to "rest in God," it is inviting us to a particular way of life resembling God's rest following the six days of Creation (Heb. 4:4). Although the Bible tells us that God rested from his works following Creation, the Bible in no way gives the impression that from that time God has been inactive. God ceased his creative work, but in no sense did he cease to carry out day by day his divine will and purpose for his creation. Jesus himself was very precise at this point: "My Father worketh hitherto, and I work" (John 5:17).

To understand the idea of rest involved here, one must remember that upon the entrance of sin into the experience of humankind, there came a curse. People now lived under the threat of death. They now had to toil and sweat to fight weeds and thorns. They were possessed by a great unrest of soul. Living in the midst of sin's curse, humankind hears the good news of the Bible—news that they do not have to remain in a state of spiritual unrest. They can become new persons in Christ (2 Cor. 5:17). A part of this new relationship means that now work ceases to become laborious toil and suddenly takes on meaningful purpose. Death ceases to be a dreaded terror because of the promised resurrection. This is the rest to which the Bible invites us. This is an opportunity to make of life a divine labor wherein all of our energies are directed toward doing the will of God. This concept is highlighted by the fact that Hebrews 4:9 uses a different word to speak of "rest" than the previous verses of that same chapter. Literally the word means "a sabbath observance." This is done to emphasize that God invites us to make of life a divine activity.

I. Resting in God is a matter of faith (Heb. 4:2).

God's recipe for life makes faith the basic ingredient. To omit faith from the mixture of life is to make vanilla pudding and leave out the vanilla flavoring. It is to make bread and leave out the yeast.

The writer of Hebrews uses the illustration of the unbelieving Israelites to warn us that faith must be a part of life: "For unto us was the gospel preached, as well as unto them: but the word preached did not profit them, not being mixed with faith in them that heard it" (v. 2). Faith is not a requirement for entrance into real life; it *is* the entrance into real life. Faith is active commitment to discipleship. A literal translation of Hebrews 4:3 indicates that "the ones believing are entering into rest." The life wherein we choose to rest our souls in God is begun by faith, not by death.

God created everything and rested. We enter into a restful relationship with him when, through faith in Christ, we are recreated. Therefore, people enter the divine activity of the kingdom of God upon conversion. But life still can be lived restlessly unless every day is lived in faith.

The fact that the congregation of Israel refused to enter the land of Canaan does not mean that each individual had refused the spiritual salvation offered by God. It does mean that it is quite possible for one to know forgiveness of sins through faith and yet hesitate from time to time to live by faith. In other words, it is possible for you to be a Christian and yet because of periodic refusals to venture forth in faith, have a certain restlessness where there should be only a restful trust. Canaan stands as an earthly illustration of the terrible possibility of God's people disobeying him in the ordinary, practical matters of life. When God opens doors of opportunity for us and we refuse to enter them, we have left ourselves no alternative but to wander around in the maze of life apart from the fullness of purpose that God offers us.

II. Resting in God has an appointed time for entrance (Heb. 4:7–9).

God's offer is good for today only. This is God's way of pressing upon us the urgency of decision. We live one day at a time because each day may be our last. We are not promised any tomorrows in which we may decide for Christ. The writer of Hebrews is eager for us to realize that his illustration of the Israelites' refusal to enter Canaan is no more than an illustration and that the rest of which he speaks is a live option today: "God again set a certain day, calling it Today, when a long time later he spoke through David, as was said before: 'Today, if you hear his voice do not harden your hearts.' For if Joshua had given them rest, God would not have spoken later about another day. There remains, then, a Sabbath-rest for the people of God; for anyone who enters God's rest also rests from his own work, just as God did from his" (vv. 7–9).

The writer reminds us that hundreds of years following the time of Joshua, God was still speaking through David, admonishing people to respond to the voice of God and to enter God's rest (see Ps. 95). If the entrance of the Israelites into Canaan under the leadership of Joshua had fulfilled God's promise of rest, then God would not have given afterward a similar invitation through David. This leads to the concluding remark in Hebrews 4:9 that indicates that each generation is offered a chance to enter into God's rest. However, the call is for today. We may not have tomorrow.

III. Resting in God is commanded by the Bible (Heb. 4:12–13).

Of all books, the Bible alone is able to help us see ourselves as we really are: "For the word of God is quick, and powerful, and sharper than any two-edged sword, piercing even to the dividing asunder of soul and spirit, and of the joints and marrow, and is a discerner of the thoughts and intents of the heart" (v. 12). Because the living God stands behind the pages of the Bible, the terms "quick" (living) and "powerful" (operative) are very fitting.

Like a razor-sharp sword, the Bible is able to cut through our self-righteousness and pride and reveal us as we really are. The Bible reveals our innermost thoughts and intentions. The word translated "discerner" is the word from which our word "criticism" comes. Literally it means to be able to properly judge. Therefore, the Bible opens us up that we may have a basis of judgment, and it demands that we see what the verdict is. Reading the Bible is an exercise for those who are ready to see the truth: "Neither is there any creature that is not manifest in his sight: but all things are naked and opened unto the eyes of him with whom we have to do" (v. 13). The Bible strips away all our pretenses and disguises. A literal reading of verse 13 reveals a word often used to speak of a butcher opening up the carcass of an animal. The idea is that God's Word lays bare our innermost thoughts. The Bible compels us to face up to our relationship to God and his invitation to enter into fellowship with him whereby our soul comes to rest and depend on him.

IV. Resting in God is made secure by Christ (Heb. 4:15–16).

The writer of Hebrews pictures Christ as our High Priest. Because of him, we are able to rest easy: "Let us therefore come boldly unto the throne of grace, that we may obtain mercy, and find grace to help in time of need" (v. 16).

Unless we are careful, we will overlook the great hope found in the phrase "grace to help in time of need." A literal translation reveals that God's grace is always present to help "in the nick of time." Any time we come to Christ for help, we can be assured that his help will come in time. Even during his earthly ministry, Jesus issued an invitation for people to find rest in him, the rest elaborated on by the writer of Hebrews: "Come unto me, all ye that labour and are heavy laden, and I will give you rest. Take my yoke upon you, and learn of me; for I am meek and lowly in heart: and ye shall find rest unto your souls. For my yoke is easy, and my burden is light" (Matt. 11:28–30).

Conclusion

The "rest" offered can be received only as a gift. Yet Jesus reminds us that the gift is not one of inactivity. Jesus reminds us that involved with "rest" is a yoke that fits. In Bible times, people often wore yokes to carry heavy burdens. A yoke that did not fit caused chaffing and galling. Jesus promises to give us his yoke, meaning that he will fit our lives to a divine purpose for which we were destined. This makes the burdens light and the journey meaningful. Since such a life stands in sharp contrast with the restless wanderings of those without Christ, God has chosen to liken it to entering into rest. The ultimate fulfillment of the divine activity we are allowed to share on this earth is, of course, heaven. Throughout eternity we will continue to participate in divine activity for the Lord. It is said that the last words of Stonewall Jackson were, "Let us cross the river and rest under the shade." God brings rest to our lives even before we cross the river.

WEDNESDAY EVENING, JANUARY 25

Title: The Problem of Practicing What You Profess

Text: "What good is it, my brothers, if a man claims to have faith but has no deeds? Can such faith save him?" **(James 2:14 NIV)**.

Scripture Reading: James 2:14–26

Introduction

James is saying: "Don't just profess it. Practice it!" To practice what you profess is difficult indeed. One wrong solution to the problem of practicing what you profess is simply to cut down your profession. Profess less, and you can practice less. This certainly is not the solution that God would have any of us use.

I. This problem arises from the inadequacy of words.

In James 2:14 the emphasis is definitely on the word "say." Words alone do not prove the genuineness of your faith. It is possible to be a "professor" without being a "possessor."

Verses 15–17 assert that words alone cannot meet the world's needs. Here is a man who needs clothes and food—not a pious testimony of one's faith. There are people in your community who do not need more sermons, but they do desperately need more lives that practice what they profess!

II. This problem is compounded by the impotency of rational belief (James 2:18–20).

Cold rational belief fails to instill power to practice what you profess (v. 18). No wonder a person finds it so difficult to practice what he professes when all he has is rational belief. An experience of saving grace alone can instill in one the power to live up to his profession.

Impotent rational belief is nothing more than mental assent to biblical truths. James says, "You believe that there is one God. Good! Even the demons believe that—and shudder" (v. 19 NIV). They believe this to the extent that they tremble, but they are still devils! Cold academic belief never changed a single life or saved a single soul!

Rational belief is rejected as invalid. "Faith without works is dead" (v. 20). The implication is that if such belief were valid, it would have helped the devil long ago.

III. This problem is solved by the unity of faith and works (James 2:21–26).

Irrefutable proof of our profession is provided when faith and works are united. When Abraham united faith and works, he did the unusual and the unexpected. And when faith and works are united in our lives, we too will do the unusual. We will go that second mile, doing what no one would ever expect us to do. Our lives are lifted out of the level of the ordinary.

The unity of faith and works in our lives indicates our allegiance (v. 25). Rahab proved that her allegiance was not with her people but rather with the people of God. She proved her faith by providing safety for God's messengers.

Conclusion

Genuine faith and acceptable works are as inseparable as the human spirit and the body. Even as the body (a symbol of faith) is dead without the spirit, so faith that is void of works is dead. The only solution is a unity of faith and works (James 2:26).

SUNDAY MORNING, JANUARY 29

Title: Christ Cleansing the Temple

Text: "Take these things hence; make not my Father's house an house of merchandise" (**John 2:16**).

Scripture Reading: John 2:12–22

Hymns: "Holy, Holy, Holy," Heber

"O Worship the King," Grant

"O Master, Let Me Walk with Thee," Gladden

Offertory Prayer: Holy Father, you have given us the privilege of being your children. You have freely forgiven our sins and graciously given us the gift of eternal life. We rejoice in the privilege of serving you and ministering to others. Help us this day to give ourselves more completely to you so that with glad hearts we may go and minister to others. Accept our tithes and offerings as indications of our love for you and as an expression of our desire to see the world come to know Jesus Christ as Lord and Savior. In his name we pray. Amen.

Introduction

The Christ we worship and serve today is the same Christ who was worshiped during the decades of the first century of the Christian era (Heb. 13:8). He is the same in his unique and wonderful person, in his redemptive purpose, in his abiding presence, in his ability and desire to meet the deepest needs of people, and in his compassion for a lost world.

Christ continues to speak to those who have ears to hear. He continues to reveal himself to those who have eyes that are willing to see. He continues to be the Bread of Life to those who have an appetite for the things of the Spirit.

According to John the evangelist, Jesus launched his public ministry by purifying the temple. This bold action revealed Christ to be something other than a meek and mild do-gooder. His action was bold, brave, aggressive, assertive, daring, radical, and revolutionary. His cleansing of the temple was a bold attack on the religious and political establishment of his day. His cleansing of the temple was a radical call for a reevaluation of the Pharisees' total approach to religion and life.

Jesus' cleansing of the temple created the hostility that was to rise up and grow until it had engineered his execution by crucifixion. Christ continued to speak and reveal himself to us through the record of this significant action at the beginning of his earthly ministry.

I. By cleansing the temple, Christ asserted his divine authority.

A. *Christ came into the temple as the Messiah.* His bold action was an assertion of his messianic authority (Mal. 3:1–3). Christ wanted the offering of the people to be pleasant and acceptable to the Lord (v. 4). There was no possibility for such under the circumstances that existed in the temple. By cleansing the temple and reestablishing worship in its purity, Jesus hoped to be a blessing to the people of his day.

B. *Christ came into the temple as the Son of God (John 2:16).* He was beginning to make the emphasis that he was the unique Son of God.

C. *Christ came into the temple as the Lord of the temple.* He was revealing himself to be Lord in the realm of worship. He was and continues to be Lord in the realm of communication with God. We learn about God best through Jesus Christ. Christ comes today to assist us with our worship. He is present to help us see, hear, and respond (Matt. 18:20).

II. While cleansing the temple, Christ expressed his holy anger.

A. *Christ was angry when covetousness and greed in the hearts of people prevented others from coming to God.* The court of the Gentiles was occupied by merchants, thus impeding the way of those who would come into the temple. People were being cut off and shut off from God.

B. *Christ was angry when hypocrites acted in such a manner as to cause people to be disgusted with the expression of religion (Matt. 23).* A hypocrite is one who wears a false face and deliberately pretends something on the outside that he is not on the inside. If there is sham and pretense in our profession of love and loyalty today, they will be discerned by those to whom we seek to minister.

C. *Christ was angry when the strong oppressed and mistreated the weak (Matt. 23:4, 14).*

D. *Christ was angry when coldhearted religious traditionalism would have prevented him from healing an unfortunate man who was suffering (Mark 3:5).*

E. *Christ was angry when the innocent were seduced into sin (Matt. 18:6).* The Christ of yesterday is the same today as he was then. We can be sure that what made him angry then makes him angry today.

Notice the pattern of the anger of Christ. Christ was never angry at wrongs done to himself. He was angry with sinners who polluted the house of God, with hypocrites who made people disgusted with religion, with oppressors of the weak, and with those who seduced the innocent into sin.

The anger of Christ was the other side of his love. Because he loved the oppressed, he was angry with the oppressor. Because he loved the people, he was angry with the hypocrites. Because he loved the innocent, he was angry with the seducers.

Christ was always eager to forgive when the guilty were willing to repent and turn to God.

III. While cleansing the temple, Christ announced his ambition.

"Destroy this temple, and in three days I will raise it up" (John 2:19) was a direct prophecy of Christ's substitutionary death on the cross and his victorious resurrection from the dead. In the significance of these events, we find our greatest needs met.

A. *Christ, by his death and resurrection, has become the meeting place of God and humanity (John 14:6).*

B. *Christ, through his church, a spiritual temple made up of living stones, is to be the meeting place of God for the whole human race.*

C. *The individual believer is to be a temple, a shrine of the Holy Spirit, where God comes and dwells.* God communicates with the individual believer and through the individual believer with an unbelieving and needy world.

Conclusion

Christ wants to be your door to God. He is the only door to God the Father. He wants to receive you, and you must receive him if you want to know the love of God as he has revealed himself as the merciful Father through Christ Jesus.

Are you willing to let your heart, your mind, your body, become the dwelling place of Jesus Christ? Are you willing to become a temple in which he dwells and through which he ministers to the world today?

If you will allow Christ to do so, he will cleanse your heart, purify your thoughts, and give your life a beauty and fragrance that will bring satisfaction to you and will be a blessing to others.

SUNDAY EVENING, JANUARY 29

Title: The Church's Biggest Problem: Stunted Christians

Text: "For when for the time ye ought to be teachers, ye have need that one teach you again which be the first principles of the oracles of God; and are become such as have need of milk, and not of strong meat" **(Heb. 5:12).**

Scripture Reading: Hebrews 5:11–6:1

Introduction

From the outset of the Vietnam War, questions were raised concerning the commitment of the South Vietnamese. There were times when the South Vietnamese did not seem to care very deeply about whether victory was obtained or not. Returning veterans indicated that it was sometimes impossible to tell who the enemy really was.

Of even greater concern is that such traits are found in great numbers of church members. The writer of Hebrews pauses in the midst of a discussion of the priesthood of Christ to direct a warning to those who claim Christ as Savior and yet resemble an army that does not care. He addresses those whose actions fail to indicate a dedication necessary for victory in the name of Christ. The church's greatest foe has never been the forces of evil but rather the weakness and immaturity of its own membership.

I. Stunted Christians shun Christlikeness (Heb. 5:11).

One might assume that any Christian would enjoy a discussion of the priesthood of Christ, but such is not the case. Rather, the writer of Hebrews finds it difficult to continue the discussion as he remembers the great bulk of Christians who have no ear for it. He indicates that although he has many things to say, they are "hard to be uttered, seeing ye are dull of hearing" (v. 11). How tragic that Christians could be described as being "dull of hearing." The word translated "dull" literally means "no push." Christians who shun Christlikeness have a sluggish mind when Christian doctrine is being discussed. Like an arm numbed when circulation is cut off, the mind can be numbed when the spiritual leadership of the Holy Spirit is stifled.

Jesus often reminded his disciples that ears were to be used to hear: "He that hath ears to hear, let him hear." The literal language of Hebrews 5:12 indicates that the people involved are personally responsible for this sluggish condition. It

43

has been brought on by neglect. They are like people who take a book to church with them to read while everyone else sings and worships. The imprint of Christ on such people is often difficult to recognize. The best television set produces only a snowy picture when the aerial is directed away from the station. There are some Christians who purposely dial God out beyond a certain point of commitment. They want to be counted among the Christians, but they have a fear of being too much like Christ.

II. Stunted Christians refuse responsibility (Heb. 5:12).

Any course of action that constantly refuses responsibility will produce a stunted Christian. The purpose behind being taught is that one may himself some day become a teacher: "Though by this time you ought to be teachers, you need someone to teach you the elementary truths of God's word al over again. You need milk, not solid food!" (v. 12 NIV). The word translated "time" is the same word from which we get "chronology." The writer of Hebrews is saying that, because of the length of time involved, the people to whom he is addressing himself should be teachers. This does not necessarily mean that every Christian should at some time teach a Sunday school class. What is meant is that all Christians should become grounded in the faith to the extent that by their words and actions they are indeed teachers.

Every young Christian goes through a period of time when he needs to be "spoon fed," but it was never intended that he should be spoon fed all his life. Here are people who, because of the length of time they have been Christians, should be mature in the faith yet still have an improper understanding of "the elementary truths of God's word." "Elementary truths" refers to the ABCs of the Christian faith. In fact, the original language indicates that these believers are morally obligated to have mastered the basic tenets of the faith by this time.

When does a person become old enough to take a place of responsibility in the body of Christ? Some people have been Christians for twenty years and still do not feel "ready" to assume responsibility. Can you imagine a man sixty years of age who continues to tell his childhood sweetheart that he plans to marry her as soon as he is able to assume that responsibility?

Only a limited amount of experience can be transmitted from one Christian to another by teaching. There comes a saturation point after which further learning must take place by doing. In his discussion of Jesus, the writer of Hebrews says that Jesus learned "obedience by the things which he suffered" (Heb. 5:8). Those Christians who never get out of the "milk" stage are those who have never decided to learn obedience by suffering for Christ. They have refused to make any real sacrifice or take any real stand. They are those who hesitate to be tied down by responsibilities.

The story of Peter Pan is the story of a young boy who fled to Never-Never Land rather than grow up. It makes an interesting fairy tale but is a rather pathetic sight when found in the church. Such people still "need milk, not solid food." As long as such people remain bottle babies, they are "not acquainted with the teaching about righteousness" (Heb. 5:13 NIV). Such people remain untried because they have never subjected themselves to the higher demands of obedience. They have never learned obedience to the point of suffering for their faith. Thus, they remain in ignorance concerning the deepest meaning of God's righteousness. They have never really had anything to do with the teaching of righteous conduct but instead always have sat and listened to words of others.

Christians who are still in the baby department are dependent on others to prepare their food for them and place it in their mouths. This prohibits them from ever being able to weigh matters for themselves and take a consistent stand on moral issues. When anything above the simplest Christian doctrine is discussed, they are at sea. Babies have no teeth and cannot chew the solid food characteristic of an adult's diet: "Solid food is for the mature" (Heb. 5:14 NIV).

Next follows a more complete description of those who are mature Christians. It has to do with their ability and willingness to choose between good and evil: they have "by constant use ... trained themselves to distinguish good from evil" (Heb. 5:14 NIV). The Greek word translated "trained" is the source of our word *gymnasium.* A person's moral awareness must be exercised if it is to be strong.

A baby's diet is completely prescribed for him. As he grows older, he learns that certain foods are dangerous. By the time he becomes an adult, he needs no one to stand by his side to show him what is good to eat and what is harmful for the body. The same is true in the moral realm. As one learns to assume responsible positions in the kingdom of God, he at the same time exercises his moral awareness and through dedicated living arrives at the time when he can stand in the midst of an ungodly society as a Christian leader.

Perhaps one of the reasons for the great increase in juvenile delinquency can be found in the great number of parents who, although naming Christ as Savior, have never arrived at a mature faith that would enable them to properly train their children. Strangely enough, people will send their children forth into life utterly unprepared to meet the moral and spiritual demands made on them. Often parents who send their children to Sunday school a few times each month assume that this is sufficient for proper spiritual instruction.

The ultimate test of one's maturity is always his behavior. During the Reformation, one group of European Christians went about wearing baby clothes and talking baby talk because of their childish interpretation of Jesus' words to the effect that people must become as little children in order to enter the kingdom. This is what happens when spoon-fed Christians are turned out on their own.

III. Stunted Christians promote stagnation (Heb. 6:1).

Christians who shun Christlikeness and refuse responsibility are promoters of stagnation. The joy offered in the Christian life is dependent on progress. There is no continuing excitement to be had by those who pack up for a summer expedition into the wilderness but decide to mill around the base camp instead of setting out on the journey. The truth is that Christians who are unhappy in their faith are Christians who have never discovered that Christ intends life to be an exciting journey into new areas of service.

One of the main themes of the book of Hebrews is that of Christian growth. New ventures of faith attempted for Christ should be the daily fare of every Christian. We need have no fear of exhausting the "unsearchable riches of Christ." When Columbus began his historic voyage, Spanish coins bearing the imprint of the Pillars of Hercules had as a motto *ne plus ultra,* meaning "nothing more beyond." After the New World was discovered, the motto was changed to *plus ultra,* "more beyond" (W. H. Griffith Thomas, *Let Us Go On* [Grand Rapids: Zondervan, 1944], 18). The only prescription for stunted Christians is the one prescribed in Hebrews 6:1: "Let us leave the elementary teachings about Christ and go on to maturity" (NIV). This admonition is couched in the passive voice and carries with it the idea of surrendering to the active pull of the Holy Spirit, allowing oneself to be borne on toward the goal to which God intends.

Conclusion

Every church problem can be traced to immaturity. God calls us out of our immaturity, and the crisis comes at the point of our obedience. We serve a Christ who became "obedient unto death." A Christian halting along the journey of faith is as pathetic as a house standing alone, half built. In light of this, let us go on!

SUGGESTED PREACHING PROGRAM FOR

FEBRUARY

■ Sunday Mornings

Continue the series of messages based on passages from the gospel of John, using "Finding the Life Abundant through Faith in Christ" as the theme.

■ Sunday Evenings

Continue the series of expository messages based on the book of Hebrews, using "The Supremacy of Christ" as the theme.

■ Wednesday Evenings

Continue the series "Personal Problems and the Practice of Pure Religion," based on the book of James.

WEDNESDAY EVENING, FEBRUARY 1

Title: The Problem of the Tongue

Text: "Out of the same mouth proceedeth blessing and cursing. My brethren, these things ought not so to be" **(James 3:10)**.

Scripture Reading: James 3:1–12

Introduction

When you visit your doctor for a checkup, he immediately does two things. First, he takes your pulse, and second, he says, "May I see your tongue?" The doctor can tell certain things about your health just by looking at your tongue.

This is an important analogy of the Christian life. Christ says to you today, "May I see your tongue?" By examining your tongue, Christ can tell what is in your heart. He can detect the condition of your spiritual health. George Duncan points out that there is a maturity the tongue reveals, a ministry the tongue fulfills, and a mastery the tongue demands.

I. A maturity the tongue reveals.

"If any man offend not in word, the same is a perfect [mature] man" (James 3:2). But we know that the tongue does not always reveal such maturity, don't we? The reason is that there is:

A. *A failure that involves the tongue.* Often we are concerned that we may say the wrong thing, yet there are times when our concern should be that we say nothing at all.

47

After Christ resurrected Lazarus from the dead, Lazarus had life but no liberty. He was still "bound hand and foot with graveclothes: and his face was bound about with a napkin. Jesus saith unto them, Loose him, and let him go" (John 11:44). Many Christians are in that same condition—they have life but no liberty; their mouths are bound.

B. *A function that requires the tongue.* Acts 1:8 spells out the function: "Ye shall be witnesses unto me." When our tongues become involved in the function, we have gained a maturity the tongue reveals.

II. A ministry the tongue fulfills.

The four metaphors mentioned in James 3:3–8—bits and rudder, fire and poison—dramatize this ministry.

A. *The ministry of direction is seen in James 3:3–4—"bits" and "helm" (rudder).* Both a bit in a horse's mouth and a rudder on a ship are used to direct, and both are small compared to what they direct. We are inclined to think that words are so small and insignificant that they really are not important. Advertisers, atheists, and radical student groups do not suffer from the delusion that words are not important. They know that destinies of nations can be determined by words. Your words (your Christian testimony) are as needed to give proper direction to society as the small rudder is needed to give direction to the huge ship. A rudderless ship is deadly.

B. *Destruction is spoken of in James 3:5–8—"fire" and "poison."* Both are destructive, but there usually is a difference: fire is accidental; poison is deliberately administered in secret. Fire symbolizes words spoken in a fit of anger or in an unguarded moment. The offender did not intend to hurt or destroy but did nevertheless! Poison illustrates that bit of gossip, those caustic remarks, that clever incrimination.

III. A mastery the tongue demands (James 3:9–12).

You should be the master of your tongue. But all too often when we fail to gain the mastery of our tongues, there is:

A. *An inconsistency that is disappointing (vv. 10–12).* A fountain should offer refreshment, but it does not; and a fig tree should offer food, but it has none! Here is an inconsistency that is disappointing! Others expected you to speak up for Christ, but you said not one word! They did not dream you would laugh, but you roared the loudest.

B. *An impossibility that is demanding.* "But the tongue can no man tame" (v. 8). This verse suggests that we cannot help ourselves; we are suffering from an incurable disease. The point is that no person can tame the tongue, but Christ can! As we die to self and let Christ live in and through us, the impossible will be accomplished by him!

Conclusion

Do you have life but no liberty? Are you well? Christ says to each of us today, "Let me look at your tongue."

SUNDAY MORNING, FEBRUARY 5

Title: Gospel Imperatives

Text: "Ye must be born again" (**John 3:7**). "Even so must the Son of man be lifted up" (**v. 14**). "He must increase, but I must decrease" (**v. 30**).

Scripture Reading: John 3:1–30

Hymns: "Faith of Our Fathers," Faber

          "Serve the Lord with Gladness," McKinney

          "Have Thine Own Way, Lord," Pollard

Offertory Prayer: Father in heaven, you are the giver of every good and perfect gift. May we give as freely as you have given to us. With these our gifts we bring ourselves to you. In Jesus' name. Amen.

Introduction

Christianity is a religion of imperatives. It is not a gospel of "maybe" or "hope so" or "if you can." It is a gospel of "you must"! The foundation on which faith is built is a solid rock, not shifting sand. The truths of God are clear-cut, dynamic, and imperative. They are never nebulous.

There are three gospel imperatives in John 3—three "musts" that arrest the attention of our hearts. The first is in 3:7: "Ye *must* be born again." This is the must of conversion. The second is in 3:14: "Even so *must* the Son of man be lifted up." This is the must of the cross. The third is in 3:30, "He *must* increase, but I *must* decrease." This is the must of consecration.

I. The must of conversion (John 3:1–7).

Nicodemus had one of the keenest minds in Israel. He was a "ruler of the Jews," a respected counselor. Yet Jesus said to the good man, "Ye must be born again." This is the first gospel imperative. But what does it mean to be born again? Nicodemus wondered if it might be a second physical birth (v. 4). Jesus said no, it is not of physical origin; it is a new life that comes from the Spirit of God. It is an act of God. In the first chapter of this same gospel, John refers to those "who were born, not of blood, nor of the will of the flesh, nor of the will of man, but of God" (1:13). Conversion is by the grace of God, not by the goodness of man. It is "willed" by God, not by man. But why must we be born again? Why aren't good works or attending church or keeping the law enough? Why isn't being a Nicodemus enough?

    A. *Because of the nature of humanity.* Verse 6 says, "That which is born of the flesh is flesh." The apostle Paul reminds us that "flesh and blood cannot inherit the kingdom of God" (1 Cor. 15:50). Conversion is a must because of the sinful nature of humans. In his Ephesian letter, Paul says we "were by nature the children of wrath" (2:3). The first two verses of this chapter describe our sinful nature. Paul says we were "dead in trespasses and sins … [and] walked according to the course of this world … fulfilling the

49

desires of the flesh." This kind of nature must be changed before we can inherit the kingdom of God. A change of nature is more than a change of clothes or a new pair of shoes. It is more than making good resolutions. It is a work that one cannot perform for fellow humans. It is an act of God.

B. *Because of the nature of the kingdom, each person must be born again.* Without the new birth, you cannot "see" the kingdom (v. 3) nor can you "enter" the kingdom (v. 5). Jesus told Pilate, "My kingdom is not of this world" (John 18:36). Jesus was saying that his kingdom does not have its origin in this world.

Remember now, Jesus stated this "must of conversion" to a man of education, reputation, and respectability. So Nicodemus, like you and like me, must be born again.

II. The must of the cross (John 3:14–15).

Jesus had lived sinlessly and toiled ceaselessly in this world. One would think that would be enough. Must there also be a cross?

A. *Sinless life was not enough.* Jesus was holy and undefiled. He went about doing good. But his holy life was not enough to save sinners. Jesus had to die and be raised back to life.

B. *Great teaching was not enough.* Nicodemus called Jesus "rabbi" and acknowledged that he was a teacher come from God. His teaching was unique; he taught with authority and not as the scribes and Pharisees. But his teaching could not save. The Son of Man had to be lifted up.

C. *Perfect example was not enough.* Jesus set a perfect example in prayer, obedience, and self-sacrifice; yet he had to die. The Son of Man had to be lifted up.

John 3 links up with Numbers 21. On the way to the Promised Land, the children of Israel murmured and complained against God and Moses, so God allowed fiery serpents to come into the camp. The serpents bit the people, and many died. God commanded Moses to make a serpent of brass and put it on a pole in the midst of the camp. Whoever believed the promise and looked on the serpent of brass was healed and lived (Num. 21:4–9). Now Jesus says, "Even so must the Son of man be lifted up" (John 3:14). In like manner, Jesus was lifted up on the cross that whoever believed and looked would live.

The cross is one of God's great imperatives. There was no other way to provide salvation, for "without shedding of blood is no remission" for sins (Heb. 9:22). Jesus prayed, "Father, if it be possible, let this cup pass from me" (Matt. 26:39), but there was no other way.

III. The must of consecration (John 3:30).

It was not easy for John the Baptist to say those words, especially when the limelight had been turned from him to another. Some of John's disciples had just reported how people were turning to Jesus (John 3:26). Once the multitudes followed John. Once they came from all the cities of Judah to hear John. Now

John was imprisoned and forgotten. Yet he said, "He must increase, and I must decrease." This is the must of consecration.

A. *He must increase.* Jesus must win over the hearts of people. His enemies must become his footstool. He must reign supreme. He must become King of Kings and Lord of Lords. John put Jesus in the right place—the first place—the place of ascendancy. Jesus said, "Seek ye first the kingdom of God," and that is what John was doing.

B. *I must decrease.* The Baptist knew his place in the divine reckoning. He early found and followed God's will for his life. His place was to announce another, to prepare the way for another, to give place to another. This is the must of consecration. John called people, not to himself, but to Jesus. His disciples left him and followed Jesus, and John was glad! John was the servant, but Jesus is the Lord. John was the voice, but Jesus is the Word. John was content to hide in the shadows of a greater one. This must of consecration is an imperative for every vessel God uses. You must be willing to deny yourself, take up your cross, and follow Jesus. Are you willing?

Conclusion

Some things are a must. Conversion is a must. You must be born again. There is no other way to God. The cross is a must. In the divine plan of reconciliation, another had to die for our sins. Consecration is a must. God cannot use a self-centered life. He can use a self-sacrificing one. Will you say, "Have thine own way, Lord, have thine own way"?

SUNDAY EVENING, FEBRUARY 5

Title: The Christian Faith Is a One-Way Street

Text: "Therefore leaving the principles of the doctrine of Christ, let us go on unto perfection.... For it is impossible for those who were once enlightened, and have tasted of the heavenly gift, and were made partakers of the Holy Ghost, and have tasted the good word of God, and the powers of the world to come, if they shall fall away, to renew them again unto repentance; seeing they crucify to themselves the Son of God afresh, and put him to an open shame" **(Heb. 6:1, 4–6)**.

Scripture Reading: Hebrews 6:1–12

Introduction

Jesus Christ described the Christian faith in terms of a strait gate and a narrow way (Matt. 7:14). Commitment to Christ is a one-way turnpike with no traffic circles and no deceptive exits. There is an assured finality given to those who begin this journey. They need not fear accidentally taking a wrong turn and finding themselves in hell instead of heaven. The "onceness" of conversion is a theme reappearing throughout this epistle and stressed by the frequent use of the Greek word *hapax*, meaning "once for all." (*Hapax* is used in Heb. 6:4 and 10:2 concerning conversion; 9:26, 28 concerning the finality of Christ's sacrifice; and 12:26–27 concerning the final shaking of all things.) The word carries the idea that "once" is sufficient and all-inclusive, requiring nothing more for completeness.

This epistle is addressed to immature Christians who at best are prone to drag their feet in spiritual progress. Later chapters indicate that they had a Jewish background and sometimes gave the appearance of looking backward toward Old Testament law rather than forward to the fulfillment wrought by Christ. Therefore, the inspired author stressed the permanence of Christian commitment in an attempt to emphasize the need for growing steadfastly toward Christian maturity. Turning back has no place in the thinking of Christ's disciples.

I. The entrance is permanent (Heb. 6:4–6).

One enters the Christian way on a permanent basis. Faith in Jesus Christ produces a new nature. Faith is a surrender, an opening of the heart's door. Once you allow the Holy Spirit to enter, you become a new person. You have a new outlook, a new set of values, a new purpose, a new peace, and a new hope. You are irrevocably changed. Jesus called the process a new birth (John 3:3). Paul declared that faith in Christ produced a "new creature" (2 Cor. 5:17). Anyone truly experiencing this "newness" would never desire to revoke it. The apostle John explained that people who appear to have departed from the faith were never really committed to it. They were false professors: "They went out from us, but they were not of us; for if they had been of us, they would no doubt have continued with us: but they went out, that they might be made manifest that they were not all of us" (1 John 2:19).

A. *God's power is at stake.* Entrance into the fold of God is permanent because of God's power to keep those who come to him for salvation. Somehow people have always found it difficult, perhaps because of pride, to believe that salvation is totally dependent on God's power rather than a person's righteousness. Through repentance and faith, a person surrenders to God's power and experiences conversion. God's power keeps the new convert day by day until the final culmination of salvation dawns with the resurrection.

In an effort to show the futility of a Christian living in doubt and uncertainty, the writer of Hebrews presents a hypothetical case (Heb. 6:4–6). The point of the argument asserts that if, after a faith surrender to Christ, God's power is insufficient to maintain the promised salvation, then all is lost. There would be no purpose in, or possibility of, repeating the process. The miracle of being born spiritually is performed by God. If God's power can fail, there remains no other hope. Let us examine these verses carefully.

There can be no doubt that Hebrews 6:4–6 describes a genuine experience of salvation. Four participles are used to describe this experience.

First, the people spoken of have been "enlightened," made to see the light, converted. Wonderful things come when one sees the light for the first time. At last joy and peace are discovered.

Another participle is used twice and is translated "tasted." It has the meaning of knowing by experience. At conversion one experiences the "heavenly gift," the gift of redemption; "the good word of God," the gospel message involving Christ; and "the powers of the world to come," the *dunamis* (a word often used of miracles in the New Testament, the root source of our words *dynamite* and *dynamo*) of the age that is about to invade time—the eternal age. A person could never be happy with the world's corn bread after having tasted eternity's golden loaves.

The fourth participle and its phrase are translated "and were made partakers of the Holy Ghost." Literally, the participle speaks of a change in character because something new has been added. This new ingredient is the Holy Spirit.

All four of these participles are modified by *hapax*, the "once for all" word already discussed. This casts over the total experience an aura of finality. This is no partial commitment lived out on the fringes, but rather a full and complete experience with nothing held back.

The whole point of this hypothetical case is that if it were possible to experience the new birth of conversion and then somehow lose the "heavenly gift," becoming the same old person as before, then nothing further could be done. No chance of a repeat performance exists. If God's power to preserve fails, then all is lost: "For it is impossible.... If they shall fall away, to renew [make them a new person again; perform the miracle of the spiritual birth again] them again unto repentance."

At stake here is not human strength to persevere, but God's power to preserve. God has already put his power on the line (John 5:24; 10:27–28; 1 Peter 1:5). If God fails, there is no other chance.

B. *Christ's atoning death is at stake.* Not only is the heavenly Father's power at stake, but also the sacrificial death of Christ. To propose that one can be converted and afterward lose the gift of redemption is to propose the utter failure of Christ's redemptive mission culminated at Calvary and triumphantly proclaimed by the resurrection. No one can be converted twice: "Seeing they crucify to themselves the Son of God afresh, and put him to an open shame."

Christ died "once for all" as the sacrifice for human sin: "By his own blood he entered in *once* into the holy place, having obtained eternal redemption for us" (Heb. 9:12). Again we find the word *hapax* used to stress finality and completeness. If Christ's sacrifice on the cross was sufficient, then the salvation experience is permanent. If salvation can be lost, if the new creation in Christ can perish, then Christ is held up for ridicule, just as he was at Golgotha, the only difference being that those responsible for his ridicule are not avowed enemies but rather those who claim him as Savior.

53

Christ plans no second redemptive death. Those implying his first crucifixion was unable to redeem them openly disgrace him. They, in effect, join with the motley crowd in Jerusalem who likewise concluded Jesus to be a deceiver. The word translated "open shame" was used to describe treatment given executed criminals whereby the body was quartered and left exposed or where the dead body was left hanging for all to see. Surely Christ must not bear this shame again at the hands of those who profess him as Lord.

II. The direction is toward Christlikeness (Heb. 6:1–2, 11–12).

The writer of Hebrews stresses the permanence of God's salvation by means of a hypothetical case in order to clear away doubts and uncertainties that often hinder Christian growth.

A. *The command.* Christians who are continually consumed with fears concerning their salvation have little strength left for making progress in the Christian life. One of the primary themes of Hebrews is expressed in 6:1: "Let us go on [be borne on] unto perfection [maturity in Christ]." To accomplish this growth, one must leave the ABCs of the faith, venturing forth into the thick of Christian warfare, "not laying again the foundation of repentance from dead works, and of faith toward God, of the doctrine of baptisms, and of laying on of hands, and of resurrection of the dead, and of eternal judgment" (vv. 1–2).

Christian maturity is our goal. The word translated "perfection" (*teleiotata*) was used by Philo to designate his most advanced students in contrast to the beginners and the middle group just beginning to make progress.

From the time of conversion, there should be steady progress in Christian maturity. The hypothetical case (Heb. 6:4–6) was given to put an end to the practice of having to be reconverted every year. I know of communities where the same people are "converted" in every summer revival. These are the people who keep trying to lay again "the foundation of repentance from dead works." The writer uses a common idiom for constructing a foundation for a house. If one spends all his time on the foundation, he will never finish the house.

B. *The challenge.* Now comes the challenge. One should follow the great models of faith, like Abraham: "And we desire that every one of you do shew the same diligence to the full assurance of hope unto the end: That ye be not slothful, but followers of them who through faith and patience inherit the promises" (Heb. 6:11–12).

The word translated "slothful" is the same word (*nothroi*) translated "dull" in Hebrews 5:11. Whereas 5:11 speaks of a sluggish mind, 6:12 refers to a sluggish numbness in keeping alive the Christian hope. Never let the assurance produced by Christian hope grow dim and tarnished. This urges us on in Christian adventure right up to the end—the *telos* (note the same root for "end" in 6:11 and "perfection" in 6:1). We are to go on, to grow in Christlikeness right up to the end—whether the end of life or the end of the age.

Conclusion

Christianity is a one-way street. You can enter only once, and having entered, the only direction is toward Christian maturity. Our resource for the journey is the power of God. In Bunyan's *Pilgrim's Progress*, Christian, by the light of day, looked back over the valley of death, through whose darkness he had just come, and saw that the narrow path was paralleled by dangerous chasms and drop-offs and that the fiends of hell lay hidden amid the rocks, and he was lost in gratitude and praise for the divine love that had carried him through. Someday we too will gaze back over life and feel the same sense of wonder. Until then, let us go on.

WEDNESDAY EVENING, FEBRUARY 8

Title: The Problem of Determining Wisdom

Text: "Who is a wise man and endued with knowledge among you? let him shew out of a good conversation his works with meekness of wisdom" (**James 3:13**).

Scripture Reading: James 3:13–18

Introduction

What is wisdom, and how does one determine it? Who is really wise? Is it that person who thinks he is a "smart operator" because he can cheat on life and get by? Is it that green college professor who is still infatuated with his doctorate and feels that at last he has a license to speak as an authority in every field, including religion, the Bible, and theology?

I. What wisdom is not (James 3:13–16).

A. *Wisdom is not arrogant.* "Are there some wise and understanding men among you? Then your life will be an example of the humility that is born of true wisdom" (James 3:13 PHILLIPS). Learning is in vain and worthless if it does not teach us to be humble in our attitude and conduct toward others.

B. *Wisdom is not divisive.* "If you have a fierce divisive spirit, even while defending your belief, you have neither genuine religion nor true wisdom" (James 3:14 PHILLIPS).

Certain pseudopious people often form private "holy clubs" within the church. Under the guise of having a prayer group, they sit around and criticize others "less spiritual" than they in the church. Some even draw around them unsuspecting young people and turn them against the older members of the church. In the name of piety and spiritual wisdom, they become divisive. This is not "wisdom from above"!

C. *Wisdom is not sensual.* "Such 'wisdom' does not come down from heaven but is earthly, unspiritual, of the devil" (James 3:15 NIV).

A prevalent attitude is, "The old idea that 'you reap what you sow' just is not true—that is, if you are wise enough to know how to get by." Cold facts refute this. For example, some people use condoms to commit fornication and call it "safe sex." They may not conceive an unwanted child or contract any sexually transmitted diseases, but have they avoided all negative consequences? What about guilt? What about shame? What about that unclean feeling? What about the loss of self-respect? You see, there is such a thing as right and wrong, regardless of the consequences.

II. What wisdom is (James 3:17–18).

A. *Wisdom is "pure," clean, and free from lustful indulgence (James 3:17).*
B. *Wisdom is "peaceable," free from self-assertion, living in peace with others and promoting peace among others (James 3:17).* This is the opposite of divisiveness and strife. Not much wisdom is required to create a "stink" in a church, for even a skunk can do that! But it takes a person of real wisdom to fill the air with the sweet fragrance of peace.
C. *Wisdom is "gentle" (James 3:17).* This speaks of being gracious in your interpretation of the actions and works of others. Such wisdom makes allowances for others.
D. *Wisdom is agreeable, "easy to be entreated" (James 3:17).* One who has such wisdom is approachable, not stubborn or obstinate.
E. *Wisdom is merciful, "full of mercy and good fruits" (James 3:17).* This characteristic of wisdom enables us to overlook wrongs done against us and graciously grant forgiveness to those who offend, while we at the same time perform every possible act of kindness.
F. *Wisdom is fair to all ("without partiality," James 3:17).* Wisdom will prevent us from being a respecter of persons. It will keep us from favoring some over others because of what they can do for us.
G. *Wisdom is unpretentious ("without hypocrisy," James 3:17).* A Christian must always act in his own character and never work under a mask.

Conclusion

"Who is a wise man and endued with knowledge among you?" You can be that person if you lay aside what wisdom is not and practice what wisdom is.

SUNDAY MORNING, FEBRUARY 12

Title: Do You Believe in Miracles?
Text: "This is again the second miracle that Jesus did, when he was come out of Judaea into Galilee" (**John 4:54**).

Scripture Reading: John 4:46–5:14

Hymns: "Come, Thou Almighty King," Anonymous

"Great Redeemer, We Adore Thee," Harris

"Glory to His Name," Hoffman

Offertory Prayer: Holy heavenly Father, we come to you today praying for divine assistance that we might gain the victory over our innate tendency to be selfish. We come praying that you would help us to recognize that you are the Giver of the ability to get wealth. Open our eyes and help us to see the need of your kingdom for financial support. Help us this day to participate in ministries of mercy and in all of the efforts to evangelize the world by means of our tithes and love offerings. Accept these gifts and bless them in the growth of your kingdom. We pray in Jesus' name. Amen.

Introduction

Jesus Christ entered the world by means of a miraculous conception. He conquered death by a miraculous resurrection. He ascended back to the Father by a miraculous ascension. He was a supernatural person. He possessed powers above those of the ordinary person.

Jesus spoke not merely for God; he spoke as God himself, for he was God in human flesh. Miracles were the normal expression of the power of his person.

Modern, sophisticated people are tempted to deny the miraculous because they are inclined either to forget, to ignore, or to eliminate God from their thinking. William Barclay has said, "Modern man is suspicious of the miraculous; he dislikes anything that he cannot explain; and he thinks that he knows so much about the universe and its working that he can say soundly that miracles do not happen. The last thing which he expects is a miracle" (*The Mind of Jesus* [London: SCM, 1960], 76). This noted scholar has declared that we might receive more miracles if we would stop insisting that miracles do not happen and begin expecting them to happen.

For us to believe in miracles, we must have faith in an unseen force behind the universe. We must believe in a personal God. Carlton Buck says it in the poem entitled "I Believe in Miracles."

> Creation shows the power of God —
> *There's glory all around,*
> *And those who see must stand in awe,*
> *For miracles abound.*
> *I believe in miracles —*
> *I've seen a soul set free,*
> *Miraculous the change in one*
> *Redeemed through Calvary;*
> *I've seen the lily push its way*
> *Up through the stubborn sod —*

I believe in miracles,
For I believe in God!

— ©1956 by Singspiration

Jesus came to release and utilize miraculous power in the lives of people. A better understanding of his ministry through miracles can be of great assistance for today. What we need today is not just a knowledge of what Christ did in the past. We need to know and respond to the Christ who wants to do things today. We must believe that the New Testament is more than just a record of what happened in the past; it is an unfolding of what can happen today in the lives of those who sincerely trust Jesus Christ and surrender themselves to his purpose and to the power he makes available to them.

The miracles of Jesus are a revelation of his power and love. In these miracles we see in action a power that is available to deal with the human situation today. We can discover in these miracles a power through which pain and suffering can be defeated and through which sin and the consequences of sin can be overcome.

It is interesting to examine the manner in which our Lord used his miraculous power.

1. Jesus used miracles to reveal something about God rather than as mere proofs of the existence of God. He assumed that people would believe that there is a God and used miracles to reveal his nature, character, and purpose.
2. Jesus used miracle power to restore that which had been lost because of the invasion of evil into the lives of people. He gave sight to the blind, hearing to the deaf, health to the ill, and even life to the dead. His was a ministry of restoring what had been lost because of sin.
3. Jesus used miracle power to reveal the divine opposition to that which harms people. Sin deprives people of achieving the destiny for which God created them.
4. Jesus used miracle power to reveal his compassion for people and his plan for them.
5. Jesus never used miracle power for his own personal needs. He rejected Satan's suggestion that he turn the stones into bread when he was hungry in the wilderness. He rejected Satan's suggestion that he cast himself down from the pinnacle of the temple to win the people's affection by an extravagant display of power. He refused to call twelve legions of angels to rescue him from the agony of the cross.

Let us look at the manner in which Jesus dealt with the man who had been lame for thirty-eight years.

I. Our Lord takes the initiative (John 5:1, 5–6).

A. *Our Lord had eyes to see suffering and ears to hear distress calls.*
B. *Our Lord did not run in apathy and indifference away from human suffering.*

C. *Our Lord deliberately went to those in desperate need.* Those who were around the pool were:
  1. Living in disappointment.
  2. Living in uselessness.
  3. Living in unhappiness.
  4. Living in helplessness.
  5. Living in despair with little hope.

II. Our Lord's probing question: "Wilt thou be made whole?"

A. *This question was needful because some people enjoy their sickness to the extent that they do not want to get well.* By this question, our Lord focused attention on the issue of the illness and the need for a cure.

B. *This question indicated his concern for the man's need.*

III. The reply of the man who was disabled (John 5:7).

A. *A confession of helplessness.*

B. *A declaration of despair and hopelessness.*

C. *A complaint against others.*

D. *A cry for help.*

IV. Our Lord's shocking command (John 5:8).

A. *Our Lord commanded that which was seemingly impossible.* He always does.

B. *His command called for an instant response of obedience on the part of the man who was disabled.* His commands always call for an instant response of obedience. Never does he suggest that we should obey him at some time in the distant future.

V. The response of the man who was disabled to the Lord's command (John 5:9).

A. *A prompt response of obedience was required, and a prompt response was made.*

B. *Our Lord's command made no provisions for a relapse into lameness. The man arose and continued to walk.*

C. *There must be a continuous use of the power that Christ makes available for us today as we seek to walk in his ways and to do his will.*

VI. Our Lord's parting word to the man who no longer had a disability (John 5:14).

A. *Sin had brought tragedy into his life in the first place.*

B. *Sin always brings tragedy into life.* Sometimes the tragedy is felt most in the one who is guilty. In other instances, others suffer because of his sin.

Conclusion

Do you believe in miracles? The apostles did. The early Christians did. Many modern Christians believe in miracles.

I believe in the miracle of God's love for us. I believe in the miracle of God's forgiveness of sin. I believe in the miracle of conversion and the gift of eternal life through faith in Jesus Christ. I believe in the miracle of God's guidance that is available to us day by day if we will follow Jesus Christ. I believe in the miracle of God's power that enables us to adjust to whatever circumstances life may bring and to live victoriously for the glory of God. I believe in the miracle of heaven at the end of the way.

With faith in the miracle-working power of Jesus Christ, let us face the future and live it for his glory.

SUNDAY EVENING, FEBRUARY 12

Title: Christian Hope

Text: "We want each of you to show this same diligence to the very end, in order to make your hope sure.... We have this hope as an anchor for the soul, firm and secure" **(Heb. 6:11, 19)**.

Scripture Reading: Hebrews 6:11–20

Introduction

Some people are by nature optimistic. Others are, by the same token, pessimistic. You often get what you expect. One person sees a rosebush in terms of thorns; another sees only the roses. One person sees the dark side of every cloud while the other looks for the silver lining. Yet genuine hope can never be based on one's subjective outlook, one's particular temperament. The person whose hope has no basis other than a general optimistic spirit is clutching a false hope, for the only valid hope is Christian hope, and temperament is not its origin.

I. Christian hope grows out of faith (Heb. 6:12).

We are admonished to be "followers of them who through faith and patience inherit the promises" (v. 12). The one great distinction belonging to Christian hope is that it is an outgrowth of Christian faith. Hope is said to produce a full assurance that in turn stimulates eager discipleship (v. 11), but faith is the mother of hope. Hope is kept alive because faith endures all disappointments. Faith does not bog down.

Abraham is the prime example of those "who through faith and patience inherit the promises" (v. 12). God's promise to Abraham (Gen. 12:1–7; 22:16) was a long-term one requiring patience. The word translated "patience" is composed of two words: "long" (*makros*) and "spirit" (*thumos*). Abraham was a "long-spirited" man, willing to wait on God's promises. He still believed God, even when driven out of the Promised Land. Though no son was born and Sarah grew old in her barrenness, he still believed God would make of his offspring a great nation.

Even when Sarah at last miraculously conceived and brought forth Isaac, the child of promise, Abraham could see God's promise of a numberless people only in the most germinal way. And as to just how his offspring would bless all nations, Abraham was never told. He did not know how, but he believed God. Abraham, like many other forerunners of faith, never saw the fullness of God's promises: "These all died in faith, not having received the promises, but having seen them afar off, and were persuaded of them, and embraced them" (Heb. 11:13). The literal figure shows them waving a greeting to these promises, which they saw in the distance. Yet because they believed, it is said of them, as it was of Abraham in particular: "And so, after he had patiently endured, he obtained the promise" (6:15).

II. Christian hope is God's standing offer (Heb. 6:18).

The writer of Hebrews literally speaks of hope as "the set-before-us hope" (6:18). Wherever we turn in this earthly melee, God sets this hope before us. We can ignore it, refuse it, or despise it, but God keeps setting it before us in an effort to gain our attention while the hourglass still contains some grains of sand.

Since the entrance of sin into the world, people have had to deal with disease and death. The fall also left people spiritually sick, victims of Satan's enticing allurements. "All have sinned" (Rom. 3:23). Moreover, "the wages of sin is death" (6:23). Our last earthly appointment is with death (Heb. 9:27). The music in every funeral home is the music of death. Every empty place in the family circle, every vacant chair, by its silence, screams out the fact of death.

The only answer to death is the hope that God sets before us—the hope of eternal life. We lay the mortal remains of our saved loved ones in the cold earth, but God promises a resurrection. They are absent from our family circle, but God's promise is that they are with him (2 Cor. 5:6–8). "Death is swallowed up in victory" (1 Cor. 15:54). Death fades away in the presence of eternal life.

III. Christian hope is an anchor amid life's storms (Heb. 6:19).

From the moment people built ships and sailed seas, the anchor became a symbol of hope. Epictetus wrote: "A ship should never depend on one anchor, or a life on one hope." Pythagoras said: "Wealth is a weak anchor; fame is still weaker. What then are the anchors which are strong? Wisdom, great-heartedness, courage—these are the anchors which no storm can shake." The Bible rises above pagan wisdom and declares that Christian hope is "an anchor of the soul, both sure and stedfast" (v. 19).

The word translated "sure" is the source of our word *asphalt*, meaning our anchor is held firmly. It cannot be dislodged, because it is grounded in heaven, beyond this crumbling earth. The reason so many hopes are torn from their moorings is that the moorings themselves are temporary. Sooner or later earthly vicissitudes shatter our self-installed anchors.

The only sure footing lies outside the physical realm to which we are committed. This age is growing old, like a tattered garment. Soon it will pass away. As Christians, our hope is anchored in the eternal. It is grounded in heaven. The writer of Hebrews uses the figure of the Holy of Holies to depict this: "Which hope we have as an anchor of the soul, both sure and stedfast, and which entereth into that within the veil" (v. 19).

The Holy of Holies was a small inner sanctuary containing the ark of the covenant, the lid of which was the mercy seat. The ark was a constant reminder of God's presence. A heavy veil one handbreadth thick, requiring three hundred priests to carry it, separated the congregation from the Holy of Holies. Only the high priest could enter, and this only once each year on the Day of Atonement in order to make intercession by the blood of a sacrificial goat. Even for the high priest, to stand in God's presence was considered a dangerous, awesome experience.

In Hebrews 6:19–20, the Holy of Holies is heaven itself. Christian hope is anchored in heaven—in the unseen spiritual realities. The veil is no longer a massive fabric but rather our human limitation. Our vision is clouded by the mortal scales over our eyes. We cannot see the solid rock gripping our anchor, but it is there—beyond the mortal veil.

Mental institutions are filled with people who staked everything on self-made hopes of one kind or another and could not stand the fearful experience of seeing those hopes dashed. Dislodged anchors drive people to drugs and alcohol and ultimately to life's garbage dump. Christians have a hope that never disappoints (Rom. 5:5). Romans reminds us that we are delivered from the despair all about us by our hope: "For we are saved by hope" (8:24).

IV. Christian hope is a person: Jesus Christ (Heb. 6:19–20).

As Socrates came to die, he spoke to his disciples the words that since have been declared the "most pathetic cry of antiquity": "I have faith in the future, and I think I see the golden islands, but, oh, that we had a stouter vessel, or a stronger word!"

Through Christ we have a stronger word and a stouter vessel. We have a living hope because Jesus Christ was raised the third day and ever lives (1 Peter 1:5). Our hope is the living Savior. When Christ ascended to the Father, our hope was firmly planted in heaven. "It enters the inner sanctuary behind the curtain, where Jesus, who went before us, has entered on our behalf. He has become a high priest forever" (Heb. 6:19–20 NIV).

Jesus is our forerunner. In the contemporary usage of the day, a forerunner was a scout, sometimes an advanced guard of an army. The Levitical high priest came before God's presence as a representative of the people but never as a forerunner. Jesus blazed the path of God. In effect, he became the path to God. Our hope is anchored in heaven because of Christ.

In ancient times every Mediterranean harbor had a great boulder deeply embedded at the shoreline as a mooring for ships within the harbor. When prevailing winds and stormy seas prevented small vessels from entering the harbor, a forerunner would carry a line ashore in a small boat. Once the line was fastened to the great rock, the vessel could be drawn to shore. Our hope lies in Christ, to whom we are grounded, who draws us ever nearer to our heavenly harbor. His death was a sacrifice for our sins, opening the way to forgiveness and eternal life.

Conclusion

But this living hope must be claimed. It is set before all people but is possessed only by those who, forsaking all other offers of hope, surrender to Christ. It belongs to those "who have fled for refuge to lay hold upon the hope set before us" (Heb. 6:18). In the background of these words lies the Old Testament cities of refuge to which lawbreakers could flee and remain safe (Deut. 4:41–42). Christ is the only refuge for sinful people—the only hope! To live without Christ is to live without hope. A faith surrender to Christ allows him to enter our lives as Lord: "Christ in [us], the hope of glory" (Col. 1:27).

WEDNESDAY EVENING, FEBRUARY 15

Title: The Problem of Selfishness

Text: "What causes fights and quarrels among you? Don't they come from your desires that battle within you?" **(James 4:1 NIV).**

Scripture Reading: James 4:1–12

Introduction

Selfishness is not a childhood disease that you will someday outgrow. Evidence of this truth is seen in that James addresses adults and reprimands them because of their childish selfishness.

I. The source of selfishness (James 4:1).

"What causes fights and quarrels among you? Don't they come from your desires that battle within you?" (v. 1 NIV).

  A. The source of quarrels is a love for sinful, selfish gratification.

  B. *You are responsible for your selfishness.*

II. The frustration of selfishness (James 4:2–6).

"You want something but don't get it" (v. 2 NIV). Here is a picture of frustration.

  A. *The frustration of unanswered prayer (vv. 2–3).* Prayer is unanswered because of unoffered prayer (v. 2) and because of unworthy prayer (v. 3).

  B. The frustration of indecision (vv. 4–6). The spirit of selfishness says one thing and the Spirit of Christ says another. You are trapped by the frustration of indecision.

   There is the frustration of indecision over friendships (v. 4). The friendships you cultivate will determine largely the degree of meaningful friendship you will have with God. We tend to take on the color of our social environment.

   Then there is the frustration of indecision over personal honesty (vv. 5–6). Perhaps James refers to Genesis 8:21, "The imagination of man's heart is evil from his youth." Are you willing to admit this? Will you or will you not be honest about yourself? If so, then there is a promise for you in the last part of James 4:6: "God gives grace to the humble" (NIV).

III. The solution to selfishness (James 4:7–12).

A. *Humility.* "Submit yourselves therefore to God. . . . Humble yourselves in the sight of the Lord, and he shall lift you up" (vv. 7, 10).

B. *Resistance.* "Resist the devil, and he will flee from you" (v. 7). Refuse to lose the battle! When some selfish urge hits you, don't give in—resist that urge. "But how can I resist the devil?" you ask. Our best example is Christ: (1) by Scripture, (2) by prayer, and (3) by surrender to God's will.

C. *Closeness to God.* "Come near to God and he will come near to you" (v. 8 NIV). As in the story of the prodigal and his father, when a soul sets out to seek the Father, the Father sets out to meet that soul. Since you tend to become like your closest friend, it is important that you stay close to God.

D. *Cleansing.* "Cleanse your hands" (v. 8). There must be the cleansing of your deeds ("hands") as well as a cleansing of your desires ("heart").

E. *Change of attitude (vv. 9–12).* Three attitude changes are required if the problem of selfishness is to be solved. First, a change of attitude toward sin (v. 9); second, a change of attitude toward others, "Never pull each other to pieces" (v. 11 PHILLIPS); and third, a change of attitude toward God's law (vv. 11–12).

Conclusion

Selfishness may be a childhood disease, but it infects adults as well. James has pointed us to the solution. Ours is the duty to avail ourselves of the answer offered.

SUNDAY MORNING, FEBRUARY 19

Title: The Claims of Christ

Text: "Jesus said to them, 'My Father is always at his work to this very day, and I, too, am working'" **(John 5:17 NIV).**

Scripture Reading: John 5:10–29

Hymns: "This Is My Father's World," Babcock

"Crown Him with Many Crowns," Bridges

"Tell Me the Story of Jesus," Crosby

Offertory Prayer: Holy Father, we pray that this day you will open our eyes and help us to see how good and how gracious you have been to us. Help us to see and to acknowledge that every good and perfect gift comes from you. We thank you for life and love and light for the road ahead. We thank you for the blessings of the past. We are grateful for your blessings upon the thoughts of our minds and the efforts of our hands. We bring a portion of the results of our labors and present them as a gift of our love to you. Bless these tithes and offerings and use them in ministries of mercy. In Jesus' name. Amen.

Introduction

Bible commentator Marcus Dods said concerning the words contained in our Scripture reading, "This five-minute talk with the Jews contains probably the most important truth ever uttered upon earth." For the first time, our Lord gave in public an explanation of his words and works so that people could know who he was and what he was trying to accomplish.

The first nine months of Jesus' ministry had been spent in Galilee. He had healed the sick and had engaged in continuous preaching and teaching. The multitudes heard him joyfully. He and his disciples were happy. He declared that God is a loving Father who hungers for the love of people. He showed that his way was a way of trust and freedom.

The Pharisees resented and opposed Jesus. Their concept of God did not include love for sinners. To them he was a legalistic God whose main concern was with the law, the temple, and the Sabbath. Religion was a restriction and a burden. Their primary concern was for the applause of people rather than for the glory of God.

Our Lord, by his actions and words, challenged the Pharisees' concept of God. He denied the truthfulness of what they thought and taught about God. He did this when he asserted his authority over the temple. He denied what they taught when he repeatedly violated their laws and traditions concerning Sabbath observance. He made bold claims that he came to fulfill the law rather than to break it. They questioned his authority, and he gave voice to some claims that only added to their animosity.

I. The uniqueness of Jesus' claims.

A. *Jesus claimed to be the promised Messiah.*
1. He had made this claim in his conversation with the Samaritan woman (John 4:26).
2. He had used the term "Son of man" concerning himself (John 1:51; 3:13–16, 35–36; 5:19–21). His Jewish listeners would recognize this as a direct claim to messiahship as revealed in Daniel 7:1–14, where the Messiah is referred to as "Son of man."

B. *Jesus asserted his lordship over the Sabbath.*
1. He encouraged his listeners to rejoice in a holiday.
2. He encouraged his listeners to rejoice in the Lord.
3. He encouraged his listeners to rejoice in doing good on the Sabbath.

C. *Jesus asserted his oneness, his perfect union with the Father (John 5:17–18).*
1. The mind of Jesus was the mind of God.
2. The words of Jesus were the words of God.
3. The actions of Jesus were the actions of God (cf. John 10:30; 14:9).

D. *Jesus asserted his life-giving power (John 5:21).*
　1. He is the giver of life in time (John 5:24–26).
　2. He is the giver of life in eternity (John 5:28–29).
E. *Jesus announced his appointment as Judge (John 5:22–23).*

Christ was to make many other claims, such as "I came down from God"; "I came down from heaven"; "I am the Son of God"; "I and my Father are one"; "He that hath seen me hath seen the Father"; "I am the Messiah"; "I am the light of the world"; "I am the bread of life"; "I am the resurrection and the life"; "I am the good shepherd"; "I am the door"; "I am the way"; "I am the true vine"; "I, if I be lifted up from the earth, will draw all men unto me"; "I have overcome the world"; and "I will come again."

II. The validity of Jesus' claims.

Were these claims true? Are they true today? How would you have reacted if you had lived in Jerusalem in AD 30?

Were these claims the result of a monstrous arrogance? Were these claims nothing more than the delusion of a pitiful hallucination? Were these words the comments of an insane, arrogant deceiver?

The claims of Jesus were then, and they continue to be, supported by unimpeachable evidence. Age after age the simple and eternal truth of these claims has been demonstrated.

A. *The claims of Jesus were verified by the witness of John the Baptist (John 5:33).*
B. *The claims of Jesus were verified by the witness of the heavenly Father (John 5:37).*
C. *The claims of Jesus were verified by his miraculous works (John 5:36).*
D. *The claims of Jesus were verified by the teachings of the Old Testament (John 5:39).*
E. *The claims of Jesus were verified by the changes wrought in the lives of those who trusted him as Lord and Master.*
F. *The claims of Christ were verified most dramatically by his victorious resurrection from the dead.* By this divine event, God gave unmistakable proof of his approval of his Son Jesus Christ.

III. Responses to the claims of Christ.

A. *Some responded with idle indifference and unconcern.*
B. *Some responded with doubts and unbelief.*
C. *Some responded with intense jealousy and hatred as a result of pride, selfishness, and prejudice.*
D. *Some received Jesus, believed in him, and followed him with a deathless loyalty.*

Conclusion

What will be your response to the claims of Jesus Christ concerning his own unique purpose? What will you do with the claims that he made concerning provisions that he has made for you through his death on the cross and through his victorious resurrection from the dead? What response will you make to his promise of forgiveness and the gift of new life for those who are willing to follow in his way?

Jesus is worthy of your confidence and love. He invites your loyalty and cooperation in doing the work of God in the world today. The response is yours to make.

SUNDAY EVENING, FEBRUARY 19

Title: Dead Priests and the Living Christ (Part 1)

Text: "Now there have been many of those priests, since death prevented them from continuing in office; but because Jesus lives forever, he has a permanent priesthood. Therefore he is able to save completely those who come to God through him, because he always lives to intercede for them" **(Heb. 7:23–25 NIV).**

Scripture Reading: Hebrews 7:1–8:13

Introduction

Hebrews alone among the books of the New Testament calls Christ a priest. Of course the concept is implied in Peter's use of "holy priesthood" to describe God's new people (1 Peter 2:5). Paul depicts Christ in terms of a mediator: "For there is one God, and one mediator between God and men, the man Christ Jesus" (1 Tim. 2:5). To be sure, there are several Old Testament references to a priestly Messiah. Zechariah prophesied: "He shall be a priest upon his throne" (Zech. 6:13). Isaiah 53 speaks of a suffering servant who will sacrifice himself for Israel's sins.

Hebrews calls Christ High Priest, not once, but numerous times (5:6; 6:20; 7:17, 21; 9:11), using the messianic terminology of the psalmist (Ps. 110:4). There must be a valid purpose behind this recurring theme, a theme so seldom implied elsewhere in the New Testament. It seems apparent that the solution lies in an awareness of the crucial situation to which the author of Hebrews addresses himself. The first Christian converts were Jews steeped in the Old Testament Scriptures and priestly traditions. These early converts continued to attend the services of the temple and synagogues. As the forces of Judaism grew more adamant, a break between Judaism and the church was inevitable. Stephen's message revealing that God was not limited to working with the physical descendants of Abraham precipitated a rupture that resulted in his martyrdom (Acts 7), followed by fierce persecution of the Christians at the hands of the leaders of Judaism (Acts 8, 9). In spite of this, we find the apostle Paul in AD 58 attending temple services at Jerusalem. Perhaps the final break came with Nero's burning of Rome, for which he made Christians the scapegoat. In the ensuing Neronian persecution, Christianity was once and for all separated from all strings to Judaism.

As the final break with Judaism came, there were, no doubt, many Jewish Christians who faltered at the prospect of forever leaving behind the Jewish traditions of their childhood training, the temple services, and the priestly rituals. At this moment of hesitation, the Holy Spirit inspired someone to write an epistle dealing with just why Christians must go on to maturity in Christ. Naturally such an epistle would need to show the superiority of Christ over the Mosaic institutions of Judaism, and particularly over the priesthood and its prescribed sacrifices. The epistle is in our canon as the book of Hebrews and delineates sharply between the Old Testament priesthood, marked by dying men replacing dying men, and the living Christ who is our High Priest. This message will deal with the priesthood composed of mortal men. Part 2, next Sunday night, will deal with the living Christ, our eternal High Priest.

I. Mortal in nature (Heb. 7:23).

The Levitical priesthood lies dead because, first of all, it was composed of mortal men who were hindered from continuance by death: "Now there have been many of those priests, since death prevented them from continuing in office" (v. 23 NIV).

The priests, being mortal men, were themselves sinful and in need of atonement. Even the high priest was no exception: "For the law appoints as high priests men who are weak" (Heb. 7:28 NIV). The major requirement for the Levitical priesthood was genealogy, not ability or character. Any man of the lineage of Aaron who was not marred by some physical defect could be a priest.

II. Temporary in purpose (Heb. 7:11 – 19).

Another reason for the decease of the Levitical priesthood had to do with God's divine purpose for its establishment. The priesthood was divinely ordained as one segment of God's total redemptive agenda. The time of its servitude was limited. When the purpose for which it was created was fulfilled, it passed from the scene.

When God chose to reveal himself to the Israelites, he was in the position of a parent who sets out to teach his toddling child. The Israelites were primitive and barbaric. To teach them the meaning of holiness was indeed a worthy undertaking. For this reason, the Old Testament is full of shadows and types, of which the priesthood is a part. Neither the Mosaic law in general nor the priestly ritual in particular was ordained as a means of dispensing salvation. In fact, salvation of the soul could be taught only by first emphasizing physical deliverance. Therefore, God delivered his people from Egyptian bondage by a mighty destruction of Pharaoh's army in the Red Sea. This great intervening act of God became the central redemptive theme of the Old Testament. Always the Old Testament prophets remind the people of God's salvation by referring to this great incident. Gradually salvation took on a spiritual aspect, though not until New Testament days was this fully seen.

We must guard against the idea that people were saved differently in the Old Testament than in the New. People have always experienced God's salvation by faith. Abraham believed God, and this belief brought him into a right relationship with God (Gen. 15:6). The nation believed God's promise to deliver from bondage, and thus they set out toward the Red Sea. By miraculously saving them from Pharaoh, God pointed toward a larger and fuller deliverance. The object of faith in the Old Testament was God's promise of ultimate deliverance. We are privileged to know the fullness of God's promised salvation as we see Christ. But the same type of faith is required today.

When Old Testament people believed God, they were at the same time committing themselves to a way of life set forth by God's law as given at Sinai. The law came to explain and delineate the life that pleased God, as well as to set up the only civil laws possessed by the young nation.

As part of the Mosaic system, the priesthood with its prescribed sacrifices played an important part. The sacrifice of animals was a constant reminder of the serious nature of sin, as well as a foreshadowing of a final sacrifice to come, by which God's promises would be fulfilled. People of faith sinned against God's law. The priestly system was there to lead them to repentance and rededication. The sinful Israelite brought an animal from his flock, which was in a sense an extension of himself, for his very existence depended on his flock, and placing his hand on the animal to complete the identification, he gave it to the priest to be slain. As the animal died, it was as if a part of the sinner died. He was reminded that the "soul who sins is the one who will die" (Ezek. 18:4 NIV) and that life is in the blood (Deut. 12:23). As the blood poured out, life poured out.

Every sacrifice pointed toward the "Lamb of God, who takes away the sin of the world" (John 1:29 NIV). In a real sense, the priestly rituals taught the serious nature of sin and helped lead people to meaningful acts of rededication much as contemporary Christians periodically rededicate themselves to the Lord's service as living sacrifices (Rom. 12:1–2).

The high priest entered the Holy of Holies once each year on the day of atonement and made sacrifice for all the people. Within the Holy of Holies he was considered to be in the very presence of God. The whole purpose of that event, in the long-range plan of God, was to prepare people to understand the sacrificial work of Christ.

III. Limited in power (Heb. 7:1).

The Levitical priesthood never offered salvation; its purpose was only to point toward fulfillment as found in Christ. Herein is found the poverty of Judaism. Without Christ, it has nothing final to offer. If the priestly ritual could have given ultimate fullness, then there would have been no need for Christ (v. 1), but it couldn't! Properly understood, the Levitical priesthood was not a failure. The Israelites forced its failure by ascribing to it a power and permanence never intended by God. When the Levitical system first became an end in itself, God sent the eighth-century prophets to preach against a cold formalism without personal dedication. Micah and Amos thundered out against social injustice. Isaiah looked past the lifeless ritual of the Israelites toward God's promised Deliverer.

When Israel persisted in their indifference, God used wicked Babylon as a chastening rod. When the seventy-year Babylonian exile was over, the captives returned to Palestine with one burning determination. Never again would they transgress God's law. It was during this era that the emphasis of the Levitical system superseded God's intended purpose and the law became, more than ever before, an end in itself. Judaism had taken an instrument of revelation and made of it the final goal.

Conclusion

The poverty of Judaism is that it leaves out Christ, God's promised Redeemer. To stop short of Christ is to spend one's life cultivating land and never sowing any seed. It is to spend a lifetime writing letters to one's betrothed, preparing a house, and planning the wedding yet never having the ceremony. Christ has come. We have no need of dead priests. Our hope is not in dying men but in the living Christ, our High Priest.

WEDNESDAY EVENING, FEBRUARY 22

Title: The Problem of Overconfidence

Text: "But now ye rejoice in your boastings: all such rejoicing is evil" **(James 4:16)**.

Scripture Reading: James 4:13–17

Introduction

There is a difference between "overconfidence" and "self-confidence." Overconfidence results from the delusion that you are capable of handling any problem all by yourself. Self-confidence in its most wholesome meaning is born of confidence in Christ and his indwelling presence. Paul's was this kind of confidence when he said, "I can do all things through *Christ*" (Phil. 4:13).

I. Overconfidence blinds you to the brevity of life (James 4:13–14).

The repetition of the word "and" four times in one verse indicates a presumptuous confidence.

A. *The brevity of life may catch you unprepared.* In verse 13 this man's main concern is to "get gain," to accumulate wealth. After all, this is the world's criteria of "success." But as long as he was busy trying to "get gain," he was not preparing to meet God. This brief life was running out, and chances were that he would be caught by death unprepared.

B. *Life is infinitesimal when compared with eternity.* It is like vapor that is but for a moment (v. 14). But as brief as life may be, it is the only life and chance you have.

II. Overconfidence encourages you to take foolish risks (James 4:13).

Many Jewish merchants were restless adventurers. They traveled from city to city in pursuit of gain. A combination of overconfidence and past successes would often encourage a merchant to take one foolish risk and lose all.

III. Overconfidence ignores the most important single factor in determining the success of your life.

What is this factor? It is the will of God. "You ought to say, 'If it is the Lord's will, we will live and do this or that'" (James 4:15 NIV). Even if we do not utter the phrase "If it is the Lord's will," in connection with every plan for the future, its spirit should always be retained.

IV. Overconfidence disregards God's law.

"No doubt you agree with the above in theory. Well, remember that if a man knows what is right and fails to do it, his failure is a real sin" (James 4:17 PHILLIPS). For a person to know the uncertainty of life and yet to live in utter disregard of the truth is for him to sin. In Luke 12:47–48 Jesus makes it quite clear that the penalty for disregarding God's law increases with increased knowledge.

God's law is immutable. It still stands. Attitudes have changed, but God's law hasn't. Interpretations have changed, but God's law hasn't. It still asserts, "The wages of sin is death" (Rom. 6:23); "The soul that sinneth, it shall die" (Ezek. 18:4); and "Whatsoever a man soweth, that shall he also reap" (Gal. 6:7).

Conclusion

You will surely stumble and fall if you try to live the Christian life in your own power. You cannot live the Christian life. No one can. God does not expect you to. He simply wants you to be crucified and then to let Christ live through you. You too will learn that you can do all things through Christ who strengthens you!

SUNDAY MORNING, FEBRUARY 26

Title: The Lord of the Storm

Text: "But he saith unto them, It is I; be not afraid" (**John 6:20**).

Scripture Reading: John 6:14–21

Hymns: "A Mighty Fortress Is Our God," Luther

"Wonderful, Wonderful Jesus," Russell

"Jesus, Savior, Pilot Me," Hopper

Offertory Prayer: Holy heavenly Father, deliver us from the tyranny of material things. Help us to live for something more significant than food and clothing and shelter. Help us to go about our daily tasks working diligently without the agony of anxiety, realizing that the heavenly Father who cares for the sparrows will not let us perish with hunger. Today we bring from the abundance that you have blessed us with that we might express our gratitude to you and that we might share with those who are in need. Bless these tithes and offerings for the preaching of the gospel and for the relief of suffering both in our community and to the ends of the earth, for Jesus' sake. Amen.

Introduction

Have you ever been out on a lake when the wind began to blow and the waves began to pitch your boat? Have you ever known the fright of insecurity that can come to one who fears that he may not be able to reach the shore? This was a recurring experience for some of the disciples of our Lord, for they made their living as fishermen in the Sea of Galilee. Under the leadership of the Holy Spirit, the apostle John used such an experience of the disciples with the Lord as one of the signs by which he sought to convince his readers that they should trust Jesus Christ as the Son of God and as the Savior who came to bring the abundant life.

John, the apostle of love, describes a number of miracles performed by Jesus that were revelations of the nature of God and his purpose for people. John begins his gospel by telling us of the eternal God who had clothed himself in human flesh. By changing water into wine at a wedding feast, Jesus declared that the best was yet to be. In his conversation with the Jewish teacher Nicodemus, Jesus sought to reveal how that life at its best without him is incomplete and unsatisfactory. In his conversation with the woman at the well, Jesus revealed that even a life in ruins can be remade into something beautiful. By healing the nobleman's son, Jesus gave expression to God's concern for Gentiles as well as Jews. By healing the lame man at the well, Jesus was declaring that there is hope for the hopeless. By feeding more than five thousand people with a few loaves and fishes, Jesus was declaring that he had come to meet the deepest needs of people rather than just feeding their stomachs.

By walking on the water and coming to his disciples in the midst of the storm, Jesus was revealing the kind of Messiah he was determined to be. He refused to accept kingship on the basis of his ability to feed the hungry. When the parallel accounts of this event are read in Matthew and Mark as well as John, we are able to get a little better picture of what had happened in our text.

The people were expecting the Messiah to be similar to Moses (Deut. 18:15). Through Moses the people had been provided with manna for their journey through the wilderness. When Jesus fed them miraculously, they immediately perceived that he was the Messiah. Evidently his disciples were a part of the campaign to crown him king on the spot because of his ability to provide bread. This is discerned as we read how "Jesus constrained his disciples to get into a ship, and to go before him unto the other side, while he sent the multitudes away" (Matt. 14:22–23; cf. Mark 6:45–46). Evidently the disciples, as they moved from group to group, suggested that Jesus was the Messiah and that he ought to be crowned as king. Jesus repudiated this kind of messiahship. With haste he had his disciples get into the boat and depart immediately. He then sent the multitude away. After dismissing them, he went alone onto a mountain to pray. He needed to pray because his messiahship was being misunderstood even by his disciples.

In the hours that followed, our Lord was to reveal his patient persistence with the disciples. G. Campbell Morgan has said, "He gave them a demonstration of His present Kingship, and that in the realm of Nature. It was as though He had said, I have refused to be crowned King upon the basis of bread, but make no mistake, I am King in every realm; King in the realm of Nature, contrary winds cannot hinder Me; the tossing sea cannot overwhelm Me. I am King" (*The Gospel according to John* [Westwood, N.J.: Revell, 1933], 103). Christ revealed himself to be Lord of the waves, Lord of the wind, Lord of the whole situation. He wants to be our Lord today.

I. The Lord of the storm prays.

A. *Our Lord prayed for himself (Matt. 14:23).* If Jesus needed to pray in a time when he was misunderstood by those dearest and nearest to him, it seems only reasonable that his followers stand in need of dialogue with the heavenly Father in prayer.

B. *Our Lord prayed for his disciples (John 17:9).*

C. *Our Lord intercedes for us today (Rom. 8:34; Heb. 7:25).*

II. The Lord of the storm watches.

A. *Our Lord saw the external dangers that confronted his disciples.*

B. *Our Lord saw the internal fears that terrified them.*

C. *Our Lord sees the entire situation in which we find ourselves today.*

Jesus' perspective is much better than ours. He knows the past as well as the present. He knows the future better than we know the past.

A pilot told of following one of the main highways across our country. Flying in a small plane at a relatively slow speed, he was able to observe traffic. He noticed that some drivers were careless and would pass while going up a hill. From his perspective above, he could look down and see how near some drivers came to a bad accident because of reckless driving habits. He said that there were times when he would have said, "No, don't try to pass now." The perspective of the pilot is an illustration of how our Lord watches us and will give us guidance and help if we are but open to his leadership.

III. The Lord of the storm comes.

A. *Between 3:00 and 6:00 a.m.* Jesus came walking on the sea to his storm-tossed and frightened disciples.

B. *Our Lord does not remain removed and aloof in our times of need.* He is concerned about us.

C. *In many instances, because of fear, we don't recognize our Lord's nearness to us.* Paul had an experience similar to that of the apostles while on his way to Rome (Acts 27:23–25). The Lord came to him to give him comfort and counsel for a difficult and dangerous time.

D. *Christ comes in times of crisis with words of assurance.* "It is I; be not afraid" (John 6:20).

IV. The Lord of the storm helps.

A. *Our Lord is a worker (John 5:17).*

B. *Our Lord is no idle, impassive bystander.*

C. *Our Lord helps on the basis of our need.*

1. To the sick he gives health.
2. To the blind he gives sight.
3. To the hungry he gives bread.
4. To the frightened he gives faith and assurance of security in his presence.

D. *Our Lord helps us according to his riches of grace.* We can count on our blessed Lord being present to help us with the responsibilities we face in marriage and rearing children. He is eager to be with the young as they develop their character and as they seek to make the choices that determine their career. He is with us to help as we earn our daily bread.

V. The Lord of the storm brought his disciples safe into the harbor.

A. *The winds ceased to blow.*

B. *The waves of the sea quieted down.*

C. *The disciples found themselves safe in the harbor.*

Conclusion

The Lord of the storm may send a storm upon those who are disobedient. Jonah experienced a terrible storm as he journeyed across the sea of disobedience. The Lord of the storm came to him and recommissioned him.

The Lord of the storm draws near to us in times when decisions are to be made. He draws near to us in times of conflict and struggle. He is willing to come on board your ship if you are willing to invite him. Edward Hopper would suggest that we pray the following prayer:

> Jesus, Savior, pilot me
> *Over life's tempestuous sea:*
> *Unknown waves before me roll,*
> *Hiding rock and treacherous shoal;*
> *Chart and compass come from Thee—*
> Jesus, Savior, pilot me!

SUNDAY EVENING, FEBRUARY 26

Title: Dead Priests and the Living Christ (Part 2)

Text: "Now there have been many of those priests, since death prevented them from continuing in office; but because Jesus lives forever, he has a permanent priesthood. Therefore he is able to save completely those who come to God through him, because he always lives to intercede for them" **(Heb. 7:23–25 NIV)**.

Scripture Reading: Hebrews 9

Introduction

Last Sunday night we noted that the Levitical priesthood, composed of dying men, was mortal in nature. Death constantly severed its continuity. Its purpose was temporary. God used it as a tool of training and revelation in preparing the way for Christ and his redemptive death. Thus, the Levitical priesthood was limited in power. It was not designed to bring salvation; it was designed to point toward salvation. Tonight we turn our thoughts to the living Christ, the eternal High Priest toward which the Levites pointed.

Whereas the Old Testament priesthood was only a segment of God's revelation and instruction, the coming of Jesus Christ is the event of the ages. He is God's promised Savior toward whom all the others pointed. To Hebrew Christians oriented toward the idea of a priesthood, Jesus is presented as High Priest forever.

I. Divinely appointed (Heb. 5:5; 7:21).

In contrast to priests whose appointment was a result of genealogy, Christ was appointed High Priest by God (5:5; 7:21). Old Testament priests all came from the tribe of Levi, but Christ's human genealogy came through the tribe of Judah: "It is clear that our Lord descended from Judah, and in regard to that tribe Moses said nothing about priests" (7:14 NIV). The writer of Hebrews wants to make clear that Christ's priesthood is not merely a continuance of the Levitical system. In fact, Christ's priesthood is more akin to that of the mysterious figure Melchizedek, who appeared unannounced, received tithes from Abram, and disappeared from the human story. Melchizedek appeared centuries before the giving of the Law. We know little about him: "Without father or mother, without genealogy, without beginning of days or end of life, like the Son of God he remains a priest forever" (7:3 NIV). What is meant here is that Melchizedek appeared without any priestly genealogy. The words translated "without father or mother" are found in Greek papyri as legal terms on birth certificates when parentage is unknown. In Genesis, a book so given to genealogy and ages, Melchizedek appears without genealogy and without giving the time of his birth or death. To say that Christ is a priest of this kind is merely to say that Christ had no genealogical claim for priesthood. Christ appeared suddenly in time, just as did Melchizedek. Melchizedek was not preceded or followed by other priests of like fashion. So also with Christ. Since Melchizedek had no successor, he was said to be "like unto the Son of God." To this degree he was like Christ. Thus, Melchizedek and Christ resemble one another in that neither was a part of the Levitical priesthood, yet each had a unique priesthood by divine appointment. Melchizedek appeared to the head of the Hebrew nation to receive tithes (which lifts the tithe above any mere Levitical requirement coming centuries later), and Christ appeared to the chosen people when they had become as the sands of the seashore (Gen. 22:17) to become their offering.

II. Perfectly suited (Heb. 7:26).

As our High Priest, Christ fits our sinful needs fully: "Such a high priest meets our need—one who is holy, blameless, pure, set apart from sinners, exalted above the heavens" (v. 26 NIV). Though without sin, he understands the temptations of us who do sin: "For we have not an high priest which cannot be touched with the feeling of our infirmities; but was in all points tempted like as we are, yet without sin" (4:15). The preexistent Christ was willing to suffer the humiliation of the incarnation in order to walk as we walk, to understand our weaknesses: "Wherefore in all things it behooved him *to be made like unto his brethren,* that he might be a merciful and faithful high priest . . . to make reconciliation for the sins of the people" (2:17).

Having graciously chosen to assume the form of human flesh, he carried the limitation to the fullest. He suffered anguish and despair: "During the days of Jesus' life on earth, he offered up prayers and petitions with loud cries and tears to the one who could save him from death, and he was heard because of his reverent submission. Although he was a son, he learned obedience from what he suffered" (5:7–8 NIV). Christ makes no demand of us that he has not already experienced. He is fitted to our need for a Savior.

III. Eternal (Heb. 7:16, 24).

We who live under death's shadow, struggle against its icy grip, and stare daily into its pale countenance have cast ourselves on the living Christ who has defeated death. As High Priest he remains forever, not by virtue of some human decree, but because on the third day he arose from the grave: "one who has become a priest not on the basis of a regulation as to his ancestry but on the basis of the power of an indestructible life" (v. 16 NIV). Levitical priests succeeded one another as death severed tenure, but "because Jesus lives forever, he has a permanent priesthood" (v. 24 NIV).

IV. Serves in a heavenly tabernacle (Heb. 4:14; 9:11).

Christ, our High Priest, has "passed into the heavens" (4:14). Having come on the scene of history as a High Priest of the "good things" presented in the gospel, he now serves in a perfect tabernacle that no hands labored to construct— a heavenly tabernacle that is utterly different from any earthly creation (Heb. 9:11). In fact, the Holy of Holies in which Christ serves is heaven itself: "For Christ is not entered into the holy places made with hands, which are figures of the true; but into heaven itself, now to appear in the presence of God for us" (v. 24). The handmade Holy of Holies constructed by Moses served to emphasize the holiness of God in contrast to the sinfulness of humans. Humans can come to God only on his terms. The Holy of Holies was a foreshadowing of the direct presence of God to be experienced in heaven—on God's terms. God's terms are bound up in Jesus Christ. To Hebrew Christians so reluctant to leave behind the image of the tabernacle, the author points forward toward heaven, which is the perfect tabernacle wherein resides the perfect High Priest. Christ is the fulfillment toward which all the paraphernalia (vv. 2–5) of the tabernacle pointed. The golden censer presented the concept of intercession. The lampstand stood in the Holy Place where only the priests assembled as a reminder that the way to God requires more than natural light. Beyond the area known as the Holy Place, beyond the veil, was the Holy of Holies, in which there was no lampstand, for people do not need light when in the presence of God. We are told there will be no need for sunlight in heaven because the Lord's presence will be illumination enough (Rev. 22:5).

The bread of the presence of God was a symbol of life sustained by God. He provided manna in the wilderness, then sent the Living Bread, Jesus Christ.

The ark of the covenant was a large wooden box overlaid with gold, the top of which was the mercy seat. The ark, together with the articles inside (Heb. 9:4), was a reminder of God's holy presence. Christ's intercession for us in heaven fulfills all that was foreshadowed by the tabernacle and priesthood.

V. Offered one sacrifice (Heb. 7:27; 8:3).

Priests offer sacrifices as part of their duties: "Every high priest is appointed to offer both gifts and sacrifices, and so it was necessary for this one also to have something to offer" (8:3 NIV). Christ too offered a sacrifice, but only one! Other high priests had to offer sacrifices in acknowledgment of their own sins before they could sacrifice on behalf of the people, but not so with Christ: "Unlike the other high priests, he does not need to offer sacrifices day after day, first for his own sins, and then for the sins of the people. He sacrificed for their sins once for all when he offered himself" (7:27 NIV).

The one sacrifice was Christ's own life: "When Christ came into the world, he said: 'Sacrifice and offering you did not desire, but a body you prepared for me'" (10:5 NIV). Since Christ had no sin demanding his death (Rom. 6:23), he could become the perfect sacrifice to pay sin's claim on life. This sacrifice was complete — never to need repetition: "Nor did he enter heaven to offer himself again and again.... Then Christ would have had to suffer many times since the creation of the world. But now he has appeared once for all at the end of the ages to do away with sin by the sacrifice of himself.... So Christ was sacrificed once to take away the sins of many people; and he will appear a second time, not to bear sin, but to bring salvation to those who are waiting for him" (Heb. 9:25–26, 28 NIV). Notice the use of the word translated "once." As previously stated, the meaning is "once-for-all," "once is sufficient." All the centuries of priestly sacrifices found their consummation in Christ's sacrificial death, leaving no raison d'être for the continuance of priestly ritual.

VI. Has power to save (Heb. 7:25).

In light of all that has been said, we have no reservation in saying: "Therefore he is able to save completely those who come to God through him, because he always lives to intercede for them" (7:25 NIV). The salvation offered in Christ is complete, reaching into every aspect of human personality. He is able to transform every segment of our lives. He experienced all the trials and temptations that we know and provides victory over them. He keeps open our way to God, for he is our way, which is what is meant by the mention of him interceding for us.

The verb "to save" (7:25) is present tense and carries here the meaning of a sustained salvation. Christ keeps on sustaining us, delivering us, saving us fully, day by day. Salvation begins with conversion but is a daily experience guaranteed by the power of the living Christ. Christ's death on the cross grants us forgiveness, but it is his living presence that provides daily assurance and strength.

Conclusion

The priesthood, like a worn-out tool, has been divinely laid aside. When we look back, we see only dead priests; when we look forward with the gospel, we see the living Christ, our eternal High Priest. The Latin word for priest is *pontifex*, meaning "bridge-builder." Earthly priests were limited. They could not build a bridge to God; they could only talk about such a project, act it out, instruct concerning the promise of it. Christ alone bridges the chasm of sin and provides a way to God. Let us follow him to glory!

WEDNESDAY EVENING, FEBRUARY 29

Title: The Problem of Fraudulent Gain

Text: "Look! The wages you failed to pay the workmen who mowed your fields are crying out against you. The cries of the harvesters have reached the ears of the Lord Almighty" (**James 5:4 NIV**).

Scripture Reading: James 5:1–6

Introduction

In law a fraud is an intentional perversion of truth to induce another to part with some valuable thing belonging to him. This is the charge that James lays at the feet of certain of those who will read this letter.

A question that these verses pose is, "Is there some gain in my life that I have obtained by fraud?" Notice three truths that these verses present concerning fraudulent gain.

I. A judgment is proclaimed (James 5:1–3).

God demands personal integrity, and when covetousness pushes integrity aside and employs fraud and deceit to obtain its desires, there is a judgment to be faced.

    A. *Judgment is impartial.* "Now listen, you rich people" (v. 1 NIV). God never confuses the "elect" with the "elite." No matter who you are or with what high esteem others may hold you, God *knows* those gains in your life that have come by fraud. His judgment falls on them!

B. *Judgment produces sorrow.* "Weep and wail because of the misery that is coming upon you" (v. 1 NIV). This is not a call to repentance; rather, it is a proclamation of judgment. He who persists in obtaining his gains, not by honesty or personal merit, but by deliberate deceit and fraud, ultimately will know the sorrow his evil way has earned.

C. *Judgment reveals the triviality of worldly gain (vv. 2–3).* How trivial are the gains for which we labor. Some have sold their souls to Satan so that they might dress in fine clothes and gain a little silver or gold. But their wardrobes are moth-eaten and their money is worthless! Christ warns of this in Luke 12:15.

II. Evidence is offered (James 5:3–4).

The word "rust" in verse 3 (KJV) shows how long the guilty have withheld wages from those to whom they were due. They were calloused and did not care for others.

Verse 4 reveals that these men had gained much but at the expense of others. Have the gains in your life been at the expense of others? Have they cost someone their reputation? Have they cost someone sleepless nights, their future happiness, or their personal purity? If so, yours has been a fraudulent gain.

III. A verdict is pronounced (James 5:5–6).

The verdict of "guilty" is clearly pronounced.

While the guilty were carelessly and greedily pampering their appetites and passions, the day of their judgment had already dawned, and they were not prepared! Like Belshazzar, they were reveling while the bloodthirsty foe was at the gate.

In gaining what they had (v. 6), they condemned, falsely accused, and murdered the righteous. For this they were pronounced "guilty" of fraudulent gain. James 2:13 became a reality: "Judgment without mercy will be shown to anyone who has not been merciful" (NIV).

Conclusion

God does not forbid you from succeeding in life. He does not sit in condemnation on personal gain. But he does demand that whatever you gain be gained in honesty and Christian fairness. The ultimate question is not "What does one have?" It is "How did he get it?"

SUGGESTED PREACHING PROGRAM FOR

MARCH

■ **Sunday Mornings**

The sermons for this month are a prelude to Easter Sunday and provide the pastor with a remarkable opportunity for leading people to appreciate the death and resurrection of our Lord. The theme for these messages is "Facing the Cross."

■ **Sunday Evenings**

Continue the series of expository messages based on the book of Hebrews using "The Supremacy of Christ" as the theme.

■ **Wednesday Evenings**

Some piercing, penetrating questions that Jesus confronted his disciples with are as relevant today as they were when he spoke them. The theme for these messages is "Questions Jesus Asked."

SUNDAY MORNING, MARCH 4

Title: The Joy of the Cross

Text: "Jesus ... who for the joy that was set before him endured the cross, despising the shame" **(Heb. 12:2)**.

Hymns: "Hallelujah, What a Savior," Bliss

"At Calvary," Newell

"Glory to His Name," Hoffman

"Must Jesus Bear the Cross Alone?" Shepherd

Offertory Prayer: Our heavenly Father, we offer to you the gratitude of our hearts for your unspeakable gift to us in Jesus Christ, our Savior. We come in worship bringing the fruit of our labors, the results of the thoughts of our minds, and the efforts of our hands in the form of tithes and offerings. As you have given yourself for us, we give ourselves to you for Christ's sake. Amen.

Introduction

We have heard many sermons on the sufferings of Christ on the cross. Words do not have the capacity to communicate the suffering that Christ experienced as he died for our sins. The loneliness of the cross was terrible. Jesus was forsaken by his friends. In the midst of his agony, he felt forsaken by God, for he cried out, "My God, my God, why hast thou forsaken me?" The shame of the cross is frequently forgotten by modern-day Christians. Crucifixion was the ultimate in insult and public contempt for a criminal. It is impossible for us even to begin to understand the horror of the cross to the sinless soul of the innocent divine Son of God.

The writer of the book of Hebrews injects into our thinking an idea that appears to be contradictory. He makes much of the fact that a part of our Lord's motive for enduring the agony of the cross was because of "the joy that was set before him" (Heb. 12:2). Is it possible that one could endure such agony, such loneliness, such shame, and such horror and yet experience joy in doing so? The writer of Hebrews says yes. There were at least three joys that led Jesus Christ to the cross.

I. The joy of glorifying God.

A. *In his great prayer, Jesus prayed, "Father, the hour is come; glorify thy Son, that thy Son also may glorify thee" (John 17:1).* To glorify means to "make known." Jesus came to the earth to make known the nature, the character, and the purpose of God. In this petition he prays that God might reveal the nature and the divine purpose of Jesus of Nazareth who was to be manifested as the Son of God in the miracle of resurrection. And Jesus, by this petition, is affirming his purpose to make known the nature and character of God by his death on the cross.

B. *What is God like?* He is the eternal Creator. He is the almighty Sovereign. He is the majestic and holy God. He is the God who is both righteous and just.

C. *The supreme revelation of the love, mercy, and grace of God is to be revealed in the display of his immeasurable love by the substitutionary death of Jesus Christ on the cross.* Jesus was eager to reveal once and for all that love and grace are at the very heart of God. He was seeking to repudiate in a manner that could not be disputed that God was totally different from that which he had been reported to be by the serpent in the garden and through all succeeding generations.

D. *The devil has misrepresented the nature and character of God from the beginning of time.* People look upon God with resentment, and they try to evade and to run from him because the evil one has slandered his character with malicious falsehoods. By his death on the cross, Jesus refutes all of these and glorifies God, makes him known, and introduces him as the God of love, mercy, and grace.

II. The joy of the highest possible personal achievement.

Could Jesus have escaped the cross? Perhaps this question is idle speculation, but it is evident that Satan thought that he could avoid the cross. Satan offered him the kingdoms of this world if he would but fall down and worship him. The heart of this temptation was a suggested escape from the cross and a convenient, inexpensive way to win the kingdoms of this world for God. Jesus rejected this suggestion and endured the cross because there was no other way to save people. In doing so, he was to achieve the highest possible destiny for his life.

A. *Apart from the sufferings of the cross, there could be no resurrection from the tomb and demonstration of the reality of eternal life.*

B. *Apart from the sufferings of the cross, there could be no crusade of love by gospel teams carrying the message of redemption to a lost world.*

C. *Apart from the sufferings of the cross, there could be for him no divine approval and exaltation at the end of the way.*

D. *His first recorded words were "Didn't you know I had to be in my Father's house?"(Luke 2:49 NIV).* From the cross, he cried, "It is finished" (John 19:30). This was not the last gasp of a defeated idealist. It was the shout of triumph of one who had fully achieved his unique and divinely ordained destiny. It was, in a profoundly sober way, a shout of joy.

III. The joy of saving souls.

A. *Jesus endured the cross to experience the joy of saving you and me from sin.* We were slaves, and he came to set us free. We were guilty, and he came to cleanse us. We were helpless, and he came to rescue us. We were in a hopeless condition, and he came and gave us life.

B. *He died for our sins.* He makes forgiveness possible. He gives new life, eternal life, spiritual life, divine life.

C. *The joy of rendering the highest possible service to you and meeting the deepest need of your heart and life was a part of the joy that led Jesus to suffer the agony of the cross.*

Conclusion

Was the death of Christ on the cross a waste as far as you are concerned? If you have rejected him, then as far as you are concerned, he died in vain. Let his death on the cross be your death to sin. Let the life he revealed on the first Easter morning be your life.

Let his example challenge you to give your life completely to the divine plan. Determine to live so as to glorify God in your daily life that others might come to your Savior and be saved by his death on the cross and be transformed by his living presence.

SUNDAY EVENING, MARCH 4

Title: The Old Covenant

Text: "But the ministry Jesus has received is as superior to theirs as the covenant of which he is mediator is superior to the old one, and it is founded on better promises. For if there had been nothing wrong with that first covenant, no place would have been sought for another.... By calling this covenant 'new,' he has made the first one obsolete; and what is obsolete and aging will soon disappear" **(Heb. 8:6–7, 13 NIV).**

Scripture Reading: Hebrews 9

Introduction

The unity of the Bible is seen in the relationship of the testaments. The readers to whom the book of Hebrews was addressed needed to be convinced of the finality of the New Testament message. Many modern readers need to be convinced of the validity and value of the Old Testament. Certain missionary groups have completely rejected the Old Testament as far as practical usage is concerned, saying that it only creates barriers in working with native Christians. Such a devaluation of the Old Testament had its earlier beginnings with a heretic named Marcion who not only rejected the Old Testament but everything Jewish in the New Testament. Another view holds that the Old Testament is useless since it was fulfilled in Judaism, not in the New Testament, saying that the pilgrimage of Israel ended in the Talmud and the synagogue. Emil Kraeling said that Christianity has as much relation to heathenism as to Judaism (James Smart, *Interpretation of Scripture* [Philadelphia: Westminster, 1961], 69–72). Adolph Harnack saw the framework of Judaism as having little or no bearing on the character of the gospel and maintained that Paul used the Old Testament only in Jewish churches (Adolph Harnack, *What Is Christianity?* [New York: Harper, 1957], 164ff.). Nazism, under Hitler, advocated the rejection of the Old Testament on the grounds that it was a Jewish book with a Jewish God. But as we will see in this evening's message, the divinely inspired testaments work together to prophesy and present the gospel of Jesus Christ.

I. The purpose of the old covenant.

The emphasis on the completeness of the new covenant set forth in Hebrews is not meant to destroy the unity of the Bible. At this point, the emphasis of J. Barton Payne is helpful. Since the death of Christ is the eternal sacrifice for the sins of any person, and since salvation always has been conditioned on one's faith in God's deliverance, Payne sees only one testament, which has both an older aspect and a newer aspect (J. Barton Payne, *The Theology of the Older Testament* [Grand Rapids: Zondervan, 1962]). Though Payne may press too far, we must never cease to affirm the unity and value of both testaments.

Following the entrance of sin into the human experience (Gen. 3), its viruslike spread provoking God to send the flood in judgment (Gen. 6), and the haughty effort of man to make a name for himself without God (Gen. 11), God set in motion his foreordained program of redemption with the call of Abraham. Abraham's faith commitment brought him into a right relationship with God (Gen. 15:6) and set forever the means of experiencing salvation. To Abraham, God set forth, though in vague dimensions, his "everlasting covenant" (Gen. 17:7). Just how God would bless all humankind through Abraham's descendants (Gen. 12:2–3) is not immediately revealed. Yet there is a sense in which the broad plan revealed to Abraham encompassed both the Old and New Testaments. Paul indicated that such is the case: "Christ hath redeemed us ... that the blessing of Abraham might come on the Gentiles through Jesus Christ" (Gal. 3:13–14); and again: "Now to Abraham and his seed were the promises made.... And this I say, that the covenant, that was confirmed before of God in Christ, the law, which was four hundred and thirty years after, cannot disannul, that it should make the promise of none effect" (vv. 16–17). Though Paul was writing to Galatian Judaizers in an effort to correct their overemphasis on the Mosaic law, or covenant, he at the same time indicated the all-encompassing nature of God's promise to Abraham.

The descendants of Abraham, being a rather primitive people, had to be led out of darkness slowly. God, in his wisdom, always begins with people right where they are. His ordained plan involved two stages—one preparatory (the old covenant given through Moses), the other final (the new covenant inaugurated by Christ). Do not confuse this with two methods of salvation. Salvation always came by the gracious act of God. People always have received that salvation by faith in God's promised deliverance. The first covenant was ordained as a means of preparing people to understand the full wonders of redemption and the full demands of discipleship as revealed in the final covenant. The two fit together in a divine unity.

II. The meaning of the old covenant.

The Hebrew word for covenant (*berith*) used in the Old Testament has the meaning of "pact" or "promise." The primary aspect of a covenant is the solemn and absolute pledge involved. God's promise to Abraham in Genesis 12 is repeated in Genesis 15 and confirmed with a solemn ceremony, making the promise a covenant, a *berith*. God's covenant with Noah that never again would civilization be destroyed by a flood was accompanied by the sign of the rainbow. At Sinai, following the giving of the Law, a ceremony of confirmation was held (Ex. 24:1–8).

When the Greek translation of the Old Testament (the Septuagint) was made, a choice of how to translate the Hebrew *berith* lay between two Greek words: *syntheke* (meaning an agreement between two people or two nations of equal rank), and *diatheke* (having to do with the orderly arrangement of affairs or disposition of property—hence often used of a person's last will and testament). Rather than risk the implication that people bargain with God on equal terms, the translators used *diatheke*, the primary idea being that God states the terms, is in charge of all disposition, all arrangements. When the Holy Spirit directed the New Testament writers to use the Greek language, he also led them to use *diatheke* to refer to covenant (*berith*). Jesus referred to "covenant" only in referring to the cup of the Lord's Supper as being representative of his blood, the confirmation of the new covenant. Though used occasionally in the New Testament, "covenant" receives its primary emphasis in Hebrews (used there seventeen of the thirty-three times it is found in the New Testament). The writer of Hebrews gives it prominence in an effort to show that the new covenant fulfills the old one and is God's last word.

III. The nature of the old covenant.

A. *Mosaic law.* Though scholars find numerous covenants in the Old Testament (covenants with Abraham, Noah, Joshua, David, and Ezra), the one most representative of the Old Testament (at times almost used interchangeably with the Old Testament), the one that bound Israel to God, was the Mosaic covenant—the law given at Sinai. It is with this one that the writer of Hebrews had to deal, for it was to this one that Hebrew converts were still clinging. Although the Mosaic covenant does not engulf all the Old Testament, it is its essence (leaving room for the early chapters of Genesis, the broad program sketched for Abraham, and the prophets who, though predicting judgment for breaking the law, pointed above legality to a personal God and his redemptive promises). As a result, there are times when "law" and "covenant" are used interchangeably (Ps. 119; 2 Cor. 3).

B. *National.* The nature of the old covenant is bound up in its purposes. For what purposes did God ordain the law? They are manifold. One that is primary has to do with the preservation of the Israelites as a nation. They needed civil laws as well as religious ones. God will not preserve a people who flaunt his holiness. The purpose for choosing a people was that they might reveal his holiness to the nations by being different—set apart. Unless they are marked by godliness, there will be no revelation. This required a separate people gathered together as a group, a nation. Therefore, many of the promises concern a land in which to dwell and have a national existence.

C. *Spiritual.* However, along with the earthly was the spiritual. The old covenant served as a nursemaid to lead people to Christ: "The law was our schoolmaster to bring us unto Christ" (Gal. 3:24). The law, with its temple, priesthood, and rituals, whispered of more to come: "The law is only a shadow of the good things that are coming" (Heb. 10:1 NIV). The contrast is between a shadow (*skia*) and the image (*eikoon*) that casts the shadow, between a pencil sketch and the living person being sketched. The many sacrifices prescribed by the law kept before all the serious nature of sin: "those sacrifices are an annual reminder of sins" (Heb. 10:3 NIV). For instance, the law declared anyone who touched a dead body ceremonially unclean and prescribed a necessary sacrifice before the defiled person could approach God in worship (Heb. 9:13). The purpose of such a command was to serve as a reminder that death is the curse of sin (Gen. 3; Ezek. 18:4). Death and sin are related. Christ, the final sacrifice, came to cleanse us completely from sin's curse: "How much more shall the blood of Christ . . . purge your conscience from dead works [righteousness apart from God defiles a person] to serve the living God?" (Heb. 9:14).

IV. The passing of the old covenant.

When Babylon sacked Jerusalem, it looked as if the covenant had ended in failure. However, we must be careful at this point. When the Bible speaks of the failure of the law, it refers to the law as misused and perverted by making it an end in itself, an idol, a substitute for faith and genuine commitment. The law was not a failure in God's plan. God's people had been taught that judgment falls on every nation that disregards righteousness—even on Israel. God was not taken by surprise by Israel's failure to live up to covenant demands. The time had come to

85

look toward the second and final episode in the divine scheme. Even as Jerusalem began to crumble, God spoke through Jeremiah about a new covenant: "Behold, the days come ... that I will make a new covenant with the house of Israel, and with the house of Judah" (Jer. 31:31). This new covenant was embodied in Jesus Christ.

Conclusion

To be in covenant with God, one must surrender to Jesus Christ. He is the divine promise of the ages.

WEDNESDAY EVENING, MARCH 7

Title: Do You Love Him?

Text: "Lovest thou me?" **(John 21:17)**.

Scripture Reading: John 21:15–22

Introduction

How many people do you know who have convinced you that they really have a deep love for Jesus Christ? Whatever the answer may be, it is not apt to be as many as say they love him. True love for him cannot be hidden or counterfeited.

One of the most personal questions ever asked by Jesus Christ was "Lovest thou me?" Even though this question was addressed to Simon Peter, it has personal meaning for us today. Some have called it "life's greatest question." If taken seriously, it causes us to take a close look at ourselves.

Do you love Jesus?

I. If you do love Jesus, your life will reveal it.

When Jesus questioned Peter, he knew that if Peter did love him, it would be revealed in Peter's life. This is also true in your life, for if you love Jesus, your life will reveal it.

A. *Your life will reveal the quality of your love.* Can you imagine a young man being happy with less than first-quality love from the girl he is engaged to marry? Of course not, because true love is revealed by quality.

   1. Your life will reveal the intensity of your love for Jesus. Jesus said to Peter, "Lovest thou me more than these?"

   2. Your life will reveal the extent of your involvement in loving Jesus. It is impossible to really love without becoming involved. Jesus knew Peter would obey if he truly loved.

B. *Your life will reveal the effect of love.* Love has a way of affecting your life and the lives of others you love. When people fall in love, they feel love's effect.

   1. Your life will reveal love's effect on your personal life. To truly love Jesus is to have your hopes, dreams, and goals affected by this love.

   2. Your life will reveal love's effect on others. Peter's love for Christ caused his life to affect the lives of other people.

Do you love Jesus?

II. If you do love Jesus, he will have first place in your life.

It would be unthinkable for persons to love Jesus and then not allow him to have first place in their lives.

A. *Jesus will have first place in your thinking.* This does not mean that you will think about nothing but Jesus. It means that Jesus will be uppermost in your mind. When Peter allowed Jesus first place, his thinking was changed. He became known as a man who had been with Jesus.

B. *Jesus will have first place in your devotion.* Peter is known for his weak loyalty and devotion, but some fail to remember that more is said in the Bible about his extreme devotion and loyalty than his weakness. The difference was that his love caused him to give Christ first place in his devotion and loyalty. For him, Jesus Christ was first even if it meant death.

Do you love Jesus?

III. If you do love Jesus, you will serve him.

Jesus asked Peter, "Lovest thou me?" and when Peter replied in the affirmative, Jesus told him, "Feed my sheep." Jesus knew that if Peter's love was real, he would serve him.

A. *You will serve Jesus willingly.* In times of great danger or need, people do not have to be asked to serve their friends or country, because they are willing and ready to serve out of their love for friends or country. A person cannot love Jesus Christ without being willing to serve him. Christians should not have to be drafted into God's service. They should be willing to serve.

B. *You will serve Jesus joyfully.* It is hard to conceive of any of the disciples not serving Christ with joy. Acts 5:41 says, "They departed from the presence of the council, rejoicing that they were counted worthy to suffer shame for his name."

C. *You will serve Jesus faithfully.* Out of love for Jesus Christ, the disciples served faithfully in all circumstances—in and out of prison, in large cities and small villages, and when the opportunity came at any time and any place.

Conclusion

Do you love Jesus? What does your life reveal?

Sunday Morning, March 11

Title: Life That Is Eternal

Text: "Jesus said unto her, I am the resurrection, and the life; he that believeth in me, though he were dead, yet shall he live: And whosoever liveth and believeth in me shall never die. Believest thou this?" (**John 11:25–26**).

Scripture Reading: John 11:18–46

Hymns: "Crown Him with Many Crowns," Bridges

"One Day," Chapman

"He Lives," Ackley

Offertory Prayer: Holy Father, help us this day to bring to you an offering in proper proportion to the manner in which we have been blessed. Help us to know that we are not blessed that we might live a life of selfish indulgence. Help us to be good managers of all that we are and all that we have as your servants. Help us to remember that we are in partnership with you in all of life. Accept our offerings and help us to give ourselves completely to you in serving others, through Jesus Christ our Lord. Amen.

Introduction

Man is a wonderful creature. He believes that it is within the realm of possibility for him to create life. He has greatly multiplied his power to provide better means of living. He has perfected methods that make instant communication around the world possible. He has greatly accelerated the rate at which he can travel from one place to another. He is even able to travel in outer space. Man does not have to work nearly as hard as he once did, and through medical research he has added years to his life. But man with all of his wonderful achievements still does not know what to do about death. He ignores it. He seeks to postpone it. He pretends that it may go away. When it does come, he decorates it and camouflages it. But still death comes as his fateful and final enemy.

Modern man's constant awareness of death, his personal death, is the greatest cloud over his life. Death comes and deprives him of his parents or of a companion or child. Without exception it comes and claims his friends. Death is always out there to cut him short of his desired perfection.

The final great sign that John selected from the life and ministry of Jesus deals with the problem of death. The event recorded in John 11 has great significance for us in this modern day if we want to face life courageously and calmly.

I. A revelation of mystery and miracle.

A. *In this wonderful chapter, we find no definition of or explanation of death.*

B. *Rather, we find here a revealing of what God has planned and provided for those of us who trust and love Jesus Christ, his Son.*

II. What does this great sign say to us?

A. *It tells us that death is but an aspect of life, just as birth is an aspect of life.* Death is not the end of things.

B. *It tells us that death is swallowed up by life, not life swallowed up by death.* Often we speak of our existence in the land of the living. In reality we live in the land of the dying. We look forward to entering into the land of the living.

C. *It tells us that personality persists beyond bodily death and that the person who has crossed over by way of death into the other life is as recognizably the same as before death came.*

D. *It tells us of an eternity in which time's incompletions may be completed.*

E. *It tells us that the resurrection is not some far-off event only, but that the resurrection begins here and now when the believer becomes identified with Christ who is the Resurrection and the Life.* Resurrection power becomes available as we seek to live a moral and ethical life pleasing to Jesus Christ.

F. *It tells us that this corruptible being can put on incorruption and that this mortal being can put on immortality (cf. 1 Cor. 15:50–57).*

G. *It tells us that victory over death has been won and that death's sting has been forever eradicated.*

III. This incident provides us with a remarkable revelation—"Jesus wept" (John 11:35).

These two words constitute the shortest Bible verse, yet there is within them a volume of significance. They present a picture of the compassionate, sympathetic heart of the Son of God who was weeping over the grief of those who were dear to him. They reveal that he is moved by our sorrow and grief today.

IV. Many believed on Jesus.

Jesus had told his disciples before they made the trip to Bethany that this whole incident should help them to have a greater faith: "I am glad for your sakes that I was not there, to the intent ye may believe; nevertheless let us go unto him" (John 11:15).

Jesus asked Martha if she had faith to believe that he was indeed the Resurrection and the Life (11:26). She gave voice to her faith in him as "the Christ, the Son of God, which should come into the world" (v. 27). Jesus discussed the significance of this miracle with her as they approached the place where Lazarus was buried: "Said I not unto thee, that, if thou wouldst believe, thou shouldst see the glory of God?" (v. 40). In his prayer to the Father, our Lord revealed the purpose behind his unique miracle of raising Lazarus: "I knew that thou hearest me always: but because of the people which stand by I said it, that they may believe that thou hast sent me" (v. 42). The result of this miracle was that many did believe on Jesus. The Pharisees concluded, "If we let him thus alone, all men will believe on him, and the Romans shall come and take away both our place and nation" (11:48).

Conclusion

By the raising of Lazarus in Bethany, our Lord reminds us that life is a continuity, with death as a stream to be crossed that only temporarily separates time and eternity.

Life must be spent eternally with Christ or without Christ. Life must be spent eternally with the forgiveness of sin or without the forgiveness of sin. Life must be spent eternally either in the company of the saved or in the company of the lost. The difference depends on a relationship with Jesus Christ. Those who know Christ as Lord and Savior will never know death. Those who do not know Christ will never see real life, for the condemnation of God will rest on them.

To believe is to accept as absolutely true everything that Jesus said and then to stake our lives on what he did and said in perfect trust. This will bring us into a new relationship with God and a new relationship with life. May this event encourage each of us to believe in Jesus Christ as the Messiah and as the Son of God who gave his life for us and who lives again that we might share his life forever.

SUNDAY EVENING, MARCH 11

Title: The New Covenant

Text: "But the ministry Jesus has received is as superior to theirs as the covenant of which he is mediator is superior to the old one, and it is founded on better promises. For if there had been nothing wrong with that first covenant, no place would have been sought for another.... By calling this covenant 'new,' he has made the first one obsolete; and what is obsolete and aging will soon disappear" **(Heb. 8:6–7, 13 NIV)**.

Scripture Reading: Hebrews 8

Introduction

The unity of the old and new covenants is seen in that the old speaks of the coming of the new: "Behold, the days come, saith the LORD, that I will make a new covenant with the house of Israel, and with the house of Judah" (Jer. 31:31).

The old covenant had a distinct part to play in God's redemptive plan. Just as John the Baptist said, "[Jesus] must increase, but I must decrease," so also the older aspect of God's covenant was scheduled to prepare the way for the final aspect.

The writer of Hebrews comments on Jeremiah's prophecy (Jer. 31:31) by indicating the ebbing purpose of the law: "By calling this covenant 'new,' he has made the first one obsolete; and what is obsolete and aging will soon disappear" (Heb. 8:13 NIV).

During the six hundred years that elapsed between the prophecy of Jeremiah and the birth of Christ, the Israelites, convinced that their Babylonian captivity was the result of breaking the law, determined it should never happen again. They were never again guilty of idolatry, but in effect they made the law an idol, hedging it about with manmade commandments. Ironically, their zealous emphasis on the details of the law occurred at the time when the old covenant, having served its time, was disappearing from God's divine horizon.

I. The dividing line.

The dividing point between the old and new covenants is the death-resurrection-ascension of Christ who became the eternal High Priest. The old began with Moses, the new with Christ. Both Moses and Christ are part of God's revelation, but they are not equal. Moses resembles a servant in the house, while Christ is Master of the house: "For this man was counted worthy of more glory than Moses, inasmuch as he who hath builded the house hath more honour than the house.... And Moses verily was faithful in all his house, as a servant ... but Christ as a son over his own house" (Heb. 3:3, 5–6).

II. The supremacy of the new covenant (Heb. 8:10–13).

A. *A clearer word.* God's revelation came in many ways through many souls at different times, but his final word came through Christ (Heb. 1:1–2). The old covenant shed much light on our relationship to God. But it was like car headlights on a dark night, shining only a short way down the road. With the coming of the full light of day, one is no longer aware of the car lights. The whole countryside, as far as the eye can see, lies in the brilliance of the streaming sunlight. The car lights do not fail with the rising of the sun, they are merely swallowed up by the greater illumination. So it is with the old covenant as it stands beside the new; the earthly is eclipsed by the heavenly.

B. *A deeper motivation.* Quoting Jeremiah, the writer of Hebrews says: "For this is the covenant that I will make with the house of Israel after those days, saith the Lord; I will put my laws into their mind, and write them in their hearts: and I will be to them a God, and they shall be to me a people: and they shall not teach every man his neighbour, and every man his brother, saying, Know the Lord: for all shall know me, from the least to the greatest" (Heb. 8:10–11).

The new covenant is not written on stone tablets, but on people's hearts. Obedience comes, not out of fear of punishment, but out of a love for Christ. To open your heart to Christ is to have the new covenant inscribed on your heart. A person with Christ in his heart is not dependent on hearsay religion or rules taught by others for a knowledge of what is right.

C. *Greater power.* The old covenant had no dynamic force, no inner power. It was not meant to have, though the Israelites made the mistake of ascribing power to it, but rather pointed toward the coming power of the new covenant: "For what the law was powerless to do in that it was weakened by the sinful nature, God did by sending his own Son in the likeness of sinful man to be a sin offering. And so he condemned sin in sinful man in order that the righteous requirements of the law might be fully met in us, who do not live according to the sinful nature but according to the Spirit" (Rom. 8:3–4 NIV). The law condemned sin on paper, but Christ conquered it in person. After Christ's ascension, the Holy Spirit came upon believers at Pentecost, marking the entrance of power into the new covenant. Disciples depend on divine strength to serve God.

D. *Better promises.* The new covenant is said to be based on more glorious promises: "He is the mediator of a better covenant, which was established on better promises" (Heb. 8:6). The new covenant goes beyond the present life, national security, length of days, and earthly deliverance, and stresses eternal redemption (v. 12). The land of promise is no longer Canaan, but heaven itself. The recipients are not only the physical descendants of Abraham, for all are invited. At last we see how all nations are to be blessed through Abraham.

E. *Final consummation.* The new covenant, embodied in Christ, is the final consummation of redemption's story: "For the law made nothing perfect [had no consummation], but the bringing in of a better hope did" (Heb. 7:19). To give emphasis to the finality of the new covenant instituted by Christ, the writer of Hebrews turns to one of the common uses of "covenant" (*diatheke*) to mean "will" or "testament": "[Christ] is the mediator of the new testament, that by means of death … they which are called might receive the promise of eternal inheritance. For where a testament is, there must also of necessity be the death of the testator. For a testament is of force after men are dead" (9:15–17). The redemptive death of Christ guaranteed the inheritance clearly set forth in the new covenant. Since Christ arose triumphant over death, he remains heir of all (1:2), making us "heirs of God, and joint-heirs with Christ" (Rom. 8:17). Everything God had in mind in his promise to Abraham finds its fullness in Christ and his gospel.

Conclusion

Is there any current value in the old covenant? Most assuredly! It stands as a holy history reminding us that God controls the destiny of nations, that he works to bring about his purposes. The old covenant serves as a sentry to halt all who would propose to live a perfect life without Christ's redemption (Rom. 3:20). The old covenant adds to the dimensions of God's grace and love his patience and steadfastness. Any person not reared in a Christian home may find the ethical pilgrimage found in the old covenant a helpful guide for his own spiritual journey toward maturity in Christ, though it should never be more than a place to begin. There is no place in God's kingdom for "Old Testament Christians."

Christ is forever God's final covenant. People accept or reject Christ on an individual basis. Jeremiah was known as the weeping prophet because the sinful condition of his people saddened his heart. But amid the tears, he spoke of a new covenant. When Christ came to inaugurate the new covenant, he too wept over Jerusalem and yearned to gather in the multitudes, but they would not come. His offer still stands today.

WEDNESDAY EVENING, MARCH 14

Title: Who Is He to You?

Text: "He saith unto them, But whom say ye that I am?" (**Matt. 16:15**).

Scripture Reading: Matthew 16:13–20

Introduction

Jesus Christ is a confronting Savior. During his earthly ministry, he confronted people, and he does so today. One of the ways he confronts people is by the use of personal questions.

During the last six months of his ministry, Jesus confronted his followers with this question: "Whom do men say that I the Son of man am?" He later made it more personal by asking, "But whom say ye that I am?"

Although you were not at Caesarea Philippi when Jesus Christ first asked the question, it still has meaning for you. You cannot escape the question "Who is he to you?"

I. It is a question concerning the nature of Jesus Christ.

One sure way of determining a person's personal theology is to find out his beliefs concerning the nature of Jesus Christ. If a person is wrong in his thinking about Jesus Christ, then his whole theology is wrong.

A. *Jesus Christ is the Son of God.* This was the response of Peter to Jesus' question (Matt. 16:16).

1. He was born of a virgin. "Behold, a virgin shall be with child, and shall bring forth a son, and they shall call his name Emmanuel, which being interpreted is, God with us" (Matt. 1:23).
2. He lived without sinning. "For he hath made him to be sin for us, who knew no sin; that we might be made the righteousness of God in him" (2 Cor. 5:21).
3. He was a revelation of God. "He that hath seen me hath seen the Father" (John 14:9).

B. *Jesus Christ is the only way of salvation.* Peter knew that Jesus Christ was not *a way,* but *the only way* of salvation for all people. In Acts 4:12 he said, "Salvation is found in no one else, for there is no other name under heaven given to men by which we must be saved" (NIV).

C. *Jesus Christ arose from the dead.* Paul wrote in 1 Corinthians 15:3–4: "For I delivered unto you first of all that which I also received, how that Christ died for our sins according to the scriptures; and that he was buried, and that he arose again the third day according to the scriptures."

D. *Jesus Christ will return the second time.* At Jesus' ascension, his followers received the promise of his return. "Ye men of Galilee, why stand ye gazing up into heaven? this same Jesus, which is taken up from you into heaven, shall so come in like manner as ye have seen him go into heaven" (Acts 1:11). "Who is he to you?" is determined by your belief about the nature of Jesus Christ.

II. It is a question concerning personal discovery.

For nearly three years, Jesus Christ worked closely with his disciples. He knew that they did not fully understand his messiahship. His question was a way he had of testing what they had discovered about him.

A. *Personal discovery is aided by Bible study.* For years the Jewish people had been looking and hoping for a Messiah to come to redeem them from their sins. Their discovery was aided by studying what the Old Testament had to say about the Messiah. When Andrew discovered Jesus Christ, he told his brother, " 'We have found the Messiah,' [that is, the Christ]" (John 1:41 NIV). Bible study will aid you in discovering Jesus Christ.

B. *Personal discovery is aided by close observation.* The disciples were able to observe Jesus Christ as he worked, prayed, taught, loved, preached, rejoiced, and died. Most of what they discovered about him came from observation. We are able to observe him as we see him at work in the lives of others and in a personal observation of his recorded ministry in the New Testament.

C. *Personal discovery is aided by God's revelation.* When Simon Peter told Jesus Christ that he had discovered him, Jesus said, "For flesh and blood hath not revealed it unto thee, but my Father which is in heaven" (Matt. 16:17). By the work of the Holy Spirit, God reveals to us his love and our need for Jesus Christ.

Conclusion

To fail to know Jesus Christ is to fail in life. Surely you will not make that tragic mistake. He is God's Son and can be your Savior.

SUNDAY MORNING, MARCH 18

Title: The Concert of Calvary

Text: "The meek shall eat and be satisfied: they shall praise the LORD that seek him: your heart shall live for ever" (**Ps. 22:26**).

Scripture Reading: Psalm 22

Hymns: "The Old Rugged Cross," Bennard

          "At the Cross," Watts

          "At Calvary," Newell

Offertory Prayer: Our Father, help us to remember daily that all good and perfect gifts come down to us from the Father of lights. May our stewardship become and remain a vital part of our discipleship. We return to you a portion of that which you have entrusted to us, remembering that you love cheerful givers. This is now our act of worship and our prayer in Jesus' name. Amen.

Introduction

Dr. Robert G. Lee has reminded us that Jesus is the theme of the Old Testament as well as the New Testament: in the Old Testament he is promised, and in the New Testament he is presented. Psalm 22 is surely one of the psalms Jesus had in mind when he said, "These are the words which I spake unto you, while I was yet with you, that all things must be fulfilled, which were written in the law of Moses, and in the prophets, and in the psalms, concerning me" (Luke 24:44).

Dr. William Pettingill has suggested that in Psalm 22 Jesus is introduced as the Good Shepherd, in Psalm 23 he is the Great Shepherd, and in Psalm 24 he is the Chief Shepherd. Dr. A. J. Gordon says that the beloved Twenty-Third Psalm is a bridge from the suffering of Psalm 22 to the glories of Psalm 24.

There are fundamental thematic emphases in this beautiful psalm.

I. The suffering of Jesus (Ps. 22:1 – 10).

The prophetic words of the psalm and the corresponding passages of fulfillment in the New Testament are most surely divinely inspired. Passages so separated in time and literary setting could not just happen.

A. *"My God, my God, why hast thou forsaken me?" (v. 1).* "And at the ninth hour Jesus cried with a loud voice, saying, Eloi, Eloi, lama sabachthani? which is, being interpreted, My God, my God, why hast thou forsaken me?" (Mark 15:34). Ten centuries before Jesus cried the words from his cross, the psalmist sang them in this gracious poem.

B. *"All they that see me laugh me to scorn: they shoot out the lip, they shake the head" (v. 7).* "And they that passed by railed on him wagging their heads" (Mark 15:29).

C. *"He trusted on the LORD that he would deliver him . . . seeing he delighted in him" (v. 8).* When the prophetic hymn came to pass, Matthew recorded it: "He trusted in God; let him deliver him now, if he will have him: for he said, I am the Son of God" (Matt. 27:43).

D. *"I am poured out like water . . ." (v. 14).* A thousand years later it came to pass, and John recorded it: "But one of the soldiers with a spear pierced his side, and forthwith came there out blood and water" (John 19:34).

E. *". . . and my bones are out of joint" (v. 14).* John recorded the fulfillment of this prophetic note when he recorded the crucifixion of our Lord: "Then came the soldiers, and brake the legs of the first, and of the other which was crucified with him. But when they came to Jesus, and saw that he was dead already, they brake not his legs" (John 19:32 – 33).

F. *"My strength is dried up like a potsherd and my tongue cleaveth to my jaws; and thou hast brought me into the dust of death" (v. 15).* Pointedly it came to pass when upon his cross Jesus cried, "I thirst" (John 19:28).

G. *"They pierced my hands and my feet" (v. 16).* This came to pass on Calvary. Luke records the postresurrection evidence like this: "Behold my hands and my feet, that it is I myself: handle me, and see; for a spirit hath not flesh and bones, as ye see me have" (Luke 24:39).

H. *"I may tell all my bones: they look and stare upon me" (v. 17).* When Jesus died on the cross, Matthew (who gives the most touching account of the cross) put it down in these words: "And sitting down they watched him there" (Matt. 27:36).

II. "They part my garments among them, and cast lots upon my vesture" (Ps. 22:18).

Again Matthew clearly records the actual events: "And they crucified him, and parted his garments, casting lots: that it might be fulfilled which was spoken by the prophet, They parted my garments among them, and upon my vesture did they cast lots" (Matt. 27:35). Here, then, are nine sets of parallel Scriptures — prophecies and fulfillments. They span the centuries in magnificent unity and beauty. Who could doubt the divine inspiration of the Bible? Who could remain unexcited in the presence of such testimony?

III. The salvation by Jesus (Ps. 22:21).

There are at least two facets of salvation suggested here.

A. *"Save me from the lion's mouth" (v. 21).* Here is pictured the imprisonment of the lost. We are caught. We are trapped. We are held captive and victim in the "lion's mouth." The figure has lost some of its appeal in our day when the only lions we see are behind the bars of zoos or circuses. But to those who encountered the lion personally, to be in the lion's mouth meant certain death. So out of imprisonment to freedom, out of capture to release, out of peril to joyful liberty, Christ delivers us.

B. *"Thou hast heard me from the horns of the unicorns" (v. 21).* It is suggested that this is a picture of impalement. The unicorn could spear its victim upon its singular horn, and the prey was helpless. To survive he must be rescued by another.

In the salvation Jesus brings, he rescues us from the impalement of our own helplessness. We cannot save ourselves: we must have help. That help is abundant in Jesus.

IV. The satisfaction in Jesus (Ps. 22:22–26).

The indisputable evidence of the validity of Christianity is that it works. Jesus satisfies.

A. *He satisfies the hunger of his followers.* "The meek shall eat and be satisfied: they shall praise the LORD that seek him: your heart shall live for ever" (v. 26). Hear Peter say, "Thou art the Christ, the Son of the living God" (Matt. 16:16).

B. *He satisfies the demands of divine judgment.* "He shall see the travail of his soul, and shall be satisfied" (Isa. 53:11).

C. *He satisfies the test of human scrutiny.* The verdict of those who have really examined Jesus impartially is forever the verdict of Pilate, "I find no fault in this man" (Luke 23:4).

D. *He satisfies the demands of his own sense of mission.* Jesus made extravagant claims for himself. They were not made in haughty arrogance. He came through on all the claims he made for himself. Hear him say with a sense of destiny, "Blessed are they which do hunger and thirst after righteousness, for they shall be filled" (Matt. 5:6).

V. The sovereignty of Jesus (Ps. 22:27–31).

Hear the drumbeats of victory. Hear the trumpets announce God's sovereignty. "All the ends of the world shall remember and turn unto the LORD: all the kindreds of the nations shall worship before thee" (v. 27). The "kingdom is the LORD's," and "he is the governor." They shall come and "declare his righteousness." The people shall "bow before him." Jesus shall reign!

Charles Crowe tells of a traffic jam in the famous Chicago Loop. The Chicago Temple is located in the Loop and is said to have atop the steeple the highest cross in the world. Each day thousands of people pass with scarcely a notice. But one day traffic choked the Loop. A thousand people had stopped to gaze upward at that cross. What was different about it this day? A man was on it cleaning it. The fact that a man was on the cross personalized it and made it attractive. There was magnetism in a man on the cross.

History's most famous cross is not an impersonal piece of historic furniture. It had the God-man on it! And because Calvary held the God-man, people still stop and look up in amazement and adoration. Will you not look to the Man on the cross for life and salvation?

Conclusion

1. Let us not be morbid but eternally mindful and grateful for the sufferings of Jesus.
2. Let us accept his salvation and find rescue both from the lion's mouth and the unicorn's horns.
3. Let us come to Jesus daily for the satisfaction of real hunger of soul.
4. Let us crown Jesus the King of Kings and the Lord of Lords in loving obedience and personal commitment.

SUNDAY EVENING, MARCH 18

Title: Willful Sin

Text: "If we deliberately keep on sinning after we have received the knowledge of the truth, no sacrifice for sins is left, but only a fearful expectation of judgment and of raging fire that will consume the enemies of God" (**Heb. 10:26–27 NIV**).

Scripture Reading: Hebrews 10:22–39

Introduction

There is a difference between acts committed in ignorance and those committed with a full knowledge of what is involved. The Old Testament differentiates between what might be called "ordinary sins" and "sins of the high hand." Certain sacrifices were prescribed for the former, but no sacrifice was delineated for the latter. Human depravity being what it is, people are going to sin. But beyond this area lies the willful, premeditated sin for which even the New Testament mentions no sacrifice.

I. The people warned (Heb. 10:32–34).

A. *They are Christians.* At first we are tempted to ask how any person could set himself willfully on a collision course with God. But on closer examination, we make the startling discovery that the people being warned are Christians.

The writer of Hebrews reminds his readers of their conversion experience at which time they "received the light" (v. 32 NIV). The literal language says clearly that they are people who have been enlightened by God. They have seen things as they really are. They have been shown Christian values. Through eyes of faith they have gained a vision of the heavenly.

B. *They have a record of past faithfulness.* One proof that the writer is addressing Christian converts is the reference to their steadfastness amid trying circumstances: "Remember those earlier days after you had received the light, when you stood your ground in a great contest in the face of suffering" (v. 32 NIV). The word translated "suffering" is the same word used to describe Christ's suffering on the cross. These people experienced a great suffering yet remained true. They accepted even the loss of personal property with a spirit of joy: "You joyfully accepted the confiscation of your property, because you knew that you yourselves had better and lasting possessions" (v. 34 NIV). The joy mentioned is depicted by a word used especially of Christian happiness.

II. The sin described (Heb. 10:22–25, 29).

A. *General characteristics.* Willful sin tramples the Song of God under foot (v. 29). Herein lies an attitude that makes one like the swine before whom Jesus warned that pearls should not be cast (Matt. 7:6). Such callousness treats Christ's death as something commonplace. The blood of the Passover lamb was sprinkled on the lintel above the door and on the posts at the sides of the door but not on the threshold lest it be trodden under foot. Such indifference is a direct insult to the Holy Spirit—"the Spirit of grace"—who makes God's grace real to us.

B. *Specific cases.* The general nature of willful sin is but a summary of the alternatives to certain exhortations clearly delineated in Hebrews 10:22–25. The writer is saying that to fail to do what he is suggesting is to willfully sin against God.

The first of three exhortations (all three are hortatory subjunctives in the progressive present and should be translated "Let us keep on drawing near," etc.) concerns personal holiness: "Let us draw near to God with a sincere heart in full assurance of faith, having our hearts sprinkled to cleanse us from a guilty conscience and having our bodies washed with pure water" (10:22 NIV). The sprinkling of the heart alludes to the sprinkling of blood set forth in the old covenant symbolizing God's power to remit sins (9:22). We must draw near God with hearts cleansed by his forgiveness made possible by Christ's final sacrifice. This cleanses us and frees us from a guilty conscience. The reference to washed bodies is undoubtedly a reference to baptism, which symbolizes the new purity found in Christ. The inner sprinkling and the outer washing is designed to include the whole being—an inner cleansing of the heart and an outward cleansing of every external action. A Christian has been cleansed inside and out by the blood of Christ.

The second exhortation concerns stability of witness: "Let us hold unswervingly to the hope we profess, for he who promised is faithful" (10:23 NIV). Our confession of faith affirms that Christ is Lord. We must remain true to this Christ. We must stand straight without bending to every adverse wind that blows, for our Lord who has promised us all things is faithful to us. Our behavior must never be determined by the crowd about us.

The third exhortation has to do with a faithful concern for the church: "Let us consider how we may spur one another on toward love and good deeds. Let us not give up meeting together, as some are in the habit of doing, but let us encourage one another—and all the more as you see the Day approaching" (10:24–25 NIV). We are to give special attention to our fellow Christians with a view to stimulating their activity for the Lord. One of the primary means of such encouragement is our faithful participation in public worship. The writer indicates that some have already taken up the dangerous habit of skipping church services. This is a warning against solitary discipleship. No doubt persecution was causing some to stay away from public identification with Christianity. Others may have been influenced by the incipient Gnosticism often encountered by the apostles, which deluded some weak converts into thinking they possessed a superior knowledge that somehow lifted them above the rank and file who might need public worship. This particular malady is still much in evidence today.

But whatever the excuse, the warning against unfaithfulness in church attendance is one of the most serious to be found in the Bible, and here is the climax of the warnings implied in the exhortations of 10:22–25. Although 10:26 ties willful sinning to any failure at the point of the exhortations, it is emphatically related to forsaking public worship. John Ruskin said the loss of worship is the greatest calamity that can befall a nation. When this happens, Ruskin said, "all things go to decay. Genius leaves the temple to haunt the senate or the market. Literature becomes frivolous. Science is cold. The eye of youth is not lighted by hope of other worlds, and age is without honour. Society lives for trifles, and when men die we do not mention them" (John Ruskin, cited in "The Epistle to the

Hebrews," in *The Speaker's Bible*, ed. James Hastings [Grand Rapids: Baker, 1961], 192).

III. The consequences involved (Heb. 10:26–31).

The willful sin is described as one committed with a thorough knowledge of what is involved: "after we have received the knowledge of the truth" (v. 26 NIV). The regular word for knowledge (*gnosis*) has a prepositional prefix here (*epignosis*), giving the idea of "full knowledge." If such is the case, "no more sacrifice for sins is left" (v. 26 NIV). This constitutes a willful turning to emptiness. Besides pointing toward Christ's final sacrifice, Old Testament sacrifices were prescribed to help believers (with faith like Abraham's) rededicate their lives and find their rightful place in God's service. The death of Christ brought about the final sacrifice and provided us with an eternal High Priest. To willfully turn from serving Christ is to take a side road to emptiness. There is no other sacrifice, no alternate way to please God or serve God.

What could a person expect if it were possible for him to be so inconsistent? "Only a fearful expectation of judgment and of raging fire that will consume the enemies of God" (v. 27 NIV). At best, this presents a dark future. One turns from serving Christ to the prospects of facing an insulted, all-powerful God.

The fearsome consequences are not spelled out in detail because God deals in manifold ways. God can reach into our most precious treasures, can touch our most sensitive feelings, if need be. Vengeance will not be meted out by someone knowing only part of the facts or having only limited means of punishment, but by God himself (v. 30). Truly we must admit, "It is a fearful thing to fall into the hands of the living God" (v. 31) while willfully sinning against him.

Conclusion

Let pagans and false converts withdraw (cf. 1 John 2:19), but the Christian has only one course—to draw ever nearer to the risen Lord; to hold fast his profession; to incite his brethren to deeper dedication by his own example, especially with regard to public worship (Heb. 10:22–25). Saving faith perseveres: "But we are not of those who shrink back and are destroyed, but of those who believe and are saved" (v. 39 NIV).

The drawing back referred to literally means "to take in sail," as a sailor would strike sail and lie becalmed rather than open the canvas to catch every breeze (W. H. Griffith Thomas, *Let Us Go On* [Grand Rapids: Zondervan, 1944], 139). God's Spirit is our wind of direction, which, when it springs up, must be allowed to drive us forth in his service. We must never strike sail, for faith is an adventure. We believe "and are saved" (10:39 NIV). The word translated "saved" is not the usual New Testament word for salvation. Literally it means "the possession of the soul." We go forward toward the goal of being completely possessed by God. Let others strive for possession; we strive to be possessed. There may be times when we are discouraged, when we feel our labors go unrewarded, when burdens become tediously heavy; but regardless of whatever vicissitudes we encounter, there is only one course that provides any solution — faithful, dedicated discipleship. Any other alternative falls into the category of willful sin.

WEDNESDAY EVENING, MARCH 21

Title: Why Did You Doubt?

Text: "O thou of little faith, wherefore didst thou doubt?" **(Matt. 14:31)**.

Scripture Reading: Matthew 14:22–33

Introduction

Have doubts been a problem in your life? Perhaps you try but are unable to shake the painful effects of doubt. Sometimes you feel that you are not much of a Christian because of your doubts. You are not alone. Most of us know too well the disorganizing power of doubt. You do not doubt the great doctrines and teachings of the Bible, but doubts come when you begin to try to apply these great doctrines and teachings to your life.

Even the disciples of Jesus were victims of doubt. They knew how upsetting doubts could be to a person. We all know about "doubting" Thomas. But Jesus never rejected the disciples because of their doubts; instead, he sought to bring help to their troubled lives. His probing question, "Why did you doubt?" was first addressed to his disciples, but it can bring you face-to-face with the "why" of your doubts.

I. Doubts come when circumstances are allowed to control you.

It had been a long day in the life of our Lord. He had fed more than five thousand people and had spent half of the night in prayer; but now he found that his disciples were in the midst of trying circumstances. In going to their aid, he walked on the waters of the Sea of Galilee. When Peter saw Jesus coming to their boat, he asked for the privilege of walking out on the water to meet him. After a good start, Peter allowed the circumstances of the wind and waves to take control, and he began to doubt.

A. *Circumstances can control you by temporarily overshadowing Christ.* Christ did not leave Peter alone, but Peter allowed the wind and waves to temporarily become more important than Christ; thus doubts came when Christ was overshadowed.

   1. When Christ is overshadowed, his commands are overshadowed (Matt. 14:19).

   2. When Christ is overshadowed, his care is overshadowed (Matt. 14:31).

B. *Circumstances can control you by challenging your personal well-being.* It is a terrifying experience to suddenly realize that your personal well-being is being challenged by forces that you cannot control. When this happened to Peter, he began to doubt.

C. *Circumstances can control you by causing your future to seem uncertain.* Peter and the other disciples gave up everything to become followers of Jesus. When trying circumstances came and their future seemed uncertain, they doubted.

II. Doubts come when fear is allowed to replace faith.

In the New Testament, a Christian's faith is described as an active trust and confidence in God and his will for an individual. This type of faith brings joy and peace to the Christian, but too often, as in Peter's case, fear is allowed to replace faith.

A. *When fear replaces faith, your courage is weakened.* Without strong courage there is usually little or no advancement in spiritual growth, evangelistic outreach, or world missions. Peter made no forward progress after fear replaced his faith.

B. *When fear replaces faith, your obedience is hindered.* It is wonderful to live in obedience to all that Christ commands, but if fear replaces faith, obedience is hindered.

C. *When fear replaces faith, your effectiveness is limited.* It is impossible to be truly effective in the work of the Lord if fear replaces faith. Peter knew only a limited amount of effectiveness in walking on the water because he allowed fear to replace his faith.

D. *When fear replaces faith, your confidence is destroyed.* The Bible says, "Commit thy way unto the LORD; trust also in him; and he shall bring it to pass" (Ps. 37:5). This is a wonderful verse, but if your faith is allowed to be replaced by fear, then like Peter, your confidence will be destroyed. There is not much you can do or will do without confidence in Christ or yourself.

Conclusion

Doubts can be defeated. When we understand why we have doubts, then we are able to defeat them. God is ready to help us with our problems.

A seven-year-old girl's faith encourages all who are troubled by doubt. After the tragic death of her parents, she prayed: "Dear God, we're sorry Daddy and Mommy had to die, but we know that you needed them up in heaven. And while they're gone, you are here to watch over us." Will you let him watch over you?

SUNDAY MORNING, MARCH 25

Title: Gathering around the Cross

Text: "And when they were come unto a place called Golgotha, that is to say, a place of a skull, they gave him vinegar to drink mingled with gall: and when he had tasted thereof, he would not drink. And they crucified him, and parted his garments, casting lots: that it might be fulfilled which was spoken by the prophet, They parted my garments among them, and upon my vesture did they cast lots. And sitting down they watched him there" **(Matt. 27:33–36)**.

Scripture Reading: Matthew 27:22–36

Hymns: "O Worship the King," Grant

"At Calvary," Newell

"Beneath the Cross of Jesus," Clephane

Offertory Prayer: Our Father, today as we see your Son on the cross, we behold the real meaning of your love for sinners such as us. In remembrance of your great gift of grace, we bring our offerings to you. May we and others be blessed through our stewardship. In Jesus' name. Amen.

Introduction

The story of Jesus' crucifixion needs little commentary. It has the power to tell its own story. My task is but to get you to come with me to "that green hill far away, without a city wall, where our dear Lord was crucified, and died to save us all." By the cords of divine love, I draw you to Calvary today.

Any public execution will draw a crowd, but on the day of Jesus' crucifixion, three enemies of the state were to be executed. Three crosses had been raised against the eastern sky, drawing a crowd to the "hill of the skull." Because it was the time of the Passover—Israel's greatest national holiday—Jerusalem, the capital city, was jammed with people. From the central cross, Jesus looked down upon a sea of faces. Who were these people gathered about the cross?

I. The soldiers (Matt. 27:27–36).

The soldiers' part at the crucifixion of our Lord was plain enough. As representatives of the Roman government, they were to carry out the orders of execution. So accustomed to cruelty and bloodshed were these men that they made a sport of the crucifixion. Because Jesus was accused of being the "king of the Jews," they pushed a crown of thorns down on his brow, stuck a reed into his hand for a scepter, and tied a scarlet mantle around his shoulders for a robe. They mocked him and said, "Hail, King!" Then they spat upon him, smote him, and led him away to be crucified.

When they reached Calvary they stretched Jesus out upon the beams of wood. They drove the nails through his hands and feet. Then the cross, with its felon fastened securely, was lifted up and into the prepared place in the ground. There the victim died a slow and torturous death by exposure, suffering, and thirst. It was maddening. With hands held fast, he was unable to defend himself against the gathering flies and insects. If he died within a day, it was merciful. But often the terrible agony lasted many hours. No wonder the Roman Cicero said, "Crucifixion is the most cruel and horrible torture in the device of men." And Tacitus said, "It is a torture fit only for slaves."

It was the custom among Roman soldiers that the personal effects of the criminal were the property of those attending at the execution. Jesus' only possession was a seamless robe that the soldiers gambled for. Having done their ghastly task of crucifixion, they sat down at the foot of the cross to divide the booty. Gambling was a favorite pastime of the soldiers, so casting lots for Jesus' robe was as much amusement as it was profit. There they sat throwing dice and joking while not a yard away Jesus hung on the cross. These men of war were completely unconscious of the great drama being played out at Calvary. They gazed unmoved and untouched on what has captured the hearts of multitudes since. They were concerned about the worth of a robe while witnessing history's greatest hour.

We, too, may gaze on the cross and see nothing. We may behold the dying Lamb of God and feel nothing. Why? Perhaps like the Roman soldiers, we are too much concerned with clothes to wear and games to play. Unmoved—while "from His head, His hands, His feet, sorrow and love flow mingled down." Unmoved! "Is it nothing to you, all ye that pass by?"

II. Passersby (Matt. 27:39–40).

Attending the execution of our Lord were the curious, the crowd followers, the passersby. They were a careless crowd moved along by waves of emotion and impulse. They acted before they thought, stumbling along after the throng. They were guilty of saying things in the midst of the masses that would never have left their lips if they were among the few. They were guilty of doing things as one of the "gang" that they would never think of doing after careful contemplation. So it is that a group of passersby became a mob set on rioting and lynching. What had changed these otherwise peaceful citizens into a mob crying for blood? Not much! They were just going along with the crowd, moving with the tide. One day it was "Hosanna," and the next it was "Crucify him." Whatever the rest were saying, they said.

Multitudes are like that today. They really have nothing against Christianity, but if the crowd isn't interested, neither are they. They have nothing against the preacher or the church, but if their crowd belittles, so do they. No wonder Jesus prayed of these kind, "Father, forgive them, for they know not what they do."

Were these passersby responsible for the crime of Calvary? Yes, a thousand times, yes. You cannot hide your guilt among the crowd. A day will come when you must stand alone before God. In that day, you will not be able to "parrot" what the crowd says. You will give an account of yourself. Nor will you be excused by saying, "Everyone else was doing it."

III. Religious leaders (Matt. 27:41–43).

After condemning Jesus before Pilate and demanding his death, these "religious professionals" followed Jesus to the place of execution. One might expect that when they had what they wanted, they would have returned to their "inner sanctum." But, no! Their thirst for revenge was so deep and their passions so strong that they gloated over every drop of blood. Forgetful of their place of dignity and reverence, they stood beside the cross to sneer and jeer. They couldn't keep their tongues quiet. "So, you are the Son of God, the King of Israel, the Messiah," they said. "If so, prove your claims." So with epithets they pelted him. "If you are so great a miracle worker, perform! Come down from the cross, and we will believe."

Jesus had met this temptation before. In the wilderness the devil said, "Turn stones into bread! Throw yourself from the roof of the temple! Miracle worker, perform!" The temptation was never stronger. He could indeed have come down from the cross, but he dared not. At a call from his holy lips, ten thousand angels would have rushed to his rescue, but as a sheep before her shearers is dumb, so he opened not his mouth.

The scribes and Pharisees were quite right when they said, "He saved others, himself he cannot save." Had Jesus saved himself, he could not have saved others. The power that kept Jesus on the cross was not the nails in his hands and feet, but his redeeming love.

Of this kind of Savior the religious leaders knew very little. They would have accepted a savior from Roman oppression, a savior from Roman taxation, a savior to lead the armies of Israel to political victory. But a bloody King on a cross they could not accept.

The spiritually shallow want a gospel of goodness and love, but they refuse a theology of blood atonement. They want to get "home" but not by the "way of the cross." They want a goody-goody brotherhood, but they will never join the company of the committed. These keep saying, "Come down from the cross and we will believe." If Christianity were only a creed to chant, a group to join, or a tradition to celebrate, they would be all for it; but they will have nothing of a religion of self-denial and cross-bearing.

IV. The penitent (Luke 23:39–43).

The penitent, represented in this confessing thief, also gather about the cross. This dying man had seen and heard it all—the soldiers cursing, laughing, gambling; the passersby shouting their taunts; the religious leaders demanding Jesus to prove his claims. All of these were terrible hindrances to faith. Yet listen to this penitent thief: "We suffer justly, we receive our due reward, but this man has done nothing amiss." The penitent admits his guilt, saying, "I have sinned!" Not too proud to ask for forgiveness, he says, "Lord, remember me." May God give you such a heart today! The heart of a penitent confesses to guilt, admits need, and accepts forgiveness.

Jesus said to this man, "Today shalt thou be with me in paradise." "Today!" What a ready salvation! "With me"! What a company! "In paradise"! What a glorious habitat! There is room at the cross for a penitent thief, and, friend, there is room at the cross for you!

Conclusion

(Have soloist or choir sing "There Is Room at the Cross for You.") Yes, millions have come, yet there is still room for one. There is room at the cross for you.

SUNDAY EVENING, MARCH 25

Title: The Necessity of Faith

Text: "Now faith is the substance of things hoped for, the evidence of things not seen.... Without faith it is impossible to please him; for he that cometh to God must believe that he is, and that he is a rewarder of them that diligently seek him" **(Heb. 11:1, 6)**.

Scripture Reading: Hebrews 11:1–13

Introduction

Christianity is not the only way of life based on faith. Rather, it is the only way of life based on faith *in Christ*. Gamblers are motivated by a kind of faith in Lady Luck. Even scientists are forced to operate on certain faith suppositions. Scientific experiments assume that matter is worth studying (Greek and Oriental philosophy deny this faith assumption), that the human mind can comprehend the realm of matter, and that there is consistency in the universe. The discipline of natural science requires human observers. When an adequate number of qualified observers corroborate the findings of one another, general conclusions are held to be valid, the primary reason being that a large number of observers have reported the same occurrences. It is at this point that we see the similarity in scientific experiments and religious experience. The Christian lives by faith but not by a blind faith. Hundreds of thousands of people from every level of society and culture since the days of Christ have reported having personal encounters with the living Christ. The gospel message invites people to come and see for themselves—to commit themselves to Christ in faith and to see if a personal encounter occurs in the process. This kind of involvement is the only real basis for life.

I. For proper perspective (Heb. 11:1–3).

If we are to find reality and come to grips with it, we must have a proper perspective. The story of the blind men touching an elephant and then seeking to describe it points up the same problem. The man touching the tail had a different concept from the one holding the trunk. The stance from which you view life is very important.

   A. *The reality of the eternal.* The Christian faith affirms that "the things which are seen are temporal; but the things which are not seen are eternal" (2 Cor. 4:18). When it comes to spiritual realities, technical empiricism, so adept at accumulating scientific knowledge, is of no help. The Bible affirms that only from the stance of Christian faith can we be aware of the eternal: "Now faith is the substance of things hoped for, the evidence of things not seen" (Heb. 11:1). In other words, faith helps us to understand that the unseen is also real. Seeing is not believing; believing is seeing.

   Faith gives substance to our spiritual hope. The word translated "substance" (*hupostasis*) literally means "to stand under." The idea of support or foundation is involved. It seems probable that here the idea of title deed is implied by the use of "substance." Faith brings to us the same assurance that comes from having the title to desired property.

But faith is never passive. Faith puts unseen realities to the test by acting on them. In the actual confrontation through commitment, the reality of the unseen is experienced, producing assurance. Jesus himself invited such testing: "If any man will do [God's] will, he shall know of the doctrine, whether it be of God, or whether I speak of myself" (John 7:17). The rule (kingdom) of God is unseen, the peace of forgiveness is intangible, life beyond death is beyond our experience, heaven is in another dimension which our human limitation cannot comprehend— yet because of an encounter with the risen Christ (also unseen to us), we are assured of the presence of the eternal.

B. *The meaning of the present.* The foundation on which one builds his life determines his general world outlook. We look about us and see, on every hand, *things.* We look up and see stars millions of light-years away. We see life and death all about us. How are we to interpret the present material universe? "Through faith we understand that the worlds were framed by the word of God, so that things which are seen were not made of things which do appear" (v. 3). In simple language, God has told us that matter is not eternal. All that we see is the handiwork of one God, our heavenly Father. This frees us from the grip of superstition and blind idolatry. We have no need to worship nature, the sun and moon, or anything else we see. All were created, as we were. Let science probe God's methodology of creation to its heart's content. We have no nervous faith that fears the truth. The only secrets that can be discovered are those planted by God for human discovery. Science is free to ask "How?" The Bible is content to limit its message to the who and the why, because these are the basic questions necessary for perspective to live the Christian life. God created all things for a purpose. We are part of that purpose, and faith begins the journey toward fulfilling God's purpose.

II. For our relationship to God (Heb. 11:4–6).

A. *Salvation of the soul.* If we are to truly find ourselves, we must first find God. This would be impossible were it not that God has already found us. He reaches out to us and bids us discover him by a faith surrender. Strangely enough, humans have never found it easy to surrender their wills to God. People much prefer to torture themselves, do penance, make religious pilgrimages, perform acts of mercy, and recite rituals. Every perversion of Christianity bears testimony to this basic fact—people fear commitment and resent it. They fear it because it obligates them and resent it because it gathers up all their devised schemes of salvation, together with their neat ledgers showing their past record of righteousness, and sends them to the incinerator. They must be obliterated. Only the righteousness of God can free a person from the guilt of his own sin. God bestows this righteousness on those who are willing to believe and to surrender body and soul to Christ in faith. We mortals do not like to declare spiritual bankruptcy. We hesitate to throw away our so-called "bargaining power." Yet there is no other way: "Without faith it is impossible to please [God]: for he that cometh to God must believe that he is, and that he is a rewarder of them that diligently seek him" (v. 6).

Before God there is no substitute for faith. Everything else is excess baggage. I remember a conversation with a friend who was honest and hardworking, who had no bad habits, whose language was free of all vulgarity, but who was not a Christian. He explained his upright life in such a way as to imply no need of forgiveness. He went so far as to say he had not committed a single sin for several months. His problem was that he was attempting to please God apart from a faith surrender. Here was a good man in many respects, but he had not been living without sin; rather, he had been guilty of the worst sin—unbelief (John 3:18). This sin is what damns a person, and he had been guilty of it every moment.

B. *Usefulness of life.* The Christian begins with faith and continues the same way. His happiness is found in doing the will of God, in being found pleasing to him every day. This requires acting out of faith. The Christian believes that the fullest life is found in complete discipleship—that God really does offer the greatest reward. He not only believes in God, he believes that God "is a rewarder of them that diligently seek him."

Whatever we give of our strength and wealth must be given out of faith or God will not accept it. God was pleased with Abel's sacrifice because it grew out of faithful commitment; he rejected Cain's because the life that offered the gift was not acceptable (v. 4).

Though Enoch is usually remembered as the man who was transplanted from earth to heaven without the dew of death on his brow, the most important aspect of his life is that "he pleased God" (v. 5). This is but another way of repeating Genesis 5:22: "And Enoch walked with God."

III. For life's decisions (Heb. 11:7 – 16).

If we are to find our destiny, we must make the right decisions. We must act on the impressions given us by the Holy Spirit. We must live by faith, discounting all cost, for the costliest thing in the world is a life lived apart from the will of God. And keep in mind that God will lead you down paths you would never chart on your own. The life of faith is a constant adventure. Since we do not know all the facts as God does, we must not expect his leadership in our lives to meet our approval. We follow him because we trust him, not because our rational calculations agree with him.

The patriarchs never saw the fulfillment of God's promises. Yet, like travelers viewing their destination from afar, they waved approval to God's promises from a great distance and willingly chose to live out life traveling in that direction:

"These all died in faith, not having received the promises, but having seen them afar off, and were persuaded of them, and embraced them, and confessed that they were strangers and pilgrims on the earth" (Heb. 11:13). Because they willingly placed heavenly promises above earthly security, they were given a coveted epitaph: "Wherefore God is not ashamed to be called their God" (Heb. 11:16).

If we are to find our destiny, our decisions must be in response to the Lord's leadership in our lives. There is no virtue in building a boat. Yet Noah is commended for carrying out such a project because it was his personal response to God's will (Heb. 11:7).

There is no virtue in pulling up all roots and moving to a new land—unless done in response to the will of God. Such was the case with Abraham (Heb. 11:8). Noah's boat project and Abraham's long trip turned out all right because the God who calls all the shots so ordered. Done apart from the will of God, both actions would have been ridiculous. The neighbors who lived next door to these two men must have had field days in chiding such religious fanatics. Certainly the actions of Noah and Abraham left them open to contemptuous pity. The point is that human vision has usually rejected God's method of bringing about divine purposes. The person of faith is not concerned about the rationality of an action, but rather about whether the action is the will of God.

Conclusion

Because these people in the faith "hall of fame" lived out life, letting God choose their place of tenure and spend their years of strength, they "all died in faith" (Heb. 11:13). Even death became merely a continuation of the adventure. The last words of Charles Frohman, who went down with the *Lusitania*, were: "Why fear death? It is the most beautiful adventure in life." What makes such an outlook possible? Faith alone! Without faith life is a meaningless maze of confused frustration and death is the most tragic of all possible occurrences. Faith is the one necessary ingredient.

WEDNESDAY EVENING, MARCH 28

Title: Do You Want to Leave Him?

Text: "Then said Jesus unto the twelve, Will ye also go away?" **(John 6:67)**.

Scripture Reading: John 6:66–68

Introduction

Would you consider Christian discipleship challenging? From a close study of the New Testament one discovers that being a disciple of Jesus is a demanding challenge.

Many of the people who followed Jesus for a while were not willing to meet the challenge. When they learned that Jesus was not going to set up a political kingdom, that he was not going to continue to give them free food, and that he would expect some commitments on their part, they stopped following him. When this happened, the real disciples of Jesus Christ faced one of the greatest trials of their lives. It had been much easier to be a follower of Jesus Christ when many were following, but now when others were refusing to follow, discipleship took on new meaning. In this context, Jesus asked the twelve disciples, "Will ye also go away?" In a real sense, as a follower of Jesus Christ, you face the same painful question, "Do you want to leave him?"

I. No, because Jesus exceeds all others.

Simon Peter and the disciples knew full well that if they refused to follow Jesus Christ, they would follow someone else who could not be of real help to them.

  A. *He exceeds all others in his identification with humankind.* It seems impossible that Jesus Christ, the Son of God, was born as a baby in Bethlehem and lived as man among us. Yet he was as much a man as any man has ever been.

  B. *He exceeds all others in his love for humankind.* No one has ever expressed love for others like Jesus Christ. The rich, the poor, the well, the sick, the righteous, the unrighteous, the educated, the uneducated, the young, the old, the master, and the slave were all objects of his love.

  C. *He exceeds all others in his willingness to help humankind.* Jesus came into a world filled with constant need, but he is not willing just to see or know the needs; he wants to meet them. The disciples knew that no one had ever helped them like Jesus. He helped them with their sins, sicknesses, sorrows, and troubles.

II. No, because Jesus alone gives eternal life.

Simon Peter's response to the question of Jesus was, "Lord, to whom shall we go? thou hast the words of eternal life." Others may offer riches, power, and pleasure, but only Jesus Christ gives eternal life.

  A. *Eternal life means that a person is no longer separated from God.* Whenever a person responds by faith to Jesus Christ, he is reconciled to God. Paul wrote, "But God commendeth his love toward us, in that, while we were yet sinners, Christ died for us. Much more then, being now justified by his blood, we shall be saved from wrath through him. For if, when we were enemies, we were reconciled to God by the death of his Son, much more, being reconciled, we shall be saved by his life" (Rom. 5:8–10).

  B. *Eternal life means that a person's sins are forgiven.* The burden of guilt because of unforgiven sins is almost more than an individual can stand. The Bible says in Ephesians 1:7, "In [Jesus] we have redemption through his blood, the forgiveness of sins, according to the riches of his grace."

  C. *Eternal life means that a person's life has been changed.* After the disciples came to know Jesus Christ, their lives were changed. Second Corinthians 5:17 says, "Therefore if any man be in Christ, he is a new creature: old things are passed away; behold, all things are become new."

1. Changed lives can be lives of joy (Phil. 4:4).
2. Changed lives can be lives of peace (Rom. 5:1).
3. Changed lives can be lives of love (Gal. 5:6).
4. Changed lives can be lives filled with purpose (Phil. 4:14).

D. *Eternal life means that a person has security.* Jesus said: "My sheep hear my voice, and I know them, and they follow me: And I give unto them eternal life; and they shall never perish, neither shall any man pluck them out of my hand. My Father, which gave them me, is greater than all; and no man is able to pluck them out of my Father's hand" (John 10:27–29).

III. No, because Jesus is the Son of God.

Simon Peter said, "We believe and are sure that thou art that Christ, the Son of the living God." We find it hard to fully understand the meaning of this statement, yet we know that in a wonderful way Jesus Christ was God's Son living among people.

A. *Being the Son of God, he can be personally known.* John the apostle describes Jesus Christ as "that which was from the beginning, which we have heard, which we have seen with our eyes, which we have looked upon, and our hands have handled" (1 John 1:1).

B. *Being the Son of God, he can be loved.* "We love him, because he first loved us" (1 John 4:19).

C. *Being the Son of God, he can be trusted.* In times of great trouble, Jesus urged the disciples to trust him. He said to them, "Let not your heart be troubled: ye believe in God, believe also in me" (John 14:1).

Conclusion

If you leave Jesus, you will solve no problems, change no lives, and help no one. Only as you commit yourself will you find a solution to life.

SUGGESTED PREACHING PROGRAM FOR

APRIL

■ **Sunday Mornings**

Continue with the theme "Facing the Cross" on the Sunday before Easter. "Easter Joy" is the theme for Easter morning and the Sundays that follow.

■ **Sunday Evenings**

Continue the expository messages based on the book of Hebrews using "The Supremacy of Christ" as the theme.

■ **Wednesday Evenings**

Continue the series "Questions Jesus Asked" as the theme for the devotional messages for those who come together for prayer and fellowship during the week.

SUNDAY MORNING, APRIL 1

Title: Triumph and Tragedy

Text: "And when he was come nigh, even now at the descent of the mount of Olives, the whole multitude of the disciples began to rejoice and praise God with a loud voice for all the mighty works that they had seen; saying, Blessed be the King that cometh in the name of the Lord: peace in heaven, and glory in the highest.... And when he was come near, he beheld the city, and wept over it, saying, If thou hadst known, even thou, at least in this thy day, the things which belong unto thy peace! but now they are hid from thine eyes" **(Luke 19:37–38, 41–42)**.

Scripture Reading: Luke 19:29–44

Hymns: "Lead On, O King Eternal," Shurtleff

"Praise Him! Praise Him!" Crosby

"Just as I Am," Elliott

Offertory Prayer: Our Father, you have declared in your Word that "it is more blessed to give than to receive." May we be doubly blessed today—receiving of your bounty in grace and now giving from our bounty to advance your kingdom. In Jesus' name. Amen.

Introduction

How rapidly the days closed on the public ministry of our Lord! Three years earlier at the Jordan River John the Baptist introduced Jesus to the multitudes by saying, "Behold the Lamb of God, which taketh away the sin of the world"

(John 1:29). From that day onward the fame of the Galilean had spread quickly throughout all the land. He was hailed as a great teacher, a miracle worker, and by some who dared, the Messiah. Wherever he moved he could not free himself from the crowds of people. They came from every quarter to see and hear him and to be healed. But not all the people held him in such esteem. As his fame grew, so did the hatred of the scribes and Pharisees. They were determined to do away with him. Now in this Passover season they plotted his death. On what we know as Palm Sunday, Jesus began his last week of public ministry on the earth.

Jesus had guarded well the secret of his messiahship. On the Mount of Transfiguration when the three disciples witnessed his glory, Jesus cautioned them to tell no one until the proper time. Now the time had come. He would let the people acclaim him King. Now the prophecy of Zechariah would be fulfilled: "Rejoice greatly, O Daughter of Zion! Shout, Daughter of Jerusalem! See, your king comes to you ... gentle and riding on a donkey, on a colt, the foal of a donkey" (Zech. 9:9 NIV).

I. A day of triumph.

The gentle spring rains had already come, and the countryside was beginning to turn green. The crocus and daffodil added their brightness to the meadow. Pomegranate and honeysuckle filled the gentle air with fragrance. What a lovely spring morning! After breakfast with friends, Jesus and his disciples left Bethany for Jerusalem. By the time they reached Bethphage, the road was crowded with pilgrims making their annual journey for the Feast of the Passover.

    A. *Preparation (Luke 19:29–34).* On the morning of Jesus' triumphal entry, he had sent two of his disciples ahead to prepare for his entry into Jerusalem. They found the colt as Jesus had instructed them, and upon loosing the animal, they were asked what they were doing. They replied, "The Lord hath need of him." Quite willingly the owner of the colt consented to its use by the Lord. Here is a lesson for us in the dedication of our possessions for the use of the Lord and his work.

    B. *Procession (Luke 19:35–38).* As Jesus seated himself on the colt, some people must have asked, "Who is this who rides in regal procession?" The disciples and others answered, "It is he who comes in the name of the Lord." The shouting of the crowd was infectious. As soon as someone began to chant "Hosanna," others took up the cry. Soon the roadway echoed with shouts of praise. As with any holiday parade, children and parents alike joined in cries of blessing. It is within reason to suppose that this holiday crowd joined in shouting portions of Psalm 24: "Lift up your heads, O you gates; be lifted up, you ancient doors, that the King of glory may come in" (v. 7 NIV). Those who went before may have cried out, "Who is this King of glory?" while those who followed replied, "The LORD strong and mighty, the LORD mighty in battle." Caught up in the emotion of the hour, some spread their garments in the way and others placed palm branches in the path.

Soon the summit of the Mount of Olives was reached. There in the morning light and splendor was the city of Jerusalem—Zion! Rising out of the Valley of Hinnom was the golden temple. About were the terraced gardens of Herod's palace. What a magnificent spectacle! Anyone could shout "Hosanna" at a time and sight such as this!

C. *Pharisees (Luke 19:39–40).* The little donkey joggled on toward the Kidron Valley. Those on the outskirts of the city now joined in with accolades about the Master. The whole valley rang with the cries of "Hosanna." So tumultuous was this Palm Sunday caravan that it seemed likely to get out of hand. Some of the Pharisees requested Jesus to rebuke the shouting disciples, but Jesus replied that if the people held their voices, the stones would cry out. The Pharisees then said among themselves, "Behold, the world is gone after him" (John 12:19). It no doubt seemed that way, for it was the day of the King's triumphal entry into the city, and everyone joined in shouting "Hosanna." Everyone was happy; everyone was in a holiday mood. Everyone, that is, except Jesus.

II. Tragedy.

In the midst of all this shouting for joy, there was one who wept. What a contrast of emotions! Shouting and weeping; triumph and tragedy! The wild demonstration of affection by the fickle multitude moved Jesus to weep. While the people shouted, "Hosanna," Jesus' heart broke into passionate lamentation: "O Jerusalem, Jerusalem, thou that killest the prophets and stonest them which are sent unto thee, how often would I have gathered thy children together, even as a hen gathereth her chickens under her wings, and ye would not" (Matt. 23:37).

A. *Lost love (Luke 19:41–44).* What we hear in these words is the agony of the Savior over a lost city. The phrase "how often" is a sorrowful summing up of the tenderest love story ever told. Never had a people been so loved as had the children of Israel. They had been called out of strange places, sheltered in Egypt, delivered from bondage, and given a land flowing with milk and honey. God had done all this for them so that they in turn might bless all the nations of the earth. God's love for them is reflected in the parables of the lost sheep, the lost coin, and the lost son (Luke 15). "How often" was a love story that started with Father Abraham eighteen centuries before. But now their day of grace was about over and they still refused God's call of love. Jesus sorrowfully said, "And ye would not."

What Jesus said to Israel that first Palm Sunday he says to us today. How often he would love and bless us, but we refuse. By every divine providence God calls us. In childhood by a mother's love and tender care, in youth by a good father's wisdom, and as we age by Christian friends and the voice of the church. The tragedy then is repeated now—"Ye would not." Enacted here is the conflict between a love that desires to save and an obstinate heart that will not respond.

B. *Lost opportunity (Luke 19:42).* "If thou hadst known … the things which belong unto thy peace." The "if" speaks of an opportunity offered and refused and lost forever. Israel had their time of visitation. They had it when God gave them Moses and the prophets, when King David stretched the kingdom from Dan to Beersheba, again when they returned from Babylon to rebuild, and now in the person of Jesus the Messiah. But they killed the prophets and stoned those who were sent to deliver them. Now they would soon crucify the Son of God himself. If only they had known!

Jesus wept that day for what Israel might have been had they remained true to her calling. But Israel missed their chance; they lost their opportunity. This is the sad story of too many lives. God has a purpose for your life. He wills only the best for you, but you must be obedient to his calling. Some of you, on this Palm Sunday, need to say yes to God's will for your lives. Do not let this opportunity be lost. For, as Jesus said, these are the "things which belong to thy peace." God's will is the way of peace and happiness for you now and in eternity.

We have seen how Palm Sunday was a day of triumph and tragedy; now we will see how it was a day of tribulation.

III. Day of tribulation (Luke 19:43–44).

While the people shouted hosannas, Jesus wept. All that the people saw was the beauty of the temple and the city, but Jesus saw something more. He saw the terrible destruction that would soon come. The people saw only the present; Jesus saw into the future. In these two verses, Jesus vividly pictures what was to happen. An enemy would come and destroy Jerusalem, and not one stone would be left upon another. Why this terrible tribulation? Jesus said, "because thou knewest not the time of thy visitation."

What Jesus predicted came true when in AD 70 Titus and his Roman army captured Jerusalem. After a siege of several months, the inner walls were breeched, and the city was put to the torch and completely destroyed. The Jewish historian Josephus summed up this day of tribulation in these words: "But for the city, it was so thoroughly laid even with the ground by those who dug it up to the foundations, that there was left nothing to make those that come hither believe it had ever been inhabited" (Josephus, *Antiquities* 5.1).

Conclusion

Do you wonder at the tears of Jesus while all the people shouted hosannas? Jesus saw and knew things that the excited crowd knew nothing about. Perhaps today, on this Palm Sunday, when we joyfully proclaim Jesus King, he weeps. He weeps because today, as long ago, there are those who refuse his love, who miss their opportunity for blessing, and who face the day of tribulation. Are these tears for you?

SUNDAY EVENING, APRIL 1

Title: People of Whom God Is Not Ashamed

Text: "They were longing for a better country—a heavenly one. Therefore God is not ashamed to be called their God, for he has prepared a city for them" **(Heb. 11:16 NIV)**.

Scripture Reading: Hebrews 11:8–19

Introduction

Children have within themselves the power to bring to their parents either the highest joy or the deepest heartbreak. A father and mother share with their pastor the news that their daughter is going to have a baby out of wedlock, and they sob, "We are so ashamed." The local newspaper reports the story of a young man jailed for drunken driving or for possession of narcotics, and his parents face the world the next day with the message engraved on their troubled brows: "We are so ashamed."

Jesus related the story of a father who had two sons whom he asked to work in the vineyard. One son immediately voiced his rebellion with the haughty statement: "I will not" (Matt. 21:28–29). I can imagine the shame the father felt at having raised a son who could be so disrespectful. In response to the father's command, the second son lightly agreed to go to work. The problem was that he never did show up in the vineyard. Here you have a case of a father being disappointed and ashamed at the conduct of both sons. The first son brought shame but afterward thought differently and reported to work in the vineyard. The father's shame was turned to pride. The second son's words brought pride to the father, but his actions later brought shame. The Bible pictures God as our heavenly Father and sets for our example the faithfulness of Abraham, who, along with other models of faith, receive the commentary: "God is not ashamed to be called their God." Let us look at such people.

I. Willing people (Heb. 11:8–9).

A. *To obey.* God can use only people who are willing to be used: "Abraham, when called to go to a place he would later receive as his inheritance, obeyed and went, even though he did not know where he was going" (v. 8 NIV). The literal language of the Bible indicates that Abraham went immediately. He didn't need any attractive travel folders telling him of enticing lands. In fact, he was not even told what land God had in mind. He went because his faith was an obedient faith.

The life of faith always begins with sealed orders that we must be willing to follow. We are allowed to open up these orders only one day at a time.

B. *To leave security behind.* "By faith he made his home in the promised land like a stranger in a foreign country" (v. 9 NIV). The journey begun by Abraham would encompass many years. He would travel from one place to another, dwelling in tents and living out the uncertain existence of an alien. Even when the time came that he could settle down in Canaan, he was forced to do it as a stranger, for the land was his in promise only.

II. Spiritually minded people (Heb. 11:10).

Only the spiritually minded are willing to give up earthly security to follow the will of God. Abraham seems to understand that only God's promises have reality, although they are unseen. He continued his wanderings because "he looked for a city which hath foundations, whose builder and maker is God." The tents in which Abraham lived throughout the years had no foundation, offered no security. Yet he believed in the reality of a heavenly city whose foundations were the work of God himself.

To the ancient Hebrew, a city was the symbol of a settled and secure condition (Ps. 107:7). The Old Testament saints understood that their greatest possession was their relationship with the living God. They understood that any earthly blessings were but visible manifestations of such a relationship. They believed in the value of spiritual treasures.

III. Trusting people (Heb. 11:13).

Concerning Abel, Enoch, Noah, Sarah, and Abraham, it is said, "All these people were still living by the things promised; they only saw them and welcomed them from a distance. And they admitted that they were aliens and strangers on earth" (NIV).

A. *In death.* A literal translation indicates that these people died "according to faith." God grants to his children a grace that gives them courage to face death and sustains them in that moment. Those who trust God are not afraid to die.

The faithful people of the Old Testament did not understand all that would be involved in God's promise of salvation, yet they waved at these promises though they were obscured by the fog of intervening centuries. The scoffers called such promises mirages in the desert of life, but the faithful recognized them as reality.

B. *In life.* The people who are able to trust God in death are those who have learned to trust him in life. This means that they do not measure their earthly success by the size of their bank account. They are content to be "strangers and pilgrims on the earth." In ancient days a great stigma was attached to aliens and strangers; they often were suspected and hated and held in contempt by the local people who no doubt were suspicious of why they had left their original home. Transients seldom have the respect of local people.

Abraham was content to spend his life on the road if that was God's will. When his wife, Sarah, died, Abraham had to bargain for a plot of ground in which to bury her. If we are to trust God, we must be willing to see ourselves as pilgrims journeying toward eternity.

The supreme test of Abraham is seen in God's command to offer up Isaac, Abraham and Sarah's only son (Heb. 11:17–19). Should Isaac be put to death, God would not be able to carry out his promise that Abraham's seed would be as numerous as the grains of sand on the shore. Yet God asked Abraham to sacrifice Isaac. Pagans often sacrificed their children. God seemed to be asking Abraham if his devotion was as great as that offered by pagans to their false gods. How true are the words of Chrysostom: "The things of God seemed to fight against the things of God, and faith fought with faith, and the commandment fought with the promise." Yet Scripture tells us that Abraham was willing to take the life of his own son, believing that God would raise him from the dead and thus continue his promise. This is trust.

IV. Loyal people (Heb. 11:14–16).

Abraham had ample opportunity to return to his own country and to go back on his commitment to God (v. 15), but he did not.

A. *Desire a heavenly home.* The reason Abraham did not betray God by going back to his homeland was simple: he was "longing for a better country—a heavenly one" (v. 16 NIV). Abraham, like every person, desired a homeland, yet he preferred a heavenly homeland to that of any earthly realm. To be sure, there are spots on earth that become dear to us. Years ago a missionary, while returning home from foreign soil, saw his child die and was forced to bury the little one at sea. He recorded the latitude and longitude of the position, longing to remember the point where his loved one rested. It is the desire for heaven and the knowledge that we will see our loved ones again that stir in our hearts the ultimate loyalty.

B. *Refuse to be traitors.* Scripture says, "If they had been thinking of the country they had left, they would have had opportunity to return" (v. 15 NIV). The literal grammar of the passage tells us that if Abraham and his family had kept on thinking of Ur, they constantly would have had opportunities to return. But loyalty prevailed.

Abraham seemed to care what God and eternity would have to say about him. He was not the kind of man who wanted to live forever with the knowledge that he had failed God and thus failed life. Not knowing when death would come, Abraham chose to live out each day in faithfulness so that if it be the last day, all would be well.

Conclusion

It is easy to live in unfaithfulness, thinking that we will make things right with God before the end comes. But we must determine that we will live each day in such a way that, should it be our last, God would not be ashamed of us. When God chose to reveal himself to Moses (Ex. 3:15), he called himself the God of

Abraham, Isaac, and Jacob. Insert your name into that statement. Would God be willing to identify himself by naming you as his child?

WEDNESDAY EVENING, APRIL 4

Title: Why Be Anxious?

Text: "Take therefore no thought for the morrow: for the morrow shall take thought for the things of itself" **(Matt. 6:34).**

Scripture Reading: Matthew 6:24–34

Introduction

Anxiety has often been called the great disease of our age. As a disease, it is no respecter of persons. It strikes the rich as well as the poor, the healthy as well as the unhealthy, the educated as well as the uneducated, the Christian as well as the non-Christian. The effect of anxiety is revealed in our lives through unusual worry, fear, and guilt.

In our Scripture reading, Jesus seeks to deal with this most difficult of diseases. By asking many questions that can be summed up in the one question—Why be anxious?—he gives much needed advice. Anxiety distracts our thinking, disturbs our worship, disorganizes our lives, and destroys our joy and peace with God. Although we sometimes feel that Jesus cannot understand or speak to our anxieties, we must never forget that he was always aware that he was a child of the laboring class; that his mother, at his birth, had brought the gift of the poor to the temple; and that from boyhood he had been accustomed to poverty. When he asks, "Why be anxious?" we can know that he understands our problems.

I. Being anxious will not provide for our bodies.

Jesus knew that many of his followers would be anxious about food for their bodies. To help them with this anxiety, he urged them to trust in him. His followers knew that God provided for the birds, but they had a problem believing that he would provide for them. They failed to see that they were more important to the Father than the birds.

Today, as well as during Jesus' earthly ministry, God provides food for his followers by giving them the ability, strength, and intelligence to work so they can buy food, or else he arranges for someone to meet their need. This truth is not for promoting undisciplined living but for disciplined living. Anxiety cannot provide food for our bodies any more than it can add minutes to our lives or inches to our height. God will meet our need for food if we will trust in him.

II. Being anxious will not provide clothing for us to wear.

Jesus' followers are subject to the same concerns as the rest of the world. They face the danger of becoming anxious about their clothing. It is easy for a person to become more interested in clothing than in Christ. More than one person has stopped attending church because he or she has nothing new to wear.

The heathen had an excuse for their anxiety over clothing: they had no loving Father to turn to. But this was not true for the Christian. Their loving Father was concerned about them and sought to help them.

As followers of Christ, we are able to see the movement of God in our lives. Our past reveals the wonderful care of a loving Father. With the writer of Psalm 124:8, we can say, "Our help is in the name of the LORD, who made heaven and earth." Our God provides for his own, and our need for clothing is not unknown to him. The God who provided for Abraham, Moses, David, Elijah, Paul, John, Peter, and multitudes of others will not fail us. Because of this truth, there is no need for us to be anxious about clothing.

III. Being anxious will not provide peace for our lives.

Henry Drummond once said, "Above all things do not touch Christianity unless you are willing to seek the kingdom first. I promise you a miserable existence if you seek it second." It is impossible to know peace if we allow anxiety to stop us from putting God first. Being anxious is a sign that God is not first. Jesus promised his followers that if they would put God first, their need for food and clothing would be met.

Conclusion

There is no justifiable reason for a Christian to be anxious. We have a Lord who will in some way provide for every need. We must simply trust and obey him.

SUNDAY MORNING, APRIL 8

Title: Good News from the Graveyard

Text: " 'Don't be alarmed,' [the angel] said. 'You are looking for Jesus the Nazarene, who was crucified. He has risen! He is not here. See the place where they laid him' " (**Mark 16:6 NIV**).

Scripture Reading: Mark 16:1–20

Hymns: "Christ the Lord Is Risen Today," Wesley

"Hallelujah! Christ Is Risen," Wordsworth

"Let Jesus Come into Your Heart," Morris

Offertory Prayer: Our Father, we thank you this Easter Day for victory over sin and death through Jesus Christ our Lord. We have a glad message to declare to our troubled world. We dedicate the gifts of your people to the purposes of the gospel throughout the world. In Jesus' name. Amen.

Introduction

Nearly a century ago, Ernest Poole wrote a novel titled *The Harbor*. The main character of the story is a bespectacled old gentleman who is impatient with life in general. He is "agin'" everything. He has a violent history and keeps repeating, "History is just news from the graveyard." From the lips of this scrooge, I take the title for this Easter message. But I shall add one word: "*Good* News from the Graveyard."

I. Good news eagerly awaited.

Easter is the one day whose sunrise is welcomed by the whole world. The arrival of other days may come with fear, but not Easter. All across the world people gathered early this morning to hear again the good news of Christ's resurrection. What makes this day so different? Why is Easter so gladly welcomed? Because Easter means "good news" and "glad tidings." This world could use some good news today. In this terrible day of war and tension among nations, of hate and prejudice among people, we could use a little good news.

II. Source of the good news (Mark 16:1–2).

Come, let us join the women on their early morning journey. Where were they going at sunrise? Scripture says that "they were on their way to the tomb" (v. 2 NIV). They were on their way to the graveyard. How universal is this pathway! All people walk this way at some point in life. With sighing and crying we walk this path of anguish. This path to the graveyard is a "trail of tears." The women came that first Easter morning to anoint the dead. The last thing they expected was to hear some good news. Who would expect good news from a graveyard?

III. Message of good news (Mark 16:5–6).

Until that first Easter, the news from the graveyard was all bad. Death was the ruler of all our destinies. We were born to die. We lived for the grave. A person's life might be fair, beautiful, and prosperous; but it was also fearful, transient, and dying. Life was like a fading flower. Life was like grass that withered and vapor that disappeared. The Bible says, "In Adam all die"; "It is appointed unto man once to die." This is the universal sentence of sin that is pronounced upon all people. One day we all will die. But the good news of Easter destroys the terror of death. In his first letter to the Corinthians, the apostle Paul wrote, "O death, where is thy sting; O grave, where is thy victory?" Because of the Easter good news, we can answer with confidence and joy, "I thank my God who gives us the victory through Jesus Christ."

A. *Jesus declares the Good News.* Jesus, the Son of God, came to put the stamp of immortality on people. He boldly declared that the grave was not the end: "God so loved the world, that he gave his only begotten Son, that whosoever believeth in him should not perish, but have everlasting life"

(John 3:16); "I give unto them eternal life; and they shall never perish, neither shall any man pluck them out of my hand" (10:28); "I am the resurrection, and the life: he that believeth in me, though he were dead, yet shall he live: and whosoever liveth and believeth in me shall never die" (11:25–26). These are the words of the Son of God! If the declaration of the truth is not enough, there is proof of immortality.

B. *Jesus proves the Good News.* Jesus died on the cross. The Bible says that he "gave up his spirit" (Matt. 27:50 NIV). He was dead all right! The soldier said he was dead. The agents of Caesar said he was dead. Joseph of Arimathea, who claimed his body, said he was dead. Make no mistake about it, Jesus died on that cross. He was not just unconscious or in a swoon; he was dead! What awful suspense there was while he lay in that tomb. Who would be master, death or life? Darkness or light? The grave or God?

All nature held its breath to see who would be victor and who would be victim, who would conquer and who would be conquered. But the good news from the graveyard was:

> Up from the grave He arose,
> With a mighty triumph o'er His foes;
> He arose a victor from the dark domain,
> And He lives forever with His saints to reign:
> He arose! He arose!
> Hallelujah! Christ arose!

C. *The disciples declare the Good News (Mark 16:7–8).* You can read the resurrection story in any of the Gospels. They all have a story to tell. The angel said to the women, "Go your way and tell," and the Bible says the women "fled from the tomb" (NIV). It seems that nearly every story about the resurrection ends in a footrace. "The women hurried away from the tomb … and ran" (Matt. 28:8 NIV). "[Mary Magdalene] came running to Simon Peter and the other disciple, the one Jesus loved" (John 20:2 NIV). "Peter and the other disciple started for the tomb. Both were running, but the other disciple outran Peter and reached the tomb first" (v. 4 NIV). These words are not by accident or invention. Those bearing good news simply cannot walk; they must run. This race at sunrise did not stop until the whole countryside knew the good news of the resurrection. What does this Easter message say?

1. Forgiveness for the past. What a dark and sinful past the disciples had! They had argued as to who was the greatest. They had slept in Gethsemane when Jesus asked them to stay awake. They had all forsaken Jesus and fled when the guards came to take him away. Peter had denied he ever knew Jesus. Yet on this Easter morning, Jesus wanted to see them (Mark 16:7). Isn't that just like Jesus? "I know you have sinned; I know you have deserted, denied, and doubted; but I still love you, and I want to see you." How do you explain this? Between their sinning and that

Easter morning was the cross. From that cross, Jesus cried, "Father, forgive them." The Bible says, "The blood of Jesus Christ his Son cleanseth us from all sin" (1 John 1:7). Friend, part of the Easter message is that God forgives.

2. Joy for the present. How disappointed and discouraged the disciples were (Mark 16:11). They had seen Jesus dead and buried. The world had come crashing down around them. There was nothing left to live for. Have you ever felt that life had lost its meaning? Has the death of a loved one robbed you of your desire to go on? Then you, like the disciples, need to listen again to the Easter good news. John 20:20 says, "Then were the disciples glad, when they saw the Lord." Their despair had turned to joy. Suddenly they were not alone; Jesus had walked back into their lives. Christ was not a memory now: he was a real and living presence. People need to discover this blessed truth about Easter. The presence of the living Lord can be real joy and peace each day.

3. Hope for the future. The good news from the graveyard is that Christ has conquered death and hell. Paul says that "the last enemy that shall be destroyed is death" (1 Cor. 15:26). And John saw in his vision that "death and hell were cast into the lake of fire" (Rev. 20:14). The disciples were glad, not just that Christ had survived the grave, but that he had conquered it. Easter took a tragedy and made it a triumph. Because of Easter we have good news to share. The last verse of Mark's gospel declares, "They went forth, and preached every where, the Lord working with them, and confirming the word with signs following. Amen" (Mark 16:20).

We join with those who witnessed the first Easter morning and declare unto you this good news from the graveyard. It is a message of forgiveness, joy, and hope.

Conclusion

You may be thinking, "I wish I had that kind of confidence and assurance. I wish I had that joy and peace." You can have it. The promise of God is this: "As many as received him, to them gave he power to become the sons of God, even to them that believe on his name" (John 1:12). The good news of Easter becomes personally yours as you accept God's gift of eternal life through Jesus Christ.

SUNDAY EVENING, APRIL 8

Title: Faith: The Surest Guide

Text: "By faith he forsook Egypt, not fearing the wrath of the king: for he endured, as seeing him who is invisible" **(Heb. 11:27)**.

Scripture Reading: Hebrews 11:24–27

Introduction

"Let your conscience be your guide" is a dangerous aphorism. A conscience can be tampered with. It can be ravished or slain. What then are we to use for our compass on this road of life? There are times when the advice of friends is helpful, but somehow they are never able to put themselves completely in our predicament. Professional counselors may give some assistance, but usually they conclude by reminding us that the decision is ours and no one else can make it for us.

Though decisions should take into account every aspect, there is such a thing as being confused by the facts. The preponderance of evidence produced by the "facts" may be misleading. Can you imagine what a computer would have put out had Moses fed it the facts of his dilemma as to whether he should remain the crown prince of Egypt or should side with the enslaved Hebrews? Let pagans base their choices on surveys and public opinion, but people of faith must decide for themselves. They must act, not because there is comforting evidence that they should do so, but in spite of the dominance of evidence that says they should not. Every major choice must be a solitary one, once we, like Moses, have "come to years" (Heb. 11:24).

Faith demands that we decide everything on the basis of our commitment to Christ. Hebrews is addressed to believers in a time of great persecution. They were tempted to cling to thoughts and practices that would hide their Christian witness and evade the spotlight of Caesar's hatred. In such a context, no greater example could be cited than Moses who, acting out of faith and against overwhelming odds, leaped into the raging torrents of his age and overcame.

I. In the choice of purpose (Heb. 11:24–25).

We are told that Moses was schooled in the wisdom of the mightiest nation of his day. Egypt was the granary of the world as well as the cradle of a mighty civilization. Egypt's might was second to none. Moses was not only the heir apparent to the throne; he was also a brilliant general, having defeated the Ethiopians during a time of national crisis. Yet he sensed that his life's purpose lay somewhere outside the royal courts of Egypt. Only a deep personal faith could cause a man to give up what Moses gave up. Acting out of faith, he stepped out to lay hold of God's purpose for his life.

   A. *Identification with God's people.* The first step in carrying out the will of God is to become identified with the people of God. It is a matter of choosing your crowd. Moses' first step involved a renunciation of his position as royal heir: "By faith Moses, when he was come to years, refused to be called the son of Pharaoh's daughter; choosing rather to suffer affliction with the people of God, than to enjoy the pleasures of sin for a season" (vv. 24–25). This is a momentous decision for a man forty years of age. This choice meant moving to the "wrong side of the Nile."

   B. *A willingness to suffer hardship.* Whereas Moses had known the pleasures at the royal court, he now traded them for afflictions. No doubt sin's pleasures were enticing, as they are today. Yet to remain in Pharaoh's court when God's call was elsewhere would have been a greater sin than mere participation in the courtly revelry.

Hardship came quickly to Moses. He was branded a murderer because he protected a Hebrew slave from the cruelty of an Egyptian soldier. He was forced to flee to the desert wastes surrounding Sinai where he was to live as a herdsman for another forty years. Genuine faith often means loneliness because the great throngs are elsewhere.

II. In the choice of reward (Heb. 11:26).

The wise man decides what he wants from life, not by the immediacy of the moment, but by the long look. Moses decided the hardships connected with the pursuit of God's will were of greater value than all Egypt's wealth. He did not make this choice by taking an inventory; he made it by looking ahead—"He regarded disgrace for the sake of Christ as of greater value than the treasures of Egypt, because he was looking ahead to his reward" (NIV).

Moses believed in the ultimate triumph of almighty God. He believed that the full life, for him, had to be lived out in conflict with Pharaoh's enslaving might. Nothing is quite as rewarding as the knowledge that you are standing in the one place on the earth that God has marked off for you and doing the one thing for which you were divinely called. The dedicated life carries with it a reward of its own.

Those who live on this side of Calvary have a deeper understanding of the eternal nature of God's reward than was spelled out for Moses, yet the rewards possible in this earthly life are still important considerations.

See Moses as he descends Sinai with a glory on his face that only God can bestow, with a melody in his heart known only to the heavenly symphonies, and ask him if he regrets his choice of rewards. See him as he stands on Mount Pisgah and gazes at the panoramic view of the Promised Land stretched out before him. But better still, see him as he steps through the door of death and finds himself in the heavenly dimension toward which his labors and prayers had pointed.

Look even further down the centuries and see Moses, together with Elijah, appearing to Jesus on the Mount of Transfiguration and discussing with the Son of God his approaching death for the sins of the world. Moses did not foresee all of this as he looked ahead, but he knew God's redemption would ultimately triumph, and he made his decisions in that light.

III. In the choice of masters (Heb. 11:27).

Though our mortal pride hesitates to admit it, complete freedom is not an option. Our freedom comes at the point of choosing under whose mastery we will live. Those who claim no master are actually at the mercy of their own base appetites. Jesus boiled the matter down to its ultimate simplicity: "No man can serve two masters.... ye cannot serve God and mammon" (Matt. 6:24). You can live for mammon (the money god) and what it can buy or for God and what he chooses to give.

We find ourselves, like Moses, standing at a fork in the road. The choice lies between God's promise to redeem and Pharaoh's promise of power. The matter is made sterner by the fact that, in choosing the invisible God, we lay ourselves open to the disdainful wrath of the very present and very visible power of the prince of this world and his pharaohs and Caesars.

Moses acted against his momentary best interests: "By faith he forsook Egypt, not fearing the wrath of the king: for he endured, as seeing him who is invisible" (v. 27). He chose to buck city hall and become an outcast. The wrath of Pharaoh could force him to flee but could not force him to stay under his mastery. The choice was one of ultimate allegiance—of serving in God's court or in the world's court. Now we are related to both, but the total picture is determined by which one we give preeminence. Neither will accept our polite nod. Each demands our heart. The surest guide for such a choice is our faith. All our decisions must be consistent with our faith commitment to Christ. The person who walks by faith is not nearly as blind as the one who takes into account merely the physical facts.

Conclusion

Suppose Moses had chosen Pharaoh as master. Instead of being inscribed in God's holy record, his name probably would be carved on the sarcophagus of an embalmed mummy, long since dragged by looters from its resting place in the inner chambers of a pyramid. Only God knew the coming fate of Pharaoh, that his lifeless body would lie half buried in the sands along the Red Sea, obscured by the scattered heap of broken chariots and dead soldiers.

The only sure guide Moses had for his decisions was his faith. The same is true for modern Christians. For in the wisdom of God, it has been decreed that "the just shall live by faith" (Rom. 1:17).

WEDNESDAY EVENING, APRIL 11

Title: Whose Neighbor Are You?

Text: " 'Which of these three do you think was a neighbor to the man who fell into the hands of robbers?' The expert in the law replied, 'The one who had mercy on him.' Jesus told him, 'Go and do likewise' " **(Luke 10:36–37 NIV).**

Scripture Reading: Luke 10:25–37

Introduction

The lawyer who sought to trick and test our Lord by questions concerning the law found himself maneuvered into what was for him an unpleasant position. To escape and salve his conscience, he raised the question, "And who is my neighbor?" Jesus responded with what we know as the parable of the good Samaritan.

Jesus concentrated the lawyer's attention not on "Who is my neighbor?" but on "Whose neighbor am I?" That is, instead of concentrating on "Who is my neighbor?" Jesus suggested that we should concentrate on being neighborly toward others.

An examination of this parable reveals that Christ still speaks through it to people of the twenty-first century. He indicts us for indifference toward the ills of a suffering, lost humanity. At the same time, he challenges us to realize life's greatest joy and to experience life's highest possibilities by practicing the attitude of the good Samaritan toward those who have become victims along life's highway.

I. The road from Jerusalem to Jericho.

Jesus tells the story of a man who fell among thieves and was left naked, wounded, and half dead.

We live in a world in which there are many who are victims of the cruelty of others.

A. *Many are lying by the highway of life, broken and bruised by the thieves of Satan.*
B. *Some are left half dead as a result of their own folly and choice of evil.*
C. *Some have been mortally wounded by the bad influence of professing Christians.*
D. *Others are broken and without hope because of past failures.*
E. *Some live broken lives because of parental failure and the enslaving habits they picked up in youth.*
F. *Some are victims of the cruelty of war.*
G. *Some are lying by the road of life because of the prejudice and hatred of others.*

II. An unneighborly spirit demonstrated.

A. *The priest came by and in coldhearted selfishness passed by on the other side of the road.*
B. *The Levite came by and demonstrated inhuman behavior.* With a cool and calculated selfishness, he hastily passed by on the other side. There was no love in his heart.

When those of us who profess to be followers of Jesus Christ show no concern for the unsaved, when we do not put forth an effort to train ourselves for effective service, when we do not support God's work with our finances, when we are critical of those who are in positions of leadership, and when we do not actively participate in ministry, we are acting with the same indifference as that exhibited in the priest and the Levite.

III. A compassionate neighbor.

A. *The Samaritan had seeing eyes and hearing ears.*
B. *The Samaritan had a compassionate heart.*
C. *The Samaritan had willing hands and a generous heart.*
   1. He chose the way of personal inconvenience that he might render service.
   2. He chose the way that led to personal expense on behalf of another.
   3. He chose to walk in a way that seemed to be unpopular, for the priest and the Levite had already set the pattern.

4. He chose the right way.
5. He chose the way that led to joy for his own heart and the way that led to health and happiness for the victim.

Conclusion

Jesus encouraged the lawyer to follow the example of the compassionate Samaritan: "Go, and do thou likewise." To be good neighbors, we must see both the spiritual and material needs of others. We must use our time and substance in helping others.

There is no way to serve our Lord except as we demonstrate love and helpfulness toward those in need. In demonstrating love for our neighbors, we demonstrate love for our Lord: "Inasmuch as ye have done it unto one of the least of these my brethren, ye have done it unto me" (Matt. 25:40).

The question is not, "Who is my neighbor?" but "Whose neighbor am I?"

SUNDAY MORNING, APRIL 15

Title: The Victory Song

Text: "Your troops will be willing on your day of battle. Arrayed in holy majesty, from the womb of the dawn you will receive the dew of your youth" **(Ps. 110:3 NIV)**.

Scripture Reading: Psalm 110

Hymns: "All People That on Earth Do Dwell," Kethe

"Jesus, the Very Thought of Thee," Bernard of Clairvaux

"To God Be the Glory," Crosby

Offertory Prayer: Our Father, help us never to become the victims of materialism. Help us, Master, to know that, for Christians, all things are sacred. We thank you for the privilege of serving you. Joyfully we return to you our tithes and our offerings, through Christ our Lord. Amen.

Introduction

We cannot recall too frequently the words of our Lord, "These are the words which I spake unto you, while I was yet with you, that all things must be fulfilled, which were written in the law of Moses, and in the prophets, and in the psalms, concerning me" (Luke 24:44). Psalm 110 is one of the psalms that undoubtedly points to Jesus. Dr. Kyle Yates said, "No human could possibly fill the picture." This psalm is quoted by every writer of the New Testament except John. There are no fewer than fifteen New Testament references to this psalm. Surely the frequency of these references challenges us to look closely at its text and truth. Through the telephoto lenses of prophetic insight, we have at least four pictures of Jesus.

I. The anointed Messiah (Ps. 110:1).

A. *Jesus is the unique Messiah. Messiah* means "the anointed one." The voice is that of God the Father to God the Son. It is from Jehovah to the Messiah. It is from the Eternal One to the Anointed One. There is only one Messiah. He is incomparable, immeasurable, and incarnate. No other one meets the demands of messianic prophecy. No other one meets the standard of heavenly approval. No other one meets the requirements of the hungering heart of humankind.

B. *Jesus is the historic Messiah.* Whatever else may be said for or against him, his historicity cannot be disputed. He really did come. His incarnation was his validation—the validation of the claims others made for him and the validation of claims he made for himself.

C. *Jesus is the contemporary Messiah.* The tense of our verb is the key to our triumph—Jesus *is*. All other leaders of world religions are gone—dead and buried. They have come, lived, and died. But Jesus *is*.

II. The conquering King (Ps. 110:1–3).

A. *A King by divine right.* Jesus is appointed and anointed by Jehovah. The ancients talked about the divine right of kings. Jesus serves by divine right as *the* King. The kingdom of God, or the kingdom of our Lord, is a dominant theme of the New Testament. But the kingdom must have a king, and Jesus is that King. The Jerusalem crowd may have been fickle in its allegiance, but it was right in its declaration, "Blessed be the King that cometh in the name of the Lord: peace in heaven, and glory in the highest" (Luke 19:38). Jesus himself acknowledged this kingship by divine right (23:2). During Jesus' mock trial, the governor asked, "Art thou the King ...?" and Jesus answered, "Thou sayest" (Matt. 27:11). And in three languages the epithet that was put above his cross by his enemies continued to speak: "This is Jesus the King of the Jews" (v. 37).

B. *A King of divine establishment (v. 2).* Not only is Jesus King by divine right; he is also King by establishment. The King was "put into business" in Jerusalem, in person, in the midst of both his friends and his enemies.

C. *A King with willing subjects (v. 3).* "Thy people shall be willing in the day of thy power" (v. 3). If a king's power is to be effective, he must rule a willing people. It is not through military power or police force or physical coercion that he rules. It is through the willingness of the subjects that his rule is effective.

D. *A King with eternal tenure (v. 3).* The kingdoms of earth crumble, and the leadership changes overnight. Thrones are overthrown, abdicated, and seized. But Jesus will reign forever. The Christian can say, "Now unto the King eternal, immortal, invisible, the only wise God, be honour and glory for ever and ever. Amen" (1 Tim. 1:17).

III. The eternal Priest (Ps. 110:4).

"The LORD has sworn and will not change his mind: 'You are a priest forever, in the order of Melchizedek'" (NIV). We can refresh our minds with the eternal priesthood of Jesus by reading again (among many other Scriptures) Hebrews 7. The priest did chiefly three things:

A. *He looked after sin.* Find the priest in the Old Testament and either his sin or the sin of another is not far away. To make an offering to atone for sin was his responsibility. To deal effectively with sin was always a large part of his job description. This Jesus did and does.

B. *He stood before the people for God.* This the High Priest Jesus did. His confrontation of people was always with a sense of divine authority. He had a "sense of sentness." He represented God; he was the messenger for God, the Word from God, and the essence of God.

C. *He stood before God for the people.* He was the Mediator whose face was no less toward the holiness of the Father because it was sensitive to the people. Thus, facing the people for the Father and facing the Father for the people, he fufilled his unique role as the perfect Priest. God and humans are assured adequate representation of each to the other in the person of our Lord.

IV. The final Judge (Ps. 110:6–7).

A. *This fact is asserted by the Bible.* Paul called Jesus the "righteous judge" (2 Tim. 4:8). Scripture tells us that Jesus has a judgment seat (Rom. 14:10), that he will judge the secrets of people's hearts (2:16), and that he will judge the quick and the dead (2 Tim. 4:1).

B. *This fact should make the sinner sober.* An old hymn declares correctly, "There's a great day coming, a great day coming, there's a great day coming by and by...." The judgments of this world are sometimes escapable. God's judgments are not.

C. *This fact should encourage the Christian.* The Christian conscience cannot help but be disturbed in our day by the rightness and the wrongness of things. But there will come a day when the books will be balanced. The scales will weigh the evidence correctly. The computers of God will compound correctly the interest of both good and evil accounts, and the final statement will be rendered. Thus, we "judge not" but leave the judgment to the Judge. And when his verdicts are in, there will be no appeal to a higher court, for there is none.

Conclusion

In the Messiah we have the one in whom "the hopes and fears of all the years are met." Let us rejoice! In the conquering King we have the holy hero of our faith. Let us sing the victory song. In the eternal Priest we have access to God's throne. Let us come boldly and frequently unto him. In the final Judge we have assurance and holy optimism. Let us leave the judgeship to him and concern ourselves with being faithful and happy witnesses.

SUNDAY EVENING, APRIL 15

Title: Why Should I Knock Myself Out?

Text: "Wherefore seeing we also are compassed about with so great a cloud of witnesses, let us lay aside every weight, and the sin which doth so easily beset us, and let us run with patience the race that is set before us, looking unto Jesus the author and finisher of our faith; who for the joy that was set before him endured the cross, despising the shame, and is set down at the right hand of the throne of God" **(Heb. 12:1–2).**

Scripture Reading: Hebrews 11:33–12:2

Introduction

"Why should I knock myself out?" "No one else cares; why should I?" "If you do a good job, no one appreciates it." It is easy for this kind of attitude to creep into one's spiritual outlook. Seldom does society repay or even notice the spiritual service rendered by Christians. Concerning the great people of faith inscribed on God's honor roll in Hebrews 11, it is said, "The world was not worthy of them" (v. 38 NIV). Phillips's translation reads: "They lost everything and yet were spurned and ill-treated by a world that was too evil to see their worth." This brings out the truth that if we expect earthly recompense for our faithfulness, we will be disappointed. Failure to acknowledge this fact is to invite grim heartbreak. Be assured of this: the world will not see your worth, and for that matter, your fellow Christians may fail to express appreciation for your labors. Should you then knock yourself out to do your best? By all means! We were never promised the appreciation of the world. Our calling does not depend on it nor seek it. We have other reasons for giving our best.

I. The glory of a divine agenda (Heb. 11:39–40).

To be a part of God's blueprint for the ages is a thrilling experience. To see the Master Draftsman unroll his plan and reveal our name inscribed on it is a reward in itself. We are offered a place in the greatest undertaking of all—God's plan of redemption: "These were all commended for their faith, yet none of them received what had been promised. God had planned something better for us so that only together with us would they be made perfect" (NIV).

These saints of the past believed in God's promise of redemption but did not live to see its fullness. To those of us living on this side of the cross was this fullness given, though we too await the final glory of eternity. God left open a place for us in his kingdom labors. We possess the good news of the ages, the greatest treasure within the reach of mortal man. We should begin every day with the anticipation that somewhere among the hours and incidents about to transpire we will find our orders for the day—our opportunity to bear witness of Christ by spoken word and personal deed. We must learn to be on instant call—to be aware of what it means to be an agent for the living God.

II. The compulsion of a sacred trust (Heb. 12:1).

To be entrusted with a great treasure is to be inspired to do your best to take care of it. As Christians, we have been given the gospel. Unlike other treasures, the only way to protect it is to share it. We stand as passers of the torch. People have suffered and died rather than allow its flame to be quenched. Hebrews reminds us that the past, to which we are indebted, looks down upon us: "Wherefore seeing we also are compassed about with so great a cloud of witnesses, let us lay aside every weight, and the sin which doth so easily beset us, and let us run with patience the race that is set before us" (v. 1).

The metaphor is that of the arena packed with spectators, giving the appearance of an encircling cloud. Yet these onlookers are more than mere spectators. The word translated "witnesses" is literally "martyrs." When persecution fell on the church, those who remained as faithful witnesses were so often put to death that to be a witness was to be a martyr. The unseen grandstands are filled with those who, in their lifetime, gave their best. Hebrews 11 is only a representative group of those "who through faith subdued kingdoms, wrought righteousness, obtained promises, stopped the mouths of lions" (v. 33). Some were miraculously delivered while "others were tortured" and "had trial of cruel mockings and scourgings.... They were stoned, they were sawn asunder, were tempted, were slain ... wandered about in sheepskins ... being destitute, afflicted, tormented" (vv. 35–37). Despite everything the forces of evil could do, "these all obtained a good report through faith" (v. 39).

It is said that in the ancient Olympic games the veteran athletes of the past had special reserved seats in the grandstands. As we spend our strength in life's arena, the challenge of knowing the past looks down on us and calls forth our best.

A. *Toward responsibility.* Why should I knock myself out? Because the sacred trust handed me by the past is a supreme responsibility. This calls for laying "aside every weight, and the sin which doth so easily beset us." Greek athletes ran almost naked. The long flowing robes worn for street dress were laid aside. The weighted shoes used in practice were discarded. Likewise, the Christian must rid his life of all encumbrances, mainly the "sin which doth so easily beset us." This means the sin that so easily surrounds us—that is always standing around us to blind our vision and hinder our movement. Like wild beasts encircling the campfire, ready to devour the sleeping victim, sin stalks us. Little sins must go if winning is important to you. What is wrong with gambling or drinking? Nothing, if you don't want to win. What harm comes from small, private acts of dishonesty? Nothing, if playing on the first team is unimportant, if integrity has no value, if your heritage has no claims on you.

B. *Toward involvement.* Once the participants have been introduced and the national anthem has been played, we have to come out on the field and play or forfeit the game. The coach takes a dim view of the player who practices with the team, vows allegiance to the team, but is too bashful to play before the crowds.

It is said that Scandinavian veterans would lead a young recruit about to put on armor for the first time to the halls of his ancestors. There the youth would gaze upon the heroes of the past and learn of their brave exploits. Thus was planted in the warrior's heart the determination to prove himself worthy of so rich a heritage. It was an effort to call forth from his troops ultimate involvement that Napoleon, in his Egyptian campaign, gestured toward the pyramids and cried, "Forty centuries look down upon you" ("Epistle to the Hebrews" in *The Speaker's Bible*, ed. James Hastings [Grand Rapids, Baker, 1961], 235).

In moments of hesitation, we must ask, "What did faithfulness cost Abraham?" "What would Moses do if he faced our decision?" "Can we hold back when thousands faced the claws of lions rather than deny Christ?" The human cost paid by the unseen witnesses about us calls us to extravagant spending for God.

III. The challenge of the risen Lord (Heb. 12:2).

Beyond the glory of a divine agenda and the compulsion of a sacred trust stands the greatest reason of all for knocking yourself out in service—the risen Lord: "Looking unto Jesus the author and finisher of our faith" (v. 2). The unseen martyrs of the past and the visible spectators about us fade into insignificance when we look toward Christ.

A. *His authority. Jesus is the "author," the pioneer of our faith.* He blazed the pathway to God. He is the one who "finishes" our faith, who brings it to fullness and completeness. Early gladiators looked beyond the crowd to the emperor for instructions. We look to Christ.

Keith Miller told of his own experience of becoming aware that he should play out his life with God as his audience. In talking with a college football coach and watching his winning team, he made a discovery. The boys gave every play their best, even on little insignificant assignments, even when the frantic fans would not notice or care. The reason was simple. Every play was filmed. The boys knew that on Monday the whole team and the coach would spend hours watching the film. Every movement would be analyzed. The same play would be viewed again and again. Minute mistakes would be discussed. The tremendous hustle of the team came because every boy was playing for his coach—not for the cheering throngs. This made every detail important (Keith Miller, *A Second Touch* [Waco: Word, 1967], 25–27).

B. *His assessment.* How did Jesus live out the divine plan in the face of mental anguish and physical torture? "For the joy that was set before him [he] endured the cross, despising the shame" (v. 2). He did what he did because of certain value assessments. To die as a common criminal was not easy for one so perfectly sensitive to righteousness. Crucifixion was one of the most painful methods of execution. He endured because he never lost sight of the joy that comes by self-giving. To die that the world might know the peace of forgiveness, that people might feel the freedom of lifted guilt, that the sting of death might be destroyed—this was enough, in our Lord's sense of values, to do what he came to do.

In moments of doubt when you wonder if you should knock yourself out for the Lord, "Consider him who endured such opposition from sinful men, so that you will not grow weary and lose heart" (Heb. 12:3 NIV). The word "consider" is equivalent to our word "analogy." Make an analogy between Christ's sufferings and yours. Compare them. "You have not yet resisted to the point of shedding your blood" (v. 4 NIV). You have not fought to the death, as did your Lord. And if called upon to do so, you must make the same assessment as Christ.

After all, we have life for one purpose—to spend it for God. Jesus warns against the refusal to "knock yourself out": "For whosoever will save his life shall lose it: and whosoever will lose his life for my sake shall find it" (Matt. 16:25).

Conclusion

It is said that Mozart's life ended like a torch burning out in the wind. He never stopped working until death stilled his hand. His thirty-sixth year, and his last one, found him busily working on the *Requiem*, the song of death. Though weak in body, he worked on it constantly. Toward the end, he shared with his wife the secret that he was writing it for himself. As he lay dying, Vienna was ringing with his fame, yet his last words were concerning the score of the *Requiem* (*Great Texts of the Bible*, ed. James Hastings [Grand Rapids: Eerdmans, n.d.], 18:462). He died consumed with his labors, and so must we. Each of us is writing his own requiem. We will never regret knocking ourselves out for the Lord.

WEDNESDAY EVENING, APRIL 18

Title: What Can I Do for You?

Text: " 'What do you want me to do for you?' Jesus asked him. The blind man said, 'Rabbi, I want to see'" **(Mark 10:51 NIV)**.

Scripture Reading: Mark 10:46–52

Introduction

Jesus performed many of his greatest ministries in an incidental manner as he traveled about the country. There was something informal and natural about the way he met the needs of those who suffered.

We do not have to be in a formal situation to experience the living presence of Jesus Christ. He walks the road not only from Jericho to Jerusalem, but also the road from Oklahoma City to Tulsa and from Frankfort to Nashville. He is as close as the air we breathe though we may not be aware of his presence.

Jesus approaches us as he approached the blind man with the question "What can I do for you?"

I. "Jesus, Son of David, have mercy on me!" (Mark 10:47 NIV).

A. *The blind beggar recognized the unique person of Jesus Christ and spoke of him as the Son of David.*

B. *The beggar was persistent in his cry for help in spite of those who tried to silence him (10:48).*

C. *Jesus was a hearer of prayer.* Above the noise of the crowd he heard the distress call of the poor blind man.

II. "What do you want me to do for you?" (Mark 10:51 NIV).

As the Christ came to the blind man, so he will come to us in the present. He has promised, "Where two or three are gathered together in my name, there am I in the midst of them" (Matt. 18:20).

We need a vital faith in the resurrected and living Christ who is the same yesterday, today, and forever. We must not consider him as merely a historical figure who lived two millenniums ago. May God give us the faith that we need to experience his presence and power and purpose today.

Jesus confronts us with his grace and power at the point of our greatest need.

III. "Rabbi, I want to see" (Mark 10:51 NIV).

We can well understand why the blind man would request above all things the restoration of his sight. He had been living in darkness. Blindness had robbed him of the privilege of looking into the face of a wife or into the eyes of precious children. He had not been able to see the beauty of a flower or the glory of a sunset. He wanted to live in a world of light rather than in a world of darkness. We can sympathize and identify with his prayer for sight.

A prayer for spiritual sight and understanding could be the greatest prayer we could offer to the Christ as he comes to us.

A. *The ability to see the spiritual poverty of our own soul could transform our lives.* Such a sight could challenge us to draw closer to our Lord, to study his Word diligently, and to find our way more often into the throne room of prayer.

B. *The ability to see the sin in our lives that is displeasing to God could be a great blessing.* Isaiah was granted a vision of the sin of his own soul (Isa. 6:5). He was convicted of his sin, confessed it, experienced cleansing, and consecrated himself to doing God's will.

C. *A vision of the spiritual resources available to believers could be one of the Lord's greatest blessings to us (Phil. 4:13).* The apostle Paul believed that Christ was present with power to help him in his times of need. His faith gave him courage as he faced difficulty and as he responded to opportunities.

Conclusion

The wonderful Savior comes to each of us with the question "What can I do for you?" If you need forgiveness of sin, ask him for it and trust him for it. If you need a greater faith in the goodness of God, ask for it. If you need the wisdom that comes only from God, ask for it. If you need strength and energy to bear the burdens of life and to face the responsibilities of life, ask for it. Our Savior wants to help you today as he helped the blind man in the past. As he served and ministered to the needs of people long ago, even so he will minister to your needs and will use you to minister to the needs of others.

SUNDAY MORNING, APRIL 22

Title: The Doxology in Solo

Text: "Bless the LORD, O my soul: and all that is within me, bless his holy name. Bless the LORD, O my soul, and forget not all his benefits" **(Ps. 103:1–2)**.

Scripture Reading: Psalm 103

Hymns: "I Love Thee," Anonymous

"Great Redeemer, We Adore Thee," Harris

"All People That on Earth Do Dwell," Kethe

Offertory Prayer: Our Father, we thank you for bringing us safely through another week. May we never take for granted the blessings that come from you. We are grateful for the bread for our bodies and the Bread for our souls. Now as we offer our gifts to you, we remember our Lord Jesus and offer both our gifts and our prayer in his name. Amen.

Introduction

Most people associate a doxology with congregational singing. It is seldom done as a solo. In Psalm 103 the writer bursts forth with single voice, singing the praises of his God.

Dr. Kyle Yates said of this psalm, "No cloud appears on the horizon, no jarring sounds, no word of complaint is heard, no note of sadness in the music comes to weaken the glad recital of praise." How can one outline a sunrise or analyze a baby's smile or diagram a mother's love? The task of outlining this psalm is comparable.

I. Praise God from whom all blessings flow (Ps. 103:1–7).

God does seven distinct things for us, each of which calls forth a song of gratitude.

    A. *God forgives (v. 3).* Alexander Pope said, "To err is human; to forgive divine." Some things God does we could have invented. Not so with forgiveness. We may have thought of reparation for sin, or of denial of sin, or of purchasing indulgence to sin, but we never would have thought of forgiveness. No quality in or out of the Bible bears the stamp of the divine any more than does forgiveness. The nature and magnitude of forgiveness primes the pump of David's own gratitude so that the rest of the psalm is a stream of praise.

B. *God heals (v. 3).* He heals all diseases. A fine physician said that God does all the healing and that he and the members of his healing profession are merely instruments in God's healing hands. This not only expresses a great truth but suggests also that we who ask God for any kind of healing also must permit him to use whatever methods and channels he chooses to effect that healing.

C. *God redeems (v. 4).* When God redeems, he is buying back what is already his. We are God's creation, but because we are lost to him through sin, he buys us back.

During the Depression a seminary student and his wife were driving to their little church. Upon arriving he observed that the spare tire and wheel had been lost from the mounting on the back of the car. No sign of the lost tire and wheel was to be found. The student gave up the hunt. About three months later he stopped at a service station for gasoline. There were his tire and wheel. Asked where he got them, the operator said he had bought them from a stranger for four dollars. He offered them to the student for what "he had in them." So the student paid the four dollars for a perfectly good tire, tube, and wire wheel that were already his. He redeemed his own. This is precisely what God does in the currency of Calvary: he redeems us who belong to him anyway. He purchases back to his own possession that which has been lost. This is redemption.

D. *God crowns (v. 4).* We sing about crowning Jesus Lord of all, and well we may, but let us not forget that there is the reverse process in the coronation of providence — he crowns us daily with the crown of "lovingkindness." Set in the crown are the diamonds of "tender mercies."

A slave stood tall and with unbending dignity at a slave auction. Asked the reason for his dignified appearance, one who knew him explained, "He is the son of a king and he refuses to forget it." So are we, crowned as heirs, and may we never forget it.

E. *God satisfies (v. 5).* The "God-shaped vacuum" in every person is never satisfied until it is satisfied in God. Ask the soul who has hungered and thirsted after righteousness, and he will tell you that God alone satisfies the longing heart. Much of life's restlessness is the result of spiritual hunger and thirst. The table of the Lord is spread with, not only good things, but with *abundant* good things.

F. *God executes righteousness and judgment (v. 6).* He rules with the character of his holiness and complete justice. Two things are to be said for his dispensation of righteousness and judgment. First, it is consistent with God's perfect nature: holy, merciful, and unspoiled. Second, it shows no favoritism. To the rich and poor, to the prominent and the obscure, to the deserving and undeserving, God is the same.

G. *God reveals his ways to people (v. 7).* "He made known his ways unto Moses, his acts unto the children of Israel." The song says, "It is no secret what God can do." Correct. But it is also no secret what he wants us to do. The frustrated cry of many this day is that they do not know the will of God for their lives. We have been reminded frequently that millions have etched in their faces the story of aimlessness. For these, life lacks purpose and goal. The God who "made known his ways to Moses" makes known his way to all. Our chief trouble is not that we do not *know*, but that there is a gap between what we know and what we are willing to do.

II. Praise him all creatures here below (Ps. 103:8–18).

God's action calls for human reaction. His revelation calls for our response. His initiative calls for our involvement. Nor are we goaded into a blind frenzy of religious spasm. Five guidelines are offered:

A. *God's mercy is contrasted with his justice (vv. 8–10).* His mercy is not the soft sanction of our sins. It is the vigorous provision for our sins. His justice is not the omnipotent pulling of his rank. It is the exercise of his eternal character and purpose, consistent with his total plan for our redemption. Such a combination makes him not only a sovereign God but also a balanced God.

B. *God's mercy is illustrated (vv. 11–12).* How high are the heavens above the earth? Nobody knows. How far is east from west? Nobody knows. Yet the limitless height of the heavens illustrates the limitless magnitude of God's mercy. The distance from east to west illustrates the distance God removes our sins from us.

C. *God's compassion is like that of a father (v. 13).* Height and breadth may be beyond us, but anyone who has known a father knows about the compassionate pity of a father. Multiply ten thousand times ten thousand the finest pity of an earthly father, and the product is the suggestion of God's compassionate fatherhood.

D. *God's permanence is contrasted with our frailty (vv. 14–15).* Even our framework—supposedly the sturdiest part of us—is dust. Our days are as perishable as the grass, and even the most beautiful of flowers is laid low by heat and wind. Not a trace is left. But over against our dust is contrasted the Rock. Set in contrast to our grass is the tree of life. And contrasted with our fragile flowers is the Rose of Sharon, whose beauty is not diminished by the years or faded by the elements.

E. *God's availability is assured for all people (vv. 17–18).* "But the mercy of the Lord is from everlasting to everlasting upon them that fear him, and his righteousness unto children's children; to such as keep his covenant, and to those that remember his commandments to do them." God is not only almighty; he is also available. We not only praise him; we can also possess him. He will be active in all people who follow him. This is the thrust of our calling to evangelism.

III. Praise him above ye heavenly host (Ps. 103:19–22).

The psalmist seems to exhaust the rooms of the earth in calling forth praise for God, so he goes upstairs to enlist more voices in the doxology he can no longer contain.

A. *There is the extent of God's kingdom (v. 19).* "All" includes all. We may be weak and frail subjects, but we are citizens of a mighty kingdom.

B. *There is the excellence of God's angels (v. 20).* They "excel in strength." They excel in obedience, "doing his commandments." They excel in responsiveness, "hearkening unto the voice of his word."

C. *There is the expression of all God's true ministers (v. 21).* Of course, this does not mean primarily any select group of the clergy. It refers to all celestial servants, but it is a happy thought that we are not excluded from the heavenly association.

D. *There is the encompassing of all creation in doxology of praise (v. 22).* From "all his works in all places of dominion" the camera is drawn back to the focus of his beginning: "Bless the LORD, O *my soul.*" The beginning and ending place of the true doxology is in the heart and life of the follower of the King.

Conclusion

1. There is valid reason for people to sing the doxology.
2. God's people do not have to wait for the music to begin. Let us start it or join it.
3. The spirit of grateful praise will improve the spiritual atmosphere of this present world.
4. The radiant, obedient, and Christ-centered life is the sweetest doxology of the soul.

SUNDAY EVENING, APRIL 22

Title: Up Against God

Text: "See to it that you do not refuse him who speaks. If they did not escape when they refused him who warned them on earth, how much less will we, if we turn away from him who warns us from heaven? At that time his voice shook the earth, but now he has promised, 'Once more I will shake not only the earth but also the heavens'" (Heb. 12:25–26 NIV).

Scripture Reading: Hebrews 12:15–29

Introduction

The text was brief: "Flunked out. Prepare Dad." It came from a college boy whose careless attention to schoolwork had wrought chaos in his academic career. His mother's reply was equally brief: "Dad's prepared. Prepare yourself."

It is strange how people keep trying to prepare God for their failures by citing the problems they are confronting. Too often we fail to see that our problems are not the trouble. We are not up against our problems but up against God.

Perhaps we know so little about God because our secular ears have tuned him out. We are pursuing shadowy goals, mirages of our own making. When people plot their own course, plan their own destiny, establish their own moral values, set up their own priorities, walk in their own strength, they are doomed to march boisterously into oblivion's shadows, where sooner or later they will land smack up against God. Hebrews warns against the course of action that leads people to fly in the face of God.

I. If you worship the temporary (Heb. 12:15–16).

The worship of things, of this present life and its passions, is serious trouble. Although the context involves Christians who are hesitant to remain true to Christ in the face of persecutions, who are placing too much value on life and too little on God, the message is an eternal one. Nothing destroys spiritual character like the worship of things.

Esau is cited as a warning: "See to it that no one misses the grace of God and that no bitter root grows up to cause trouble and defile many. See that no one is sexually immoral, or is godless like Esau, who for a single meal sold his inheritance rights as the oldest son" (vv. 15–16 NIV).

Esau forever stands as the man who saw the satisfaction of human appetites as an end in itself. "Today" consumed his every thought. The birthright he forfeited involved the first rank in the family, a double share of the inheritance, and the privilege of offering sacrifices and leading in worship following the death of the father. But more than this, it involved a place among the patriarchs through whom God's promises to Abraham were transmitted.

Esau's sad predicament stands as a solemn warning against a worldly spirit: "Afterward, as you know, when he wanted to inherit this blessing, he was rejected. He could bring about no change of mind, though he sought the blessing with tears" (Heb. 12:17 NIV). At this point, Esau's personal relationship to God is not being discussed. The thrust of this verse is that Esau could find no way to undo what he had done. He had made a deal! The repentance came not from seeking God's forgiveness, but rather from a desire to reverse the past. His tears were of no avail. We cannot recall the past and relive it.

II. If you ignore Christ (Heb. 12:22–24).

Another aspect of the life that is on a collision course with God's wrath is an indifferent attitude toward Christ and his Gospel. The writer of Hebrews reminds his readers of the present location. They are confronted with Zion (v. 22), the highest elevation in Jerusalem. The term came to represent God's heavenly city, the assembly of God's people, and hence the church itself. One term is stacked on another to give emphasis to the fact that individual Christians are confronted with the church as well as Christ (vv. 22–24).

The contrast is between the giving of the law at Sinai (Heb. 12:18–21) and God's final revelation in Christ. Sinai was an awesome experience with its thundering and quaking. Since God's presence was on the mountain, the people were warned not to touch it, for if they did, they would die. Though the voice of God was speaking, it was an earthly kind of revelation, mediated through the man Moses. God's final voice in Christ demands even more urgent attention (v. 25).

People stand at the last stage of the agenda of God's divine revelation. The final word has been spoken in Christ. The last covenant has been established. Old Testament covenants were ratified by the sprinkling of animal blood, but the last covenant was ratified by the blood of Christ shed at Calvary (v. 24). Abel's blood stands as a reminder of the murderous evil of sin-controlled man. Christ's blood speaks to us of God's offer of forgiveness and transformation.

III. If you discount the eternal (Heb. 12:22–28).

Closely akin to an indifferent attitude toward Christ's commands is the careless life that discounts the eternal nature of God's kingdom and of life itself. Above all others, the Christian is called upon to make high-risk investments in following God's will.

The Christian has a kingdom that cannot be destroyed, but neither can it be seen. We must commit our lives to the eternal: "Therefore, since we are receiving a kingdom that cannot be shaken, let us be thankful, and so worship God acceptably with reverence and awe" (v. 28 NIV).

God's unseen kingdom, however, does have a visible instrument—the church. Therefore, you cannot separate loyalty to God from faithful activity in the church. Not only are we confronted by Christ, but also by the calling to serve in the church (vv. 22–24). The Israelites could not refuse to enter Canaan without disobeying God. Their destiny and usefulness lay in Canaan. They could not serve just as well in the wilderness. Their attempt to do so was marked by the tombstones of every person over the age of twenty who turned back.

At Sinai, God's voice shook the earth, but there is coming a moment when all things will be sifted by shaking and only the eternal will remain. Referring to Haggai 2:6, the writer of Hebrews elaborates: "At that time his voice shook the earth, but now he has promised, 'Once more I will shake not only the earth but also the heavens'" (v. 26 NIV).

The word translated "shake" refers to the trembling motion of an earthquake and is the root of our term *seismograph*—a measurement of the earth's quivering. "Yet once more" contains the little word *hapax*, which carries the meaning of "once and for all." There is the definite note of finality inherent in it. The word has already been used to speak of the "onceness" of a genuine salvation experience (Heb. 6:4) and the complete finality of Christ's sacrifice for our sins (9:26, 28). The author elaborates: "The words 'once more' indicate the removing of what can be shaken—that is, created things—so that what cannot be shaken may remain" (12:27 NIV).

With the birth of Jesus, the shaking began. The unseen sieve, gripped by the hand of God Almighty, began to move back and forth. Jesus upset those taking pride in their man-made traditions. This is why he declared that he never came to bring peace—meaning the peace of the status quo. The first tremors were noticed as he died on the cross. The intervention of God at Sinai was accompanied by the trembling of the earth (v. 26). But the final travail will involve the removal of everything temporal, that only the eternal may remain.

The Bible always pictures the end of time in terms of the complete upheaval of nature (Rev. 6:13–17). Hebrews began by stating that heaven and earth are temporary in God's scheme (1:11–12).

Conclusion

Why is it that God has chosen to make the temporary visible and the eternal invisible? Perhaps to demand that we trust him enough to believe his intangible promises. Perhaps this is the only way we can have real freedom of choice. We are not overawed by a dazzling heavenly display. The facts are revealed to us in God's Book, and we are left to make our decision as free agents.

It all boils down to this: cling to God and the eternal, or cling to this perishing world. If you choose the latter, you are up against God!

WEDNESDAY EVENING, APRIL 25

Title: Where Is Your Faith?

Text: "And he said unto them, Where is your faith? And they being afraid wondered, saying one to another, What manner of man is this! for he commandeth even the winds and the water, and they obey him" (**Luke 8:25**).

Scripture Reading: Luke 8:22–36

Introduction

Jesus encouraged people to have great faith in God. He taught people to have faith by means of the marvelous words he spoke. He encouraged a greater faith by the miraculous works he performed. He sought to instill faith by the remarkable life he lived. He demonstrated his faith by dying on the cross. He thus expressed his confidence that the Father would raise him from death.

We live in a time that emphasizes faith in oneself. Emphasis is placed on the importance of material security to the extent that many people trust in their material resources. Others have put their confidence in science for a solution to the problems of life. Still others have put their faith in their own common sense and judgment. People always experience disappointment when they place the confidence that should be reserved only for God in something less than God.

I. A misplaced faith is the besetting sin of us all.

We have a tendency to forget God and then become overwhelmed with the difficulties and the problems of life. We put confidence in material possessions, in military power, or in human ingenuity.

    A. *Faithlessness was the "undoing sin" of ancient Israel.*

    B. *Lack of faith was the sin that plagued the disciples and hindered them from being channels of God's power.*

    C. *Faithlessness deprives the church of today of spiritual power and significant achievement.*

    D. *It is the sin of faithlessness that causes the unsaved to remain lost and away from God (John 3:18, 36).*

II. The tragic results of little or misplaced faith.

    A. *Without faith it is impossible to please God (Heb. 11:6).*

    B. *Without faith imaginary dangers darken the pathway ahead.*

    C. *Without faith prayer is an undiscovered privilege.*

    D. *Without faith service for God appears to be an impossible task.*

III. Misplaced faith grieves the heart of God.

    A. *It disappoints his love.*

    B. *It questions his power.*

    C. *It hinders his purpose.* When Jesus visited his hometown of Nazareth, he was unable to do any mighty works there because of the residents' unbelief.

IV. Growing a great faith.

    A. *Make your little faith a matter of prayer.* Join with the apostles who prayed, "Lord, increase our faith" (Luke 17:5).

    B. *Study God's Word to increase your faith.* "So then faith cometh by hearing, and hearing by the word of God" (Rom. 10:17). Read the Bible not merely as a record of the past but as a revelation of what can happen in the present when we have faith and live the life of obedience.

    C. *Use the faith that you have.* Our Lord said, "If you have faith as small as a mustard seed, you can say to this mulberry tree, 'Be uprooted and planted in the sea,' and it will obey you" (Luke 17:6 NIV). Our faith may not be as great as it should be; however, it will become greater if we use the faith that we do have.

    D. *Cling to the promises of God.* The Bible contains many of the promises of God. We can develop a greater faith if we will find these promises and trust in them. As God proves trustworthy, our faith in him will increase with the passing of the years.

Conclusion

Examine your faith. Is it misplaced? Are you putting your confidence in something less than the living Lord who commanded the winds to cease their blowing and the waves to cease their raging? If so, you will experience disappointment in life.

Put your confidence in God. Use the faith that you do have. Pray for a greater faith. Obey his commandments and experience his blessings, and you will discover that yours is a growing faith.

SUNDAY MORNING, APRIL 29

Title: Do You Know Him?

Text: "For the which cause I also suffer these things: nevertheless I am not ashamed: for I know whom I have believed, and am persuaded that he is able to keep that which I have committed unto him against that day" **(2 Tim. 1:12)**.

Scripture Reading: 2 Tim. 1:8–12

Hymns: "Blessed Redeemer," Christiansen

"I've Found a Friend," Small

"O How I Love Jesus," Whitfield

Offertory Prayer: Dear Lord, help us to remember every manifestation of your grace. We are totally unworthy of your love. Thank you for hearing our prayer in the time of trouble. We are grateful for you cleansing our sin and directing our lives. The eloquence of your love is evident in your numberless material gifts to us. Help us to refuse to take these blessings for granted. We dedicate our money to you as well as our lives. Teach us to give ourselves and our substance as your Son has given himself for us. We pray in Jesus' name. Amen.

Introduction

Do you know Jesus Christ?

Whenever the apostle Paul affirmed his knowledge of Christ, he was not speaking primarily of knowing him doctrinally or historically. Rather, his declaration was that of knowing Jesus Christ vividly, personally, immediately, and authentically. The presence of Jesus Christ was a personal reality in his life. Knowing Christ is a matter for individuals to determine through a personal faith in him.

Paul said, "I know whom I have believed." The question for you to consider in this message is, Do you know Jesus Christ?

I. Do you know Jesus Christ in commitment of your sins for forgiveness?

Paul had deposited his sins in the Lord Jesus Christ. He was confident that Christ would keep them until the day of judgment. A person's initial knowledge of Jesus Christ comes through confession of sin and personal commitment of those sins to him.

The Bible is replete with the call of people to repentance. Repenting includes the entrustment of sin into the keeping power of the Savior. The apostle John tells us that if we confess our sins, God is faithful and just to forgive us our sins

(1 John 1:9). No person ever comes to know Jesus Christ until he is willing to entrust his sins to the Savior. This is the essence of the prayer of the publican, "God be merciful to me a sinner" (Luke 18:13).

Somewhere I read of a brilliant young atheist who was arguing with an elderly Christian. He said to the older man, "I have learned that the Bible is only myth and folklore. Jesus Christ only fainted on the cross. Geology reveals that no God created this world but that all of life came by evolution. Philosophy ridicules the dualism of a devil and a God. Old man, renounce your superstitious Christian faith and become an enlightened tweny-first-century citizen."

The old Christian answered, "I know nothing of philosophy, geology, or science, but answer me one question. I once was an unfaithful husband, an abusive father, a drunken workman, and a moral derelict. One evening I stumbled into a little mission. I heard a preacher tell of one called Jesus who could change a man's life and help him start all over again. I fell on my knees and asked this Jesus to save me. When I stood up, I felt all clean inside. I went home to be a faithful husband, a kind father, a decent citizen, and an honest workman, and I've never touched a drop of liquor since. Now young man, if there is nothing to Christianity, would you please explain what happened to change me?"

The young man stammered. "Well, that's one question we've not been able to answer yet."

Do you know Jesus like that? Have you had the miraculous power of God make you a new person through your personal knowledge of Jesus Christ? John the apostle indicates that we can know that we have Jesus Christ and that we have eternal life (1 John 5:13). Do you know Jesus because of what he did when he became a substitute on the cross for you, receiving your punishment in order that he might save you eternally? Has Jesus changed you, redeemed you, and made you a new creature? Have you given Jesus Christ your sins and entrusted him to cleanse you and forgive you?

II. Do you know Christ in commitment of your life?

Paul counted everything as loss for the excellency of the knowledge of Christ. He stated that he had suffered the loss of everything in order to win the knowledge of Jesus. "That I may know him, and the power of his resurrection, and the fellowship of his suffering, being made conformable unto his death; if by any means I might attain unto the resurrection of the dead" (Phil. 3:10–11).

Is your life committed to witnessing? Jesus spoke with a common woman of the streets at Jacob's well. As they visited together, conviction of sin came into the woman's heart, and she realized that she was talking to the Savior of the world. While Jesus spoke to her, something happened inside her soul that changed an impure, immoral individual to be as white as fresh-fallen snow. The woman went back into the city where she lived. There she cried with fervor and enthusiasm, "Come, see a man, which told me all things that ever I did: is not this the Christ?" (John 4:29).

Do you know Jesus? Are you calling with enthusiasm and fervor for people to come and see him? Do you know him like that?

Is your life committed to faith? Nicodemus once came to Jesus and asked him concerning the miracles that he performed. He assumed that Christ had to be from God. Jesus made a strange reply. He told him that unless one was born again, he could not have any part of God. Nicodemus found this to be incredible. Jesus told him that being born again was as much a mystery as the blowing of the wind, but just as real. In so many words, Christ was saying that knowing God was a deep mystery of life. It could not be understood by finite human reasoning. Knowing God comes only through faith in him. We do not understand all the implications of the cross, the resurrection, the creation of the world, nor the coming judgment. But if we accept Jesus Christ by faith, we will know him as Savior. This is made explicit in John 3:16 and in Ephesians 2:8–9. Do you know him through personal faith?

Is your life committed to following Christ? On one occasion, Christ had explained to a great crowd of people that to follow him one must make him his Lord. He declared that faith and trust meant total commitment and unreserved dedication. This means that Christ himself was to live in the person and the person was to crown Jesus as Lord of all. This was a difficult teaching, so difficult that upon hearing the words, hundreds turned away from him. Jesus then turned to his disciples and asked, "Will you also go away?" Peter replied, "Lord, to whom shall we go? You have the words of eternal life. We believe and know that you are the Holy One of God" (John 6:68–69 NIV). Do you share Peter's conviction that Jesus Christ is the only one in whom people can find eternal life? Is he your Lord? Do you know him like that? Are you committed to following him?

Is your life committed to Christ in the time of sorrow? Mary and Martha grieved because of their brother's death. He had been in the grave long enough that his body had begun to decay. Jesus came to these two and wept with them. He shared their sorrow. He walked with them down through the valley of the shadow of death. Martha said to him, "Lord, if you had been here, my brother would not have died." Jesus replied, "I am the resurrection, and the life. He who believes in me will live, even though he dies; and whoever lives and believes in me will never die" (John 11:21, 25–26).

Do you know Jesus Christ in the hour of sorrow wherein he provides a peace that passes understanding and a joy unspeakable? Do you know him in the assurance of his presence, power, and love? Paul said, "I am persuaded, that neither death, nor life, nor angels, nor principalities, nor powers, nor things present, nor things to come, nor height, nor depth, nor any other creature, shall be able to separate us from the love of God, which is in Christ Jesus our Lord" (Rom. 8:38–39). Do you know him like that?

The psalmist had great certainty of his knowledge of God when he said, "I will say of the LORD, He is my refuge and my fortress: my God; in him will I trust" (Ps. 91:2). Do you know him like that?

Conclusion

Do you know Jesus like that? You can know Christ today if you will confess your sins to him and express faith in him. You can know his marvelous change within you as you entrust your life to him. If you do not know him, will you accept him today as your personal Savior? Genuine knowledge of Christ brings the reality of peace. He puts a song in the heart. He gives assurance to the soul. You can know him today.

SUNDAY EVENING, APRIL 29

Title: What Means a Changeless Christ?

Text: "Jesus Christ the same yesterday, and today, and forever" **(Heb. 13:8)**.

Scripture Reading: Hebrews 13:1–14

Introduction

When God's final shaking destroys the temporary and reveals the eternal (Heb. 12:27), there will be one source of stability—Jesus Christ. Through him we will transcend the limits of time and cross over the golden span to eternity. Amid constant flux and change stands the changeless Christ. Through the last Old Testament prophet, God affirmed: "I the LORD do not change. So you, O descendants of Jacob, are not destroyed" (Mal. 3:6 NIV). Our hope is in the changeless Lord. Pagan religions have capricious, arbitrary deities, but the God of all is dependable.

I. The Christian stance is changeless (Heb. 13:1–4).

The ethic and outlook set down by Christ are always current. In spite of technological and cultural progress, human nature remains the same. Sin continues to wreak its usual havoc in lives, producing its usual selfishness and hatred.

A. *Love.* In such a world as ours, the Christian is called upon to love: "Let brotherly love continue" (v. 1). A vital part of love includes hospitality to those outside our realm of acquaintance: "Be not forgetful to entertain strangers: for thereby some have entertained angels unawares" (v. 2). To be sure, in our day when hotels are abundant, we can scarcely understand the predicament faced by travelers in the New Testament world where inns were known for their exorbitant rates, filth, and bawdy characters. Early Christians began the practice of carrying letters of recommendation from their home congregations in order to find open doors in Christian homes along their journey. When all the public facilities were of such ill repute, a Christian home was a haven to the weary traveler. Today there is still a place for Christian hospitality to those in need. Certainly there is a place for Christian hospitality in the local community as a witness to "strangers" who live down the block. The Christian home has a tremendous opportunity to witness for Christ.

B. *Compassionate fellowship.* The New Testament church was known for its fellowship as expressed by the term *koinonia*. It is a fellowship formed by the Holy Spirit's presence that enables Christians to share both joys and sorrows. When one member suffers, all suffer. When one rejoices, all rejoice: "Remember them that are in bonds, as bound with them: and them which suffer adversity, as being yourselves also in the body" (v. 3). The author writes at a time when Christians are tempted to withdraw from the church because of impending persecution (10:24–26). Instead of withdrawing, they must stand together and, if need be, suffer together.

C. *Moral absolutes.* Today's morality advocates a type of decision making that allows any violation of the Christian moral code, in certain situations, if love demands it. Jesus Christ is presented in Hebrews 13:8 as the one great absolute, and his expressed morality is timeless. The author of Hebrews singles out the matter of sexual morality for emphasis since human lust has ever made this a crucial issue in life: "Marriage should be honored by all, and the marriage bed kept pure, for God will judge the adulterer and all the sexually immoral" (v. 4 NIV).

A great deal is said in this short verse. Marriage is declared to be the only legitimate expression of sexual relations. Within marriage, sex finds its fulfillment and divine purpose. In marriage a man and woman become one flesh in the eyes of God and give themselves completely to one another. Generally, fornication refers to sexual relations outside of marriage, and adultery refers to illicit relations on the part of those given in marriage but going outside that relationship to satisfy their passions. Briefly, this reminds us that premarital sex is immoral, that extramarital sex is immoral, and that homosexuality is immoral, since it does not come within the divine bounds of one man and one woman joined together in the marriage bond.

II. The source of strength is changeless (Heb. 13:5–6).

Believers in every age have been strengthened by Christ's promise: "I will never leave thee, nor forsake thee" (v. 5). Christ never ducks out on us. When Joshua was given the place of leadership left vacant by Moses, the Lord said: "As I was with Moses, so I will be with thee: I will not fail thee, nor forsake thee" (Josh. 1:5).

The greatest contender with God for man's obeisance is mammon (Matt. 6:24). Mammon, if worshiped, will rob you of all contentment. Hence the admonition: "Let your conversation be without covetousness; and be content with such things as ye have: for he hath said, I will never leave thee, nor forsake thee" (Heb. 13:5). The word translated "covetousness" literally means "lover of money" and is parallel with the word "lover of brother" in Hebrews 13:1, translated "brotherly love." The Christian is to be a brother lover, not a money lover.

III. Salvation is changeless (Heb. 13:9, 12).

A. *Means of salvation.* Every generation is confronted with "all kinds of strange teachings" and is warned against being influenced by them (v. 9 NIV).

Hence the admonition: "It is good for our hearts to be strengthened by grace, not by ceremonial foods, which are of no value to those who eat them" (13:9 NIV). The foundation for the heart's assurance must ever be the grace of God. Neither the ritual laws of Judaism nor modern-day legalism can bring salvation, for spiritual cleansing comes only by the grace of God through Christ.

Salvation by grace through faith has ever been an affront to people. Many prefer to believe they can contribute to their salvation through good works.

Legalists who advocate salvation by works or ritual have no part in Christ's altar, which was his cross on Calvary: "We have an altar from which those who minister at the tabernacle have no right to eat" (Heb. 13:10 NIV). The Jews of Jesus' day failed to see that their sacrificial ritual was only a prophetic foreshadowing of the one ultimate sacrifice at Calvary. Only the death of Christ makes atonement possible. Though priests could usually eat the meat of sacrificial animals, on the Day of Atonement they could not. The sacrifice was burned outside the camp (Lev. 16:27). Only the blood was kept in the sanctuary. In like fashion, Jesus gave his body "outside the city gate" in providing for the atonement of sins (Heb. 13:12 NIV).

B. *The object of salvation.* Currently we see in the religious arena much discussion as to what is to be saved. The social gospel has been resurrected and again is making its bid for recognition. The question is simple: "Are we to seek to change lives through personal conversion or to change social institutions?" The social gospelers would hold to the latter; the Scripture would advocate the former. If we are to preach the gospel, we must decide whether to preach it to institutions or people.

At the heart of the matter lies the question of sin. If sin is personal, then people must have God's forgiveness and experience a spiritual rebirth. The Bible affirms this to be the mission of the church. To be sure, redeemed people will seek to improve social institutions, but better social institutions will not solve the human problem of guilt. Lord Eustace Percy once said, "To think of changing the world by changing the people in it may be an act of great faith: to talk of changing the world without changing the people in it is an act of lunacy" (*Christianity Today*, May 24, 1968, 5).

The degree to which the trend away from personal evangelism has clouded the issue of the church's message is illustrated by an incident during the Tell-Scotland campaign in the mid-1950s. The movement's headquarters at Glasgow received a letter from a minister from the north in which he said all the committees were organized, the plans laid, and the promotion in operation. However, he had one question: "Pray tell me," he wrote, "what are we to tell Scotland?" (Leighton Ford, *The Christian Persuader* [New York: Harper and Row, 1966], 93).

Conclusion

Though disciples in every age must find new ways to minister, the basic demands of discipleship remain the same: "Let us, then, go to him outside the camp, bearing the disgrace he bore" (Heb. 13:13 NIV). Jesus ever calls us out of the security of our cherished self-righteousness, out of the human plans we have laid, to a journey of faith akin to that of Abraham's.

Discipleship will always be, simply stated, following Jesus. Life is a pilgrimage: "For here we do not have an enduring city, but we are looking for the city that is to come" (Heb. 13:14 NIV). And so as we come to the close of this epistle, we see vividly set before us the figure of the changeless Christ beckoning us on. It is said the word *Hebrew* means "one who has crossed over" (W. H. Griffith Thomas, *Let Us Go On* [Grand Rapids: Zondervan, 1944], 183). God called Abraham to cross the Euphrates on faith. He called Moses to lead the Hebrews across the Red Sea to freedom. He called Joshua to lead his people across the Jordan into the Promised Land. This same Lord now calls us to follow him. "Let us go on."

SUGGESTED PREACHING PROGRAM FOR

MAY

- ## Sunday Mornings

    The theme for this month's sermons is "Seeking to Be Christian in Our Home Life."

- ## Sunday Evenings

    "The Christian and Controversy" is the theme for this month's Sunday evening sermons.

- ## Wednesday Evenings

    The messages suggested for Wednesday evenings are based on the objectives the apostle John had in mind when he wrote his first epistle. His objectives meet definite needs in our lives today. "Why John Wrote These Things" is the theme for these five messages.

WEDNESDAY EVENING, MAY 2

Title: John Wrote to Enrich Fellowship

Text: "That which we have seen and heard declare we unto you, that ye also may have fellowship with us: and truly our fellowship is with the Father, and with his Son Jesus Christ" **(1 John 1:3)**.

Scripture Reading: 1 John 1

Introduction

To know an author's purpose can aid one immeasurably in understanding the letter or the book that has been written. If we want to understand more fully the truth of the Bible, we should seek to know the purpose that was guiding the author of the book or passage that we are reading. This purpose is not always stated explicitly.

The apostle John stated his controlling purpose for the gospel that bears his name near the end. "But these are written, that ye might believe that Jesus is the Christ, the Son of God; and that believing you might have life through his name" (John 20:31). We need to remember this controlling principle as we read the gospel of love, the gospel of the Spirit. John was seeking to win converts to Jesus Christ with his gospel.

When we read John's epistles, we discover that while his ultimate purpose may have been to win converts, his immediate purpose was something else. He was writing to those who already were believers in Jesus Christ. He was seeking to refute some error that threatened their spiritual life and fellowship. He was seeking to instruct them in ways that would lead to spiritual maturity. We discover that John had a number of specific objectives or purposes. We can profit greatly by discovering these objectives and responding to them. John's purposes meet some specific needs in our lives today.

A study of John's first epistle will reveal that John's first objective was to increase fellowship.

The Greek word *koinonia*, translated "fellowship," is one of the great words of the New Testament. It occurs twenty different times in the New Testament, and four of these occurrences are found in 1 John. There is no one word in the English language that can carry the full meaning of the word translated "fellowship."

The root meaning of *koinonia* is "participation," or "communion." It is also translated "partnership." It refers to a sharing of something with others and to a close relationship with others. It would assert that there is no such thing as a solitary Christian.

I. Our fellowship is with the Father.

Through the grace of God we have the privilege of becoming his children through faith in Jesus Christ. In this experience he imparts to us his divine nature. We have a greater capacity to love and trust him. We have an inward inclination to obey him.

Fellowship with God is basic to Christian fellowship.

II. Our fellowship is with Jesus Christ.

As believers in Christ, we share in a common conversion experience through faith in Christ. He imparts to us his nature. He reveals to us his will. He gives to us his command. He blesses us with his presence and power.

III. We are to have fellowship with one another.

We share a common sinful nature that causes us to need Jesus Christ as Lord and Savior. We share in a common conflict with evil and with Satan that causes all of us to need to stay close to Jesus Christ. We share in a common conversion experience through faith in Christ that makes us brothers and sisters. We share in a common commission from our Lord that places us under a spiritual debtorship to proclaim his love and grace and mercy to a lost and needy world.

A. *God the Father wants our fellowship with him to be deepened and enriched.*

B. *Christ the Son wants our fellowship to be richer and fuller.*

C. *The Holy Spirit dwells within the heart of each of us to increase our fellowship with one another in prayer, worship, praise, and proclamation.*

Conclusion

Let each of us respond to the riches of the fellowship that God wants us to have both with himself and with each other. Let us guard against any attitude or habit that would harm our fellowship with each other. Let us put forth a positive effort to extend Christian fellowship to strangers who may come into our midst.

Christian fellowship is the greatest treasure that a group of believers can enjoy. It is the gift of God created by the Holy Spirit. John wrote his epistle to increase fellowship among believers with God the Father and with Jesus Christ his Son.

SUNDAY MORNING, MAY 6

Title: God's Good Man

Text: "And he shall be like a tree planted by rivers of water, that bringeth forth his fruit in his season; his leaf also shall not wither; and whatsoever he doeth shall prosper" **(Ps. 1:4)**.

Scripture Reading: Psalm 1

Hymns: "Who Is on the Lord's Side?" Havergal

"My Jesus, I Love Thee," Featherstone

"Blessed Assurance, Jesus Is Mine," Crosby

Offertory Prayer: Our Father, let true thanksgiving be more a mark of our daily living than a mark upon our calendar. For our food, our clothing, and our houses, we thank you. Most of all, we thank you for Jesus and the redemption we have in him. For his cause and for his glory we offer our gifts today. We lift this prayer in his dear name. Amen.

Introduction

The Bible almost begins and ends with trees. Someone has suggested that the heart of the gospel may be found in Adam behind a tree, Jesus upon a tree, and the redeemed in heaven under a tree.

Psalm 1 is a tree poem. Kyle Yates has suggested that perhaps Jesus took his text for the Sermon on the Mount from this psalm. There is not time here to do justice to a parallel reading of these two great pieces of literature, but if you have not read and compared Psalm 1 and the Sermon on the Mount, a great personal blessing awaits you. Each passage tells about the character, the influence, the conduct, and the destiny of the good and the bad life.

I. Characteristics of the good man (Ps. 1:1–2).

A. *Negatively (v. 1).*

1. God's man does not get his advice from evil men. He "walketh not in the counsel of the ungodly." The guiding influences of his life are not from the enemies of God. He does not adjust his conduct to their patterns.

2. God's good man does not hang out with the wrong crowd. He does not loaf around with the unrighteous. He is not too good to associate with

sinners, but he does not so adopt their habits that he feels entirely at home with them. The good man may penetrate the darkness as a light, but he does not dwell in darkness.

    3. God's good man does not become a scoffer in the area of spiritual things. He holds God's way and God's Word in high esteem. God's good man is never found in the seat of the scornful.

  B. *Positively (v. 2).*

    1. God's good man enjoys doing what God wants done. The delight he has is not merely one of admiration: it is one of participation. He not only likes to know what the law of God is, but he likes to do it.

    2. God's good man follows a daily devotional program of self-improvement. He meditates on God's law day and night with the desire to bring himself up to its standards. The real follower of God studies, prays, works, and seeks to improve himself as long as he lives.

II. Comparison of the good man (Ps. 1:3).

"And he shall be like a tree...."

  A. *Both are planted.* It is not by accident that the tree is by the water. It is planted in a certain place for a certain purpose. The good man is not an accident. He is planted. There is purpose in his location and in his life.

  B. *Both are provided.* The tree is planted by the river of water; otherwise it would die for lack of sustaining moisture. The good man is not planted in the desert to die. Above the ground as under the ground there is a river to supply his need.

  C. *Both are productive.* The tree brings forth fruit, and the good man brings forth fruit. Jesus once came upon a certain fruit tree and found "nothing but leaves." He said that some people are like that tree: "Ye shall know them by their fruits" (Matt. 7:16). He then repeated his statement at the end of this same comparison: "Wherefore by their fruits ye shall know them" (v. 20).

  D. *Both are permanent.* The tree is an evergreen. "His leaf also shall not whither." In the tree and in God's good man, life does not come and go. The Holy Spirit provides a spring of life in God's good man that flows continually.

  E. *Both are prosperous.* This does not mean that there are no lean years or crop failures. It does mean that a good tree and a good man are planted to succeed, and the total influence of each will be one of victory and success as God provides their needs.

III. The contrast with God's good man (Ps. 1:4–5).

Let us not forget in our ecumenically minded day that God's Word not only unites but that it also divides. "For the word of God is quick, and powerful, and sharper than any two-edged sword, piercing even to the dividing asunder of soul and spirit, and of the joints and marrow, and is a discerner of the thoughts and intents of the heart" (Heb. 4:12). Contrasted with the good life is the bad life, the ungodly life.

A. *The bad life is unanchored (v. 4).* For the righteous, the roots of the tree keep it fixed in the wind. But the bad life is like the chaff that the wind easily blows away.

B. *The bad life is unsafe (v. 5).* It will not stand in the final judgment day. This is the opposite of permanent prosperity of the good life.

C. *The bad life is unacceptable (v. 5).* Sinners may place themselves in "the congregation of the righteous," but they are not acceptable to God until they are changed within. People may affiliate superficially, but God will separate finally.

IV. The conclusion of God's good man (Ps. 1:6).

The explanation of God's good man is God's work in and for him. God watches over the plans of the good man, and the good man permits God to do it. Not only does God watch over the plans of the good man, but he watches over his paths. Both in his plans and in his performance God is with his man.

The paths of the evil man lead to doom. It is not so much the *way* of the ungodly that will perish as it is that the man himself will perish.

Conclusion

There are but two ways for us. Each is vividly described in the Scriptures. It is up to each of us to choose the way we will go.

SUNDAY EVENING, MAY 6

Title: The Christian and Controversy

Text: "Do not think that I have come to bring peace on earth; I have not come to bring peace, but a sword" **(Matt. 10:34 RSV)**.

Scripture Reading: Matthew 10:24–39

Introduction

How involved should the Christian be in controversial matters? How involved should the church be in controversial issues? Should the Christian try to avoid controversy at all costs, or does his faith have something relevant to say? Does his faith compel him to act?

I. Conflicts can hardly be avoided.

The church should be faithful in its proclamation of the gospel, and the fullness of the gospel has serious implications for the life of people in their society and for their nation. If this were not so, why would Jesus have said, "Think not that I am come to send peace on earth: I came not to send peace, but a sword. For I am come to set a man at variance against his father.... He that findeth his life shall lose it: and he that loseth his life for my sake shall find it" (Matt. 10:34–39)?

The apostle Paul was not being merely rhetorical when he wrote the following lines to a young person in the Christian life: "I have fought a good fight, I have finished my course, I have kept the faith" (2 Tim. 4:7). Paul was referring to his faithfulness to the gospel—in living for it, in preaching and teaching it day and night. There were problems in the days of the early church that required Paul to stand up and be counted. It has been said that wherever Paul went he was involved either in a prayer circle or in a riot—and the two are not always mutually exclusive.

Jesus manifested his righteous indignation and anger at wrongs in his society. To be sure, he never would have been crucified if he had avoided the controversial. He was too dangerous to have around, so he was condemned and crucified—not only as an unusual, or unorthodox and dangerous religious leader, but as one who was thought to be too revolutionary. The Jewish leaders could not stand Jesus confronting them with the disturbing will and love of God, so they crucified him.

Conflict is not necessarily evil. It can be evil, especially if it is not dealt with promptly and positively. But some conflict is basic to life. Biologists and others who study life tell us that people learned and grew through conflict with their environment; conflict compelled people to seek knowledge that they might gain some mastery over their surroundings. Throughout history one idea has been challenged by another, and in the ensuing conflict either one or the other was victorious or the two merged into a new and entirely different idea. Thesis, antithesis, synthesis—these form the polarity and the movement of life.

Life is action; action is something in conflict with something else. Take, for example, married life and family life. How can two people, even when they are in love, and especially when they are joined by children, ever expect that the home will not have conflict? By the very nature of the case, conflict is not only inevitable, it is natural and basic. A bad marriage can be one in which there is the absence of conflict. One such marriage is pictured in a cartoon of a man and his wife at work in the kitchen. The mild and meek husband, in a burst of real bravery, ventures to observe: "One thing I don't like, dear, is when you ask me a question, then you answer the question for me, and then you disagree with me!"

Going back to the question "How can a Christian avoid conflict?" he cannot, unless he avoids life around him and puts his faith in the lock box of sentimental pietism.

II. Dealing with controversy.

Conflict must be faced honestly and realistically. We do the greatest damage to ourselves and others when we try to avoid conflict that cannot—or should not—be avoided. Loving our enemies and praying for those who despitefully use us is not negated by our facing the issues that make us enemies. Going back to the thought of marriage, conflict is not what destroys marriage, but avoidance of the issue does. Harbored feelings, hidden resentments, unevaluated indifferences—these can destroy a marriage and wreck family living. A good family discussion is not to be avoided when one is needed. When a family faces the issues, there likely will be differences of opinion, but sweeping conflict under the proverbial rug, refusing to discuss it, hiding from it in sweet, sentimental talk—this is what builds up into a huge explosion in many instances. Then comes the drifting apart and the feeling of "I just can't stand to live with him [or her] any longer." Inability to love physically, emotionally, and spiritually often is a consequence. More marriages are destroyed by a couple's failure to face the issues than are destroyed because they fight too much. However, this should not be taken as an encouragement to pick a fight with your spouse. It is to say that it is better to face an issue than to avoid controversy that needs attention. The same truth applies concerning great public issues confronting a community or a nation.

Conclusion

"I have fought the good fight," wrote Paul. This should be written across the life of every Christian and every church. The nature of the Christian's faith demands our involvement in life. L. Wilson Kilgore once said that it is better to get into trouble with the world seeking to do God's will than to get into trouble with God because we are afraid to do his will in our world. Let us never forget that the central symbol of our faith is a cross.

WEDNESDAY EVENING, MAY 9

Title: John Wrote to Increase Joy
Text: "And these things write we unto you, that your joy may be full" (**1 John 1:4**).
Scripture Reading: 1 John 1

Introduction

The apostle John is explicit at the point of his objective in writing his first epistle. In our text, he declares that he has written to increase joy—the joy of the readers of this epistle along with his own joy.

Joy is much richer and deeper in quality than happiness. Human happiness is the result of happenings that bring pleasure and delight, but joy is a gift from God that can cause the heart to overflow even in adverse circumstances.

It is significant that on the night before our Lord was crucified he said, "These things have I spoken unto you, that my joy might remain in you, and that your joy might be full" (John 15:11). Jesus described his own life as one of joy. Some of us have overlooked this characteristic of our Lord. We have thought of him as a man of sorrows and acquainted with grief. We remember him weeping over the city of Jerusalem. We need to remember that his personality was winsome and attractive and magnetic to the extent that people chose to follow him to the point of death. He described himself as a bridegroom, and bridegrooms are usually happy. He was described by his enemies as being a winebibber and a glutton. Behind these criticisms there is the observation that our Lord loved to be with people during happy and festive occasions.

Is your life characterized by joy? If not, you have failed to enter into your spiritual heritage. You have missed something that God has for you.

John mentioned many things that should contribute to our joy.

I. We can experience the joy of fellowship (1 John 1:3).

II. We can experience the joy of forgiveness and cleansing (1 John 1:9).

III. We can experience the joy of an adequate Savior (1 John 2:1–2).

IV. We can experience the joy of divine sonship (1 John 3:2).

V. We can experience the joy of the indwelling Holy Spirit (1 John 3:24; 4:13).

VI. We can experience the joy of knowing that God loves us without measure (1 John 4:9).

Conclusion

A careful study of these wonderful blessings that are ours through faith in Jesus Christ should cause our hearts to overflow with indescribable joy.

The world about us is hungry for a joyful way of life. Christ came to fill our hearts with joy. That kind of Christianity is contagious.

SUNDAY MORNING, MAY 13

Title: The Prayer of an Ambitious Mother

Text: "Then came to him the mother of Zebedee's children with her sons, worshipping him, and desiring a certain thing of him. And he said unto her, What wilt thou? She saith unto him, Grant that these my two sons may sit, the one on thy right hand, and the other on the left, in thy kingdom" (**Matt. 20:20–21**).

Scripture Reading: Matthew 20:20–28

Hymns: "Love Divine, All Loves Excelling," Wesley

"God, Give Us Christian Homes," McKinney

"Make Me a Channel of Blessing," Smyth

Offertory Prayer: Our heavenly Father, we thank you for your blessings upon us through the home. May our tithes and offerings be used to bring about the conversion of boys and girls, men and women, who will be able to serve you better in their homes. Bless this act of worship as each of us brings of our material substance to express our gratitude and to indicate our sincere concern for the advancement of your kingdom through Jesus Christ our Lord. Amen.

Introduction

Many have tended to join with the other ten apostles in an attitude of hostility toward Salome, the mother of James and John, because of her preferential consideration of her sons. It is significant to note that while Christ corrected her, he did not berate, criticize, or condemn her.

Let us look at this remarkable mother of two men who were to serve their Lord and their generation in such a manner as to be famous after two millenniums. We should remember that she was not divine. She was imperfect like other mothers. However, there must have been something uniquely different about her, for her two sons were among the first who were selected and who responded to our Lord's invitation to discipleship (Matt. 4:21–22).

While nowhere do we find a direct reference to the fact that the mother of James and John was named Salome, a careful consideration of all the passages in the New Testament seems to imply that this was her name. There is some tradition that would indicate that Salome was a sister of Mary, the mother of Jesus. If this is true, then James and John were cousins of Jesus on their mother's side. We cannot be dogmatic at this point.

I. Salome was a mother of great faith.

A. *Salome had great faith in Jesus Christ or else she would not have made her request for preferential treatment of her sons.* It is possible that her faith was colored by the nationalistic and materialistic expectations that were so prominent in the minds of Jewish people in that day and time. Even if this were true, it indicates that she had faith in Jesus Christ.

B. *Salome had faith in the ability and faithfulness of her sons.* She had high expectations of them. She believed that they were capable and could be trusted. Modern-day mothers need to have a great faith in the potentiality of their children. Dr. M. E. Dodd said concerning his mother, "My mother had a kingdom in her heart and empires in her imagination when she thought of her children and their potential."

II. Salome was a woman of warm devotion.

A. *Salome had a warm love for Jesus Christ that indicated itself in the critical and dangerous time when he was going to the cross.* "And many women were there beholding afar off, which followed Jesus from Galilee, ministering unto him: Among which was Mary Magdalene, and Mary the mother of James and Joses, and the mother of Zebedee's children" (Matt. 27:55–56). Her genuine faith and warm love were manifested by her presence at the tomb as it began to dawn toward the first day of the week (Mark 16:1).

B. *Salome had a great and exalting love for her sons.* We cannot criticize her for this. Instead, she deserves to be commended.

How do you spell the word *mother*? It has been suggested that the best way to spell mother is L-O-V-E. How do you spell the word *love*? It has been suggested that the best way to spell love is M-O-T-H-E-R.

III. Salome was a woman of warm spiritual ambition.

A. *Salome came to Jesus worshiping him.*

B. *Salome came to Jesus with a prayer.*

C. *Salome listened and learned as much as it was possible for her to grasp at that particular time.*

D. *Salome accepted correction from the Christ (Matt. 20:22).* Is ambition for our children sinful? In some instances, the answer would be yes. In other instances, the answer would be no.

If Salome was thinking only of position, power, and prestige, her ambition was selfish. On the other hand, perhaps she wanted her sons always to be near Jesus Christ. Possibly she sincerely wanted them to be of assistance to him. Perhaps she wanted them to be totally involved in his work in the world.

Jesus proceeded to explain what one must be and do to be great in the kingdom of God (Matt. 20:26–28). All would agree that James and John met these conditions.

It is highly possible that Salome was of great assistance in helping her sons to become the servants of Jesus Christ that they did become.

1. James, the son of Zebedee and Salome, became the first of the apostles to experience martyrdom (Acts 12:1–2). Evidently James learned the lesson of humility and self-sacrifice well to have followed his Lord to the point of death.

2. John became the "apostle of love." He was the apostle to whom our Lord committed the care of his mother while on the cross (John 19:25–27). According to the best traditions, John served lovingly, faithfully, and significantly until the last decade of the first century of the Christian era. He spent his last years in the city of Ephesus. From there he was exiled to the island of Patmos where the living Lord gave him the visions recorded in the book we know as Revelation.

Behind these two significant men, we need to recognize a mother who was ambitious for her sons. Likewise, mothers of today should be ambitious for the conversion of their children, for the development of Christian character in their children, and for the entering into of Christian marriages and God-pleasing vocations for their children.

Conclusion

On this Mother's Day those of us who are husbands and fathers should rededicate ourselves to daily prayer for the mothers of our children. We need to encourage them, express our gratitude for them, and assist them.

On Mother's Day, each of you who is a mother would do well for yourself and for your children if you would accept your role as a teacher for God. God has blessed you with children that you might disciple them, dedicate them, and discipline them for his glory and for the good of humankind in the world today. If you would be a true teacher for God, you must give yourself to genuine worship of the Lord Jesus Christ. You need to go into the throne room of prayer day by day for wisdom, grace, guidance, and help. You need to have faith in the presence and power and purpose of the Holy Spirit as he works in your own heart and through you to bless your home and your children.

SUNDAY EVENING, MAY 13

Title: Can Churchgoing Be Sinful?

Text: " 'Go to Bethel and sin; go to Gilgal and sin yet more. Bring your sacrifices every morning, your tithes every three years. Burn leavened bread as a thank offering and brag about your freewill offerings — boast about them, you Israelites, for this is what you love to do,' declares the Sovereign LORD" **(Amos 4:4 – 5 NIV)**.

Scripture Reading: Amos 4

Introduction

Regular attendance at church worship services is one of the normal characteristics of one who is considered to be genuinely Christian. Is it possible that we have emphasized regular attendance at worship services at the cost of something else? Is it always wise to judge the quality of one's faith in terms of his loyalty to the stated services of the congregation with which he worships?

Something is wrong with the emphasis that leaves the impression that regular church attendance is the hallmark of excellence as far as Christian involvement is concerned. To accept the idea that mere church attendance is a full expression of one's faith is to live under the illusion that the rest of the week is outside the will and concern of God.

On one occasion our Lord used irony to portray the emptiness and meaninglessness of ritualistic prayer and worship (Luke 18:10 – 12). A Pharisee came before the Lord and thanked the Lord that he was not like others. A publican who was also in the temple was vividly aware of his unworthiness and made a sincere plea for pardon. He had a genuine experience with God. His experience was a transforming one with the living God, while the experience of the Pharisee only confirmed him in his pious self-righteousness.

Amos used great irony and invited the people of his day to go to the temple and to increase their sinfulness. Evidently there was something radically wrong with their worship activities. Is it possible that we fall into the same category?

I. When quantity is substituted for quality, a church is in great danger.

It is one thing to assemble a crowd. It is something entirely different for that crowd to become a congregation of worshipers. The individual must not assume that because he is a part of the crowd that he has had a genuine experience with God.

Instead of being primarily concerned with the quantity of the crowd that is worshiping together, the emphasis needs to be placed on the genuineness of the faith and commitment of those who have come together for an experience with God.

II. When form is substituted for content and when externals are accepted for spiritual realities, the church is in danger.

Amos lived in a time in which the places of worship were crowded with those who had come to bring their offerings and sacrifices. They went through the pomp and ceremony of worship. These experiences were very satisfying to the people involved. However, God was not only disturbed but also displeased. The worship activities of the people were not productive of moral and ethical conduct on the part of those who went to the places of worship.

We need to question the genuineness of any experience that we consider to be a worship experience if it is not productive of a change in our lives or in the lives of others about us.

III. When the bringing of tithes and offerings is substituted for a total commitment to the living God, a church is in danger.

One of the perils that we all face is the peril of substituting a part for the whole. Some people labor under the erroneous idea that if they are regular in attendance at worship services and if they are faithful in bringing their tithes and offerings, then they have fulfilled their obligation to God and have met their responsibility for a lost world. The bringing of tithes and offerings is of vast importance but is just a part of the whole of the commitment of the genuine Christian. These should be symbols of our complete dedication to the will of God and to the ministry for him in every area of life including the so-called secular part of life.

We must guard against the idea that one-seventh of our time and one-tenth of our money belongs to God and that we are free to do as we wish with the balance.

IV. A church is in great danger if it becomes an end in itself.

Christ placed the church in the world to be a channel through which his redemptive work could be carried forward. He did not intend for it to become a repository into which he would bestow his blessings and on which people would bestow their affection and energy.

The church is not to be thought of as a shrine that exists for its own purpose. Instead, it should be thought of as a force through which the people of God unite and cooperate with each other in doing the work of God in today's world.

We need to correct our impressions concerning church work and the work of the church. There is much confusion at this point. To teach a Sunday school class, to sing in the choir, to work with a youth group probably falls in the category of church work rather than the work of the church. The work of the church is that which the people of God do during the week in the community and in the world.

Conclusion

The people of Amos's day were great as far as doing church work was concerned. They flocked to the temple on the Sabbath and on feast days. They brought offerings in abundance. And they probably were greatly surprised to learn that God was not pleased with these (Amos 5:21–23). God was primarily concerned with a moral and spiritual response from his people. Because God is a moral God, he was concerned about their making a moral response to his will (v. 24).

We must beware lest our worship activities as individuals and as a church become an empty form that does not produce moral change within our lives.

WEDNESDAY EVENING, MAY 16

Title: John Wrote to Prevent Sin

Text: "My little children, these things write I unto you, that ye sin not" (1 John 2:1).

Scripture Reading: 1 John 2

Introduction

John the beloved apostle writes from the perspective of a pastor. He writes to those whom he considers to be his spiritual offspring. His loving heart is concerned that they experience the very best and that they avoid everything that would be detrimental to their spiritual welfare.

In our text, John comes right to the point concerning his objective in writing. He declares that he is writing to encourage them to avoid sin. Phillips translates our text as follows: "I write these things to you (may I call you 'my children'—for that's how I think of you) to help you to avoid sin." John was warning them against the danger of falling into sin. The tense of the verb in the original language suggests that he had primary reference to isolated acts of sin rather than to a continuous state of sin. He recognized that there was constant danger of their falling into individual acts of sin. Later he emphasized that the born-again child of God does not continue to live in sin (1 John 3:4–10).

I. The possibility of falling into sin.

John was aware that it is possible for his readers to fall into sin. He spoke repeatedly of the evil one who would destroy us if it were in his power to do so.

John was refuting the error of the Gnostics who taught that sin did not affect the spirit, that sin was not really sinful.

II. To commit sin is to contradict the new nature.

Later John insisted that sin is of the devil and that it is contradictory to the nature of a born-again Christian to live in sin. He spoke of those who "went out from us, but they were not of us; for if they had been of us, they would no doubt have continued with us: but they went out, that they might be made manifest that they were not all of us" (1 John 2:19).

III. Acts of sin displease the Father.

IV. Sin must be avoided because sin is self-destructive.

By its very nature, sin destroys that which is finest and best in life. This is why God cannot condone or tolerate sin. His love requires that he oppose sin in its every form.

Conclusion

John would insist that every believer accept personal responsibility for avoiding sin. We can best do this by being sensitive and responsive to the presence of the divine Spirit living within our hearts. We can greatly strengthen our spiritual life by making much of God's Holy Word. We must recognize the terrible destructive nature of sin itself and abhor it. We must flee from it. We must refuse to tolerate it. We must not condone it. We must look to Jesus Christ for deliverance not only from the penalty of sin but from individual acts of sin in our daily life.

SUNDAY MORNING, MAY 20

Title: How Christian Is Your Home?

Text: "Let the word of Christ dwell in you richly in all wisdom; teaching and admonishing one another in psalms and hymns and spiritual songs, singing with grace in your hearts to the Lord" **(Col. 3:16)**.

Scripture Reading: Colossians 3:12–21

Hymns: "Have Faith in God," McKinney

"God, Give Us Christian Homes," McKinney

"Happy the Home When God Is There," Ware

Offertory Prayer: Holy Father, you who art the Creator and the Sustainer of life, we come to you with gratitude for the inner disposition that causes us to want to worship you. We thank you for the inward prompting of your Holy Spirit that would draw us closer to you. As an act of worship, we bring our tithes and offerings for the advancement of your ministry of mercy in the world. Help us to be more grateful for your generosity toward us. Bless both these gifts and the givers. Bless those who will be blessed by the gifts. In Jesus' name we pray. Amen.

Introduction

As we consider the Christian home, we face the peril of accepting a part for the whole. Could it be possible that some of us have accepted a counterfeit for the genuine article? We also need to be cautious lest we accept a substitute for a genuine Christian home.

I. What is a Christian home?

A. *Is it a home that merely maintains high moral standards?*
B. *Is it a home where all the members believe in the existence of a supreme being?*
C. *Is it a home where all of the family members are listed as church members?*
D. *Is it a home where everyone goes to church every Sunday?*
E. *Is it a home where all of the family members have been converted?*
F. *Is it a home where religion is a form to be maintained and a duty to be carried out that produces no glow to gladden the heart or grace to sustain the spirit?*
G. *Is it a home where there are certain moral restrictions imposed on the children?*

We are using the word *Christian* as an adjective rather than as a noun. An adjective is used to "denote a quality of the thing or to specify a thing as distinct from something else." When the word *Christian* is used as an adjective, it denotes a quality that is distinctive about the noun to which it is attached. When we ask, "How Christian is your home?" we are referring to a home that is distinctively different.

II. How would you define a Christian home?

A Christian home has been defined by Olin T. Binkley as having at least the following three characteristics.

A. *A Christian home is a home where Christ is known, trusted, and obeyed.* It is a home in which Christ lives as Savior, Lord, Friend, and Teacher.
　1. The husband loves his wife sincerely and steadfastly even as Christ loved the church (Eph. 5:25).
　2. The wife reverences her husband and recognizes him as the head of her household (Eph. 5:21–24, 33).
　3. The children respect and obey their parents in the Lord (Col. 3:20).
B. *A Christian home is a home where the husband and wife love each other sincerely and steadfastly.* The vows they made before God and the state on their wedding day are treated as an unconditional commitment to each other as long as life lasts.

　　The love that should prevail between a husband and wife will manifest itself on the sexual level, the social level, and the sacrificial level. God gives his smile of approval to the romantic attraction of the husband and wife for each other. The husband and the wife should conduct themselves so as to maintain the respect and appreciation of their companion. If married love is to reach its highest level, it must be characterized by a spirit of sacrificial self-giving on the part of each to the other and for the other.

C. *A Christian home is a home where there is a creative relationship between the parents and the children.* The husband and the wife have a spiritual responsibility to help each other to be the best Christians they possibly can be. In turn they have a responsibility to provide spiritual nurture and encouragement to their children as well as provision for their material needs. The parents must not delegate to the church the sole responsibility for the spiritual training and discipline of their children. Parents must recognize their responsibility for the spiritual training and discipline of their children.

Children need to recognize that they have a responsibility to God for assisting in making the home Christian. It is the will of God that they respect and obey their parents. If they would be pleasing to their Lord, they must recognize the authority of their parents. Children need to overcome their inherent tendency to be selfish and to put forth an effort to grow toward spiritual maturity that involves responsible action within the home.

If there is a generation gap that exists, it is a two-way gap. It can be bridged only when both parties put forth an effort to communicate with each other.

III. Making the home more Christian.

To maintain a creative relationship between parents and children, we will need three gifts and activities.

A. *We need the gift and activity of faith.*
1. Faith in God (Heb. 11:6).
2. Faith in self.
3. Faith in each other.
4. Faith in the future.

B. *The gift and activity of hope.*
1. Hope based on the goodness and faithfulness of God.
2. Hope based on character and commitment to Christ.
3. Hope based on the presence of God in the hearts of others and in our own hearts.

C. *The gift and activity of love.* Three Greek words are used to communicate the nature of love. *Eros* refers to sensual or sexual love. This type of love is emotional and instinctive. While it may be selfish, it also can be pure, genuine, and noble between a husband and wife who love each other sincerely and steadfastly. *Philia* is social love, or brotherly love. It is based on the worth detected in another or on similarity of interest and feeling. It means "I sincerely like you." *Agape* is sacrificial, self-giving love, the Calvary kind of love. It always puts the best interest of the other ahead of the interest of self. All three of these types of love are in the plan of God for the Christian home.

Conclusion

If we want to have faith, hope, and love in abundance, we need to let Jesus Christ dwell in our hearts and in our homes as Savior, Lord, Teacher, and Friend. He will assist and encourage us.

Yours can be a Christian home if you will trust and obey Christ and if you will love your companion sincerely.

If there is one in your home who does not know Jesus Christ as Lord and Savior, then trust him for guidance and help as you seek to give your Christian witness and as you seek to lead that one to know your Savior as Lord and Master.

SUNDAY EVENING, MAY 20

Title: Power, an Arena of Controversy

Text: "For I am not ashamed of the gospel; it is the power of God for salvation to every one who has faith" **(Rom. 1:16 RSV)**.

Scripture Reading: Romans 1:8–17

Introduction

Our series "The Christian and Controversy" continues tonight. Conflicts coming out of differing views and value systems are unavoidable. The Christian should concern himself with these great issues, and his behavior should be characterized by kindness and love, intelligence and integrity. Tonight we will deal with the issue of how we acquire and use power to achieve noble purposes.

I. People of power.

In the not-so-recent past, the command posts of Untied States society were held by the state, the corporation, and the military. The family, the church, and the school had been ancient and revered centers of power, but then the time came when they stood in the wings while the "big three" occupied the stage. The ramparts of power were held securely by the politicians, the corporation executives, and the generals. Furthermore, the big three reached such size that their aims, purposes, and decisions were solidly interlocked. The war lords, the corporation chiefs, and the political directorates kept a wary eye on one another from their lofty summits at the pinnacle of power. One could scarcely act without the check and balance of the other two.

There have been two classic ways of judging how these people use their power. One side sees them as mere pawns in the onward rush of history. Fate is the executor of power according to this view. The other side perceives the people in power as ruthlessly shaping passing history with no regard for the inner demands of the events, let alone for the people who may suffer.

In time, the power of the big three was successfully challenged by the masses. The masses learned that they are not the prisoners of history, but the tillers who use the plow to help change history and bring needed improvements. As someone has said, "Force is the midwife of every old society pregnant with a new one." In many nations, the force of massive peaceful demonstrations cracked the foundations of the big three. This in itself is not anarchy. Power is in the process of redistribution, and that is disturbing to a lot of people.

II. Power and purpose.

Power is simply the ability to influence the actions and decisions of others. American society operates most smoothly when it is functioning on the basis of a consensus. Most people prefer a consensus to a simple majority. The search for a consensus automatically vests power in the minority, but it does not take power away from the majority.

If we have the Christian perspective, we will keep in mind God's purpose for the world of people — to live as a family as sons and daughters of himself and as brothers and sisters of one another. Whatever power we have available, it should be used for that purpose. But be aware of the risks. God limited himself, choosing to have a world of free persons, not puppets. To the extent that one is truly Christlike, he has some power to help make the world a harmonious society. Power is related to purpose.

A bull is a powerful animal in the arena, but it has no power to preserve delicate antiques in a china shop. The gentle hands of a woman would be power for that purpose. The huge diesel locomotive is powerful for pulling a train but not for teaching a child the alphabet. A gun is a powerful instrument for the killing of an enemy, but for taking two men on the opposite sides in a war and making friends of them it has no power at all.

III. Power for people.

Paul makes the claim in the text that the gospel mediates the power of God, and he was not ashamed of it. The word *gospel* came from an old English word used to translate the Greek *evangelion*, which meant "good tidings." In the New Testament it meant good news about the Christ, the proclamation of the saving event of which Jesus' life, death, and resurrection were the center. God has acted for people's salvation, and that is good news.

This good news, the gospel and its proclamation, is the *power of God*. Jesus had declared that "the Son of man has power on earth to forgive sin," and he promised to those who followed him a sharing of this gift (Matt. 9:6, 8; Acts 1:8).

Conclusion

When men and women in Christ's name become a medium of reconciliation among people, they appropriate the power of God. He has given us this ministry (2 Cor. 5:18).

WEDNESDAY EVENING, MAY 23

Title: John Wrote to Provide Christian Assurance

Text: "These things have I written unto you that believe on the name of the Son of God; that ye may know that ye have eternal life, and that ye may believe on the name of the Son of God" **(1 John 5:13)**.

Scripture Reading: 1 John 5

Introduction

Some sincere believers and followers of Jesus Christ do not believe that they can have assurance of eternal life until the judgment day. They labor under the mistaken impression that eternal salvation is a result of the grace of God on one hand and human effort and achievement on the other. When these people are conscientious, they have to admit that in many areas of Christian growth and ministry they have fallen far beneath their potential. They also have to admit that some attitudes and actions that have characterized their lives reflect poorly on the name of their Lord. Consequently, they live in both fear and hope. They fear that they will miss heaven and spend eternity in hell. They hope that perhaps their death will come at a time when all sin has been confessed and they can go out to meet God without any unconfessed sin that would condemn them.

John specifically declared that one of his purposes for writing this epistle was to provide assurance of eternal life to those who were believing in Jesus Christ as the Son of God and as the Savior who came to take away their sin. The apostle did not want any believers to be in doubt concerning their relationship with God. He would declare to us that the heavenly Father is eager that each of his children rejoice in and respond to the implications of their sonship and the gift of eternal life.

I. Lack of Christian assurance is hurtful.

A. *The absence of assurance can arrest the growth of the new convert.*

B. *Lack of assurance robs the believer of the joy that should characterize one who is a member of the family of God.*

C. *Lack of assurance can cripple a believer's usefulness.* It would be impossible to give a winsome witness concerning Jesus Christ if one did not have the assurance of an abiding relationship with him.

II. The causes for a lack of assurance.

A. *A misunderstanding of the way of salvation causes many believers to feel insecure in their relationship with God.* If one believes that salvation is the result of his own faithfulness and obedience following a conversion experience, he cannot help but feel insecure.

An awareness that eternal life is the free gift of the grace of God by faith in Jesus Christ can be most helpful at this point (Eph. 2:8–9).

169

B. *Lack of assurance may be due to divine chastisement.* The Bible repeatedly teaches us that the heavenly Father chastises his children when they act in a manner that contradicts their new nature and reflects on their relationship with the heavenly Father (Heb. 12:5–13). Chastisement is actually a proof of sonship rather than an indication that we are no longer the children of God. Sin in the life of the child of God affects his fellowship rather than his relationship with God. Confession and correction bring both cleansing and a restoration of the fellowship that was once enjoyed with the heavenly Father.

C. *A lack of Christian assurance may be due to an expectation of a particular type of emotional experience in connection with conversion that has not been forthcoming.* Nowhere does the Bible teach us that we all must have a certain emotional feeling in the initial experience of receiving salvation.

D. *Lack of assurance may be due to insufficient faith in the promises of God.* There is no way by which a believer can continue to have assurance of salvation if he is uninformed concerning the provisions and promises of God as contained in the Scriptures. One must base his assurance of salvation on the promises of God rather than on his own achievements or his own feelings. Feelings fluctuate. Faith must be placed in the promises of God, and these must be treated as facts of experience.

III. A check list for Christian assurance.

John gives us a number of tests by which we may examine our own faith and spiritual experience. He lists some of the identifiable marks or distinguishing characteristics of those who are members of God's family. These characteristics are inward and spiritual yet expressed outwardly.

A. *Christian assurance can be enjoyed by those who have a continuing inward desire to be obedient to the commandments of our Lord (1 John 2:3–4).* The absence of such a sincere desire should cause us to be concerned about whether we have experienced the new birth.

B. *Christian assurance can be enjoyed by those who have a continuing love for their Christian brothers and sisters (1 John 3:14).* If a person believes that he has a basis for a hope of salvation and does not find within his heart a genuine love for the people of God as they engage in worship, witness, and work, he should be doubtful concerning the genuineness of his faith and the basis for such a hope.

C. *Christian assurance can be enjoyed by those who have an awareness of the abiding presence of the Holy Spirit within their hearts (1 John 3:24; 4:13).* The apostle Paul declared also that the Holy Spirit assures the believer of his relationship with God through faith in Christ Jesus (Rom. 8:14–17).

D. *Christian assurance can be enjoyed by believers who accept the testimony of the Scripture as being divine truth (1 John 5:11–12).* Lack of confidence in the teaching of the Scripture at this point will rob us of the joy of assurance that the heavenly Father desires that we have.

Conclusion

John declared that one of his objectives in writing this epistle was that believers might have assurance of salvation. If you are a genuine believer, a study of this epistle and an honest examination of your own spiritual experience can help you to experience the joy of assurance. If you are among those who have had some kind of an emotional experience that has not produced real change, then a study of this epistle will help you to see that what you really need is to put your trust in Jesus Christ, experience the new birth, and become a child of God.

SUNDAY MORNING, MAY 27

Title: The Choices of Youth

Text: "Trust in the LORD with all thine heart; and lean not unto thine own understanding. In all thy ways acknowledge him, and he shall direct thy paths" **(Prov. 3:5–6).**

Scripture Reading: Hebrews 11:23–27

Hymns: "Glorious Is Thy Name," McKinney

"Give of Your Best to the Master," Grose

"Arise, O Youth of God," Merrill

Offertory Prayer: Holy heavenly Father, your Holy Spirit has come to dwell within our physical bodies to make us holy and to reproduce within us the character of your Son Jesus Christ. Help us to make ourselves fully available to him as he seeks to work your work within us. We come bringing the fruits of our labors, asking your blessings upon them in advancing the work of your kingdom among people. We offer these gifts through Jesus Christ our Lord. Amen.

Introduction

With pride and joy we come to the day when high school seniors are recognized as having completed a course of study. We come to this day with praise for our Lord for his blessings upon us. We come with praise for those who have achieved success in this portion of their lives. We should offer gratitude and praise to teachers who have made their distinctive contribution. We come to this day with hope and anticipation, for the future holds great promise. We come to this day with earnest prayer for divine guidance for you as you begin making the decisions that will determine your destiny.

Life is made up of choices as well as consequences. There are some circumstances concerning which you have had no choice whatsoever. You could not choose your parents, and you could not choose the nation into which you were born. You could not choose the date of your birth or the world situation into which you were born. The past has been formed by the choices made by your parents and your response or reaction to these choices. Now a new door is opening for you. A new era is beginning. You will enjoy more freedom in the future than you have in the past. With this new freedom will come a great increase in responsibility. I hope today that you are mature enough to accept responsibility for your choices.

The new world you face can be exciting and satisfying. The road you choose will lead to your destiny. Your responses to circumstances will determine your decisions. It is only proper that your pastor and your parents come to this day with prayers for you.

I. We pray that you will choose to serve God rather than mammon.

"Ye cannot serve God and mammon" (Matt. 6:24). We live in a secularized world where the scientific approach to life is emphasized. Great emphasis is placed on achieving material success.

A Hindu merchant in Hong Kong was observed burning a candle before an image at the beginning of the business day. Inquiry revealed that he was making a sacrifice to the money god. He believed that the money god could give him financial success. He declared that this was the first thing on his agenda each morning. The world's strong emphasis on economic success would encourage you to live your life dedicated fully and completely to the search for mammon.

A. *Live for something more than profit.*
B. *Live for something more than position.*
C. *Live for something greater than power.*
D. *Live for something more than privilege.*

II. We pray that you will choose to sow to the Spirit rather than to the flesh.

"Be not deceived; God is not mocked: for whatsoever a man soweth, that shall he also reap. For he that soweth to his flesh shall of the flesh reap corruption; but he that soweth to the Spirit shall of the Spirit reap life everlasting" (Gal. 6:7–8).

A. *In our flesh we are kin to the animal kingdom.*
B. *In our mind and soul we are related to God.* While living in the flesh, in the world, we must recognize that our higher nature is in the realm of the Spirit. We are something more than intelligent animals walking around on two feet.

The person is made in the image and likeness of God. He has an inner hunger that cannot be satisfied with anything except a knowledge of and a relationship to the Creator God.

As you give attention to preparing your mind, do not forget your soul. Determine that you will not be content with a childhood concept of God. As your knowledge of the world increases, make certain that your knowledge of God deepens and grows.

III. We pray that you will choose to enter the narrow gate of disciplined living rather than the broad way of shallow drifting.

" 'Enter through the narrow gate. For wide is the gate and broad is the road that leads to destruction, and many enter through it. But small is the gate and narrow the road that leads to life, and only a few find it" (Matt. 7:13–14 NIV).

A. *No one becomes a scholar automatically or accidentally.* Scholarship is the result of a desire that is followed by a decision to make diligent inquiry and comprehensive study of some field of knowledge. This requires discipline.

B. *One does not become an outstanding athlete accidentally.* One may possess a wonderful physique and have splendid muscular coordination. However, these do not constitute athletic prowess.

C. *One does not become a medical doctor merely because he has desire.* Desire must be matched with decision and discipline. To follow the course of study that leads to a medical degree requires that one eliminate many available electives and options.

The mighty minority who achieve significance are those who live a disciplined life. Jesus speaks of the gate being small and the way being narrow that leads to the abundant life. He has reference to that narrow gate of decisiveness and the disciplined life of dedicated living. No one can become a dedicated Christian apart from the discipline that makes the will of God the top priority of life.

IV. We pray that you will choose to serve rather than to be served.

"For even the Son of man came not to be ministered unto, but to minister, and to give his life a ransom for many" (Mark 10:45).

How do you define success? Do you think in terms of stocks and bonds, farms and property? Do you think in terms of a beautiful home and the latest model automobile? Do you define success primarily in terms of the things that you can acquire and enjoy?

If you want to find the highest success possible, you must do so by defining success in terms of service to others. Jesus warned his disciples against the error of thinking of greatness in terms of exercising authority and control over others. He said, "Whosoever will be great among you, let him be your minister; and whosoever will be chief among you, let him be your servant" (Matt. 20:26–27). Jesus paints for us a word picture of a man who thought of success in terms of being served rather than serving. The rich farmer was eminently successful in planning and following a procedure that produced an abundance of material things. These things made it possible for him to be served by others. The divine verdict is that this man followed a policy of foolishness because he thought only in terms of himself. He forgot God, he forgot others, and he forgot eternity. He was living to be served rather than to serve (cf. Luke 12:15–21).

V. We pray that you will choose the will of God as the road map for life.

"Thy kingdom come, Thy will be done in earth, as it is in heaven" (Matt. 6:10).

A. *The will of God is not something to be avoided at all cost.*

B. *The will of God is not something that we must endure with dread.*

C. *God's will is all-inclusive and comprehensive, and it leads to the highest possible joy and achievement in life.*

D. *God's will is always ultimately best for us and best for others.* God is a good God. He loves us to the extent that he gave his Son to die for us on the cross. All of his purposes and plans for us are purposes of love. To find the will of God for your life is life's greatest discovery. To do the will of God in your life is life's greatest achievement.

Conclusion

As you face the future, I would suggest to you that Christ is the way for you. He is the way out from the guilt and from the power of sin. He is the way through an unknown, uncertain tomorrow. He is the way to abundant life, to the life that leads to the highest possible usefulness and happiness. Christ is the way to the Father. In all of your ways acknowledge him, obey him, follow him, and trust him.

SUNDAY EVENING, MAY 27

Title: On Helping to Reduce Controversy

Text: "God ... gave us the ministry of reconciliation" (**2 Cor. 5:18 NIV**).

Scripture Reading: 2 Corinthians 5:16–21

Introduction

Certain conflicts are of the essence of life and cannot be avoided. They should be faced honestly and realistically. We have an opportunity today to create a world community where people will relate to others on the basis of justice and brotherhood to a greater degree than we have known before. But for such a world to become a reality, our sharp controversies will have to be reduced. The Christian faith offers some help.

I. First, heartrending controversy will be reduced if we see that reconciliation with the adversary may offer greater dividends than victory over him.

The apostle Paul said, "God gave us the ministry of reconciliation." What would happen if Christians were to put reconciliation in place of primacy? Our nation's self-defense and domestic war on crime are unrealistic goals apart from reconciliation. We must strive for reconciliation first of all with God, then with ourselves and others.

II. Second, controversy can be reduced when we concentrate on the causes of trouble rather than declaring war on the symptoms.

Understanding and dealing with the causes of our troubles is more important than punishing the offenders. We, and especially people in policy-making positions, need to know what provoked the trouble. What fosters drug abuse and violence? As ambassadors of Jesus Christ, we need to go to the root of the trouble and deal with individuals in love and in the power of the Holy Spirit.

III. Third, controversy will be reduced when we think in terms of redemption rather than destruction.

Jesus saw his enemies in a wholly new way. His enemies were not very different from those abroad in our world. There were zealots about him who said, "Better dead than Roman." Jesus responded by saying, "If a Roman forces you to go one mile, go with him two miles."

Jesus does not ask us to minimize or gloss over the evil in the enemy. He makes the assumption that the enemy can be changed; therefore, we should find out how to do it. He is not to be destroyed; he is to be redeemed.

IV. Fourth, controversy will be reduced when Christians see themselves as imperfect.

This is the easiest proposition to evade, for we can point to the evil in others to distract attention from ourselves. No man and no nation find it easy to admit being part of the problem and not a part of the solution. Personal relationships often are fractured on the rocks of self-righteousness. One historian has said, "If we get rid of arrogance, we can get rid of war."

Conclusion

Reconciliation to God is our basic need. Without it, we are estranged from God. With it, we are reconciled to God and to our fellow humans. Nothing less can take us safely across the seas of misunderstanding.

WEDNESDAY EVENING, MAY 30

Title: John Wrote to Recommend Perseverance

Text: "I write these things to you who believe in the name of the Son of God so that you may know that you have eternal life" (**1 John 5:13 NIV**).

Scripture Reading: 1 John 5

Introduction

John addressed his letter to those who already had put faith and trust in Jesus Christ as the Son of God. This experience of faith and trust brought them into the family of God (1 John 3:2). As the children of God, eternal life was a present possession for them (1 John 5:11–12).

In our text, John is insisting on the continuing nature of a genuine faith in Jesus Christ. Genuine faith must be thought of as something that continues in the present as well as being something that was exercised toward Jesus Christ in the past. The New English Bible translates our text as follows: "This letter is to assure you that you have eternal life. It is addressed to those who give their allegiance to the Son of God."

John declares, "The victory that defeats the world is our faith, for who is victor over the world but he who believes that Jesus is the Son of God?" (1 John 5:4–5 NEB). Is yours a continuing faith? A growing faith? A faith that produces victory in your own heart and life?

I. We must trust Christ to take care of the past (1 John 2:1–2).

Christ died for our sins. He was our substitute on the cross. He bore the penalty of our guilt (Isa. 53:5–6).

II. We must trust Christ in the present.

Christ has promised to be with us in all of our ways and throughout all of our days (Matt. 28:20).

In declaring himself to be the Light of the World, Jesus promised those who would follow him that they would not walk in darkness but would enjoy the light of life (John 8:12). By his Spirit he guides us and directs us in our choices from day to day.

The apostle Paul faced life in the confidence that he could adjust himself in a victorious manner to a variety of different circumstances. He was persuaded that Christ would help him in all circumstances.

We must trust Jesus Christ in the present for deliverance from the power and practice of sin even as we trust him for deliverance from the presence of sin in the future.

It is just as necessary that we trust Jesus today for full salvation in the present as it is that we trust him for salvation from the past and salvation in the future.

III. We must trust Christ to provide for the future.

No one can know what the future holds. The only thing certain about the future, from a human standpoint, is its uncertainty. The believer is to face the future with faith in Jesus Christ rather than with a fear that paralyzes and frustrates.

A. *Christ has promised to be with his followers to the end of the age (Matt. 28:20).*

B. *Christ sought to comfort his apostles with a precious promise concerning the home at the end of the way (John 14:1–3).*

By its nature, the Christian life is a life of faith that expresses itself in faithfulness to Jesus Christ.

Conclusion

John encouraged faith in Jesus Christ because of what Jesus had already done for those who would trust him, for what he was able to do in the present for and through those who would trust and obey him, and because of what Jesus Christ is able to do in the future.

Christ is dependable and trustworthy. Trust him fully.

SUGGESTED PREACHING PROGRAM

JUNE

- ### Sunday Mornings

    Continue with the theme "Seeking to Be Christian in Our Home Life."

- ### Sunday Evenings

    The messages for Sunday evenings this month are directed to professing followers of Christ. An appeal is made to practice what we profess. "When the Church Is Really the Church" is the theme.

- ### Wednesday Evenings

    The messages are based on four warnings found in the First Epistle of John. "Words of Warning from the Apostle of Love" is the theme.

SUNDAY MORNING, JUNE 3

Title: The Door to Abundant Living

Text: "I am the door: by me if any man enter in, he shall be saved, and shall go in and out, and find pasture" (**John 10:9**).

Scripture Reading: John 10:1–10

Hymns: "For the Beauty of the Earth" Pierpoint

"Happy the Home When God Is There," Ware

"Let Jesus Come into Your Heart," Morris

Offertory Prayer: Heavenly Father, you have given us your love. You have revealed your love in the gift of your Son Jesus Christ. We experience your love day by day through the abiding presence of your Holy Spirit. You have blessed the labors of our hands. Today we return to you a tithe and an offering of our love to indicate our gratitude. Bless these gifts to the proclamation of your love and mercy to the ends of the earth. In Jesus' name we pray. Amen.

Introduction

Jesus' role is likened not only unto a shepherd but to a gate and its keeper. Jesus claims to be the doorway into the presence of God.

In John 9 we have a record of how the Pharisees cast the man who had been born blind out of the temple because he was speaking words of appreciation and commendation of Jesus Christ. By that action they were claiming that the temple with its traditions and rituals was to be the door into the presence of God.

Christ came saying, "I am the door." He claims the authority to determine who will be members of the flock of God. He is in control of both the membership and the ministers within God's church.

Christ claims to be the doorway into abundant living. By the word *abundant*, he places emphasis on quality rather than on mere quantity. Eternal life is more than everlasting life. Eternal life is the very life of God, fullness of life in the here and now as well as in the future.

I. Christ is the Door out.

Jesus defined his ministry in terms of "preach[ing] deliverance to the captives" (Luke 4:18).

A. *Christ is the door out of the slavery of sin.*

B. *Christ is the door out of the condemnation that sin brings (John 3:17–18).*

C. *Christ is the door out of the worst possible failure. No one likes to be a loser.* The worst failure that one can experience is spiritual failure: "For what shall it profit a man, if he shall gain the whole world, and lose his own soul?" (Mark 8:36).

D. *Christ is the door out of a destructive, negative attitude toward oneself.* Many people are rejecting themselves and are guilty of thinking destructively concerning themselves. Our Lord would lead each one out of attitudes that are negative and destructive by revealing the extent of his love for us.

II. Christ is the Door through.

A. *Christ is the way through an uncertain future.*

B. *Christ is the way through the desert of difficulties that may be before us.*

C. *Christ is the door through the curtain of death.*

III. Christ is the Door in.

A. *Christ is the door into divine sonship (Gal. 3:26).*

B. *Christ is the door into true significance.*

1. Christ reveals our worth in the eyes of God.

2. Christ reveals the value of our soul.

3. Christ reveals the extent to which God was determined to save us. A number of years ago, a man lost his life during the wintertime on the golf course. He attempted to retrieve a golf ball from the surface of a frozen lake. The ice collapsed, and he fell into the frigid water. Before help could arrive, he perished. He did not intend to sacrifice his life to retrieve a golf ball. Christ, however, deliberately gave his life to retrieve us from sin.

C. *Christ is the door into perfect security.*

1. Through Christ we can enjoy security in the present.

2. Through Christ we can enjoy security in the future.

IV. Christ is the Door up.

A. *Christ is the door up to the highest possible manhood and womanhood that we can experience in life.* If you were to look for the most queenly women and the most kingly men on earth, you would find them among those who are the followers of Jesus Christ.

B. *Christ is the door up to God.* There are many evidences for the presence and power of God that are discernible in nature. However, if one would come to know God as Father, he must do so in and through faith in Jesus Christ.

C. *Christ is the door up to heaven.* There is only one way to heaven. That way is Jesus Christ. Jesus said, "I am the way, the truth, and the life: no man cometh unto the Father, but by me" (John 14:6).

Conclusion

If the temperature is frigid and if one is in danger of freezing, he must do something more than just know where the door to warmth is. He must enter the door. If a storm is coming and there is a great threat of a downpour of rain, one needs to do something more than just know where the door to security is. He needs to enter the door. Christ comes and declares that he is the door to all that is finest and best in life and that he is the doorway to God.

The Christ who is the door comes to the door of our heart. He wants to come in and occupy the deepest zone of our being. As we let him come in, he becomes the doorway through which we enter into fullness of joy and into the very life of God.

SUNDAY EVENING, JUNE 3

Title: Since the Church Is of God

Text: "He destined us in love to be his sons through Jesus Christ, according to the purpose of his will" **(Eph. 1:5 RSV)**.

Scripture Reading: Ephesians 1:3–10

Introduction

In one of Charles Schulz's *Peanuts* cartoons, Lucy shouts, "Do you understand?" Linus puts his hands over his ears and says, "Yes. I understand! You don't have to yell at me!" Lucy reflects. "Perhaps you're right.... Perhaps I shouldn't yell at you so much, but I feel that if I talked to you quietly as I am doing now [and again she shouts], you'd never listen!"

This is reminiscent of generations of robust, aggressive, evangelical Protestant preaching. The practice of "laying the truth on the line" and turning up the volume is not to be downgraded if done with integrity. Most of us have heard the story of the preacher who wrote on the margin of his sermon notes, "Weak argument—get louder here." Christianity is more than something to be *preached* and something to be *heard.* Kierkegaard pointed this out: "Christianity, by becoming a direct communication, is altogether destroyed. It becomes a superficial thing, capable neither of inflicting wounds, nor of healing them."

We who have been redeemed through Jesus Christ are the church of God, and therefore it is our responsibility to go beyond "turning up the volume" when presenting God's Word. When we become Christians, we step into a sacred community where we are to serve others. The church is of God, not of human origin.

I. Since the church is of God, we should not resist self-examination.

The quaint old church on Main Street or in the suburbs, U.S.A., is facing many crises. The church has been a captive church swallowed up in a middle-class culture. Often it has acted as if its sole task is to do whatever the world wants done and to do it on the world's terms. Afraid to live in terms of its own integrity, the church adopts what has been called a "flirtatious response," trying to con the world into noticing its presence by all kinds of tricks.

In Robert Bolt's drama *A Man for All Seasons*, the concluding scene has the Common Man step to the edge of the stage just after the godly Thomas More has been beheaded for defying for conscience' sake the wrathful Henry VIII. The Common Man says to the stunned audience: "I'm breathing.... Are you breathing, too?... It's nice, isn't it? It isn't difficult to keep alive, friends—just don't make trouble—or if you must make trouble, make the sort of trouble that's expected."

Here is our problem, at least in part. Any trouble the church has caused modern society is the kind that is expected, like passing resolutions at conventions. Jesus came to bring a sword, but we have been busy pin-pricking. Jesus overturned the tables of the money changers in the temple, but we have only hinted gently that they might be offending God. Lukewarmness often is considered virtuous; economic and social application of the gospel is sometimes rejected as subversive, as though communist inspired. Ministers, in far too many instances, have unwittingly sold out in the defense of an oppressive status quo and then wondered why their members ask, especially before the new wears off, "Have you heard our fine preacher?" Our Christian fathers in the first century did not flinch at the charge that they "upset the world"! What heirs we have turned out to be! We cannot bring ourselves to upset the apple cart, let alone the world.

Self-examination is necessary for the church in each generation. Some good and exciting things are taking place now as a result of such reflection. More good things ought yet to come.

II. Since the church is of God, it must learn and remember what God wants it to be.

The New Testament records the early Christians' convictions about the purpose of the Christian life, community, and witness. It is more of a shout of joy than a closely reasoned theological argument. It invites people to come and see what God has done in Jesus Christ.

In the opening sentences of Paul's letter to the Ephesians, he is refreshing the memory of his readers of their joy in their newfound faith, and then he gives this reason for it. "[God] destined us in love to be his sons through Jesus Christ … for he has made known to us … [his] plan for the fulness of time, to unite all things in him" (Eph. 1:5, 9–10 RSV). God is summing up all things in Jesus Christ; he is bringing all things into clear focus in him. All things, as they are brought into their true relationship with him, also are brought into their true relationship to one another and so into an all-embracing harmony.

These early Christians meant business when they said they had found God in Christ or had been found by God in Christ. The one whom they called Lord was Lord in fact as well as name, not only of their lives but of the entire universe. Such a saving experience and such a sense of mission ushered them into a community, the church, under the guidance of the Holy Spirit. The church is not a chance creation of a group of people who happened to make up their minds that they wanted to stand for certain things. They found a mission for living and the strength to carry that mission to the ends of the earth. We belong to the church not simply when our names are on the membership book but when we feel deeply a part of the power of the love of God that brings all things into focus in Jesus Christ.

III. Since the church is of God, it calls for and is deserving of our love, loyalty, and support.

Conclusion

When you choose Christ in such a way that he truly becomes the center of your life, you put yourself in the sphere where you not only act but are acted upon. This kind of living is not passive. It goads you to your best and haunts you at your worst. It summons you up into what you could be and to forgive what you have been. It invites you to compassion and brings pain upon you. It bids you laugh at your own insignificance; it gives you a sense of your own importance. It calls you into the lives of the unlovable; it enables you to get along without their love. It drives you to the heart of sorrow; it puts you alongside joy as well. Since the church is of God, be a part of it.

WEDNESDAY EVENING, JUNE 6

Title: Beware of the Profession That Does Not Produce Practice

Text: "And hereby we do know that we know him, if we keep his commandments. He that saith, I know him, and keepeth not his commandments, is a liar, and the truth is not in him" (**1 John 2:3–4**).

Scripture Reading: 1 John 2:1–11

Introduction

John uses strong language to tell us that we should be highly suspect of our profession if it does not produce practice. John is not suggesting that we apply this test to others; rather, he is giving us a checklist by which we may test the genuineness of our own relationship with God.

He is warning us against the peril of self-deception. He would save us from the great disappointment of spending eternity away from God because we put faith in a profession that did not result in practice.

The unbelieving world has no confidence in a profession of religion that does not result in practice. Sermons that walk around in shoes and express themselves in action are far more convincing than a mere articulation of words.

I. A profession of faith is essential.

By a profession of faith, we identify ourselves as believers. We commit ourselves to Jesus Christ and separate ourselves from unbelievers. We take our stand with God and declare our intention to do his will.

The importance of a profession is seen in the words of our Lord. "Whosoever therefore shall confess me before men, him will I confess before my Father which is in heaven. But whosoever shall deny me before men, him will I also deny before my Father which is in heaven" (Matt. 10:32–33).

Our Lord spoke also concerning the worthlessness of a profession of faith that was empty and superficial and did not lead to the doing of the will of God: "Not everyone that saith unto me, Lord, Lord, shall enter into the kingdom of heaven; but he that doeth the will of my Father which is in heaven. Many will say to me in that day, Lord, Lord, have we not prophesied in thy name? and in thy name have cast out devils? and in thy name done many wonderful works? And then will I profess unto them, I never knew you: depart from me, ye that work iniquity" (Matt. 7:21–23).

II. The practice of our profession.

John encourages his readers to place great faith in their profession, providing it expresses itself in at least two different ways.

A. *Keeping the commandments of God.* In this epistle great emphasis is placed on the significance of a deep inward desire to obey the commandments of God. The word "commandment" appears fourteen different times in these five short chapters. John insists that you can test the genuineness of your profession of faith and you can become assured of a vital, living relationship with God only if you find deep within your heart a sincere desire to be obedient to all of his commandments.

We should give more serious and prayerful consideration to the commandments of God. These are not the biased rules of a capricious God. The commandments of God are revelations of the great spiritual and moral principles that undergird the universe itself. One who ignores, violates, or transgresses the commandments of God does so to his own destruction. To be disobedient to the laws of God brings destruction in the realm of the spirit comparable to the destruction wrought in physical life when one ignores the laws of gravity and jumps off a cliff.

B. *Loving our brother.* This entire epistle places emphasis on giving expression to our faith in a genuine love for our brother. One who makes a profession of knowing Jesus Christ but does not practice a love for his brother is self-deceived (1 John 2:9–11).

    Our love for our brother and sister is not to be limited to a vocal expression of affection. John calls for a practical demonstration in benevolent care on the part of one who makes a profession of faith (1 John 3:16–18). He advises that we reexamine our profession of faith if it does not express itself in practical ministries of mercy toward the unfortunate, for by such ministries we indicate our kinship with God. The absence of a social and economic expression of our profession of faith indicates that we are self-deceived and in great danger of entering eternity without a saving faith in Jesus Christ.

Conclusion

    Is your profession of faith a profession that proves itself in your practice? Are you a living, walking, serving sermon? Does your walk match your word? If so, rejoice and praise God. If not, reexamine and reevaluate your spiritual condition. Perhaps you have never been born again. Perhaps you have drifted and need to rededicate yourself and begin living a life that would be pleasing to the Lord whom you once trusted but whom you since have neglected.

SUNDAY MORNING, JUNE 10

Title: The Challenges before Us

Text: "And Caleb stilled the people before Moses, and said, Let us go up at once, and possess it; for we are well able to overcome it" **(Num. 13:30)**.

Scripture Reading: Numbers 13:26–33

Hymns: "Come, Thou Almighty King," Anonymous

          "Have Thine Own Way, Lord," Pollard

          "I Would Be True," Walter

Offertory Prayer: Our Father in heaven, we rejoice that our Savior came into this world to rescue us from the waste and disappointment of sin. Today we give of ourselves that others might come to know him as their personal Savior from sin and as a wonderful companion for the road of life. Accept and bless these tithes and offerings that others might hear the gospel and respond by faith so that your name might be honored and glorified. In Jesus' name we pray. Amen.

Introduction

    The story of Moses sending the twelve spies into the Promised Land is one of the most thrilling incidents in the Bible. Their report, split ten to two, may well be a parallel of today's church members. Would we say that only two out of twelve are really faithful Christians?

When the ten gave their report, they created such confusion in the camp that it was with great difficulty that Joshua and Caleb were able to get the floor to present the minority report. Their faith in the power of God and his ability to help people should inspire Christians everywhere to dedicate themselves completely to the Lord and trust him for the results. I see six wonderful challenges in the report of Joshua and Caleb.

I. The challenge of cooperation — "Let us."

A. *Working together is the key to success in any endeavor.* The job is too great for a few, so "let us" do it together — teamwork.

B. *Cooperation made Pentecost possible.* "And when the day of Pentecost was fully come, they were all with one accord in one place" (Acts 2:1). What if that had been in our day when the 120 had gathered in the Upper Room? The record would be something like this: "The meeting was called for the first day of the week, but so many things interfered, that of the company of 120 only 40 could be present. Peter and his wife had bought a cottage on Lake Galilee and were away from the hot city over the weekend. Bartholomew had guests and, of course, could not come. Philip and his family had been up late the night before and overslept. Andrew had a business conference about a new fishing boat. James had to stay home and cut the grass." Result? No Pentecost!

II. The challenge of activity — "Go."

A. *Cooperation says, "Let us go."* There is action — something to be done. It was Sunday morning in the Doe household. The parents were not interested in the church and its program, but they wanted their son to have the advantage of the church's activities. The mother had dressed little Joe for Sunday school. On the way out, he paused in front of his dad as he sat before the TV in his sweats and T-shirt, coffee in hand. "Dad, may I ask you a question?" "Sure, son," he replied. "When am I going to get old enough not to have to go to church either?" The father hesitated a moment then said, "Wait a minute, son, and I'll go with you." Without a doubt, that was the right answer — "Go."

B. *Look into another home:* A little girl with shining eyes and face all aglow said, "Daddy, it's almost time for Sunday school. Let's go." "Oh no," said Daddy, "not today. I've worked hard all week, and I must have one day of rest. I'm going down to the river where I can relax. The fish will be biting today. Now run along; don't bother me. We'll go to church another day." Months and years roll by, but Daddy no more hears that plea, "Let's go to Sunday school." Those childhood days are over, and Daddy is growing old. Life is halfway through when he finds time to go to church. But what does his daughter say? She says, "Not today. I stayed up late last night, and I just have to get some sleep. Besides, I look a fright."

C. *Should parents insist that their children go to Sunday school?* Yes. How do you answer Junior when he comes to breakfast Monday morning and announces rebelliously, "I'm not going to school today"? Junior goes! What about when he comes in dirty and says, "I'm not going to take a bath"? Junior takes a bath! How do you answer when Junior gets sick and says, "I'm not going to take medicine." Junior takes it! Why then are some parents timid in the area of their children's spiritual guidance and growth? Are you going to let your child wait and decide what church to go to when he is old enough? Quit kidding! You didn't wait until he was old enough to decide whether he wanted to go to public school or until he made up his mind whether he wanted to be a clean or healthy person. What should you say when Junior announces that he does not like Sunday school or church? Just be consistent. "Junior, in our home we all attend Sunday school and church, and that includes you." Your firmness and example here will furnish a bridge over which youthful rebellion may travel into rich and satisfying experiences in personal Christian living.

III. The challenge of advance — "Up."

A. *One of the greatest challenges America has ever had is before us now — winning the world for Christ.* The world is becoming more pagan each year. The challenge to total commitment to service for Christ is before us.

B. *To go "up" means work — lots of it — and I believe that Christians are capable of it if they set their minds to doing it.*

IV. The challenge of urgency — "Now."

A. *Years ago a prominent American Christian asked a native Chinese, "Why has Christianity lost to communism in your country?"* The studied answer was, "Because the Communists have a philosophy, a program, and a passion." They believe in something, they plan how they may appeal to others, then they work with a passion, even to giving their lives. Christianity has the first two — a philosophy and a program, but tragic beyond words is our absence of *passion.* The apostles had it: "Beaten ... they departed ... rejoicing that they were counted worthy to suffer shame for [Jesus'] name" (Acts 5:40–41).

B. *Our philosophy is infallible truth.* Our program is divine. Our passion is such that we have to plead for our members to attend worship regularly on the Lord's Day. If one-third of the members agree after high-pressure preaching to give 10 percent of their income, we count it success. No wonder so few members lead anyone to Christ in their lifetime. When our passion for Christ and his cause is sufficient to produce the practice of "he that loseth his life for my sake shall find it" (Matt. 10:39), then Christianity will overcome the world.

C. *Somewhere among your acquaintances there is someone who has not taken Christ as personal Savior.* Somewhere in our busy lives we have promised ourselves that sometime we will invite that someone to come to our church. But we have put it off or have forgotten that promise. For some of us, time is running out. Someday it will be too late to speak to that person about becoming a Christian. Either we may be gone or that someone may die before accepting Christ as Savior. Let us talk to that someone today and invite him to come to church and to Christ. "Let us go up now."

V. The challenge of conquest—"Possess the land."

A. *Isn't it wonderful to accomplish something—to get it done?* Most church members who find fault, who are unhappy, who find so many things to clutter up their lives, who stir up trouble, and the like have themselves to blame. They make excuses when they ought to make good.

B. *It is easy to quit, but it is often difficult to keep on going when the going is tough; that makes a real man or woman. Joshua and Caleb said, "Let us go possess the land."* Beloved, let us enter on a spirit of conquest for God. Let us resolve that with his help we are going to do our share in reaching people. Let us not be making excuses when we ought to be making good.

VI. The challenge of ability—"We are able."

The ten spies said, "They are too big for us. We can't do it." Joshua and Caleb answered, "We are able, for we have God on our side." What do you say?

Conclusion

The experiences of Joshua and Caleb and the subsequent results of entering the Promised Land should inspire all of us to trust the Lord to do what he promises. Victory is ours.

Sunday Evening, June 10

Title: On Knowing a Church by Its Fruit
Text: "By their fruit you will recognize them" **(Matt. 7:20 NIV).**
Scripture Reading: Matthew 7:15–23

Introduction

Jesus once said that people are like trees: they can be judged by their fruit. "Are grapes gathered from thorns or figs from thistles?" he asked. "So, every sound tree bears good fruit, but the bad tree bears evil fruit.... Thus you will know them by their fruits" (Matt. 7:16–20 RSV).

"Fruit" is more than outward acts; it is inner motives relentlessly showing themselves in the course of time by word and conduct. Fruit grows slowly, but it loudly proclaims the tree. Thus, the test is one of inner and outer Christlikeness proved by time—the eyes of Christ being the judgment. "Fruit" is a major term in the New Testament, and while it includes works, it must never be equated with outward works. The tree is judged good or bad according to the kind of fruit it produces. The bad tree is not a rotten one, but the wrong kind. The word is used in the parable of the net in Matthew 13:48. The bad fish are not diseased, but the wrong kind, inedible.

These words of Jesus about the danger of false teachers are somewhat surprising. We might have expected him to say, "You will know them by their beliefs, their interpretations of texts, their fidelity to creeds. Or you will know them by the company they keep or the way they baptize." But not so. He said we could distinguish the false prophet from the true one by his fruit, by the temper he displays, by the spirit that he manifests, by the character that he reveals, by the deeds that he does, by the life that he lives. Paul wrote to the Galatians, "The fruit of the Spirit is love, joy, peace, patience, kindness, goodness, faithfulness, gentleness, self-control" (5:22 RSV).

A man who prides himself on his orthodoxy but is uncharitable, bitter, and hard is a dangerous man. Certainly we should attach importance to right beliefs, but keep in mind Jesus' warning, "Many will say to me in that day, 'Lord, Lord, did we not prophesy [preach, teach] in your name, and cast out demons in your name, and do many mighty works in your name?' And then will I declare to them, 'I never knew you; depart from me, you evildoers'" (Matt. 7:22–23 RSV).

People are like trees, Jesus said; they can be judged by their fruit. Churches are people, and if people are like trees, so are churches. We know them by their fruit. Great churches produce great fruit, and by examining the fruit, we learn about the church. Our Lord's church is a world-embracing fellowship of those who acknowledge Jesus Christ as Lord and seek to be his followers. The church exists to be the carrier of the gospel of Christ; a church is or is not a church in the fullest sense to the degree that its members are faithful to this mission.

To be a carrier of the good news of Jesus Christ is a many-sided task. It takes many forms and requires that many channels be opened. How can we know if a church is becoming what our Lord expects? By its fruit. What fruit, then, does a good church produce?

I. The first fruit of a good church is worship.

A church announces its worship times, and we usually refer to these times as worship services, a rather odd use of words in the opinion of some people who define the words as somewhat opposites and say that a person cannot do one while doing the other. As I see it, the words *worship* and *service* are not contradictory—they go together properly. A Christian congregation unites in a "service" of worship not primarily to serve themselves and go away feeling better after "getting a lift," but to serve and honor God. This by no means excludes the call to the service of others, which, beginning at the house of worship, should extend out into daily life in the workplace and home. Yet it is quite different from worship as a psychological exercise, the inducing of a meditative mood for a pleasant feeling of well-being. The Greek word *leitourgia*, from which the word *liturgy* is derived, though it can be applied to any corporate service of worship, is itself derived from words that mean "public work." Not only does this suggest that the worship of God is a form of service, but the word for "public" suggests that the whole people of God—ministers, choirs, and congregations alike—are to do something about it.

Regrettably, the worship service of the church for some people is nothing but a strange interlude between getting the children ready for Sunday school and cooking the Sunday dinner, or between reading the newspaper and taking an afternoon nap. It is the process of sitting back and watching the ministers and the worship band perform. And when this is the case, we judge the worship service as we judge a motion picture or a baseball game. Is it a good show or isn't it? Has it been entertaining or hasn't it? Did we like the players or didn't we? And when the service is over, it may have been a pleasant meeting, a helpful talk, or a clever performance; but it certainly has not been worship.

The thoughtful Christian regards the worship of the church as both an attitude and an act. It involves an attitude of awareness, a conscious entrance into the presence of God as "the personal Spirit, perfectly good, who in holy love creates, sustains, and orders all." But it is more than attitude; it is action, too. It involves adoration of God's glory and thanksgiving for God's will. It involves confession of one's own sins, petition for one's own needs, and intercession for others.

II. A second fruit of a good church is evangelism.

Evangelism is the battle for souls and central loyalties. It is what Jesus intended when he told his disciples to let their light so shine before all that others might see their good works and give glory to their heavenly Father. It is what Jesus intended when he sent them out with the command to "preach as you go" and when he commissioned them to "make disciples of all nations." It is what Jude meant when he urged the early Christians to "contend for the faith."

Evangelism is telling the truth about God with a persuasiveness designed to win people to his fellowship. It is proclaiming the glad tidings of Jesus Christ in the hope of helping people to understand that the victory over sin, which people could never win for themselves, is daily being won for them by one who was crucified long ago.

Evangelism takes many forms. There is a place for mass evangelism through the voice and appeal of a Christian evangelist who views this as his particular calling, providing it is done with integrity and without hysteria. Evangelism is also a quiet pastor in a church service, a teacher in a Sunday school room or at a social, a parent talking to a child, a workman talking to his friend, a college student chatting with her peers, or young people sharing their thoughts and feelings—with a view to winning people to a commitment to Jesus Christ the Lord. Evangelism is the outward probing of the church as the church invades the world with the good news of God's love.

III. A third fruit of a good church is education.

It is a major function of a church to appropriate, understand, and transmit its Christian heritage, applying the eternal truths of the gospel and the funded wisdom of the past to the contemporary needs of persons. The major source of this Christian heritage is the Bible, and many churches try to make the study of the Bible as comprehensive and helpful as possible through the work of the Sunday school.

Christian education involves the stimulation of human growth in its highest and noblest forms—the enlightenment of the mind, the kindling of the heart, the drawing out of the real person. The tragedy is that often such programs are devoted to entertaining trivialities or to themes that are wholesome in themselves but have no basic Christian rootage—such as sports, flower arranging, or quilt making. The fruit of education coming from a good church provides an opportunity to see and understand the world as God has made it. It requires probing after truth, rejoicing when truth has been found, and gladly sharing with others both the riches of the gospel's past and individual contemporary discoveries that tell us that God is still at work among his people.

IV. A fourth fruit of a good church is service.

James put it this way, "If a brother or sister is ill-clad and in lack of daily food, and one of you says to them, 'Go in peace; be warmed and filled,' without giving them the things needed for the body, what does it profit? So, faith by itself, if it has no works, is dead" (2:15–17 RSV). Henry Drummond said, "To grow up in complacent belief that God has no business in this great groaning world of human beings except to attend to a few saved souls is the negation of all religion."

The church has no right to ignore human suffering and need. When it sees injustice, it must rebel; when it confronts deprivation, it has compassion. Wherever human need exists unmet, a church too proud to try to meet it is dead. The need may be to improve poor housing conditions, or to help a person find a job or get legal counsel, or to help a child feel wanted. In other words, we are to give a cup of cold water in Jesus' name.

V. A fifth fruit of a good church is fellowship.

Some would say that fellowship should come first, but I think the last place is its rightful place—not because it is unimportant, but because it is quite superficial unless its roots are in the soil of worship, evangelism, education, and service. We can have fellowship in almost anything we do, from climbing mountains to collecting antiques, but the only fellowship that marks a great church is the fellowship of men and women who are doing the Lord's business through that church.

Conclusion

According to these fruits, what can we know about our church? Is it a good church?

There are some blossoms on the trees; and if warmth of concern and sunshine of work, prayer, and cooperation are provided, good fruit can be harvested.

WEDNESDAY EVENING, JUNE 13

Title: Beware of the Lure of the World

Text: "Love not the world, neither the things that are in the world. If any man love the world, the love of the Father is not in him. For all that is in the world, the lust of the flesh, and the lust of the eyes, and the pride of life, is not of the Father, but is of the world. And the world passeth away, and the lust thereof: but he that doeth the will of God abideth for ever" (**1 John 2:15–17**).

Scripture Reading: 1 John 2:12–21

Introduction

John wrote to help his readers avoid the disaster of being lured to destruction by the world.

I. The world against which John warns us.

John uses the term "the world" more than all the other New Testament writers combined. He uses this term seventy-nine times in his gospel and twenty-three times in 1 John. Curtis Vaughan has stated that this term

> has at least three different significations in the Johannine writings: (1) It is used of the world of nature, the created order, the material universe (John 1:10; I John 4:17). This world, with its changing seasons, majestic mountains, restless seas, and verdant fields, is a thing of beauty and is to be acknowledged as such by Christians (cf. Ps. 8, 19 et al.). (2) It is used of the whole human race thought of as a world fallen into sin and in need of redemption. This world God loves (John 3:16); He feels its burdens and is sensitive to its needs (I John 2:2; 4:9). (3) It is used of unbelieving, pagan society thought of as a rebel order embodying the influences and forces hostile to God (I John 5:19; John 14:30; 15:18–19; 16:30). John saw this world ranged in opposition to the people of God and threatening their very existence on the earth. It is this world which the Christian is not to love. (Curtis Vaughan, *I, II, III John* [Grand Rapids: Zondervan, 1970], 53)

II. The appetites of the world.

A. *The lust of the flesh.* We are warned against living solely for the gratification of our earthly nature. Here the word "flesh" stands for our human nature as corrupted by sin. "Lust" refers to the unlawful and sinful desires produced by our lower nature. We must not live merely for the satisfaction of the appetites of our lower nature.

B. *The lust of the eyes.* We must guard against living for and loving that for which our eyes crave, that which brings satisfaction and gratification to the eye. Temptation often comes to us through seeing that which appeals to the lower nature and that which would bring gratification to human pride.

C. *The pride of life.* We must guard against that which makes a contribution toward the proud display of life. We must not live for vainglory and for the vain grandeur that the world has to offer. We must not live for the glamour of a pretentious life.

III. The devil's offer of the world.

In our Lord's temptation experience, the devil offered to him all the kingdoms of the world and the glory of them providing he would fall down and worship him (Matt. 4:8–10). Jesus resisted this temptation and declared that one must worship God only and nothing less than God.

The devil uses the world today to tempt the children of God in an effort to lead them to spiritual destruction. Perhaps the following considerations can assist us in rejecting his offer of the world to us.

A. *The world is perishing.* The words of our text declare it. The world is not permanent. It will not last forever. Only those who do the will of God will abide forever.

B. *The world does not really satisfy.* The securing of wealth, the enjoyment of pleasure, or even the earning of honor do not satisfy the deepest hungers of the human heart.

C. *The world is something that you will leave behind you at the day of death.* You cannot take the world with its appetites and ambitions with you to heaven. The treasures of the world are not the treasures of heaven.

D. *The world is dangerous.* That is the whole point of our text. We need to recognize that the world would capture our imagination, monopolize our energy, and lead us away from God.

Conclusion

This world is not our home. We are only passing through. We must beware lest we fall into a trap set for us by the devil. Slowly but surely he would use the world as bait to lure us further and further away from the will of our loving Father.

It is in the world that we serve God and seek to win people to faith in Jesus Christ. It is not the will of our Lord that we be taken out of this world at this time but rather that we should live in this world a victorious life of worship, witness, and service (John 17:15–17).

SUNDAY MORNING, JUNE 17

Title: "Your Father Which Is in Heaven"

Text: "If ye then, being evil, know how to give good gifts unto your children, how much more shall your Father which is in heaven give good things to them that ask him?" **(Matt. 7:11).**

Scripture Reading: Matthew 6:6–15; 7:1–11

Hymns: "God, Our Father, We Adore Thee," Frazer

"O God, Our Help in Ages Past," Watts

"Jesus Is Tenderly Calling," Crosby

Offertory Prayer: Our heavenly Father, help us to see how richly and abundantly you have bestowed your blessings upon us. Help us to recognize your loving purpose in all of the events that happen and all of the gifts that you bring into our lives. Help us to accept life as a trusteeship. Help us to prove our love with lives that are dedicated to your glory. Bless the gifts that we bring today for the advancement of your kingdom. In Jesus' name we pray. Amen.

Introduction

On this Father's Day we can most profitably give consideration to "our Father … in heaven." *Father* is the supreme name for God.

The name *Father* occurs in the Gospels more than 150 times. The term *Father* is in the first recorded utterance of Jesus: "Didn't you know I had to be in my Father's house?" (Luke 2:49 NIV), and Jesus used this title for God in his last dying cry: "Father, into your hands I commit my spirit" (23:46 NIV). Jesus placed his main emphasis on helping his disciples to accept and to respond to the God who reveals himself as a loving Father. To grasp this understanding of the nature of the eternal God can impart faith to our hearts. It can create love and motivate service.

What kind of Father is the God whom Jesus came to reveal?

I. Our heavenly Father loved with a perfect love (Matt. 5:45, 48).

A. *The love of God finds its source in the nature of God rather than in the loveliness of his children.*

B. *God loves us in spite of our sins (Rom. 5:8; 1 John 3:1).* Sometimes in a performance-oriented society, we drift into the erroneous idea that somehow we must merit the love of the heavenly Father. This we can never do outside of faith in and response to the lordship of Jesus Christ.

The eternal God continues to love the unlovely with a perfect love.

II. Our heavenly Father is instantly available at all times (Matt. 6:6).

A. *We can enter into the throne room of God's gracious presence at any time we are willing to recognize him as both Lord and loving Father.*

B. *The practice of pure religion and worship should be natural and regular rather than formal, stilted, and unnatural.*

III. Our heavenly Father rewards his obedient children (Matt. 6:6).

A. *Much is said in the New Testament about the rewards that the heavenly Father bestows on his children for their faithfulness and obedience.*

B. *Jesus affirms that the heavenly Father always hears the prayers of his children.* Some people doubt this. Perhaps this is because they fail to recognize that God's answer may be yes or no or it may be "not yet." Sometimes the wisdom of the loving Father declines our request because that which has been requested would prove to be harmful. Sometimes the answer is "not yet" because we are not equipped to manage or to utilize that for which we request.

C. *God's greatest rewards are inward and spiritual.* They are invisible to the naked eye of the beholder.

IV. Our heavenly Father chastises his children (Heb. 12:6–13).

A. *The heavenly Father will not condone or tolerate sin in the life of his children without chastening them.* He does this for the good of his children as well as for the advancement of his kingdom.

B. *God chastises us in order to produce spiritual growth and fruitfulness (Heb. 12:10–11).*

C. *As the children of God, we need to recognize and respond positively to the chastisement of the heavenly Father (Heb. 12:5, 12–13).*

V. Our heavenly Father provides for his children (Matt. 6:26).

A. The heavenly Father makes ample provisions for the sparrows.

B. The heavenly Father clothes the lilies of the field in all of their beauty.

The heavenly Father can be trusted to provide his children with the necessities of life. The sparrows work, but they do not worry. The lilies perform their function and send forth their fragrance and beauty into the air. God takes care of them, and he will take care of us.

VI. Our heavenly Father forgives sin (Matt. 6:12, 14–15).

A. *Our heavenly Father is eager to forgive sin.*

B. *Sin in the life of the child of God affects his fellowship with God and with others.* It hinders his service and deprives him of heavenly rewards. God is eager for each of his children to sit in judgment on their sins and to renounce them and forsake them. When we come to look at our sins as God looks at them, he grants us his forgiveness and cleansing.

C. *We must be forgiving toward those who sin against us if we are to experience God's free and full forgiveness.*

VII. Our heavenly Father gives good gifts (Matt. 7:11).

A. *The gifts of the heavenly Father are always good.*

B. *The gifts of the heavenly Father are always appropriate.*

C. *The gifts of the heavenly Father are always perfect.*

Conclusion

Every day should be Father's Day. "This is the day which the LORD hath made; we will rejoice and be glad in it" (Ps. 118:24). We should give to our heavenly Father our complete trust and faith, a warm and steadfast love, a glad and enthusiastic obedience.

Jesus Christ is the way to the Father (John 14:6). We can see the majesty, the mystery, and the power of God in nature. It is only in Jesus Christ that we learn of his love and of his merciful Fatherhood. Come to God this day through Jesus Christ. Let him become your Father.

SUNDAY EVENING, JUNE 17

Title: A Christian in Politics

Text: "You shall love the Lord your God ... and your neighbor as yourself" (**Luke 10:27 RSV**).

Scripture Reading: 1 Peter 2:13–17

Introduction

"Politics is a dirty business"—the old American shibboleth lingers on. The notion that politics is dirty is as persistent and universal as government itself. Simply to mention the word is to evoke visions of corrupt payoffs, dishonesty, and evil scheming. There seems to be no need to prove that politics is dirty, because all people simply accept it. For late-night talk show hosts, it is always open season on politicians.

Public opinion surveys have revealed that while most parents would be pleased if their child became a senator or president, few approved of the idea of their child becoming a "politician." Bizarre tales of the downfall of churchmen who dared to enter the arena are available as documentation. How often have we heard, "He may be a good man when he enters politics, but if he gets in office he won't be good long." So the response to a Christian being in politics generally is negative. Consequently, it has been observed that while saints are engaged in pious introspection, burly sinners run the world.

Such assumptions, thoughts, and actions that would divorce Christianity from politics are wrong, disastrously wrong. It weakens government and increases probabilities of corruption in high places, and it makes Christianity an irresponsible escapism devoid of the courage and moral fiber so characteristic of Jesus of Nazareth. There are some good, solid reasons why Christians should be in politics. Before coming to that, though, one should try to understand first that the notion that politics is dirty is a myth.

I. The notion that politics is dirty is a myth.

If politics is dirty, why do we never hear it said that democracy is dirty? Politics is the process by which people govern themselves in a democracy. In the sense that all humankind is dirty or sinful, it is true that the politician is dirty or sinful. By the same wrong reasoning, you could say that banks or schools or businesses or churches or hospitals are dirty because sinful people run them. But the myth implies that only politics deserves this label.

The myth persists for two reasons. One is simply that the work of politicians and governmental officials is far more visible to the public than that of most other occupation groups. City councils, state legislatures, the Congress, and various commission and board meetings are required by law to be open to the curious gaze of the public, including prospective opponents at the next election. This is not true of meetings of bank directors, corporation executives, labor unions, or church deacons. It is "operation goldfish bowl" for the government but not for most other segments of society. I am not suggesting that any of this should be changed, but recognition of it should explain at least in part the unfavorable image reserved for politics.

A second reason the myth that politics is dirty persists lies in our double standard of morality. We condemn behavior in politicians and other public officials that we take for granted in everyone else. When a company gives a free trip to Bermuda to a governmental official, we cry "dirty politics" but not "dirty business." It was the businessman who offered the bribe or payoff, but only the politician receives the stigma. Gift giving is an acceptable business practice, sometimes in the form of trips, from suppliers to business purchasing agents, justified as developing goodwill. But gifts to government purchasing agents are considered corruption and bribery.

Take, as another example of our double standard, the instance of the son of a doctor or lawyer or businessman being brought into the profession or business. He is given a healthy head start and is pushed gently but inevitably to the top. We expect this, and few, if any, eyebrows are raised. In fact, we rather admire the family loyalty and togetherness. But what if a government official should do this for his son, especially in his particular division of government? We do not comment on family loyalty but cry "nepotism."

The process of running government, that is, politics, is no more dishonest or dirtier than the process of running a factory or store, a bank or school, or even a church. Because of its life in a goldfish bowl, the governmental process may actually be a bit cleaner and more honest than the process of running most other social institutions.

II. A Christian in politics? Yes, if you want to be true to the full implications of your Christian faith.

Christian commitment, commitment to the lordship of Jesus Christ, means involvement in, not withdrawal from, all the great issues of life. Jesus said that we are the salt of the earth and the light of the world. Salt does not do any good if it is kept in the sack on the shelf. Light does not prevent stumbling if it is kept under wraps. "Thou shalt love the Lord thy God with all thy heart, soul, mind and strength. This is the first and great commandment. And the second is like unto it: Thou shalt love thy neighbor as thyself" (Luke 10:27).

What does it mean to love one's neighbor in the kind of world we live in today? Jesus taught that we should feed the hungry, clothe the naked, give drink to the thirsty, and minister to the sick. Millions of Americans, Asians, Africans, and Latin Americans are starving and in need of clothing and medical attention.

As long as there is need, Jesus' teaching remains in force. Christians with hearts of compassion constantly will be seeking ways to help the illiterate to read. They will help the sick to become well and the well not to become sick, the economically disadvantaged to learn how to earn a living. They will seek to help victims of racial discrimination find open doors, children to grow up somewhere other than in rat-infested slums, and all people to be free from the ravages of war.

Giant evils are abroad in the world. Major causes of human suffering are disease, war, poverty, unemployment and underemployment, exploitation, racial discrimination, population explosion, and pollution. In many ways, one's love of neighbor is still shown by one individual to another. The story of the good Samaritan is reenacted by individuals and local churches. But these giant evils are too complex for this alone. Governmental action against these giant evils has become one practical way to work for the accomplishment of certain of the ethical teachings of Christ. Politics is the art and science of government, the process of determining who gets what, when, and how. It is the process of translating social pressures into public policy and concrete action.

This process could not function without power. To speak disparagingly, therefore, of all "power politics" is to reveal a serious lack of understanding of political realities. Political power in its best sense is the ability to put a policy into effect and to fit that policy into a concrete program. The government of a community, state, or nation maintains a preponderance of political power. It cannot tolerate any group within it with more power than itself. The moment any group emerges with more power than the government, it immediately becomes the government. To separate power from politics is like separating cold from ice.

A Christian in politics? Yes, emphatically yes, if you want to be true to the full implications of your Christian faith.

III. A Christian in politics? Yes, but be alert to the hazards.

There is real difficulty in many instances in knowing how, as a Christian, one can relate the law of love to the world of politics. On the one hand, we can see Christian love, *agape*, represented by Christ on the cross — utterly self-sacrificing, self-giving, other-regarding love. On the other hand, we see the calculating world of politics, where *accommodation*, *negotiation*, and *compromise* are the words we characteristically use to describe how a course of action is determined. How can one be true to the selfless Christ on the cross and have anything to do with the process of political horse trading?

Space and time do not permit an attempt to answer the question here other than to point it out as a hazard. I would observe, too, that the core and agony of the dilemma is in any group decision process including the family and the church. To stay out of the political arena because it is hazardous would be to sin against this love that motivates us.

A. *There is the hazard of evil compromises.* Not all compromises are evil. Where democracy prevails, no one can have his own way entirely. Personal liberty has to be compromised. Absolute liberty would produce anarchy. Interests conflict, and good people with the finest intentions may differ widely in their value judgments. Choices have to be made about what programs and projects will benefit or suffer from the amount of money available. Conflict, controversy, and compromise are simply hard, cold realities in the kind of world we live in. To turn away from them is to turn away from cross-bearing.

Some compromise is evil, however. To compromise one's Christian convictions by misrepresenting the condition of a car when selling it, or withholding vital information that would alter the outcome of a business transaction or public project is clearly wrong. One ought to be committed to honesty, to the public welfare, to a way of loving and caring. One ought to be committed to objectivity insofar as it is humanly possible, getting all the necessary facts available that bear upon the matter at hand before reaching a conclusion. Compromises in these things are evil, and admittedly, it is often a thin line between the evil and the good.

B. *Another hazard in politics to which the Christian should be alert is the wrong use of power.* While power politics is essential, its purpose is not principally to keep one in power. This primary method of getting things done has as its main purpose the public good.

C. *Another hazard is in the assumption that since one is a Christian he always has the best or right solutions and answers.* The Christian may be more sensitive to human aspects of the situation than the expert, and he may be helped by his faith to ask deeper questions than the expert is likely to ask. But this sensitivity and this questioning cannot take the place of expert knowledge and specific experience. For example, Christians might agree that this nation's farmers need a fairer chance for an income commensurate with their hard work and investment. But the Christian faith as such cannot give the technical answer about what types of farm price-support programs Congress should pass, if any.

D. *Another hazard to a Christian being in politics is the temptation to use and adapt his political skills to vent his prejudices.* Many sad stories from the American political scene would fill volumes on this subject. Not only is there hazard of venting one's own prejudices through political activity, but there is the ever-recurring temptation to gain advantage for one's candidate or candidacy by appealing to the prejudices of the voters. Thus, one group is pitted against another group—city dwellers against country people, rich against poor, labor against management, white against black, South against North, Midwest against East, ad infinitum.

E. *The hazard of idolatry.* Political activity can be allowed to become one's first love. The political arena can replace the church, and one's image as the people's choice may be that before which one bows down to worship.

Conclusion

Dr. Foy Valentine, in his book *Citizenship for Christians* ([Nashville: Broadman, 1965], 82), has pointed out that religion and politics do not mix in the sense "that the gears of the church ought not to engage the cogs of the state, and vice versa." They do mix in the sense that spheres of concern and action have some overlapping. A Christian, then, should become informed on the issues and vote intelligently. Some Christians should run for office. Some should work with special interest groups. All Christians owe their highest loyalty to God.

WEDNESDAY EVENING, JUNE 20

Title: Beware of False Prophets

Text: "Beloved, believe not every spirit, but try the spirits whether they are of God: because many false prophets are gone out into the world" (**1 John 4:1**).

Scripture Reading: 1 John 4

Introduction

John wrote his epistle from the perspective of a loving pastor concerned for the welfare of his spiritual children. He was eager to help them find fullness of fellowship and joy in their faith. He was eager to warn them against the teachings of false prophets who were posing a serious threat to the very life of the Christian faith.

Gnosticism is the name given to the philosophy and system of ethics that threatened to destroy the ideas that undergird the Christian faith. This system of heresy was a combination of Greek philosophy and Oriental mysticism. This philosophy held that only the spirit of man is good and that all matter is evil. The Gnostics believed that the God of light was spirit and that he did not create a world in which evil existed. This philosophy posed a threat to Christianity that was both theological and ethical. The Gnostics did not believe that God could possibly become flesh because flesh was considered to be evil. Consequently, they denied the incarnation. This erroneous doctrine also had ethical implications that were contradictory to the teachings of Christ. The Gnostics did not believe that there was a vital relationship between the spirit and the flesh, that the actions of the flesh in any way affected the spirit. Consequently, there was no emphasis on righteous conduct among the Gnostics.

The Gnostics treated Christianity as they would have treated any other religion—they accepted and sought to absorb it. They sought to give it new content.

The Gnostics claimed to know God and to belong to God. They taught that one entered into relationship with God through esoteric knowledge that was communicated by those who had been initiated into the various secrets of the cult.

I. The teachings of the false prophets.

A. *The false prophets taught that the Messiah did not become flesh (1 John 4:2–3).*
The Gnostics believed that the Messiah came upon Jesus the man at his baptism and left him before his crucifixion. They believed that Jesus was

199

just a man and that it was impossible for the eternal God of light to clothe himself in human flesh.

Throughout this epistle John declares and affirms that Jesus Christ, the promised Messiah, became flesh and lived among men (cf. 1 John 1:1–2).

B. *The Gnostics did not connect conduct with their creed.* John insists that there is an inseparable relationship between what we believe and how we should live (1 John 2:6). John warns against any erroneous doctrine that would separate creed from conduct. He declares that genuine Christianity expresses itself in ethical conduct similar to the conduct of the Christ.

II. Testing the spirits.

A. *In our text, John is warning his readers against being misled by the teachings of false prophets.* It is interesting to note that he places responsibility on the listener for determining whether the prophet is a true or false prophet.

A prophet was one who claimed to speak for God. John gave one great test that was to be applied to those who claimed to be a spokesman for God: "Every spirit that confesseth that Jesus Christ is come in the flesh is of God" (1 John 4:2). This was a direct attack on Gnosticism. John was saying that you can differentiate between the true and the false by the attitude they have toward Jesus Christ.

B. *Jesus warned against false prophets.* He emphasized the test of the fruit of their teaching (Matt. 7:15–20). The good prophet's message produces good fruit. The false prophet's message produces evil fruit.

C. *The apostle Paul warned against false apostles who were the incarnation of Satan himself (2 Cor. 11:13–15).*

The devil uses false prophets today to deceive and mislead. He seeks to communicate erroneous concepts of God to the minds of people. He seeks to lead us astray in our conduct and to encourage us to accept the wrong goals for life.

Conclusion

There are voices about us that would encourage us to live the secular life and to forget God. They declare that one can sin and escape suffering. There are voices that affirm that if you would find the full, happy life, you can do so by smoking a particular brand of cigarette, wearing a certain brand of clothing, carrying a certain model of cell phone, or drinking a suggested brand of beer. There are voices that make no claim to speak for God, yet they claim to offer solutions to the ultimate problems and questions that confront humans. In a real sense, these voices are the voices of false prophets.

Each of us needs to examine our concepts of God in the light of the teachings of the Word of God. We need to examine our conduct by the example and teachings of Jesus Christ. Each of us needs to go into the closet of prayer that we might hear the still, small voice of the Spirit of God. These habits can help us to escape being misled by a false prophet.

SUNDAY MORNING, JUNE 24

Title: God's Good Earth

Text: "The earth is the LORD's and the fulness thereof: the world, and they that dwell therein" (**Ps. 24:1**).

Scripture Reading: Psalm 24:1 – 10

Hymns: "Praise Ye the Lord, the Almighty," Neander

           "The Spacious Firmament," Addison

           "This Is My Father's World," Babcock

Offertory Prayer: Our heavenly Father, we come now to bring our tithes and offerings to you. Help us to recognize the necessity of giving our total selves to you. Help us to place all that we are on the altar in sincere worship. Help us to give our minds, hearts, hands, and energy. We offer to you our tongues that we might praise your grace and that we might tell the story of your love to others. Bless these gifts to the advancement of your kingdom, to the relief of human suffering, and to the salvation of souls. In the name of Jesus we pray. Amen.

Introduction

A number of people rejoiced greatly many years ago when there seemed to be a groundswell for an annual observance of Earth Day. It is time for all of us to take a good look at what we are doing to the land in which we live, the water we drink, and the air that we breathe. Extended drought conditions in Southern California led to restrictions on the use of water that meant a change in lifestyle for millions of people. Oil spills like the Exxon *Valdez* incident in Alaska and the British Petroleum oil rig explosion in the Gulf of Mexico have destroyed natural resources and imperiled wildlife.

A farm boy became greatly disturbed when the lovely river near his home became the dumping place for industrial waste. The creosote content was so strong that the fish were no longer edible. Such has been repeated in many rivers across the country.

One evening a father was planning a trip for his family. When he discovered he did not have adequate maps, he remembered that his child had a globe that might be helpful. He went to the child's room to secure it, and as he was tiptoeing out, he was detected by the child, who saw the globe by the light in the hallway. He sat up in bed and said, "Daddy, what are you doing with my world?" The boy's question to his daddy is an appropriate one to each of us. Whose world is it, and what are we doing with it?

Many answers have been suggested to the question, "Whose world is it?"

I. The earth is the earth's.

There are some who believe that the earth is but an accident in the universe without a creator and without a divine sustainer. According to these materialistic evolutionists, the earth came from nowhere and is not going anywhere. It is nothing more than just a wonderful accident.

II. The earth has been claimed by the devil (Matt. 4:8–9).

In our Lord's experience of temptation, he was confronted by the devil with an offer of the kingdoms of the world as a gift on condition that he fall down and worship him. The devil was claiming the power to be able to give the world to him if he would reject his divine mission.

Jesus speaks of the devil as being "the prince of this world" (John 12:31). Paul speaks of the devil as "the god of this world" (2 Cor. 4:4). The devil is a usurper. If he is the prince of this world and the god of this world, it is because he has laid claim to that which belongs to God. If he is the prince of this world and the god of this world, it is because people have given him that position.

III. Communists believe that the earth belongs to the state.

A. *The right to hold or to own property is said by communists to be the basic evil that has plagued the world.* Consequently, in the communist system there is no ownership of property and no right of inheritance.

B. *In this system, the mind, the soul, and the body of a person are to be regulated and controlled by the state.*

C. *Because of terrible tyranny in the economic, political, and religious realms, communist revolutionaries rejected both religion and the right to own property.* They deified the state and gave to it the authority that belongs only to God.

IV. Some believe that the earth belongs to humanity.

A. *Laws have been established regulating the rights of ownership and trusteeship as far as property is concerned.*

B. *The Bible recognizes and safeguards people's right to the fruits of their labors.*

The world is so beautiful and so desirable that there are some who give to it the worship that belongs only to God. A question raised by Jesus is appropriate at this point. "What shall it profit a man, if he shall gain the whole world, and lose his own soul?" (Mark 8:36).

We need to beware lest we be overcome with a covetous spirit that would cause us to define our purpose for being in terms of acquiring material things. In the parable of the rich farmer, whom God called a fool, Jesus seeks to warn us against the peril of living for earthly values alone (Luke 12:13–21).

V. The earth is the Lord's.

The tense of the verb in our text is of great importance. It declares that "the earth *is* the Lord's." It does not declare that "the earth *was* the Lord's at the Creation." Neither does it affirm that "the earth *will be* the Lord's during the millennium." It does not even say that "the earth *would be* the Lord's if man had not stolen it." It affirms that the earth is the Lord's *now*. This may sound absurd to you, but it is true.

A. *God is the Creator of the earth.*

B. *God is the Lord, the controller, and sustainer of the earth.*

C. *God is the owner of the earth and all things therein.* There never has been a time when a "For Sale" sign has been placed on the earth. The implications of this truth are of great significance. This means that my body, my mind, my possessions, my relationships, and my business belong to God.

D. *God is the Judge of the world (Acts 17:31).* Scripture tells us that when God created the earth, he "saw that it was good" (Gen. 1:10). The great Creator God has given us freedom.

With the gift of freedom we must assume responsibility and trusteeship for our actions in the world God has made. We are responsible not only to society, but also to God for the way that we live in and treat his world.

E. *God is the redeemer and the restorer of the earth.*

1. Christ came to redeem the world (John 3:16).
2. The last book of the Bible paints a picture of the time when there will be a new heaven and a new earth (Rev. 21:1). Sin will have been removed, and the curse of sin will be no more.

Conclusion

The God of grace and mercy is eager to cleanse us from the pollution of sin. He is eager through Jesus Christ to cleanse our minds and our hearts from the evil taint of sin. He is eager to put purity and the cleansing of heaven in our hearts now. He holds out to us a promise of an eternal home that will be free from the pollution of sin (Rev. 21:27).

The earth is the Lord's. All who dwell on the earth belong to him by right of creation. His ownership should be recognized and responded to. Through Jesus Christ people can find their way into the presence and favor of God.

SUNDAY EVENING, JUNE 24

Title: The Risks Involved in Being Religious

Text: "You are the salt of the earth" (**Matt. 5:13 NIV**).

Scripture Reading: Matthew 5:13–16

Introduction

Once a large city church with an ambitious recreational program attracted young people from other churches through its swimming pool, bowling alley, gym, and other athletic facilities. One boy's parents and pastor became concerned and persuaded him to return to his own church. The boy, with some reluctance, was explaining to the youth director and friends why they would not be seeing him around the recreation-centered church again. He concluded his explanation with a question spoken in sadness and disgust, "Ain't religion hell?"

And sometimes that is the way it is. Religion can, on the one hand, be unpleasant and distasteful, or on the other hand, it can be attractive and strengthening. The term *religion* has a wide variation of meaning. Some published sermon titles, for example, are "God versus Religion," "Let's Have Less Religion," "Can Religion Save Us?" "Vital Religion," "Folk Religion and Biblical Faith," "Personal Religion," ad infinitum.

How we regard religion depends on where we stand, which way we look at it, and how we define it. There are risks involved in talking about religion—the risk of being misunderstood and the risk of being understood. The term *religious* is used in this message in the sense of living a sincerely dedicated Christian life. There are risks involved. The danger is that we will mistake the forms of Christianity for Christianity itself, go through the motions but miss the meaning, or lose our awareness and appreciation of the ultimate values to which we give outward homage.

This risk was recognized by the prophets. God's message came through Amos to the people of his day: "I hate, I despise your feasts, and I take no delight in your solemn assemblies.... Take away from me the noise of your songs; to the melody of your harps I will not listen. But let justice roll down like waters, and righteousness like an overflowing stream" (Amos 5:21, 23–24 RSV).

The writer of Ecclesiastes, whose faith never quite overcomes his fears that all of life is a "vanity of vanities," has this admonition on watching carefully our spirit in our acts of worship: "Guard your steps when you go to the house of God; to draw near to listen is better than to offer the sacrifice of fools; for they do not know that they are doing evil" (5:1 RSV). In other words, we who handle or come close or live close to holy things must take care lest we substitute repeated forms and patterns for the real thing.

Jesus compared the formal religious life of the Pharisees to whitewashed tombs—outwardly beautiful, inwardly full of dead men's bones. But he also warned Peter, James, and John, and the other disciples to beware lest their own faith should lose its sharpness and vitality: "You are the salt of the earth; but if the salt has lost its taste...."

Some of you may have difficulty with this metaphor because you know that chemically pure salt is always salt. Pure sodium chloride does not deteriorate. But Jesus' words must be interpreted in their original setting to get the full force of what he meant. The salt with which Jesus was familiar was a crude composite such as would be familiar on the shores of the Dead Sea or the Mediterranean Sea. This salt could be so adulterated as to be essentially lost. A great deal of it would not be salt at all, but other crude material. Piles of it would be out in the open, and rain might wash the salt out and there would be nothing left but the dross—with no true saltiness left. Such residue was absolutely worthless.

Jesus is saying that mild religion, far from being of partial value, is of utterly no value. We may continue to go through the motions; we may continue the structure, the system, the program, the institution, and the organization. But eroded religion is of no value at all.

Consider more specifically these risks that are involved in being religious:

I. First, the risk of growing insensitive to God in public worship and in private living.

We may be regular church attendees, and we may be able to repeat the Lord's Prayer with the congregation without a bobble. We may sing the hymns and go through all the forms and parts of the worship service and still have little or no awareness of God. We can be present but quite insensitive to what God is trying to do. Our conscience would bother us if we did not pay our respects to God at fixed times and places. But the hands of our watches drag along so mercilessly slow, like something crawling through a desert of uneventfulness as though lame in both feet.

Ministers, choir members, ushers, Sunday school workers, and people who attend regularly may think of a worship service as something we put on for the benefit of others. We become merely professionals leading, or if you are in the pew, you are part of the props that enhance worship for others. So, while we are numbered with the religious, we find ourselves becoming onlookers or observers, mere critics of the message or the music, the messenger or the musicians, without examining ourselves in the light of the service's theme, without an awareness that God makes his way to our door and seeks entrance to our thoughts and lives. Whether we are ministers or laypersons, there is the ever-present inclination for those of us who attend faithfully to think of public worship as a time for others to be changed while we ourselves neither expect nor desire to be changed.

This same insensitivity to God may show up, too, in our personal devotional life. Because we are active workers in the church, we are used to living with the Bible—in the preparation of sermons, devotionals, and Sunday school lessons. We may not think it necessary that we feel the cutting edge of its message of judgment and reconciliation. And because we are required so often to pray or we join in the public prayer of another, we may lose sight of a need to approach our heavenly Father in privacy. The attitude "I keep prayed up" becomes the first step to the unconscious conclusion "I have no need for prayer."

A risk involved in being religious is that one may grow insensitive to God in public worship and in private living.

II. A second risk is insensitivity to people, to their suffering, their sins, their needs, and their possibilities.

We can make our church work (or other charitable and benevolent work) a substitute for coming to grips with the multitude of personal and social problems about us. Such outward, pretended love of God without concern for others is merely a rationalized, high-level form of self-love.

We know that Jesus was sensitive to persons—to blind Bartimaeus beside the road, to a desperate woman who touched the hem of his garment in a crowd, to another woman by a well, to Zacchaeus up a tree, and to little children in their mothers' arms. We know, too, that we as Christians are called to be sensitive to others and their needs. But even as we give ourselves to helping them, it becomes easy to "grow weary in well-doing" and to ease back on personal, costly involvement—mostly in time and energy and emotion, if not in finances. And so we find ourselves helping people in general and losing sight of persons in particular. We will hire people on the church staff to do it, or we will hire our denomination's mission forces to do it.

III. A third risk involved in being religious is insensitivity to opportunity.

When things are difficult on the local church scene or in our personal lives, we can easily allow ourselves to slip into complacency, find comfort in reliving the past, and thus miss today's opportunities. Or, if all things look rosy around us, we can become satisfied in our "blessings" and become unresponsive to the challenge of each new day. Past performance will not take the place of present needed action. Each day must find us wrestling with creative ways of witnessing for our faith in order that the gospel might go forth.

Conclusion

If we recognize the risks involved in our Christian faith and work, it will enable us to be more open to him who helps us to overcome. We can, then, be the salt of the earth, giving flavor to human relationships and that quality that preserves what is good.

WEDNESDAY EVENING, JUNE 27

Title: Beware of Idolatry

Text: "Little children, keep yourselves from idols. Amen" **(1 John 5:21)**.

Scripture Reading: 1 John 5

Introduction

The closing words of the apostle John may come as a shock to the casual reader. The writer assumes the role of a spiritual father giving counsel to his children. He warns them against the peril of giving first place in their love and loyalty to idols. Throughout the epistle he addresses his readers as believers and as followers of the Lord Jesus Christ. To these he says, "Little children, keep yourselves from idols." He tries to put them on the alert against accepting substitutes for the true God.

The New English Bible translates these words as follows: "My children, be on the watch against false gods." The Amplified Bible says, "Little children, keep yourselves from idols—false gods, [from anything and everything that would occupy the place in your heart due to God, from any sort of substitute for him that would take first place in your life]. *Amen. So let it be.*"

I. Modern idols.

An idol has been defined as anything that comes between the soul of a person and the true God. That which a person puts first in his life is his object of worship. When the true God does not have first place, we cannot escape from the truth that one has become an idol worshiper. Modern-day idol worshipers do not bow down before stone images. They are too refined and cultured for that.

A. *Have you made a god out of success?* Instead of desiring to be saints, some of us hunger for the privilege of being a success so that we can enjoy all of the gadgets our society has to offer. Success is defined in terms of material values and possessions.

B. *Have you made a god out of society?* Are acceptance and approval by the group of supreme importance to you? Are the decisions that determine your destiny made on your understanding of the will of God or on the basis of what the crowd wants you to do at the present?

C. *Have you made a god out of science?* Some say that only ignorant and lazy people will look to God for help. These people believe that modern man can solve his own problems and answer his own questions.

We live in a day in which science has performed feats that are almost miraculous in nature. However, in the final analysis, science provides us only with tools with which the mind can work. We need to let God tell us how to use these tools. Unless human minds are ruled by the Spirit of God, we may destroy ourselves with the discoveries of science.

II. Substitute gods cannot meet the deepest needs of life.

A. *Substitute gods are a poor substitute for the real thing.*

B. *Substitute gods are helpless in our time of deepest need.*

C. *Substitute gods will always disappoint in the time of need.*

D. *Substitute gods usurp the place that belongs to the true God.*

III. Worship the true Lord only.

John was encouraging his readers to beware of the peril of letting anything usurp the place that belongs to the Lord Jesus Christ who alone is worthy of our genuine worship.

A. *Christ alone can be depended on in all times and under all circumstances.*

B. *Christ alone is worthy of the supreme love and loyalty of the believer's heart.*

C. *Christ alone is the Messiah, the Savior who came to save us from sin.*

D. *Christ alone is the living Lord who deserves our supreme love and loyalty above country, above family, and above occupation.*

Conclusion

Beware of worshiping a substitute god. All substitute gods are false gods. The besetting sin of ancient Israel was the sin of idolatry. They let the nature gods usurp the place that belonged to the true God. Let us learn by their mistakes and refuse to follow their example. Let us give heed to this warning from the apostle of love and avoid the peril that is always present—the peril of giving to something less than God the love and loyalty that belong only to God.

SUGGESTED PREACHING PROGRAM FOR

JULY

■ **Sunday Mornings**

"Some of the Great Questions of the Bible" is the theme for a series of topical sermons that deal with questions that are relevant for the individual, the church, and our country.

■ **Sunday Evenings**

A series of topical sermons based on passages of Old Testament Scripture is suggested. The theme is "Old Testament Stories That Present a Christian Message."

■ **Wednesday Evenings**

"God's Eternal Purpose of Redemption" is the theme for the Wednesday evening devotional messages. They emphasize that while God's methods may change, his purpose has been constant through the ages.

SUNDAY MORNING, JULY 1

Title: What Makes a Nation Great?

Text: "Righteousness exalteth a nation: but sin is a reproach to any people" (**Prov. 14:34**).

Scripture Reading: Proverbs 14:12–34

Hymns: "My Country, 'Tis of Thee," Smith

"America the Beautiful," Bates

"The Star-Spangled Banner," Key

Offertory Prayer: Our Father, today we celebrate the independence of our nation. We are grateful for America, and we pray that you will bless our president and all those who lead us as a nation. We pray that you will receive the tithes and offerings we give to you. Bless them and use them for your glory. They are given from hearts of gratitude. In Christ's name we pray. Amen.

Introduction

The United States of America is a great nation. We have been preserved these many years by God. We have grown in numbers, wealth, and power. America has a surplus of the necessities of life and offers the freedom of opportunity. Truly we are a God-blessed nation. What has made America great?

I. A nation becomes great when that nation has the right kind of citizens.

The people of America have helped make America great.

A. *God-fearing citizens make a nation great.* Dr. J. D. Grey said in an address before a Kiwanis International Convention in Seattle, Washington, June 15, 1952: "The founders of our nation were, in the main, a God-fearing, God-honoring people. They were not the renegades, the back-wash, the off-scourings of the nations of Europe. Among the fifty-six signers of the Declaration of Independence, 47 of them were graduates of Christian colleges, eight of which were functioning in our land before 1776. But even prior to this, when the Pilgrims were about to land at Plymouth Rock, they bowed their knees before Almighty God in grateful recognition of His blessings upon them in bringing them to a safe harbor, and in that spirit they dedicated to Him their endeavors in this new land."

B. *Freedom-loving citizens make a nation great.* The people who came to the shores of America were people seeking freedom. The framers of the Constitution of the United States were freedom-loving people. America's name has been made glorious because our citizens are people who love freedom and want freedom for all people.

C. *Sacrificial-living citizens make a nation great.* In crises Americans have shed precious blood to protect America.

II. A nation becomes great when the citizens establish the right kind of institutions.

A. *Homes.*
B. *Churches.*
C. *Schools.*
D. *Businesses.*
All of these great institutions have contributed to America's greatness.

III. A nation becomes great when the citizens are righteous.

The writer of Proverbs said, "Righteousness exalteth a nation: but sin is a reproach to any people" (14:34).

A. *What are some of the evils that threaten America today?*

1. Atheism. Atheism manifests itself in many ways. Millions in America say they do not believe in God. Millions more claim they believe in God and Christ but live like pagans, ignoring God in their thinking, planning, and living.

2. Materialism. Many Americans have made materialistic objectives their goal. They spend their lives getting things.

3. Socialism. The equal distribution of the wealth of America is the *summum bonum* to the socialist. Equal rights before the law and a fair opportunity are not enough. Under socialism thrift is penalized and laziness is rewarded.

4. Alcoholism and drug abuse. Substance abuse in America has become a major problem. Social pressure, business pressure, and spiritual empti-

ness have caused many to become slaves of drink, prescription drugs, and illegal drugs.

5. Secularism. There has been a concerted effort in America to take God out of schools, government, and other areas of public life. One of the enemies of America is secularism.

6. Violence. H. H. Hobbs shared the following story: "A newspaper writer tells of going to a crowded theater in New York the night after Senator Robert Kennedy died. The movie glorified a man who delighted in shooting people in the head while they were on their knees pleading for life. As he put his gun to a horrified victim's head and pulled the trigger, the audience laughed. After killing a priest, someone in the film remarked, 'I don't like that. It is bad luck to kill a priest.' The audience laughed heartily as though it was viewing a comedy rather than a tragedy. What is happening to our world? We want blood, blood, and more blood."

Since that time television and movie violence has escalated dramatically. Violence threatens our nation.

7. Evil forces, demon forces, threaten America. Paul said, "The Spirit clearly says that in later times some will abandon the faith and follow deceiving spirits and things taught by demons" (1 Tim. 4:1 NIV). It seems as if satanic forces have invaded our nation. Heavy metal music and New Age mysticism seem to be the order of the day.

8. Humanism threatens America. Public schools and colleges and the media are propagating the idea that oneself is one's god. From this false teaching stem other evils such as abortion and euthanasia.

B. *What will save America from these evils and make us strong and great?* The writer of Proverbs has the answer for us—righteousness!

1. Righteousness is required by God. A nation will be punished for its sins. America must repent of its sins, because God requires righteousness.

2. Righteousness will bless a nation.

3. Righteousness is found in following Christ. National righteousness will follow where there is submission to Christ. We must repent of our sins and put our faith in Jesus Christ if we want to be righteous.

Conclusion

God will bless America if we turn to Christ, our only hope, our sufficient Savior.

SUNDAY EVENING, JULY 1

Title: Bring Back My Samuel

Text: "Then said the woman, Whom shall I bring up unto thee? And he said, Bring me up Samuel" **(1 Sam. 28:11)**.

Scripture Reading: 1 Samuel 28:7–11

Introduction

Conduct of many people within our nation makes pertinent the question: Can a democratic society survive? What were once hallowed institutions and respected offices have become objects of disrespect and scorn. When we reflect on what this "nation under God" would be without our founding fathers' great spirit of responsibility and freedom, one thought occurs: Are we letting our foundations for greatness and our hope for creative living slip from us?

King Saul was blessed with the great prophet Samuel. Samuel had been God's vessel through whom Saul was chosen as king. He had been available to assist Saul on every occasion. Because the people had praised Saul and his enemies had melted before him, he had no need for Samuel.

The day came when Saul's magic sword failed. Now he stole from the battlefield under cover of darkness and in disguise, headed for Endor. At Endor lived a witch who claimed to call up the dead. Saul begged of her, "Bring me up Samuel." He was saying: "Give me another chance to benefit from God's prophet." Let us learn before our Samuel is taken from us.

I. Fads cannot be substituted for foundations.

    A. *A country is not great today because of world popularity.*

    B. *A country is not great because of what it has done for her citizens.*

        1. Greatness consists in what individuals do for the common good.

        2. Government reflects people and their purposes.

    C. *A country is great because of the principles on which it was formed and the character of those forming it.* Our institutions are as strong as we who serve.

II. Economic and social adjusting cannot replace individual self-reliance.

    A. *Good government, as good churches, cannot be measured by what is done for its members.*

        1. Both are channels through which we serve.

        2. Both are institutions in which we grow.

        3. A healthy citizen serves rather than demands service.

    B. *There are nations and churches at Endor's cave.*

        1. Many hearts ache today in those who live under totalitarian rule. How they would love their freedom again.

        2. There must be deep sorrow in church leaders who have confused others in hearing God's clarion call.

    C. *What a multitude of individuals crowd about the witch's cave.*

        1. Unfaithful marriage partners.

        2. Dishonest business associates.

        3. Drunkards.

III. In God's grace we have our Samuel.

    A. *We have a chance to build a better world.*

    1. What generation has had so great an opportunity to influence others?

2. A restless world is begging for the answers.
    B. *The Christian church has never before enjoyed adherents with such wealth, education, and position.*
    C. *The witnessing Christian has never before had such tools to serve the living God.*

Conclusion

Try for a moment to hear Saul as he is winning his battles and someone says, "You need Samuel."

"Why?" he queries. "Samuel is an old, worn-out man [institution]. I'll always win. I have so many opportunities now that I don't know which to choose. I'm the greatest king and soldier alive. Why do I need Samuel?" Endor's cave is a humiliating trip for a spirit like that.

Today you need Jesus Christ. You have every reason to trust him. You have opportunity—this hour is yours. I pray that you will not reject him. I pray that you will not some day go to the witch's cave trying to call back a chance that is gone, trying to "bring up your Samuel."

WEDNESDAY EVENING, JULY 4

Title: God Chooses to Bless

Text: "Now the LORD had said unto Abram, Get thee out of thy country, and from thy kindred, and from thy father's house, unto a land that I will shew thee: And I will make of thee a great nation, and I will bless thee, and make thy name great; and thou shalt be a blessing: And I will bless them that bless thee, and curse him that curseth thee; and in thee shall all families of the earth be blessed" **(Gen. 12:1–3)**.

Scripture Reading: Genesis 12

Introduction

Does God have a purpose for the individual believer in today's world? Does God have a specific purpose for a local congregation of believers? If he has such a purpose, how is it to be discovered?

Both Old Testament Israel and the early church believed that the eternal God does have a purpose for individuals and for all humankind in today's world. This faith gave meaning and direction to life. To discover God's eternal purpose should be the desire of every believer.

The Old Testament is a testimony to the fact that God does have a purpose in the world. He is working out this purpose in and through his people. God's eternal purpose was first revealed to Abraham and then repeated to the patriarchs. It was restated through Moses to the nation of Israel and then interpreted and applied by the prophets. It came to fulfillment in the person and life of Jesus

Christ and is being continued through the church in the present. God will continue to work out his purpose until the Lord Jesus Christ returns.

I. God's sovereign choice (Gen. 12:1).

God first revealed his purpose of redemption to Abraham. By God's sovereign choice, Abraham was chosen as the point of beginning for the nation that would carry on God's purpose of redemption and salvation. We are safe in assuming that God chose Abraham because he was the most usable man available. Abraham was by no means perfect, but God chose him as an instrument for the accomplishment of his redemptive purpose in the world.

II. God's promise to his chosen servant (Gen 12:2–3).

In the revelation of God's purpose, there was a promise to bless the chosen. While the promise included protection, guidance, and material substance, the chief blessing to Abraham was spiritual.

A. *Abraham was to enjoy fellowship with God.*

B. *Abraham was to be God's coworker.*

III. God's commission to his chosen servant (Gen. 12:2).

With the promise of special blessings, God laid upon Abraham a heavy responsibility: "And thou shalt be a blessing." This is no mere statement of a fact; it is a divine command. Abraham was promised the blessings of God that he might be a blessing to others. God was declaring that with every blessing there is a corresponding responsibility and opportunity.

A. *The tragedy of Israel.* The descendants of Abraham laid claim to the promises of God but neglected to respond to the opportunities and responsibilities that went along with God's commission.

B. *The tragedy of the modern church. In many respects the modern church is making the same mistakes as did ancient Israel.* We want to claim the promises of God while neglecting to respond to the commission of our Lord to evangelize the whole world.

The promise of the presence of our living Lord to meet the deepest needs of our lives can be claimed only when we are living in obedience to his commission to carry the message of salvation to our individual world and to the big world in which we live (Matt. 28:18–20).

Conclusion

When God said, "In thee shall all the families of the earth be blessed," he was declaring that his loving purpose is all-inclusive and universal in application. At the beginning, God was determined to bless the whole world by means of his chosen servant Abraham and those who would follow in his train.

God's eternal purpose has not changed. He continues to desire to bless the whole world. He will bless those who cooperate with him in this eternal purpose of redemption.

SUNDAY MORNING, JULY 8

Title: Can We Have Revival Today?

Text: "And he said unto me, Son of man, can these bones live? And I answered, O Lord God, thou knowest" **(Ezek. 37:3)**.

Scripture Reading: Ezekiel 37:1–14

Hymns: "Revive Us Again," Mackay

"Lord, Send a Revival," McKinney

"Pentecostal Power," Homer

Offertory Prayer: Our Father, we are grateful for the privilege we enjoy of worshiping you today. We are grateful for the salvation we have in Christ our Lord. We bring our gifts out of hearts of gratitude and pray that they will be blessed and used by you. We give them not because you need them but because we love and adore you. Let us rejoice in the blessedness of giving. In Christ's name we pray. Amen.

Introduction

The weird picture so impressively presented in this Scripture passage is a picture of the children of Israel in Babylon. To properly understand the passage before us, we must recall the background to the passage. Jeremiah the prophet, in the city of Jerusalem, had preached the unpopular message of submission to the king of Babylon as the only way for Israel to survive as a nation. Zedekiah, the king, rebelled, and Nebuchadnezzar returned to put down the rebellion and brought an end to Judah. This took place in 587 BC. It was a tragic hour when the walls around the city were broken down, the houses burned, the temple destroyed, and additional people were dragged away into captivity.

Ezekiel and ten thousand exiles had been living in a concentration camp in Babylon. He began to serve as a prophet in 593 BC, and for six years he sought diligently to break down false hopes of an early return to Palestine and to prepare the people for the tragic news of the destruction of Jerusalem. With the temple and national life gone, God's people presented a pitiable picture. The people were as dead as dry bones scattered on the surface of a deserted battlefield. The people said of themselves: "Our bones are dried up and our hope is gone; we are cut off" (Ezek. 37:11).

What a tragic picture! Can Israel live again? With weirdness, with realism, and with drama, the prophet presents the heartening news that Israel may hope to live. Even dry bones, without sinew and flesh and blood, can live.

Can we have a revival today? Many say no. Others say, "Don't you know that the day of revivals is over?" Revivals are passé if we listen to others instead of to the Lord. Ezekiel's vision should teach us that we can have a revival; a revival is possible. Using Ezekiel's vision as a suggestion, let us note some revival truths.

215

I. The desperate condition.

A. *The dry bones of Ezekiel's day.* The people in the Scripture passage point out their desperate condition: "Our bones are dried, and our hope is lost; we are cut off for our parts" (Ezek. 37:11). In these words, we have the clarion condition of the people. There is death, despondency, and despair everywhere. Surely they needed a revival.

B. *The dry bones of today.* There are dry bones to be found in every church, and they are easy to recognize.

1. There are lazy bones in our churches. They will do anything to keep from going to work for the Lord.

2. There are jaw bones in our churches. They are always talking, rendering lip service. They talk much but do little.

3. There are wishbones in our churches. They wish others would do all the work. They wish others would give the money for the youth building or for some other undertaking.

4. There are skull bones in every church. They are the hardheads who will not and cannot be changed. They are satisfied if minor changes are made but are hardheaded about major changes such as new methods of teaching God's Word, new ways of doing the Lord's work, and new techniques in witnessing.

5. There are knuckle bones in every church. They take delight in criticizing all who try to work for the Lord. They rap, rap all the time.

6. There are backbones in every church. They are the nerve center of the church. They work for the Lord and get behind every church program and push until the work is done.

Can we have revival today? There is real need for revival today as there was in Ezekiel's day.

II. The divine course.

God has a way for everything. We would do well to heed and follow the course outlines for Ezekiel.

A. *"Prophesy upon these dry bones, and say unto them, O ye dry bones, hear the word of the LORD" (37:4).* Ezekiel was a God-called and Spirit-led prophet, and he must have shuddered at the appalling sight of dry human bones—"very many" and "very dry." Ezekiel said, "So I prophesied as I was commanded" (v. 7). Here we have the crux of the matter. "O ye dry bones, hear the word of the LORD" (v. 4). Madness? Yes! Insanity? Yes. He said to the bones, "Hear!" though they had no ears. To save our faces, we modify God's commands, and thus we lose face. Ezekiel obeyed God; and God, as always, responded. But note that Ezekiel did not mistake commotion for creation, action for unction, nor rattle for revival. "There was no breath in them" (v. 8). It was then that Ezekiel was told the next step in the divine course.

B. *"Prophesy unto the wind, prophesy, son of man, and say to the wind, Thus saith the Lord God; Come from the four winds, O breath, and breathe upon these slain, that they may live.* So I prophesied as he commanded me, and the breath came into them, and they lived, and stood up upon their feet, an exceeding great army" (37:9–10). When we prophesy as God commands, life will come to dry bones; life will come to defeated, despairing, despondent souls!

III. The delightful consequences.

The consequences of Ezekiel's prophesying are evident in the Scripture passage.

A. *The dead come to life (37:14).*

B. *God's people serve him (37:14).*

C. *God's people know that God is the Lord (37:6).*

The same thing will happen the day we proclaim God's Word and depend on the Holy Spirit to bring life to our words.

Conclusion

God has not changed; he has not lost his power; he is not dead. He is the same yesterday, today, and forever (Heb. 13:8). Let us ask God for a revival, and let us follow his directions for that revival.

SUNDAY EVENING, JULY 8

Title: The Call of the Blood

Text: "And when Hadad heard in Egypt that David slept with his fathers, and that Joab the captain of the host was dead, Hadad said to Pharaoh, Let me depart, that I may go to mine own country" (**1 Kings 11:21**).

Scripture Reading: 1 Kings 11:14–22

Introduction

David's great army trampled over Edom and in a short while put to the sword all its male population. Hadad was a child in the reigning family and would have died with the rest had not an old patriot secretly escaped with him to Egypt. Here he did well and gained favor to the extent that he married the queen's sister. He found contentment and prosperity in his position. All was excellent with his young son, Gennubath, and his devoted wife until one day news came that David had died and that the great soldier Joab had been slain. Immediately a great longing arose in Hadad to go back to his own people. A call of the blood which he could not deny or quiet seized him, and he cried, "Let me depart that I may go to my own country."

To all our lives come calls that shape our destinies by reason of our responses to them.

I. The call of temptation.

A. *Pharaoh pleads with Hadad, "What hast thou lacked with me?"*

217

1. For every noble thought to achieve, there is an accompanying thought of ease.
2. Paul observes, "The good that I would I do not: but the evil which I would not, that I do" (Rom. 7:19).

B. *Temptation is not always to do evil; sometimes it is not to do.*
1. Hadad did not complain of Egypt. Life there had been good.
2. Easy living cannot be a substitute for life's mission.

II. The call of memory.

A. *The voices that call across the years cannot be hushed.*
1. Hadad had never lost his view of the red cliffs of Edom nor forgotten the hushed silence of a night near the Dead Sea.
2. For a homesick Edomite boy, a king's palace can be a prison.

B. *The voice of memory may not be reasonable, but it is real.*
1. The memory of the barren rocks of Edom is a poor exchange for the palace of Egypt.
2. We may fill the years with successive victories, but we ever hold memories to give activities true value for us.

C. *There is a call of the blood that is claiming, "Howbeit, let me go."*

III. The call of dedication.

A. *The call of Edom is sometimes drowned in the clamor of Egypt's activity.*
1. The heart of each person is restless until it rests in God.
2. You may eat at the king's table and still be in exile.

B. *The claims of Christ are "the call of the blood."*
1. Our kinship in Christ.
2. Christ's call for our loyalty.

Conclusion

If you today could but hear a call like that of Hadad! Perhaps you never meant to drift from the Master's love and be seduced by comfort or lust. If you only could hear; the calls of memory and of dedication can drown the present roar of temptation. Is there surging up in you a desire to go back to the Edom of simple trust in Jesus as Lord and Savior of your life? Then with the young prince say, "Let me depart, that I may go to mine own." "Out of my bondage, sorrow and night, Jesus, I come to Thee."

WEDNESDAY EVENING, JULY 11

Title: God Repeats His Plans

Text: "And the LORD said, Shall I hide from Abraham that thing which I do; seeing that Abraham shall surely become a great and mighty nation, and all the nations of the earth shall be blessed in him?" **(Gen. 18:17–18).**

Scripture Reading: Genesis 18:16–33

Introduction

On many different occasions, God reminded Abraham of the divine purpose behind his calling. In every time of crisis or need, God came to Abraham and repeated the promise and illustrated its meaning in a variety of ways.

I. God shares his purpose (Gen. 18:16–19).

This divine soliloquy reveals again the high purpose of God for Abraham. The patriarch was to receive new truth from God that was to be taught to his descendants concerning both God's nature and God's purpose.

  A. *God shared with Abraham the secret of his decision to destroy the wicked city of Sodom.* Through sharing in this secret, Abraham was to learn the divine attitude toward wickedness and ungodliness.
  B. *Abraham also was to learn of the divine compassion and willingness to give even the most undeserving people every possible opportunity for forgiveness and redemption.*

II. God reveals his patience (Gen. 18:26ff.).

The compassion and redemptive purpose of God is revealed in his willingness to spare Sodom for the sake of ten righteous persons. If even ten righteous persons could be found in the city, this would be indicative of the fact that there was hope for others.

  A. *God was revealing that he could not and would not tolerate wickedness and ungodliness indefinitely.*
  B. *God also was demonstrating that judgment would not fall until people were beyond hope of redemption.*

III. God responded to Abraham's plea of intercession (Gen. 18:24–32).

  A. *God was pleased with Abraham's concern for the people of Sodom.* Abraham's concern for the inhabitants of the city was but a faint shadow of the concern in the heart of the heavenly Father for a lost world.
  B. *God blessed and encouraged Abraham's concern for others.* He indicated his approval by continually reducing the number whose presence would be sufficient to provide a basis for hope for others to experience redemption. The God of Abraham is the same yesterday, today, and forever. He cannot tolerate and condone ungodliness and wickedness. He is infinitely patient. He is seeking to work through us to bring the message of redemption to a needy world. This message of redemption produces purity of character and holiness of life. Ten people of the right kind in Sodom really could have made a difference with the blessings of God upon their efforts.

Conclusion

Are you among the "ten" righteous persons upon whom God is depending to communicate his great redemptive purpose in the world today? He needs you like he needed Abraham. He needs you like he needed the apostles. We all are needed to help God in his effort to redeem the world from sin.

SUNDAY MORNING, JULY 15

Title: How Can You Identify a Disciple?

Text: "By this shall all men know that ye are my disciples, if ye have love one to another" **(John 13:35)**.

Scripture Reading: John 13:33–35; Mark 12:28–34

Hymns: "Love Is the Theme," Fisher

"Love Lifted Me," Rowe

"I Love to Tell the Story," Hankey

Offertory Prayer: Our Father, we are grateful that Christ loved us and gave himself for us. We thank you for the unspeakable gift of salvation. We rejoice in the opportunity to serve you. Out of hearts filled with love we bring our tithes and offerings and pray that they will be used to bring honor and glory to the name of Christ. Fill us with the Holy Spirit that we may manifest your love to sinners. We pray in Jesus' name. Amen.

Introduction

"Which is the first commandment of all?" (Mark 12:28). How would Jesus answer the question? The question was a familiar one, for it had often been raised in professional circles. The Law was loaded with commandments. One rabbi said there were 613 commandments, 248 affirmative and 365 negative. Numerous attempts had been made to set forth the heart of the Hebrew religion. David listed eleven items (Ps. 15:2–5), Isaiah listed six (Isa. 33:15), Micah listed three (Mic. 6:8), and Habakkuk listed one (Hab. 2:4). What would Jesus say to the scribe who asked the question?

Jesus' answer to the scribe is a masterpiece. " 'The most important one,' answered Jesus, is this: "Hear, O Israel, the Lord our God, the Lord is one. Love the Lord your God with all your heart and with all your soul and with all your mind and with all your strength." The second is this: "Love your neighbor as yourself." There is no commandment greater than these' " (Mark 12:29–31 NIV).

The now famous answer by Jesus came from Deuteronomy 6:5 and Leviticus 19:18. Both the first and second commandments demand the exercise of love. We must love both God and fellow humans if we are Christians. No one can profess love for God and hate one's fellow humans. The apostle John said: "If a man say, I love God, and hateth his brother, he is a liar: for he that loveth not his brother whom he hath seen, how can he love God whom he hath not seen? And this commandment have we from him, that he who loveth God love his brother also" (1 John 4:20–21).

In fact, Jesus said, "By this shall all men know that ye are my disciples, if ye have love one to another" (John 13:35). If we would be known as disciples, we must be distinguished by that which distinguishes Jesus—love for others.

I. Love is a new commandment from the Lord (John 13:34).

Archbishop James Ussher, on a memorable occasion, called this new commandment the eleventh commandment. It is recorded that having heard of the simplicity and beauty of the ordering of Rev. Samuel Rutherford's home, he resolved to visit it for himself. One Saturday night he arrived alone at the manse and asked for entertainment over the next day. A simple but hearty welcome was accorded him; and after partaking of the frugal fare, he was invited to join the household in religious exercises that ushered in the Lord's Day.

"How many commandments are there?" the master asked his guest, wholly unaware who he was.

"Eleven," was the astonishing reply, at which even the servants were startled, regarding the newcomer as a prodigy of ignorance. But the man of God perceived the rare light of character and insight that gleamed beneath the answer and asked for a private interview. This issued in the invitation to preach on the following day. To the amazement of the household, so startled on the previous night, the stranger appeared in the master's pulpit and announced as his text the words on which we are meditating, adding, "This may be described as the eleventh commandment" (F. B. Meyer, *Gospel of John* [Grand Rapids: Zondervan, 1952], 202).

Why is Jesus' command called the eleventh or new commandment? Is it not simply the old commandment: "Thou shalt love thy neighbour as thyself"? I think not. It is a command to love one another as disciples. Hatred among Christians is unchristian. We love one another because of our union with Christ and because of mutual devotion to his will.

II. Love is the badge of discipleship.

A. *Christians love God.*
   1. Christians love God with the whole of their affections—"all thy heart."
   2. Christians love God with their whole life—"all thy life."
   3. Christians love God with the whole realm of thought—"all thy mind."
   4. Christians love God with the whole energy of their beings—"all thy strength."

B. *Christians love one another.* Christians are known not by dress, not by a long face, not by a pious whine, not by a negative attitude, not by wealth, not by learning, but by love for one another. The unbeliever does not love. The devil does not love because the essence of his nature is malice, envy, hatred, and revenge. Christians take on the nature of Christ—they love one another.

III. Love is the pattern of living for Christians.

Christ walked in love, and the Christian must do the same. Paul said, "Be imitators of God, therefore, as dearly loved children and live a life of love, just as

221

Christ loved us and gave himself up for us as a fragrant offering and sacrifice to God" (Eph. 5:1–2 NIV).

Christ showed the way for his disciples. He set an example of walking in love. One of Jesus' disciples betrayed him, but Jesus still loved him. Another disciple denied him, but Jesus loved him all the more. One disciple disbelieved his identity and resurrection, and Jesus asked him to put his fingers into the nail prints. John the apostle said, "It was just before the Passover Feast. Jesus knew that the time had come for him to leave this world and go to the Father. Having loved his own who were in the world, he now showed them the full extent of his love" (John 13:1 NIV).

Hatred is positive proof that one is not a disciple. Love is the pattern of living for Christians.

The regular monthly meeting of a well-known infidel club was scheduled to be held in London a couple of generations ago. A noted lecturer had been engaged to deliver a scathing attack on Christianity. In introducing the speaker, the chairman dared anyone to answer him at the conclusion of his message, and he assured the visitor that they were all of one mind on the matter of atheism.

As the applause died down at the conclusion of the address, a humble laborer arose and said:

> I have been a member of this club for five years. You all know me. Some of you have been in my home. Six months ago I lost my work, and I was ill, too. Not one of you came near me, though my illness was known here. But someone came, and that man and his wife nursed us and provided for us; otherwise my wife and I would not be alive today. That man was a city missionary whom I had driven from my home with threats. When I was well enough to think, I asked myself why he had been so kind to me, and I could not tell. So I asked him, and he told me he had done it for the love of Christ.
>
> Now that is my answer to the speaker. I say that a religion which will bring a man to the bedside of one who has hated and cursed him, and returns good for evil, love for hate, is a good thing for this troubled life, and I have taken it for myself. I have seen it in operation, and I know it is good." (R. L. Middleton, *Take Time!* [Nashville: Abingdon, 1949], 69–70)

A. *God's greatest gift to us is Jesus Christ.* God's love for man is revealed in Jesus Christ. Jesus said, "For God so loved the world, that he gave his only begotten Son, that whosoever believeth in him should not perish, but have everlasting life" (John 3:16). He also said, "Greater love hath no man than this, that a man lay down his life for his friends" (15:13). Paul said, "But God commendeth his love toward us, in that, while we were yet sinners, Christ died for us" (Rom. 5:8).

B. *Love for God is our greatest gift to God.* Paul listed for us the gifts given by the Holy Spirit: wisdom, knowledge, faith, healing, miracles, prophecy, discerning of spirits, tongues, and interpretation of tongues (1 Cor. 12:8–11). He ends 1 Corinthians 12 with these words: "Eagerly desire the greater gifts" (v. 31 NIV). Then he goes on to talk about love and concludes chapter 13 with these words: "And now these three remain: faith, hope and love. But the greatest of these is love" (v. 13 NIV).

Let us use this best of all gifts to love the best of all persons, Jesus Christ, our Lord.

Conclusion

Let us obey the commandments of God: Love him, love disciples, love our neighbor!

SUNDAY EVENING, JULY 15

Title: Timely Voices

Text: "So David received of her hand that which she had brought him, and said unto her, Go up in peace to thine house; see, I have hearkened to thy voice, and have accepted thy person" **(1 Sam. 25:35)**.

Scripture Reading: 1 Samuel 25:1–35

Introduction

During the periods of a nation's stress, the character of her citizens is most clearly seen. How vividly this is illustrated in the warrior David and the rich farmer Nabal.

It had been a drawn-out war. David and his troops had not only to continually pursue the enemy but to guard the farmers and their flocks on the home front as well. When finally the enemy was chased far enough so that respite was possible, camp supplies had dropped to the minimum. David sent his quartermaster sergeant to the nearby Nabal with a request for supplies. Nabal's reply to the request was shocking. "Shall I then take my bread, and my water, and my flesh that I have killed for my shearers, and give it unto men of whom I know not whence they be?" (1 Sam. 15:11). A report on this answer fired the wrath of David. This was one farmer who would pay his taxes! With select troops and with swords flashing, David descended the mountain intent on slaying every male of the household.

Nabal's wife was named Abigail. She was as wise as he was stupid. Upon hearing of her husband's foolishness, she made preparation and rushed out to meet the angry David. Because of her quick action and appropriate words, a terrible disaster was avoided. Her well-timed words are wisdom to us as well as to David.

I. Abigail spoke words of common sense.

A. *She pointed out that Nabal was a fool, both by name and practice.* The world is full of Nabals; you cannot kill them all.

223

B. *She convinced David that his profession and character were above being stained with the worthless blood of Nabal.*

II. Abigail spoke words of spiritual consideration.

A. *David was "in the hand of God."*
   1. He did not have to deal vengeance. "Vengeance is mine saith the LORD."
   2. He did not have to judge.

B. *David was "bound in the bundle of life with God."*
   1. His vocation was by God's leadership.
   2. His victories were by God's choosing.

III. Abigail spoke words of divine purpose.

A. *She wished her words to be identified with God's will.*
   1. "When the LORD shall have dealt with my lord, then remember thine handmaid" (v. 31).
   2. David said, "Blessed be thy advice [tact]" (1 Sam. 25:33).

B. *She gave herself to divine leadership in her association with David.*

Conclusion

Many men praise God today for the timely voices that came from some Abigail. It may have been mother, sister, or wife, but in the nick of time, when some Nabal was about to pay for his foolishness, the message came. Like David we say, "If you had not come quickly to met me [something tragic would have happened]" (see 1 Sam. 25:34 NIV).

The end came soon for Nabal. "It came to pass about ten days after, that the Lord smote Nabal, that he died" (1 Sam. 25:38). With a bubbling heart of gratitude, David dropped to his knees to utter, "Blessed be the LORD, that ... hath kept his servant from evil" (v. 39).

Can you look back over the critical moments of life and hear timely voices? Often the still, small voice was the voice of God. He has visited you in Christ Jesus and can walk with you and talk with you. Today he speaks: "Come now, and let us reason together, saith the LORD: though your sins be as scarlet, they shall be as white as snow; though they be red like crimson, they shall be as wool" (Isa. 1:18).

WEDNESDAY EVENING, JULY 18

Title: God Continues His Purpose
Text: "And ye shall be unto me a kingdom of priests, and an holy nation" **(Ex. 19:6)**.
Scripture Reading: Exodus 19:1–6

Introduction

Abraham was expected to pass on to his descendants the great truths that God revealed to him. In addition to Abraham, the covenant purpose was declared to Isaac and repeated to Jacob. The blessings of God rested on these descendants of Abraham. Near the end of Jacob's life, his family moved into Egypt where they were to live in comparative peace and prosperity until a change in the ruling dynasty reduced them to slavery. The Lord, the God of Abraham, Isaac, and Jacob, selected Moses to be the deliverer of his people from slavery. By a series of plagues, the Egyptians were convinced of the power of Moses' God. The children of Israel were convinced of Moses' divine appointment to be their leader and deliverer. The plagues were more than just natural catastrophes. Each plague was a contest that revealed the superior power of the God of Moses to the gods of the Egyptians. The climax in this contest was a knockout blow to Pharaoh and the gods of Egypt. This demonstration of the power of Moses' God caused Pharaoh to demand that the Israelites leave immediately.

In due time, Moses brought the people to Mount Sinai where they were to be formally organized and recognized as a nation. Through Moses, God offered to them a covenant relationship that was a continuation of the promise made to Abraham, Isaac, and Jacob.

The covenant relationship was to be based on God's gracious act of redeeming them from the bondage and slavery of Egypt (Ex. 19:4). It is said that the mother eagle will soar around and fly underneath her fledgling eaglets while they are in the process of learning how to fly. If necessary she is always there to provide the needed support on her extended wings to prevent them from plunging to their death. In the same manner, God declared that he had been with the distressed Israelites and that he had brought them to their present place for his own purposes.

God called Moses to the mountaintop in order that he might communicate with him a message for the people at the foot of the mountain. On the basis of his redemptive act of delivering them from slavery, God was calling them into a covenant relationship. He states the requirements that will be necessary if they are to fulfill his purpose for them.

I. Obedience to his commands.

"Now therefore, if ye will obey my voice indeed, and keep my covenant" (Ex. 19:5). The response of the people of God to the purpose of God required both faith and obedience. By faith they entered into the covenant, and by obedience they kept the covenant. This had been true in the case of Abraham. In obedience he departed from his homeland because of his faith in the promises of God. God always has desired and required that his children be obedient if they are to be useful.

II. Recognition of his ownership.

"Then ye shall be a peculiar treasure unto me above all people: for all the earth is mine" (Ex. 19:5). "A peculiar treasure" indicates a precious possession that has been acquired at great cost. God was declaring that, although all the earth was his, he would have the people of Israel to be his own possession in a precious and personal way.

In order for the Israelites to fulfill their part of the covenant, they needed to recognize God's total ownership of all they were and of all they possessed.

III. Interpreters of God's nature.

"And ye shall be unto me a kingdom of priests" (Ex. 19:6). The function of a priest is to mediate between God and humankind. The priest interprets God and his ways to humankind, and he represents humankind in the presence of God. As a kingdom of priests, Israel was to serve as a mediator for the other nations, making God known to them. As priests they also would be responsible for bringing offerings and petitions to God on behalf of the other peoples of the earth. This had been God's purpose for Abraham and was to be God's purpose for Israel.

IV. Dedication to God's purpose.

"And an holy nation" (Ex. 19:6). As a "holy nation," the Israelites were to be dedicated completely to the purposes of their God. This dedication to God would produce a difference between them and the other nations of the earth. The primary idea in this concept is that they were to be completely available as a redemptive instrument through which God would bless the world.

Conclusion

God's eternal purpose of love has been the same from Creation to the present. Different people and different methods have been used through the ages for the accomplishment of that purpose. As God blessed Abraham and Israel, so he has blessed the church today. As God held Abraham and Israel responsible, so does he hold the church responsible now. God chose Abraham that he might be an instrument of blessing to others. God chose Israel that Israel might be a blessing to others. God has chosen each of us and blessed us that we might be instruments of his loving purpose in our world today.

SUNDAY MORNING, JULY 22

Title: Is Life Worth Living?

Text: "This day I call heaven and earth as witnesses against you that I have set before you life and death, blessings and curses. Now choose life, so that you and your children may live" (**Deut. 30:19 NIV**).

Scripture Reading: Deuteronomy 30:11–20

Hymns: "Living for Jesus," Chisholm

"Footsteps of Jesus," Slade

"Savior, Like a Shepherd Lead Us," Thrupp

Offertory Prayer: Our Father, you are our Creator, Helper, Guide, and Redeemer. You have blessed us in so many ways. Today we thank you for all you have done for us and in us and through us. Take the gifts we give today and use them to bring blessings to others. In Jesus' name. Amen.

Introduction

We have much to make us happy, yet there is much misery and unhappiness in the world today. A philosophy of pessimism broods over the land. More young people are taking their lives than ever before. Many are saying life is not worth living.

Moses said to Israel years ago, "Choose life, so that you and your children may live" (Deut. 30:19 NIV). God wants people to live. In fact, Jesus came to this earth that people "might have life, and that they might have it more abundantly" (John 10:10).

I. Why are some saying that life is not worth living?

A. *Some say life is not worth living because of brevity.* The Bible points to the frailty and brevity of human life. The psalmist said of life: "In the morning it springs up new, by evening it is dry and withered" (Ps. 90:6 NIV). James said: "What is your life? You are a mist that appears for a little while and then vanishes" (James 4:14 NIV). Life indeed is short, but that does not mean it is not worth living. Old age does not mean success in living, nor does an early death indicate a wasted life.

B. *Some say life is not worth living because of its confusion.* James said, "For where envying and strife is, there is confusion and every evil work" (3:16). People are confused as to the meaning of life, the purpose of life, and the goal of life.

C. *Some say life is not worth living because of man's inhumanity to man.* Someone has described our world thus: "The world today is a world of mechanical perfection and moral disillusionment, a gadget world, where every step is made more comfortable and every night more horrible." Rioting, terrorism, bombings, killings, and wars are causing some to say life is not worth living.

D. *Some say life is not worth living because of the materialism of the day.* Materialism, with its greed and grind, with its promise and poverty, with its hurrahs and despairs, is crushing into the dust and mud of this earth not only the bodies but the spirits of men and women as well. Some are saying that life is not worth living because they cannot obtain all of the things of the world they would like to have. We need to remember what Jesus said: "Watch out! Be on your guard against all kinds of greed; a man's life does not consist in the abundance of his possessions" (Luke 12:15 NIV).

II. Why is life worth living?

A. *Life is worth living because Christ loves you (John 3:16; 15:13).*

B. *Life is worth living because Christ died for you (Isa. 53:5–6; Rom. 5:8; 1 Peter 2:24–25).*

C. *Life is worth living because with Christ life is eternal and abundant (John 3:36; 10:10; 1 John 5:11–12).*

D. *Life is worth living because Christ lives and he expects us to live too (Rom. 12:1–2; Heb. 12:1–2).* A few years ago I visited the ancient city of Pompeii. When the city was destroyed, many were buried in the ruins who were found in different situations. Some were found in the streets as if they were attempting to make their escape. Some were found in deep vaults as if they had gone there for security. Some were found in lofty chambers as if to hide from the lava. Where did they find the Roman sentinel? He was found at the city gate where he had been placed by his captain, and his hand was still grasping his weapon. While the heavens threatened him, while the earth shook beneath him, while the lava rolled, he stood at his post; and there, after a thousand years had passed away, he was found. So let us Christians live and stand at the post of duty because Christ lives and wants us to live and serve him.

Conclusion

Choose life and live! With Christ life can be lived victoriously. Life is worth living when Christ is Lord and Savior.

SUNDAY EVENING, JULY 22

Title: A Fool on Purpose

Text: "And he changed his behavior before them, and feigned himself mad in their hands, and scrabbled on the doors of the gate, and let his spittle fall down upon his beard" (**1 Sam. 21:13**).

Scripture Reading: 1 Samuel 21:10–15

Introduction

David was once a fool on purpose. King Achish of Gath was a real threat to David's life. The only possible escape was to be worthless to the king, so David "feigned himself mad." The scheme worked, and with the exception of some smashed dignity, David was none the worse for the wear. For David, a man after God's heart, a musician, a soldier, a man of international renown, to make such a choice demands our interest. It sets our minds aglow to prospects of what life may hold, especially a life related in faith to God.

I. A king on the run.

A. *David fled to protect Saul.*

1. The evil spirit in Saul forced David either to kill him or to flee from him.

2. "David strengthened himself in Jehovah." Sometimes running takes more courage than standing.

B. *David was running with God, not from Saul.*

II. A king in the wrong hands.

A. *God's leading into deep water could be to teach us to swim.*
1. The eagle dropping her young to teach them to fly.
2. Jeremiah's potter—"marred to make."

B. *God's responsibility is where he leads; ours is what we do there.*
1. Dealing with Achish was David's problem; he solved it well.
2. In adverse circumstances, God will "mount a guard over our minds," but we must make our own decisions.

III. A king becomes a fool on purpose.

A. *God measures by man's heart, not his appearance.*
1. We confuse life assignments by our false standards of ability, achievements, and favors.
2. Often God has to deal drastically to break through our arbitrary alignments.

B. *God does not always choose dignified roles for us.*
1. This was David's biggest problem; with his neck as the alternative, however, it seemed good.
2. There is no difference in David's escaping by swinging a sword or playing an idiot, except to his pride.
3. God led David to destroy one enemy with a sling and another enemy with a trick.
4. In serving Christ there is great risk to dignity.
5. In God's test our skills are not as important as our self-control.

C. *The way of the cross has been called "foolish."*
1. It is not God's dignity but love that we see there.
2. "Christ crucified ... the wisdom of God" (1 Cor. 1:24–25) is seen by some as foolishness.
3. Paul saw in this cross "the power of God unto salvation" (Rom. 1:16).

Conclusion

David, in becoming a fool on purpose, became someone we can appreciate and understand. Somehow we can see the great heroism of his soul as he stands there in the shadow of death, inwardly smiling as he puts on his mad act. What courage his strong heart has as he is entertained in hearing Achish scold his servants for bringing a fool before him. Mentally he is occupied planning his next battle's strategy as they unceremoniously kick him from the premises. What set of soul; what power of God rests in such a man!

Have you ever dared to be a fool for Jesus' sake? Have you so trusted God that his serenity and peace continually abide in you? Do you dare come down off your pedestal of dignity? It is a risk; do you dare try?

WEDNESDAY EVENING, JULY 25

Title: God Illustrates His Continuing Program

Text: "And she said unto her mistress, Would God my lord were with the prophet that is in Samaria! for he would recover him of his leprosy" **(2 Kings 5:3)**.

Scripture Reading: 2 Kings 5:1–15

Introduction

The miraculous healing of Naaman, the captain of the host of Syria, was a dramatic reminder to Israel that the concern of God is not restricted to one country or one race but is as wide as the world. If Naaman could become a worshiper of the God of Israel, it would follow logically that other people of the world could come to know him. If God would use his power to heal Naaman from the hated nation of Syria, it would follow that God was interested in other nations too. God was using the testimony of a slave girl who was a prisoner of war to bring about a miracle of healing in the life of a foreigner in order to rebuke the attitude of narrow nationalism and religious exclusiveness that was causing the people of Israel to isolate themselves from other nations.

I. God used the testimony of an Israelite slave girl.

The testimony of an unknown slave girl dramatically illustrates the redemptive purpose of God for Israel as a nation. This little maiden had been taken captive in one of the expeditions that the Syrian army had made into the land of Israel. She became a servant of the wife of Naaman, the commander-in-chief of the army of Syria. Her faith in God manifested itself in a concern for the physical well-being of Naaman, who was afflicted with leprosy. She expressed her concern and gave her testimony concerning her God and his prophet. By so doing, she was the means of bringing health, happiness, and faith to a man who most of her people considered to be completely outside of the concern of God. By her testimony, she became the instrument of making Israel's God known among the heathen.

II. The ministry of God's prophet (2 Kings 5:9–12).

Jehoram, son of Jezebel and king of Israel, was helpless and distressed when Naaman appeared at his gate with a letter from the king of Syria requesting a cure for the captain of his army. Jehoram had no solution for this perplexing problem.

The prophet Elisha took the initiative and sent a message to the king, instructing him to send Naaman to the prophet's house. Through Elisha God would graciously show his presence, power, and purpose to Israel and to Syria alike. The Syrian warlord was to discover the power of the God of Israel and to experience a miraculous healing that would cause him to become a worshiper of the true God.

"Elisha sent a messenger to say to him, 'Go, wash yourself seven times in the Jordan, and your flesh will be restored and you will be cleansed'" (2 Kings 5:10 NIV). At first Naaman was insulted and angered by what he considered to be a degrading suggestion from the prophet. He correctly reasoned that the waters of Damascus were better than those of Israel. It was only normal for him to think that his suggestion was designed to humiliate him. He turned away in anger. The plan suggested for a cure was entirely too simple. It did not agree with his preconceived ideas and expectations of what ought to be done for a person of his lofty position.

God's way of healing Naaman of his leprosy was so simple that there was no legitimate excuse for its rejection. The means used for effecting the cure was intended to direct his attention to the true God rather than to a king, a prophet, or a magic ceremony.

A. *The way of faith.* The instructions of the prophet emphasized the necessity of faith and humility on the part of Naaman. The nearest route from the city of Samaria to the Jordan Valley would involve a journey of twenty-five miles. By the journey and by the repeated dippings in the river, Naaman was required to exercise faith.

B. *The way of obedience.* Because of the command of the prophet, the encouragement of his servants, and his own personal need, Naaman dipped himself seven times in the Jordan. By a miracle that could be ascribed only to the power of Israel's God, the leper was made clean. In striking contrast to his former diseased and defiled condition, this mighty man of valor found himself healthy and clean.

Conclusion

God had used the testimony of an obscure slave girl in a foreign country as a means of communicating the truth concerning his power and willingness to exercise that power on behalf of man. God had used one of his prophets as a means of communicating specific instructions to a great man concerning what he must do if he would be clean. The mighty military leader of Syria exercised faith in the instructions that were given him concerning the will of God. His faith and obedience made it possible for God to do something wonderful for him and for others also.

God wants to continue his program through your testimony. He will use your life and your witness. Great things can be accomplished through you if you will but trust him and obey him.

The accomplishment of God's great redemptive purpose in the world waits on our faith and obedience. We should follow the example of the unnamed slave girl and let God do wonders through us.

SUNDAY MORNING, JULY 29

Title: What Kind of Religion Do You Have?

Text: "As John's disciples were leaving, Jesus began to speak to the crowd about John: 'What did you go out into the desert to see?'" **(Matt. 11:7 NIV).**

Scripture Reading: Matthew 11:2–15

Hymns: "Living for Jesus," Chisholm

"Beneath the Cross of Jesus," Clephane

"Give of Your Best to the Master," Grose

Offertory Prayer: Dear Lord, you are our Friend, our Refuge, our Strength, our Redeemer, and our Hope. Our trust is in you. We praise your name today for the many blessings you have given us, especially life's greatest blessing of salvation. We ask that you receive our tithes and offerings and use them for your glory. We pray in Jesus' name. Amen.

Introduction

John the Baptist, the forerunner of Jesus, was sent by God to prepare the way for the coming of the Messiah. John was of priestly descent on both his mother's and father's line. His father, Zechariah, was a priest of the course of Abijah, and his mother, Elizabeth, was of the course of Aaron (Luke 1:5). His birth took place about six months before the birth of Jesus. The angel of the Lord appeared to Zechariah and told him that his prayer had been answered and that his wife would bear him a son whose name was to be John.

John was a mighty preacher of judgment and repentance. Jesus was baptized by John, and it appears at this time that John recognized him as the Messiah. A little later, John said of Jesus, "Look, the Lamb of God, who takes away the sin of the world!" (John 1:29 NIV). When Jesus began making disciples, John the Baptist said, "He must increase, but I must decrease" (3:30).

Finally, John the Baptist was put into prison by Herod because he preached that it was wrong for Herod to have his brother Philip's wife, Herodias (Matt. 14:3). John had been in prison approximately seven months when he sent two of his disciples to Jesus to inquire whether he was really the Messiah. This inquiry seems strange, and a number of reasons have been put forth for it. John had lost heart and needed encouragement. His disciples needed assurance that Jesus really was the Messiah. John expected the messianic kingdom to be ushered in cataclysmically and could not understand why it had not happened. Some have suggested that John felt neglected while others were being helped and blessed.

When the disciples of John came to Jesus, they asked, "Are you the one who was to come, or should we expect someone else?" (Matt. 11:3 NIV). In answer Jesus said, "Go back and report to John what you hear and see: The blind receive sight, the lame walk, those who have leprosy are cured, the deaf hear, the dead are raised, and the good news is preached to the poor. Blessed is the man who does not fall away on account of me" (vv. 4–6 NIV).

As soon as the messengers of John left Jesus, he pronounced a glowing eulogy of John. In this eulogy Jesus spoke of the kind of religion John had. His kind of religion had made him a truly great man, for Jesus said of him, "I tell you the truth: Among those born of women there has not risen anyone greater than John the Baptist" (Matt. 11:11 NIV).

What kind of religion did John the Baptist have? What kind of religion ought we to have?

I. A religion of conformity?

" 'What did you go out into the desert to see? A reed swayed by the wind?' " (Matt. 11:7 NIV).

A. *John the Baptist was no conformist.* He was not a reed shaken with the wind. Reeds were plentiful in the Jordan Valley where John preached. The reeds by the Jordan bent with the wind, but not so John. He was no ordinary prophet. He was no fickle doubter. He was a man who did not conform to the ways of the world.

B. *Christians do not have a religion of conformity.* Paul said, "Do not conform any longer to the pattern of this world, but be transformed by the renewing of your mind. Then you will be able to test and approve what God's will is—his good, pleasing and perfect will" (Rom. 12:2 NIV). Peter said, "As obedient children, do not conform to the evil desires you had when you lived in ignorance" (1 Peter 1:14 NIV). Christians avoid conformity not by oddity of dress and manners, but by inward transformation. Our lives, like John the Baptist, should be marked by decisiveness, constancy, and courage. The world will not listen to a Christian who is like a reed shaken by the wind.

II. A religion of ease and privilege?

" 'What did you go out to see? A man dressed in fine clothes? No, those who wear fine clothes are in kings' palaces' " (Matt. 11:8 NIV).

A. *The religion of John the Baptist was not one of ease and comfort.* He was no weakling, no self-seeker. He refused to play courtier to Herod. He went to prison rather than choose a life of ease and comfort. Some courtiers who attached themselves to Herod laid aside their plain dress and wore the gorgeous raiment of courtiers.

B. *Christians are not those with a religion of ease and comfort.* They are soldiers of the Christ. They put on the whole armor that they might withstand in the evil day. They deny themselves that they might be true followers of Christ. They follow him, knowing that all who live godly in Christ Jesus will suffer persecution. They are faithful till death.

III. The religion of a prophet-plus.

" 'Then what did you go out to see? A prophet? Yes, I tell you, and more than a prophet. This is the one about whom it is written: "I will send my messenger ahead of you, who will prepare your way before you"'" (Matt. 11:9–10 NIV).

A. *John the Baptist was an inspired man who spoke of God.* The people regarded him as a prophet (Matt. 21:26). He possessed all the great qualities of a prophet: a speaker for God, a man of truth, a man of moral conviction, a fearless man, a man of zeal and righteousness. Jesus said he was indeed a prophet, and something exceedingly more than a prophet. In fact, he was the fulfillment of Scripture (11:10). One of the great things about John the Baptist was that he had a message to tell and live.

B. *Christians are to speak God's message to men.* We are to be witnesses for him. We are to proclaim the salvation found only in Christ, our Lord. We are to announce that Christ is indeed the Messiah, the only Messiah. In him is life everlasting. In him we find there is more to life than living; there is abundant living.

Conclusion

Larry McKenzie, 1951 polio poster boy, whose picture and story have been used by the National Foundation for Infantile Paralysis to help thousands of other stricken children, is also making his testimony as a Christian count in helping others.

In his tour of the country in behalf of the polio drive, the Christian lad frequently told of his love for the Lord Jesus. Now his testimony has been printed in a tract, "Rise Up and Walk," which is being published and distributed by the American Tract Society.

Says Larry in the tract, "I met many famous people on my tour—president of the United States, Harry S Truman; J. Edgar Hoover, chief of the Federal Bureau of Investigation; and others, but I think often about the time I will meet the Lord Jesus, and until then I really want to serve Him any way I can" (Walter B. Knight, *Knight's Master Book of New Illustrations* [Grand Rapids: Eerdmans, 1956], 736).

May our Lord help us to serve him and witness for him!

SUNDAY EVENING, JULY 29

Title: Playing Dolls with a God

Text: "And Michal took an image, and laid it in the bed, and put a pillow of goats' hair for his bolster, and covered it with a cloth" **(1 Sam. 19:13).**

Scripture Reading: 1 Samuel 19:8–17

Introduction

Ours is a day when religion is used for our own purposes. Michal is our mother in this custom. She was the daughter of Saul and the wife of David.

There was a generation gap between Saul and David, and Michal was caught in between. Having no real faith, she used all the religious symbols she knew to obtain her desires. She could fall prostrate before her teraphim in worship, or she could put it to bed and tuck it in as her doll. She reminds us of Christians who watch for black cats or toss salt over their shoulders. Although we are prone to deny it, our faith really is not what we profess, but it consists of those things in which we believe. As Michal, we use God to serve us in our emergencies. There are lessons that we learn from Michal's experience.

I. If our faith is to remain vital, we must maintain reverence.

A. *This image could be used to fool Saul's men but could never again inspire worship.*

B. *When in our cleverness we use religion, we wreck the foundation of our morality.*

C. *Reverence in worship is not following formal requirements but exercising faith.*

II. If our lives are to have power, we must have reality in faith.

A. *Michal had to bolster and cover up her image.*

1. Often we have to pretend to keep our religious practices popular.

2. God was less concerned with protocol when he sent his Son to sinners.

B. *Simple faith may make a dedicated person appear simply faithful.*

1. Skills in religious practices are but developed creature activities.

2. God's ways are not human ways, and sometimes God's ways appear foolish to natural people.

3. A living God is not always discernible to those "dead in trespasses and sin."

III. If we are to experience redemption, we must know God as redeemer.

A. *David never saw Michal's act of saving his neck as God's redemption.*

1. We do not deny that David needed help. The help that Michal afforded was transitory.

2. David saw this act as but a means to a greater end.

B. *Salvation to David was to be in God's will.*

1. Saving faith is a definite thing. It is a personal action.

2. Receiving the mercy of God is not sufficient. One must trust God in his mercy.

Conclusion

Who has not experienced with Michal the feeling that the insensate harshness of situations causes the forfeiture of character? The heartless Saul or the devastating hurricane or overpowering lust would make our lot appear to be a meaningless collision of blind forces. Are we not justified to seize any object or idea, even God himself, and bring it into play that we may win the day? It is at this point that the Christian faith speaks to us. In Jesus Christ we stand victorious. This does not imply that every foe is crushed beneath our heel or that every battle is for us a victory. We are victors in that his Spirit in us overcomes—even death. To know a living God who ever stretches his eternal purposes before us is to have the solution for life's perplexities. He can be our toy only for the hour but our redeemer forever.

SUGGESTED PREACHING PROGRAM FOR

AUGUST

■ **Sunday Mornings**

Continue the series "Some of the Great Questions of the Bible."

■ **Sunday Evenings**

Continue the series "Old Testament Stories That Present a Christian Message."

■ **Wednesday Evenings**

A series of expository messages based on Peter's first epistle is suggested for the balance of the calendar year. "Encouragement and Counsel for Difficult Times from a Seasoned Veteran of the Cross" is an appropriate title for this series of devotional messages.

WEDNESDAY EVENING, AUGUST 1

Title: God's Chosen People

Text: "Peter, an apostle of Jesus Christ, To God's elect, strangers in the world, scattered throughout Pontus, Galatia, Cappadocia, Asia and Bithynia" (**1 Peter 1:1 NIV**).

Scripture Reading: 1 Peter 1:1–2

Introduction

Peter wrote his first epistle to help his readers recognize the greatness of their salvation and make a proper response to God's redemptive purpose for their lives. He encouraged them to believe that the blessings of the past and the glories of the future make the difficulties and the unpleasantness of the present worthwhile. He attempted to blow a bugle for drooping spirits in a time when it was dangerous and costly to be a follower of Jesus Christ.

Apparently the occasion for this epistle was a wave of persecution that threatened the life of the church (1 Peter 1:6–7; 3:14; 4:1, 12–19). Peter himself had known persecution at the hands of both religious and civil authorities (Acts 5, 12). He was thus preeminently qualified to be used by the Holy Spirit to communicate God's message to a persecuted people who needed to remain faithful in order to fulfill God's redemptive purpose in their lives.

It is believed that the epistle was written during Nero's persecution of Christians in the Roman Empire during the early AD 60s. This persecution gradually moved out into the provinces of the empire. The existence of the church was threatened. God's redemptive purpose required that his servants respond with loyalty under fire. The apostle employed language such as the Jews used to refer to their own people scattered among the nations outside Palestine. All true Christians were addressed as constituting the people of God. Peter was affirming that Christianity is the true Judaism. He addressed his readers, not as Jews or as Gentiles, but as the people of God and as the chosen instrument through which God would bless the world. He urged that they recognize their privileged relationship to God and their position of responsibility for the continuation of the saving work of Jesus Christ. He reminded them of the spiritual riches that were in store for them in the future.

I. The chosen people of God.

Peter begins his epistle by affirming that Christians are the "elect," the chosen people of God. As God had chosen Abraham as an individual and Israel as a people, so he has chosen Christians for redemptive service. God has bestowed upon the followers of Christ the high honor and great responsibility of communicating the message of his grace and love to a needy world.

The church is not an organization of human origin; it was born in the heart of God. It has a divine purpose to fulfill—the salvation of people. Each believer should rejoice over the privilege of being included in the purpose of God.

II. Consecrated by the Holy Spirit.

By the activity of the Holy Spirit, God's people have been convinced of their need for a Savior and have received the miracle of the new birth wrought in their hearts. By the Holy Spirit's work of sanctification, that is, his continuing work of delivering them from the power of evil and producing within them the graces of Christ, they are being prepared for effective service for the Lord.

III. For obedience to Jesus Christ and sprinkling by his blood.

The Old Testament mentions the sprinkling of blood upon three significant occasions.

A. *It was a symbol of cleansing when a leper was declared healed of his leprosy (Lev. 14:1–7).*
B. *It was a symbol of being set apart for priestly service (Lev. 8:30).*
C. *It was used in the establishment of a new covenant relationship between God and his people (Ex. 24:1–8).*

Likely these three ideas are wrapped up in the phrase the apostle Peter uses: "sprinkling by [Jesus'] blood" (1 Peter 1:2 NIV). By the blood of Jesus Christ, God's sinless Son, the Christian is cleansed of sin, is set apart for a priestly ministry for God, and is obligated to a covenant life of loving obedience and service to God.

Conclusion

God the Father, God the Son, and God the Holy Spirit work upon and within believers for their individual well-being and also for the spiritual well-being of others who can be reached through their ministry.

We are God's chosen people. He has chosen us for our own good and for the good of others. We should respond to his purpose with faith and obedience.

SUNDAY MORNING, AUGUST 5

Title: Are We Hiding from God?

Text: "And they heard the voice of the LORD God walking in the garden in the cool of the day: and Adam and his wife hid themselves from the presence of the LORD God among the trees of the garden" **(Gen. 3:8)**.

Scripture Reading: Genesis 3:1–19

Hymns: "Come, Thou Almighty King," Anonymous

"Holy, Holy, Holy," Heber

"O Worship the King," Grant

Offertory Prayer: Our heavenly Father, we thank you for the opportunity to share with you what we have. We give and ask you to bless our gifts and use them for your glory. We acknowledge that you are our Maker, Redeemer, and Friend. Bless us as we worship with our tithes and offerings. In Jesus' name. Amen.

Introduction

Adam and Eve were happy at first in the garden of Eden, the beautiful home provided for them by their loving God. They had not been there long before Satan appeared as a serpent, insidious and artful. He raised the question as to whether God was kind in withholding from Adam and Eve the right to use the good things by which they were surrounded. After winning a hearing, Satan persuaded Eve to eat of the fruit of the tree in the midst of the garden. Then Eve persuaded Adam to eat of the tree. Their eyes were opened, and they knew they were naked. So they sewed fig leaves together and made themselves aprons and hid themselves from the presence of God.

Sin always brings guilt and separates us from God. It causes us to turn from God and flee from his presence.

The question for us today is: Do we really want God? The prophet Isaiah said, "Seek the LORD while he may be found; call on him while he is near" (Isa. 55:6 NIV). It is logical to believe that God is seeking us, and if we seek him, we will experience that wonderful relationship of fellowship. However, not all people want him. Some, like Adam and Eve, are hiding from God.

I. Are we hiding from God in our failure to repent of our sins?

Jesus said, "Repent and believe the good news!" (Mark 1:15 NIV).

What is repentance? Repentance is not remorse, not self-reproach, not fear of consequences, not the mere sense of sin, and not a negative attitude. Repentance is a change of mind resulting in a new positive direction that affects the

239

whole of life, including the use of our time, money, leisure, talents — our all. Often we do not want God because of our failure to repent of our sins.

II. Are we hiding from God in our pursuit of knowledge?

Many are not Christians because they say they cannot understand Christianity. They profess they do not understand the new birth, regeneration, salvation. Some are not Christians because they say they do not understand the virgin birth, the divinity of Christ, his miracles, the cross, or the resurrection.

The difficulties in the way of a person finding God and becoming a Christian are rarely intellectual. Jesus does not ask people to give allegiance to a creed as a condition of salvation. He asks people to repent of their sins and put their trust in him. Seldom is it an intellectual difficulty that stands between a person and God. It is usually some personal sin the person does not want to give up.

It is one thing to know about God and quite another thing to trust him and live in daily contact with him. It is one thing to be able to answer all of the questions concerning God and another thing to say as Job said, "Though he slay me, yet will I trust in him" (Job 13:14).

III. Are we hiding from God in our church activities?

There is a difference between service that is an expression of our relationship with the Lord and service that is an attempt to evade a right relationship with the Lord. Some are rendering service, running errands, and giving money to the church in an attempt to avoid surrender of self. Jesus said, "If any man will come after me, let him deny himself, and take up his cross, and follow me" (Matt. 16:24). Many are hiding from God by a failure to surrender self.

Saul of Tarsus was a mighty man who rendered passionate service before his surrender. Evidently God was trying to speak to him but could not until he struck Saul blind on the Damascus road (Acts 9:8). Like some of us, Saul was religious before he found the Lord. Are we hiding from God in our religious activities?

IV. Are we hiding from God in our familiarity with Christianity?

Some church members are so familiar with words, phrases, and expressions that describe a religious experience that they feel they have experienced all there is to experience. The most difficult people in the church to do anything with are those who do not believe there lies anything beyond them that they do not already know. One of the things that holds back progress in the churches today is the presence of vast numbers of people who have had no real experience with God and believe there is nothing beyond that which they have found. They are the ones who have had only small doses of Christianity and have failed to experience abundant life in Christ.

V. Are we hiding from God in our failure to come to grips with reality?

Too often we have said, "Come to Christ and everything will be all right." Have we been guilty of leading people to believe that Christianity is a flowery bed of ease and that a Christian will not experience the shocks of this hard world? Christianity is not a bed; it is a cross. Christianity is not to be lived on a lounge; it is to be lived in the arena of conflict and hard knocks. To expect to find peace, rest, and comfort without cross-bearing is to seek an illicit shelter of the soul. Christianity is not escape; it is conquest. When a person comes to Christ and accepts him as Savior, he is put in touch with amazing resources that will enable him to be victorious. The man who has found God has not insured himself against trouble, but he has found one who will show him how to turn trouble into triumph.

VI. Are we hiding from God in our refusal to get right with our fellow humans?

Some do not follow the Lord because they do not want to get right with their fellow humans. There is no such thing as reconciliation with God unless we are reconciled with our fellow humans. The apostle John said, "Anyone who claims to be in the light but hates his brother is still in the darkness" (1 John 2:9 NIV). "This is how we know who the children of God are and who the children of the devil are: Anyone who does not do what is right is not a child of God; nor is anyone who does not love his brother" (3:10 NIV). "If anyone says, 'I love God,' yet hates his brother, he is a liar. For anyone who does not love his brother, whom he has seen, cannot love God, whom he has not seen" (4:20 NIV).

I heard a woman say of a great Christian worker, "I hate him! I hate him!" I said to her, "It is impossible for you to hate him and be a Christian, for Christians do not hate." The person who hates others and excludes them cannot find God.

Conclusion

Are you hiding from God? What is your reason for hiding? You may be like Adam and Eve, and you may have broken one of God's commands. Forsake your sin and turn and be reconciled to him.

SUNDAY EVENING, AUGUST 5

Title: Redeeming the Fringes

Text: "In the plain of Jordan did the king cast them, in the clay ground between Succoth and Zarthan" **(1 Kings 7:46)**.

Scripture Reading: 1 Kings 7:45–51

Introduction

The detailed account of building and furnishing the temple seems remote, of little interest to us, and probably would not be read were it not in God's Word. It is refreshing, however, to wade through the engineering specifics and suddenly have a unique aspect of character in God's great servant pop to the surface.

What can be added to the greatness of the mighty Solomon? But here it is, and Solomon is even greater to us now that we have noticed it.

In mastering his kingdom, Solomon added to the production of his vineyards, grain fields, and forests. These achievements were noted and lend to his recognition as the wisest of kings. We almost missed the fact, however, that he also brought production from the wasteland of his kingdom. He mined the heretofore worthless clay pits between Succoth and Zarthan. It is the king who can "redeem the fringes," who can develop the seemingly worthless, who is really king of all the kingdom.

This challenge, received and answered by King Solomon, is to each of us. Have we redeemed life's fringes?

I. We are directed to develop talents.

A. *Life is a trust; its terms are met in living to the fullest.*
B. *We are born equal.*
C. *Jesus illustrates the required attitude toward talents.*
D. *Often we see as talent only that which is marketable.*

II. The Christian life is a growth in relationships.

A. *The ancient concept of "brother's keeper."*
B. *Who is my neighbor?*
C. *Roles in family life.*
D. *The life motivated by love.*

III. Our challenge to redeem the fringes.

A. *Times of trouble and distress.*
  1. A financial problem can bring us into a new stratum of life to serve.
  2. A certain distress may identify us with one needing to share our experience.
B. *Periods of deep sorrow.*
  1. This which can be wasted time also may be growth time.
  2. An old woodsman once said, "Most births occur in the valley."
  3. Deep understanding of life often comes out of crushing experiences.
C. *Seasons of sickness and pain.*
  1. We try to shun them and pray for health.
  2. We are prone to think of such times as misfortune.
  3. We forget that "all things" can work together for good.

Conclusion

The gospel of Christ is a call to redemption. It is not a recognition of the good in life. It is a proclamation that the worst can be reclaimed. The heavy clay soil of sorrow, sickness, and sin that people pray be removed from them can be the place where the Master forms his choicest vessels. From the clay pits he has brought them: a cursing fisherman who denied knowing him, an immoral woman under the hail of flung stones, a synagogue official breathing out curses against Christ's church. To the foulest, deepest pits went the King of Kings. In the stiff clay of Calvary, he worked until sin was defeated. He has brought out as many precious vessels as would yield to his undying love. Every vessel, whether of purest gold, burnished brass, or molded clay, rejoices in a King who "redeemed the fringes," even to the pits of clay.

WEDNESDAY EVENING, AUGUST 8

Title: Our Wonderful Salvation
Text: "Blessed be the God and Father of our Lord Jesus Christ" (**1 Peter 1:3**).
Scripture Reading: 1 Peter 1:3–5

Introduction

The apostle Peter was overwhelmed with gratitude for the blessings of God as revealed in and experienced through the death and resurrection of the Lord Jesus Christ. By calling attention to these, Peter sought to strengthen his readers and encourage them for enduring the trials they faced.

I. The new birth (1 Peter 1:3).

The Christian is one who has experienced a birth from above, a birth in the Spirit. He received new life, eternal life, in a miracle wrought by the Holy Spirit.

In the new birth, the believer receives the very life of the eternal God in the depths of his being. He is a new creation. He receives the nature and character of God in embryonic form. He is now a child of God as well as a creature of God.

II. To a living hope (1 Peter 1:3).

The pagan world was a world without hope. It was with a chill that people considered the future. They saw themselves as the helpless victims of a cruel fate, and old age was dreaded with horror. Death reigned as a king over all, and the thought of such destroyed much of the joy of living. Many regretted that they had been born; others wished that they had died in infancy. There was nothing but darkness in the future of the pagans.

The gospel was to change this attitude of hopelessness for those who believed, making hope a reality for those who lived in despair. The gospel assured believers that oblivion was not their destiny. Their lives were given a new dimension.

III. By the resurrection of Jesus Christ from the dead (1 Peter 1:3).

The resurrection revealed that Christ's death on the cross had not been a mere accident or tragedy. The resurrection was a dramatic demonstration of the fact that the penalty of sin had been paid and that the righteousness of God was fulfilled completely through the sacrifice that had been made on the cross.

The resurrection declared that death had been conquered and that eternal life was a reality for those who would trust Christ as Savior and Lord.

Jesus' followers could face the future without fear or even blind resignation to the inevitable. With joy and faith they could face death itself as a doorway that would lead into the presence of God.

IV. Unto an inheritance (I Peter 1:4).

To Jewish Christians the word *inheritance* contained a rich meaning. The Jewish people had looked upon the Promised Land as their divine inheritance. Peter used three great words to describe the Christian's inheritance.

A. *This inheritance is incorruptible.* The word means "unravished by an invading army." The devil and all his angels cannot ravage the promised land of the Christian.

B. *This inheritance is undefiled, or stainless.* It has never been defiled or polluted by moral evil.

C. *This inheritance "fadeth not."* In contrast to flowers that wither and fade, our heavenly inheritance does not die.

V. Reserved in heaven for you (I Peter 1:4).

The Christian is no mere creature of his day. His life has a dimension other than the visible. Through Christ death has been conquered. Heaven, a life of endless fellowship with God, is a living reality that gives significance to the present.

VI. Kept by the power of God through faith (I Peter 1:5).

On our way through the world with its evil forces, we are protected by the power of God. Our faith in him makes it possible for him to stand over us like a military bodyguard through all our days.

VII. Unto salvation ready to be revealed in the last time (I Peter 1:5).

The New Testament speaks of salvation in three tenses: past, present, and future.

A. *Believers were saved from the penalty of sin in the past when they received Christ as Lord and Savior.*

B. *Believers are presently in a process of being saved from the power and practice of sin in their daily lives by the operation of the indwelling Spirit.*

C. *Believers will be saved completely from the presence of sin when the Lord returns for his own.*

Conclusion

The apostle Peter did not have words adequate to describe the wonderful salvation that we have through Jesus Christ. It is ours to share. It is ours to enjoy. The more we enjoy and share it, the more we will have to enjoy and share.

SUNDAY MORNING, AUGUST 12

Title: "What Shall I Do Then with Jesus, Who Is Called Christ?"

Text: "Pilate saith unto them, What shall I do then with Jesus, who is called Christ? They all say unto him, Let him be crucified" **(Matt. 27:22)**.

Scripture Reading: Matthew 27:11–38

Hymns: "I Love to Tell the Story," Hankey

           "Praise Him! Praise Him!" Crosby

           "My Savior's Love," Gabriel

Offertory Prayer: Our Father, we reverently pause to thank you for your love for us. We are grateful that you loved us so much that you sent your Son to die for us while we were sinners. Help all people everywhere to come to Christ for salvation. Enable us to love you more and to serve you effectively. In Jesus' name. Amen.

Introduction

If I were to ask you what the great question of the day is, I presume I would get a variety of answers. Some would say ecology is the great question of the day. What are we going to do about the pollution in the world? Some would insist that inflation is the great question of the day. How are we going to cope with rising costs? Some would say that caring for the elderly is the great question of the day. How can we adequately care for the needs of the elderly? Some would insist that educating our youth is the great question of the day. What can be done to channel them in the right direction? We could go on and on.

To be sure, these questions are important, but there is a question of vastly greater importance: "What shall I do with Jesus, who is called Christ?" It is not a new question. Pontius Pilate asked it nearly two thousand years ago. Much depends on the right answer to this question. The right answer means that one will have everything worth having for time and eternity. The wrong answer means that one will lose everything that is worth having.

What will be ours if we answer this question right?

I. If you do the right thing with Jesus, who is called Christ, you will have deliverance from the power of sin.

Everyone who is an unforgiven sinner lives under the dominion of Satan. He has power over the sinner's life. The Bible teaches us that Jesus Christ can set a person free from the grip of Satan and make him a child of God: "If the Son sets you free, you will be free indeed" (John 8:36 NIV). The apostle John said of Jesus: "He came to that which was his own, but his own did not receive him. Yet to all who received him, to those who believed in his name, he gave the right to become children of God—children born not of natural descent, nor of human decision or a husband's will, but born of God" (1:11–13 NIV).

II. If you do the right thing with Jesus, who is called Christ, you will receive forgiveness of your sins.

Paul, the great militant and missionary apostle, said: "... to the praise of his glorious grace, which he has freely given us in the One he loves. In him we have redemption through his blood, the forgiveness of sins, in accordance with the riches of God's grace" (Eph. 1:6–7 NIV). The ground for forgiveness by God is the atoning death of Christ. Any person who will repent of his sins and put his faith in Jesus Christ as Lord can have forgiveness.

    A. *Christ has power to forgive sins (Matt. 9:6).*

    B. *There is forgiveness for the vilest sinner.*

        Ralph Fultz, a man who was associated with Clyde Barrow and Bonnie Parker in crime, a bank robber for twenty-five years, was sentenced to more than five hundred years in prison. Christ saved him, and Christ can save you.

    C. *Forgiveness can be had now (1 John 1:9).*

III. If you do the right thing with Jesus, who is called Christ, you will have peace in your soul.

    A. *There are many things that rob a person of peace:*

        1. Sin.

        2. Conscience.

        3. Calamity.

        4. Fear of people.

        5. Illness.

        6. Death.

        7. Thoughts of eternity.

    B. *Jesus Christ can give a person peace.* Jesus said, "Peace I leave with you, my peace I give unto you: not as the world giveth, give I unto you. Let not your heart be troubled, neither let it be afraid" (John 14:27).

        Paul said, "Therefore being justified by faith, we have peace with God through our Lord Jesus Christ" (Rom. 5:1).

IV. If you do the right thing with Jesus, who is called Christ, you will have eternal life.

What is eternal life? What are some of the characteristics of eternal life?

    A. *Eternal life is life of the highest knowledge.* "Now this is eternal life: that they may know you, the only true God, and Jesus Christ, whom you have sent" (John 17:3 NIV).

    B. *Eternal life is fullness of life.* Jesus said, "I have come that they may have life, and have it to the full" (John 10:10 NIV). John, the beloved apostle, said, "This is the testimony: God has given us eternal life, and this life is in his Son. He who has the Son has life; he who does not have the Son of God does not have life" (1 John 5:11–12 NIV). Eternal life in all its fullness is like the life of God as revealed in his Son Jesus Christ.

C. *Eternal life is endless life.* The words "eternal life" mean quite literally "age long." An age is the longest time the human mind can conceive clearly. The words "eternal life" therefore came to mean endless duration. Eternal life is life with Jesus Christ forever. The best-loved verse in the Bible says, "For God so loved the world, that he gave his only begotten Son, that whosoever believeth in him should not perish, but have everlasting life" (John 3:16).

V. If you do the right thing with Jesus, who is called Christ, you become an heir of God and joint heir with Jesus Christ.

A. *The inheritance is for all true believers (Eph. 3:6).*
B. *The inheritance is guaranteed by the giving of the Holy Spirit (Eph. 1:14).*
C. *The inheritance is the kingdom of God with all its blessings (Matt. 25:34; 1 Cor. 6:9; Gal. 5:21).*

VI. If you do the right thing with Jesus, who is called Christ, you will have great joy.

There are many joys for the believer:
A. *The joy of communion with God (1 John 1:3).*
B. *The joy of feasting on God's Word (Ps.1:1–3; Jer. 15:16).*
C. *The joy of witnessing (Prov. 11:30; Dan. 12:3; Matt. 4:19).*
D. *The joy of suffering for Christ (2 Tim. 3:12).*
E. *The joy of victorious service (Matt. 16:24; Phil. 4:13).*

Conclusion

If you have not received Jesus as your Savior, then do so now. Do the right thing with Jesus and have all of these things and many more.

SUNDAY EVENING, AUGUST 12

Title: Good-bye to Glory

Text: "She named the child Icabod, saying, The glory is departed from Israel: because the ark of God was taken, and because of her father in law and her husband. And she said, The glory is departed from Israel: for the ark of God is taken" **(1 Sam. 4:21–22).**

Scripture Reading: 1 Samuel 2:29–36; 4:1, 10, 17

Introduction

The heartrending theme of this story is that a nation, a church, a home, or an individual may lose the glory of God.

The aged Eli had been indulgent with his two immoral sons. As a result of their conduct, the whole nation of Israel had strayed from Jehovah. Disrespect for the ancient symbols of worship had resulted in the degeneration of character and in a general weakening of the people. A longtime enemy, the Philistines, took this as an occasion to wreak havoc on them.

News reached Eli that his sons, Hophni and Phinehas, were killed in battle and that the ark of God was in enemy hands. It was too much for the old man; in his grief he fell from his seat to his death. This disastrous news was brought to Phinehas's wife at the time her baby was to be delivered. In shock and sickness of heart, she could only whisper the name to be given to her newborn child, "Ichabod." This name conveyed the dying mother's distress. It meant "the glory is departed." From the emotion-filled moments of this young woman's death, some age-long principles seem to take on added importance.

I. The destiny of a nation is often affected by the conduct of her people.

A. *The destruction of Sodom and the plea of one righteous man.*

B. *Nineveh and her repenting people.*

C. *The conditions of Jehovah's covenant.*

D. *God in Genesis: "If ye do well."*

E. *Contemporary conduct in the United States.*

II. The conduct of the citizenry often imitates that of the leaders.

A. *Biblical historical records during the period of the divided kingdom.*

B. *Aggressive nations of the past century.*

C. *American leaders and their following.*

III. God's glory departs when his will is not proclaimed.

A. *The role of the Old Testament prophet.*

B. *Early Christians before the civil authorities.*

C. *Christians of the twenty-first century and the "Word of God."*

Conclusion

" 'They will fight against you but will not overcome you, for I am with you and will rescue you,' declares the LORD" (Jer. 1:19 NIV). More and more we believe this less and less. Ours is a day in which we want to divorce both our national and personal relationships from God. We think we can avoid responsibility if we deny the divine plan. The fact is that God has been and is good to us. We have not deserved the loving-kindness and tender mercies that he has showered on us. We are responsible to act because of what has happened. We must confess the high noon of God's glory shining on us. It is ours to work "while it is yet day." We can expect his continued blessings only as we announce his claims.

WEDNESDAY EVENING, AUGUST 15

Title: Joy in Trials

Text: "Wherein ye greatly rejoice, though now for a season, if need be, ye are in heaviness through manifold temptations" (**1 Peter 1:6**).

Scripture Reading: 1 Peter 1:6–12

Introduction

Many modern Christians labor under the mistaken idea that faith in God and faithfulness to God should give them some kind of an immunity from trials, troubles, and difficulties. Experience reveals that there is no such immunity except from the consequences of the sins that we would have committed if we had not made Jesus the Lord of our lives.

When we examine the writings of the New Testament, we find that the followers of our Lord often found themselves in the midst of great trials and troubles over which they had no control. There can be no question about the fact that often they were tempted to give up the struggle and quit. It was a dangerous time in which to be a follower of the Lord Jesus Christ. Such is true in some portions of the world today. All of us need to study the New Testament to discover how these early followers of our Lord faced persecution and troubles triumphantly. Peter thanked God for the possibility of having joy within the heart even in the midst of the trials that threatened the life of the churches of Asia Minor.

I. Faith on trial (1 Peter 1:6–7).

The troubles that were to fall upon the Christians would be a test of the genuineness of their faith in Jesus Christ. By remaining faithful and steadfast under pressure, they would prove to themselves, to their Lord, and to the unsaved world that their experience with God was more precious than gold. This evidence of their faith and commitment would bring great glory to their Lord. When Christ returns he will bestow upon them great praise, honor, and glory.

II. Faith and faithfulness (1 Peter 1:8–9).

A. *Genuine faith is the faith that demonstrates itself in faithfulness.*

B. *Genuine faith enables the believer to experience the joy and blessings of God's presence and power in the present and the fullness of salvation in the future.*

III. The faith and faithfulness of the prophets (1 Peter 1:10–12).

Peter reminded his readers that through the centuries God had used the prophets to communicate his message of love and mercy toward people. These servants of God had labored in hard times and under painful circumstances as the Spirit of God led them. They had been inspired to speak of the sufferings of Christ, even when they could not fully comprehend all that their message implied. This message had been so wonderful that the curiosity of the angels had been aroused. These heavenly creatures desired to look into what God was doing in the human race.

Conclusion

Peter wrote to his Christian friends who were scattered abroad, and to us, seeking to encourage a positive response to the mercy and purpose of God for his servants during difficult times. He knew that they would not be able to understand everything that happened to them. He sought to encourage them by assuring them that they were a part of God's continuing purpose of saving people from the waste and ravages of sin. He insisted that they exercise faith and faithfulness even when it was difficult to do so.

SUNDAY MORNING, AUGUST 19

Title: Whose Voice Do You Hear?

Text: "And the LORD came, and stood, and called as at other times, Samuel, Samuel. Then Samuel answered, Speak; for thy servant heareth" **(1 Sam. 3:10)**.

Scripture Reading: 1 Samuel 3:1–20

Hymns: "Speak to My Heart," McKinney

"Breathe on Me," McKinney

"I Am Resolved," Hartsough

Offertory Prayer: Dear Lord, it is a glorious privilege to have a part in your work through our tithes and offerings. We give you our gifts today from hearts of love and gratitude. We thank you for every good and perfect gift that comes down from above. Bless and use our gifts. For Jesus' sake we pray. Amen.

Introduction

The days of Eli were a dark period in Israel's history. There was no settled government. Anarchy exposed the people to the assaults of the enemies and heathen about them. Idolatry deprived them of the one thing that might have given them stability and courage. The tabernacle remained, but old Eli, with his two reckless and licentious sons, Phinehas and Hophni, showed the weakness of ceremonialism to stay the tide of passion and selfishness.

But God had pity on sinful Israel. He desired to communicate himself to them. How could he do it? People had grown cold and callous with their own concerns. It seemed as if in Israel there was only one who could be receptive to the voice of God—youthful Samuel. Doesn't God always speak to the simple, the humble, the childlike, the ones ready to receive him? The things that were hidden from the learned and pious were revealed to a youth. Thus began a long line of prophets who were open to the vision, voice, and truth of God.

Whose voice do you hear?

I. Some hear voices but not the voice of God.

It is evident that Eli heard voices but not the voice of God. The Bible says, "In those days the word of the LORD was rare; there were not many visions" (1 Sam. 3:1 NIV).

There was a period when nothing happened. The only voices Eli heard were the voices of his sons and the voices of his enemies.

There are many voices heard today.

A. *The voice of nations.*

B. *The voice of politics.*

C. *The voice of science.*

D. *The voice of race.*

E. *The voice of sex.*

F. *The voice of relevancy.*

G. *The voice of false religions.*

All of these voices and many more speak and desire to be heard. Whose voice will you hear? Whose voice will you listen to? Whose voice will you heed?

II. Some hear the voice of God.

"The LORD called Samuel: and he answered, Here am I" (1 Sam. 3:4).

A. *The voice of the Lord can be heard.* "One night Eli, whose eyes were becoming so weak that he could barely see, was lying down in his usual place. The lamp of God had not gone out, and Samuel was lying down in the temple of the Lord, where the ark of God was. Then the Lord called Samuel. Samuel answered 'Here I am'" (1 Sam. 3:2–4). Eli was the one in Israel to whom a revelation should have come. God's priest and God's judge should have been able to hear the voice of God. But another is preferred: the voice comes to Samuel, and Eli is superseded. The voice comes to the pupil, not to the teacher. Yes, God does speak, and his voice can be heard!

B. *The voice of the Lord is heard in the place of worship.* It is important to note that the voice of God was heard in the temple by Samuel. Even though there was sin and corruption in the temple, God could still speak. I believe God still speaks in the place of worship. He called Samuel by name. God has a perfect knowledge of each soul, and he can call you by name.

C. *The voice of the Lord is heard often or more than once.* God speaks more than once. He speaks with ever-increasing impressiveness. Like Samuel he may have to speak four times, but he does speak.

D. *The voice of the Lord should be received immediately with reverence, humility, and obedience.* Samuel confessed himself to be a servant. He was dedicated to God as his servant and is ready to hear and obey. When one hears and receives the Lord with reverence, humility, and obedience, what a difference it makes in one's soul and in one's purpose in life.

E. *The voice of the Lord sometimes reveals a message of judgment.*

1. The judgment of the Lord is startling and horrifying to people (1 Sam. 3:11).

2. The judgment of the Lord comes after warnings already given (1 Sam. 3:12).

3. The judgment of the Lord will be complete (1 Sam. 3:12).

4. The judgment of the Lord is deserved (1 Sam. 3:18; James 4:17).

5. The judgment of the Lord is permanent and irrevocable (1 Sam. 3:14).

F. *The voice of the Lord reveals a message that is sometimes painful to deliver.*

1. The message was not given hastily or rashly (1 Sam. 3:15).

2. The message was given truthfully, faithfully, and without reserve (1 Sam. 3:18).

3. The message was followed by a beneficial effect (1 Sam. 3:18).

   a. A similar spirit was shown by Aaron (Lev. 10:3).

   b. A similar spirit was shown by Job (Job 1:21).

   c. A similar spirit was shown by David (2 Sam. 18:14–15, 32–33).

   d. A similar spirit was shown by Hezekiah (2 Kings 20:19).

   e. The voice of the Lord must be heeded, or ruin and disaster will follow (1 Sam. 4:11–22).

Conclusion

Let each of us believe that God still speaks. Let us acknowledge God's voice, listen to his directions, and do his work. Will you hear the voice of God, or will you listen to other voices?

SUNDAY EVENING, AUGUST 19

Title: A Harvest Hanging

Text: "And he gave them into the hands of the Gibeonites, and they hanged them on the mountain before the LORD, and the seven of them perished together. They were put to death in the first days of harvest, at the beginning of the barley harvest" (**2 Sam. 21:9 RSV**).

Scripture Reading: 2 Samuel 21:1–14

Introduction

When circumstances impinge on our personal interest, guilt feelings within us bring us to conclude, "It is God's punishment." It may be, but if God is responsible for all the maladies for which he is accused, he is kept pretty busy doing evil against sinners. During the reign of King David, there occurred a drought of three years. The religious fathers in their formal council concluded that God was angry because of the action of Saul in breaking a treaty with the tribe of Gibeon. David was advised to approach the offended Gibeonites and to "make things right." The demand of the heartless Gibeonites was that five sons of Merab (Michal) and two sons of Rizpah be slain. This sordid request of the fanatically mad Gibeonites was fulfilled as a religious act. We learn a lot about human nature then and now from this emotion-filled Hebrew story.

I. Often the weak, not the guilty, must pay for society's wrongs.

A. *These seven sons and two wives of Saul were in no way guilty of sin against the Gibeonites.*

B. *Merab and Rizpah, the most innocent of all, paid the highest cost of suffering.*

C. *The fact that the drought brought on hunger was assumed to be an acceptable reason for making people suffer.*

D. *In many world societies today, individuals are proclaimed guilty if ample finances are not available to "determine" them otherwise.*

II. Frequently God's action is ascribed to the wrong cause.

A. *The drought was not broken because of the slaying of seven descendants of Saul.*
   1. The cause of war is not to be glorified because brave men die in it.
   2. Behind war are sin and evil that require such drastic action.

B. *The drought was broken because of God's compassion toward fidelity and love.*
   1. Rizpah, in her sackcloth high on the hill, watching over the slain bodies, had power with God.
   2. A mother's tears brought more rain than a king's bargain.

C. *God's requirement for human attitude is "a broken and contrite heart."* He has no traffic with the deal seeker.

III. God at Golgotha sheds light on God at Gibeon.

A. *With God, love is victorious.*
   1. King David bowed in defeat as he recognized the iniquity of his order.
   2. King David demanded an honorable burial for all the sons.
   3. The drought ended in answer to a mother's devoted vigilance.
   4. A mother's tears had to wash the face of God so that people could see it.

B. *With God, the crowd can be wrong.*
   1. When calamity comes, its victims may be the most innocent.
   2. Often the guiltiest try to direct blame.

Conclusion

There is a moving comparison between this mother and son on Gibeon and a mother and Son on Golgotha. As they look down on the parched fields of the world, they see the weary reapers facing spiritual famine "year after year." The unrelenting heaven holds back its rains of mercy, and people shrivel more and more into egotistical nothingness. But that hour came, that hour when love triumphed and the long drought was broken. At that time, God's love showed through and his mercy showered down.

Will we ever come to see—to see why love is crucified? Why do we continue to hurt? We could be ever so thankful for the Rizpahs if from them we could all learn that sins of the past cannot be atoned for by reprisals among the living. Only in the spirit of love can the mercy of God fall as gentle rain and the long drought end.

WEDNESDAY EVENING, AUGUST 22

Title: A Call to Holy Living

Text: "But as he which hath called you is holy, so be ye holy in all manner of conversation; because it is written, Be ye holy; for I am holy" (**1 Peter 1:15–16**).

Scripture Reading: 1 Peter 1:13–16

Introduction

Peter wrote to remind Christians of every age that, as Israel was redeemed from the bondage of Egyptian slavery by the blood of the lamb on the night of the Passover, so they have been redeemed by the blood of Christ, the Lamb of God (1 Peter 1:18–20). As Israel is called to a holy life of redemptive service for God, even so for the Christian the bestowal of divine privileges implies the assumption of redemptive responsibilities.

Peter issued a challenge to his scattered Christian friends that they dedicate themselves completely to a life of devoted service to God. This exhortation is based on the great salvation they have experienced through the redemptive sufferings of Jesus Christ (1 Peter 1:11).

I. "Wherefore gird up the loins of your mind" (I Peter 1:13).

Israel was instructed (Ex. 12) to eat the Passover feast with their loins girded and with their shoes on their feet in anticipation of an immediate departure for the Promised Land.

Peter encouraged the Christian sojourners in an alien world to "gird" up their minds. He bade them and us to bring every thought into harmony with the revealed will of God. Sobriety is to characterize the conduct of those who have been called out of the empire of evil where once they lived in sin. Hope for ultimate victory through Jesus Christ is to be the guiding light that leads them as they make their journey through the difficulties of the present and future.

II. "As obedient children" (I Peter 1:14).

To be chosen by God and redeemed from the slavery of sin is not only a privilege to be enjoyed; it is also a responsibility that must be assumed. The children of God are forbidden to conduct themselves in a manner that would compromise the good name of their heavenly Father. They are urged to sever themselves from their former manner of life.

III. "Be ye holy; for I am holy" (I Peter 1:16).

Peter challenged the followers of Christ who constituted the new Israel, the chosen ones, to be a holy people. He quoted the divine imperative for holiness that was at the heart of the genuine faith of Israel (Lev. 11:44–45; 19:2; 20:7, 26).

The root idea in the word "holy" as used by Peter is "different" or "set apart," in the sense that Christians are to be consecrated, dedicated without reservation to the will of God.

Conclusion

The apostle Peter was challenging those who would read this epistle to consider themselves as the chosen people of God, separated from profane activities and consecrated to the service of God. They are God's special people and, as such, the character of God is to characterize their attitudes, their ambitions, and their activities.

By dedicating ourselves completely to the service of God, we avoid the peril of being totally self-centered and being involved in the work of the devil. The best way to overcome evil is to be overcome and captivated by doing good in the service of God. This requires desire, decision, dedication, and determination. The Holy Spirit will so lead us if we will let him.

SUNDAY MORNING, AUGUST 26

Title: Am I My Brother's Keeper?

Text: "And the LORD said unto Cain, Where is Abel thy brother? And he said, I know not: Am I my brother's keeper?" **(Gen. 4:9)**.

Scripture Reading: Genesis 4:1–15

Hymns: "From Greenland's Icy Mountains," Heber

"I Love to Tell the Story," Hankey

"Send the Light," Gabriel

Offertory Prayer: Dear God, it is written in your Book that God loves a cheerful giver. It is also said that it is more blessed to give than it is to receive. Help us to be cheerful givers, and may we be blessed by our giving. Now bless the gift and the giver. In Jesus' name. Amen.

Introduction

One of the great questions of the Bible is the response of Cain to an inquiry of the Lord: "Am I my brother's keeper?" (Gen. 4:9).

Cain was the first son of the first couple mentioned in the Bible, Adam and Eve. The name Cain means "possession." Eve said when Cain was born, "I have gotten a man from the LORD" (Gen. 4:1). She was expressing the joy of her possession, Cain, and the joy of participating with God in giving birth to life. Cain was a farmer by occupation. After the murder of his brother, he fled to Nod, built a city, and became the ancestor of the following: Jabal, forefather of tent-dwelling cattle keepers; Jubal, forefather of musicians; Tubal-Cain, forefather of smiths; Lamech, a man of violence and progenitor of the Kenites (Josh. 15:57).

Abel was the second son born to Adam and Eve. The name Abel means "breath," "transitoriness," "shepherd," "herdsman," and "son." He was a keeper of sheep and is described as a righteous man (Matt. 23:35). He offered to God a lamb of his flock, which was accepted, while Cain's offer of produce was rejected.

When Cain murdered his brother Abel, the Lord said to Cain, "Where is Abel thy brother? And he said, I know not: Am I my brother's keeper?" (Gen. 4:9). The answer to this great question is a resounding, "Yes! I am my brother's keeper!"

Let us examine this great question and the lessons that come from it.

I. The question "Am I my brother's keeper?" addresses itself to one's attitude.

Note from the beginning that making an offering to God is a natural thing. There was an offering to God long before the institution of sacrifice by Moses. It seems to be evident that God had "respect" unto the offerings because attitudes were involved. "And the LORD had respect unto Abel and to his offering" (Gen. 4:4). "But unto Cain and to his offering he had not respect" (v. 5).

Abel represents one who responds to God's revelation, comes to God on God's terms, and submits to God's will. Cain represents one who comes to God on his own terms, refusing to do what does not suit him or commend itself to his judgment.

Micah wrote about attitude: "He has showed you, O man, what is good. And what does the LORD require of you? To act justly and to love mercy and to walk humbly with your God" (6:8). Cain's attitude not only was wrong toward God, but it was wrong toward Abel, whom he murdered.

How is your attitude?

II. The question "Am I my brother's keeper?" addresses itself to a form of godliness without power.

Someone said, "The minister sees the best side of a man, the lawyer the worst, and the physician the real." If you want to know what a person's worship is worth, see him after the services are over and he is outside the church. Cain killed Abel when church was over, after a worship experience.

Cain's anger shows that his worship was a form of godliness without power. If his offering had been made in the right spirit, there would have been no killing. Cain refused to heed the warning of God: "If you do what is right, will you not be accepted? But if you do not do what is right, sin is crouching at your door" (Gen. 4:7 NIV). If Cain had had a real case of religion and not a form of godliness without power, he never would have murdered his brother.

III. The question "Am I my brother's keeper?" addresses itself to acceptability.

Some offerings are more acceptable to God than others. God looked with favor on Abel's offering and with disfavor on what Cain brought. The Scripture hints concerning the preference but gives no real reason for it. The preference may have been due to the different dispositions of spirit in the brothers; the substance of the offerings—flesh not fruits; and the method of the offering—the firstfruits by presentation only and the firstling of the flock by sacrifice, by death and presentation.

Had Cain really accepted God? God would have accepted Cain's offering if Cain really had given God his life. The Scripture reveals Cain as a wicked person, "Do not be like Cain, who belonged to the evil one and murdered his brother. And why did he murder him? Because his own actions were evil and his brother's were righteous" (1 John 3:12 NIV). If you accept Christ as the Lord of your life, then it follows that your offering will be acceptable to him and your brother will be acceptable to you.

IV. The question "Am I my brother's keeper?" addresses itself to the revelation of people as sinners.

Our sin may go unnoticed by others, but God takes account of every sin. He said to Cain, "Your brother's blood cries out to me from the ground" (Gen. 4:10 NIV).

Biblical writers point out that God knows us as sinners (Num. 32:23; Gal. 6:7–9). And our sins not only are known by God, but he will punish us because of them. Cain said, "My punishment is greater than I can bear" (Gen. 1:13). Unless our sins are taken to God and straightened out, they will lie at the door ready to strike at any moment.

V. The question "Am I my brother's keeper?" addresses itself to responsibility.

The question is taken usually to refer to physical well-being. This meaning can be justified by the Scripture passage. We do have duties to perform in behalf of those unfortunate ones who need food, clothing, shelter, and healing.

The question really points not so much to the physical as to the spiritual. Cain was proud of himself, and like an exhibitor at a contest, he portrayed his offering as an estimation of his endowed abilities. On the other hand, Abel was a true child of God. It does not seem unjust to Cain to say that his sacrifice, however good in itself, was not prompted by a faith that rested in and responded to God's revelation of his will. Abel's offering was offered in faith. "By faith Abel offered unto God a more excellent sacrifice than Cain, by which he obtained witness that he was righteous, God testifying of his gifts: and by it he being dead yet speaketh" (Heb. 11:4).

Abel knew he was responsible to God and to his fellow human!

VI. The question "Am I my brother's keeper?" addresses itself to witnessing.

The only right answer to the question "Am I my brother's keeper?" is yes. We are responsible for people's souls as well as their lives.

The Bible teaches us to witness (Prov. 11:30; Ezek. 3:17–21; Dan. 12:3; Matt. 28:19–20; Acts 20:26–27). We have been redeemed, and we are to point others to the Lamb of God who takes away the sin of the world. We have been saved to win others to Jesus as Lord and Savior. We have been chosen that lost men everywhere might have the gospel.

Conclusion

Are you a witness? Do you witness to your mate, your children, your neighbors, your friends, your acquaintances? Give witness to your saving faith today. Proclaim Jesus as Lord, Savior, and Master of your life!

SUNDAY EVENING, AUGUST 26

Title: Sackcloth on the Flesh

Text: "When the king heard the woman's words, he tore his robes. As he went along the wall, the people looked, and there, underneath, he had sackcloth on his body" (**2 Kings 6:30 NIV**).

Scripture Reading: 2 Kings 6:24–30

Introduction

For Paul, "to know Christ and him crucified" was to see one's spiritual need. In a most amazing manner, this Samaritan king in his conduct during the Syrian siege projects the spirit of the crucified Christ.

The heartless plan of the Syrians was to starve the citizens until they exposed themselves, then slay them. Privation with extreme suffering became so severe that cannibalistic practices began. One woman bargained with her neighbor to eat the neighbor's son one day and then her son the next (1 Kings 6:28). When, on the following day, the son was hidden, the cheated woman appealed to the king. As the king came to know the extent of their destitution, he was utterly crushed. In his deep grief, he lay hold of his royal robe and rent it asunder. Gazing on him, the people discovered that underneath, next to his flesh, he wore the chafing sackcloth. The king had been suffering with them all the time, and they had not known it. This realization of a suffering king brought new life to a weary, emaciated people. It is similar to the realization of the sin-sick who for the first time understand "Christ died for the ungodly."

I. Encouragement in the presence of God.

A. *The Samaritan king on the wall was a comfort to the beleaguered people.*
   1. The people took comfort in knowing that the king felt their pain
   2. A king who identifies with his subjects is a king who will be followed.
B. *God came to us when our battle was at its worst.* He exposed himself in the way he came to us.
   1. "God was in Christ," and we love him for having taken that route.
   2. In Christ, God was wounded in the siege and suffered with us.
C. *"She had hidden [her son]," cried the deceived woman* (2 Kings 6:29 NIV). God revealed his Son.

II. Power in the act of God.

A. *The king did not strengthen the people with a speech.*

1. Jesus was a great teacher, but this did not make him our Savior.
2. He not only spoke the gospel—he was the gospel.

B. *It was the supreme deed of Jesus that has power to transform.*
   1. It was the depth of Christ's sacrifice that revealed the depth of God's love.
   2. Who would not love a King like that?

III. Transformation in identity with God.

A. *"I have been crucified with Christ and I no longer live, but Christ lives in me" (Gal. 2:20 NIV).*

B. *Identifying in the death of Christ is to share in his life.*

C. *The new creature.*

D. *Paul's concept of the Christian as adopted.*

Conclusion

We find in this ancient story the meaning of the death of Christ. When the battle was fiercest, our Savior and Lord came upon the wall, and through the torn robe on Calvary, we could see God's glorious love. "The people looked, and there, underneath, he had sackcloth on his body." We would never have known the heart of God but for Calvary. Many a person who has looked has never been the same since.

Life does not stop with the understanding and accepting of God's creative love. It was to those defenders out on the city's walls that the king's act was the most meaningful. For the Christian it is in following the living Christ that the purpose of God is realized. In days when the human spirit has sagged, we need a powerful gospel. That gospel has its roots in the Lord God, and we may see it through the sackcloth at Calvary.

WEDNESDAY EVENING, AUGUST 29

Title: A Call to Spiritual Growth

Text: "As newborn babes, desire the sincere milk of the word, that ye may grow thereby" (**1 Peter 2:2**).

Scripture Reading: 1 Peter 2:1–3

Introduction

The apostle Peter did not labor under the erroneous idea that the new birth immediately produces a mature Christian. As in the realm of the physical, so it is in the spiritual: a birth produces an infant.

The apostle challenges his readers to respond fully to the potential that is theirs because of their spiritual birth into the family of God: "You have been born again, not of perishable seed, but of imperishable, through the living and enduring word of God" (1 Peter 1:23 NIV).

Peter urges his readers to beware of the peril of assuming that the spiritual birth experience will automatically assure spiritual maturity. He stresses the importance of a positive response to the call of God to become spiritually mature and competent as the servants of God.

I. "Laying aside" (1 Peter 2:1).

The words of 1 Peter 2:1 can come as a real shock to the person who labors under the false assumption that the new birth alone is the ultimate in God's plans for his children.

Peter declares that those who have been called into the family of God must lay aside the wicked ways of the heathen world in which they have lived and in which they continue to sojourn. As if it were a contaminated garment, infected with a fatal disease, ungodliness is to be stripped off. The Christian is to divest himself of all evil—two-faced trickery, false pretense, envyings, and unkind remarks about others. These are but illustrations of the things that must be laid aside if believers will truly be God's people in the world.

II. "As newborn babes" (1 Peter 2:2).

Peter did not assume that those to whom he addressed his letter already were spiritually mature. He was realistic in recognizing that if they would become the servants of God, they must be involved in a continuing process of spiritual growth. He emphasizes the supreme importance of a sustained spiritual diet involving the "spiritual milk" in the Word of God.

The Word of God had been used by the Holy Spirit to effect Peter's readers' spiritual birth into the family of God (1 Peter 1:23–25). By eating and drinking this "sincere [spiritual] milk of the word," they could nourish the growth of the life that God had imparted to them in the new birth.

Conclusion

There is no way for the new convert to grow if he neglects or refuses to feed his soul on the milk and meat of the Word of God. The new birth is made possible by the preaching of the Word of God (1 Peter 1:23). It is by obeying the Word that believers purify their lives (v. 22). These things are possible because the Word of God has the life of God in it (vv. 24–25).

Spiritual growth makes fullness of joy, as well as effective service, possible. Spiritual growth points toward victory and a quality of life that is pleasing to the heavenly Father. It is the will of our heavenly Father that each of his children be in a process of continuing spiritual growth. When we cease to grow, we begin to die.

SUGGESTED PREACHING PROGRAM FOR

SEPTEMBER

■ Sunday Mornings

The sermons for Sunday mornings in September have an evangelistic focus.

■ Sunday Evenings

"The Church in the New Testament" is the theme for a series of messages based on Paul's first epistle to Timothy. In a time when the church is under attack, we need a better understanding of the nature and ministry of the church to fulfill our Lord's purpose for us in the present.

■ Wednesday Evenings

Continue the series of expository messages based on Peter's first epistle, using the theme "Encouragement and Counsel for Difficult Times from a Seasoned Veteran of the Cross."

SUNDAY MORNING, SEPTEMBER 2

Title: Go Home and Tell

Text: "Go home to your family and tell them how much the Lord has done for you, and how he has had mercy on you" (**Mark 5:19 NIV**).

Scripture Reading: Mark 5:1–20

Hymns: "To God Be the Glory," Crosby

"I Love to Tell the Story," Hankey

"Wherever He Leads I'll Go," McKinney

Offertory Prayer: Gracious God, our heavenly Father, you have provided all things necessary for the saving of people everywhere—your great love, the gift of your Son, and the blood of the cross—now it is up to us. May we dedicate our time, talent, and treasure that people everywhere might hear and believe the gospel. In Jesus' name. Amen.

Introduction

For Christ, in all his earthly ministry there was no escape from people in need. From every quarter they came with their requests for help and healing. And he never turned them down. His heart was always moved by the pull of the people. The day's activity recorded in Mark 4 and 5 is no exception. It was a day spent in healing and teaching. Now, at the end of the day, completely exhausted,

Jesus sought retreat in a boat on the waters of Galilee. So physically spent was the Master that he soon fell asleep. Suddenly, without warning, a storm swept down upon the disciples and Jesus. At their cry for help, Jesus awoke, rebuked the winds and the sea, and called for calm. By morning light the boat was pulled ashore in the land of the Gadarenes.

I. The demoniac (Mark 5:1–4).

As soon as Jesus stepped ashore, he was met by a man who was possessed by demon spirits. What a sad spectacle! Each of the gospel writers adds a little to the horrible description. Matthew says that the man was fierce and that his madness made the way impassable for travelers. Luke says he wore no clothes, had no home, had no friends, and lived among the tombs. Mark says that day and night he cried and cut himself with stones. Unwanted and friendless, he now lived the life of a beast. Alone, he lived among the dead! What a wretched piece of humanity was this man called Legion!

Modern forms of Gadara's madman of the tombs are not hard to find. The drunkard, the drug addict, and the sexually perverse are all demon possessed. Like the demoniac, they are hopeless and helpless without God. Only the grace of God can free them. It is not enough to clean up a madman and clothe him; he must be freed from the demons that possess his heart.

II. The Savior (Mark 5:6–8).

The demoniac of Gadara had been watching Jesus' boat from the rocky cliffs. The wild storm of the night with its lightning, thunder, and fierce winds were but an outward manifestation of his troubled heart. Now in the morning calm, Legion watched Jesus and the disciples pick their way among the rocks. Suddenly the madman cried out, "What do you want with us, Son of God? Have you come here to torture us before the appointed time?" (8:29 NIV). The demons in this man recognized that Jesus is the Son of God. Ah, if we had even the sense of the devil, we would know who Jesus is! What did the demons mean by "before the appointed time"? Before the time of judgment. There is a day coming when the devil will get his due. The evil spirits know their days are numbered.

    A. *The demons' request.* "The demons begged Jesus, 'Send us among the pigs; allow us to go into them'" (Mark 5:12 NIV). The demons would rather dwell any place, even in swine, than to be cast into the pit, the "place of the destroyer." The pit is a place of wailing and darkness. Jesus said we should do anything to keep from going to the pit. Lose your eye or arm, but do not let your whole body be cast into the pit. What a warning this ought to be to unbelievers today!

    B. *Jesus' command (5:8, 13).* Can Jesus with a word command the demons? Yes. What no other power on earth can effect, Jesus can. He is able to deliver you.

    C. *The demoniac healed (5:15).* What a contrast between this verse and the beginning of the story! At the beginning, the madman lived in the tombs, could not be bound, and cried day and night with torment. Now he was seated, calm, clothed, and in his right mind. No wonder the people of Gadara were afraid! They had seen a miracle; they had witnessed the mighty power of God to deliver.

III. From madman to missionary (Mark 5:18–20).

The request of this man just "saved by the grace of God" was a natural one. He had just been delivered from a legion of demons and had been given a new life. It is natural that he would want to be with his Savior. There is indeed something wrong with a person who has been saved and then does not want to follow the Savior.

A. *The commission (v. 19).* Jesus said to this man, "Go home." The man volunteered to follow Jesus, but Jesus told him to go home. To others Jesus had said, "Follow me," but not to this one. Why not? The people of Gadara had requested Jesus to leave (v. 17). It was their polite way of saying, "Get out of town." Christ had to go. Suppose this new convert left with Jesus! There would have been no one left to tell of the great things Jesus had done (see v. 19). If this man did not stay home and tell, the whole countryside would have no witness to the power of God. His presence at home would be a constant sermon. He would be a living epistle of God's grace.

This is what our town needs—someone to go home and tell. We need a whole country full of "home" missionaries.

B. *The missionary (v. 20).* The new Christian obeyed. He went home and began to tell the story of what God had done for him. He did not wait for a class on how to win the lost. I doubt if he knew the "ABCs of salvation." But he knew God had touched his life with grace, and he wanted to share the good news. Did it work? It must have, because Luke concludes the story with these words: "Now when Jesus returned, a crowd welcomed him, for they were all expecting him" (Luke 8:40 NIV). This is the kind of missions we need today. Believers everywhere must "go home and tell." Will you?

Conclusion

As in Jesus' day, there simply are not enough "preachers" to go around. If the gospel is ever to be told "to every creature," each believer must "go home and tell."

SUNDAY EVENING, SEPTEMBER 2

Title: The Church and Its Doctrine

Text: "Paul, an apostle of Christ Jesus by the command of God our Savior and of Christ Jesus our hope, To Timothy my true son in the faith: Grace, mercy and peace from God the Father and Christ Jesus our Lord" (**1 Tim. 1:1–2 NIV**).

Scripture Reading: 1 Timothy 1:1–20

Introduction

The church was first and foremost in the mind, the heart, and the work of the apostle Paul. His first concern on entering a new field was to lead people to Christ Jesus as Savior and to establish a church. Everything he wrote was either to a church, for use in a church, or to help regulate the affairs of a church. He says, "Christ also loved the church, and gave himself for it" (Eph. 5:25). The same could be said for the apostle.

In his first letter to Timothy, Paul gives instructions to his young convert concerning the organization of the church and how its members should conduct themselves. This particular church had many problems, and Paul seeks to find a solution for them. Paul tells the church how to deal with heresies and discusses the church's doctrine, worship, organization, and pastoral ministry.

Now with this overview in mind, let us look in detail at the first chapter, which we can entitle "The Church and Its Doctrine."

I. The greeting from Paul (I Tim. 1:1–2).

A. *The man who wrote. Paul, as was the custom of the day, immediately identified himself.* He was writing from prison, where he awaited execution. This was not a new experience for the apostle. He had been imprisoned in Philippi, Caesarea, Jerusalem, Ephesus, and now in Rome. He was truly "the prisoner of Jesus Christ."

1. The name he bore—he calls himself Paul. This was the Gentile name he used. He had been Saul, but when he met Jesus Christ on the road to Damascus and became a new man with a new mission (to the Gentiles), he gradually dropped the Jewish name and became Paul.

2. The calling he received—"an apostle of Christ Jesus." Paul was proud of his apostleship. There were times when he had to defend his calling, because he had enemies who questioned his authority. Christ had uniquely appeared to him and called him. The church had set him apart by divine direction of the Holy Spirit.

    Paul is not unique in this calling. The word *apostle* means "a sent one." Actually, all of us are "apostles"—ones sent by God to minister in his name.

3. The Master he served—"our Savior ... Christ Jesus." All that Paul did was for Christ. He could boldly assert, "I have been crucified with Christ and I no longer live, but Christ lives in me" (Gal. 2:20).

4. The hope he possessed—"Christ Jesus our hope." Because of the hope Paul possessed, he had a certainty and assurance in every circumstance. Christ was his hope, and he is our hope—our only hope. He is our hope of salvation, of abundant life, and of eternity.

B. *The son he loved.* Paul was writing "to Timothy my true son in the faith." He had led Timothy to the Lord and, consequently, held him dear to his heart. Timothy had been a constant companion of the apostle and a trusted coworker. He had entrusted Timothy with many special responsibilities in caring for the needs of the churches.

C. *The blessings he desired.* Paul wanted Timothy and the church to experience the best—"Grace, mercy and peace from God the Father and Christ Jesus our Lord."

   1. "Grace, mercy and peace"—what a trilogy of blessings for anyone—"grace" for every need, "mercy" for every failure, "peace" for every circumstance. How we all need these! We can have them if we come boldly before the throne of grace.

   2. "From God the Father and Christ Jesus our Lord." This is the source of all blessings. It is to him we owe our lives and our obedience. He is our Father, to whom we can take our every need. And he is our Lord, to whom we must give our entire person.

II. Paul's warning concerning error (I Tim. 1:3–11).

Paul placed Timothy in Ephesus to guard the flock of God against error. As the shepherd, he must protect the sheep from the enemies of the gospel who would destroy. Timothy was to see that a false gospel was not taught. Paul warned him of this. He believed that to be "forewarned is to be forearmed."

A. *The nature of the error (vv. 3–10).* The error being taught was that which we know as Gnosticism. Paul notes two characteristics of this doctrine.

   1. Wrong creed. The Gnostics were teaching false doctrine. The law was good, but they were making it bad. They had perverted its purpose. Paul says elsewhere, "The law was our schoolmaster to bring us unto Christ" (Gal. 3:24).

   2. Wrong conduct. Because the Gnostics' faith was in error, their lives were in error. Paul illustrates this by listing in verses 9 and 10 some of their practices.

B. *The gospel is the standard (vv. 10–11).* All doctrine is to be tested by the "glorious gospel of the blessed God." It had been committed to his trust. The church not only is responsible for knowing the truth, but also for embodying the truth and for propagating it.

C. *Love is the antidote (v. 5).* Paul says that whatever the problem, the difficulty, or the command, love is the answer. Some have seen in the listing of sins in the above verses an enumeration of the Ten Commandments. (William Barclay, for one, develops this thought.) The first four commandments deal with one's relation to God, while the last six deal with one's relation to his neighbor. When Jesus said that the first commandment was to "love thy God," he covered the first four commandments. When he gave the second commandment, "to love thy neighbor as thyself," he covered the last six. Love is the antidote for all.

III. The testimony Paul gave (I Tim. 1:11–17).

Paul always bore his personal testimony concerning what Christ had done for him (vv. 11–14).

A. *Paul's testimony of thanksgiving.* He began by giving thanks to God.

1. He enabled me. Paul was not boasting. If it had not been for the grace of God, he would have been doing as the Gnostics were. He remembered what he was before he met Christ. Now he could "do everything through him who [gave him] strength" (Phil. 4:13 NIV).

2. He entrusted me. He "considered me faithful, appointing me to his service" (1:12 NIV). Paul had been a blasphemer, persecutor, and insulter, yet God trusted him in spite of this. Now the privilege of service was his. In like manner, this same experience is ours. We are ambassadors for Christ by his grace. He has committed to us the ministry of reconciliation.

3. He "exampled" me. If I may coin a phrase, Paul was saying that his life was an example to be used by God. If he could save and use one such as Paul, he can save and use anyone.

B. *Paul's testimony concerning Christ (v. 15).* This is "a trustworthy saying" (NIV) — one you can base your life on. Paul frequently uses this expression (3:1; 4:9; 2 Tim. 2:11; Titus 3:8). This probably was a common phrase currently in use by the early Christians.

1. "Christ Jesus came." This expresses Christ's preexistence. It emphasizes the incarnation of our Savior.

2. "To save." This emphasizes his mission. The angel declared, "You are to give him the name Jesus, because he will save his people from their sins" (Matt. 1:21 NIV).

3. "Sinners." This includes all of us. Paul calls himself the "worst" one. We all feel this when we have seen Christ Jesus.

IV. The charge to Timothy (1 Tim. 1:18–20).

Paul was saying, "Let me remind you why I gave you this responsibility and the burden that rests on your shoulders. Remember you are:

A. *To "fight the good fight" (v. 18 NIV).* This is the picture of a soldier engaged in conflict — not on the parade ground, not simply guarding a treasure, and certainly not on furlough. He was to meet the enemy and overcome him. If he and we do this, we can say at the end, "I have fought the good fight" (2 Tim. 4:7 NIV).

B. *To "hold on to faith" (v. 19 NIV).* Others had made shipwreck of the faith, such as Hymenaeus and Alexander (v. 20), but Paul was persuaded that Timothy would do better things.

C. *To have a "good conscience" (v. 19).* Paul spoke of those whose consciences were seared — hardened. Timothy, however, was to be sensitive to every convicting action of the Holy Spirit and every guiding movement of Christ Jesus. Only in this manner could he fulfill his mission.

Conclusion

For a church to be effective, its doctrine must be pure. It must hold tenaciously to the faith. It must teach and preach the gospel. This means that the leadership and members must *know* and *do*. It takes both.

The gospel simply stated is given in verse 15, "Christ Jesus came into the world to save sinners" (NIV). He came to save you even as he did Paul. Receive him today.

WEDNESDAY EVENING, SEPTEMBER 5

Title: A Call to Priestly Service
Text: "You are ... a royal priesthood ... that you may declare the praises of him who called you out of darkness into his wonderful light" **(1 Peter 2:9 NIV)**.
Scripture Reading: 1 Peter 2:4–10

Introduction

In words saturated with quotations and concepts from the Old Testament, Peter discusses the nature and the function of the church as it faces and responds to Jesus' great commission. He challenges his readers to recognize and respond to their high and holy privileges and responsibilities. He declares that the purpose of God and the promises of God as made to Israel in the past are now applicable to those who constitute the church. The true nature and functions of the church are not always known and understood even by its members. We often make a partial response to our Lord's purpose for us rather than a total response.

The functions of the church have been described in terms of worshiping, witnessing, teaching, and ministering. The manner in which we implement these functions will vary from person to person and from church to church.

All of us who consider ourselves members of the church could profit greatly by understanding the nature of the church from the viewpoint of its Founder and the early leaders in the Christian enterprise. Peter, the spokesman for the apostles on so many different occasions, writes of the church in the following manner.

I. The Living Stone.

Christ, the Living Stone, is the foundation on which the church is built, being constituted of born-again believers who are the "lively," or living, stones.

Jesus had applied to himself the words of Psalm 118:22 (see Mark 12:10–11). His use of this figure of speech provides the background for understanding Acts 4:11–12 and Ephesians 2:20–22, as well as Peter's reference to "a living stone."

Christ, the Stone that had been rejected by the high priests and by the people of national Israel, is chosen by and precious to God. Though dishonored by men, he is held in the highest esteem by God.

II. Living stones.

Those who receive Christ, the Living Stone, as Lord and Savior, themselves become living stones. As living stones connected to and built on Christ, they constitute the new spiritual temple of God. Each one is to offer up a spiritual sacrifice that is acceptable to God (Rom. 12:1).

III. A chosen generation.

As Israel was a chosen people, even so the church, the followers of Christ, are God's chosen servants. They are chosen to bring forth fruit to the honor and glory of God (John 15:16).

IV. A royal priesthood.

Those who know Jesus Christ as Lord and Savior constitute a royal priesthood. They are such because they belong to Christ and are obligated to serve him as their King. They are to function as priests, go-betweens for God and people. As believers are filled with the Spirit and obey the Spirit, God will be able to reach the unbelieving world through them. At the same time, the unbelieving world will come to know about God through those individual believers. This is our priestly function, which is also evangelistic in nature.

V. A holy nation.

As a people who belong to a holy God, believers have been set apart for redemptive service. Believers now constitute a holy nation whose citizenship is in heaven (Phil. 3:20). Each of us needs to recognize the obligations as well as the privileges of belonging completely to our Lord.

VI. People belonging to God.

Believers are "a people for God's own possession." Jesus has redeemed believers by his own blood on the cross of Calvary.

Conclusion

Peter applies to the church the titles and functions Moses had applied to Israel (Ex. 19:5–6). The church is the new Israel. It is the successor to both the privileges and responsibilities of the old Israel.

God intended for the nation of Israel to render both a priestly and a proclamation ministry. Peter declares that these new people of God are to offer "spiritual sacrifices, acceptable to God through Jesus Christ," and to "declare the praises of him who called [them] out of darkness into his wonderful light" (1 Peter 2:5, 9 NIV).

This dual ministry calls for the full dedication of each believer's total faculties in a service of love to God. This service will manifest itself in compassionate concern for the world that does not know God. Such a ministry should characterize every church today.

SUNDAY MORNING, SEPTEMBER 9

Title: The Greatest Need of All

Text: "Jesus answered and said unto him, Verily, verily, I say unto thee, Except a man be born again, he cannot see the kingdom of God" **(John 3:3)**.

Scripture Reading: John 3:1–16

Hymns: "Guide Me, O Thou Great Jehovah," Williams

          "I've Found a Friend," Small

          "Ye Must Be Born Again," Sleeper

Offertory Prayer: Our holy Father, we worship you in Spirit and in truth. We approach you with an offering of love and gratitude. We invoke your blessings on these tithes and offerings to the end that others might enthrone Christ as Lord of life and experience the miracle of the new birth. We thank you for your blessings on us in every area of life. Help us to be more worthy of your gracious generosity. In Christ's name we pray. Amen.

Introduction

Much is being said and written these days about the needs of people.

I. People have many needs.

A. *People need to work.* Work is good. Every boy and girl wants to succeed in life's work. The Bible pays honest toil a great tribute. Jesus was a working man.

B. *People need wealth.* This is especially true in these days of skyrocketing prices. You know this when you buy groceries. But testimonies of those who have reached the summit of wealth are unanimous in that wealth does not meet the deepest need of humanity.

C. *People need some recreation.* Recreation eases the strain of living and gives us time to unwind. Jesus took time out to rest and pray.

D. *People need good health.* An old proverb says, "He who has health has hope, and he who has hope has everything." Health is a great asset, but some are happy who do not have good health. Good health is not the best thing in life.

E. *People need an education.* No person would argue this. We make many sacrifices to obtain it. Proverbs places a premium on knowledge and wisdom.

F. *People need to know that they are loved and needed.* This is a basic instinct inherent in human beings. Perhaps the reason there are so many suicides is because many feel unloved and unneeded.

II. What then is the greatest need of people?

It is to be saved. People need redemption from their sins and the wreckage caused by them. We are part of a mutinous world where rebellion against God is the order of the day.

Four things God wants you to know:

A. *You need to be saved.* "Except a man be born again, he cannot see the kingdom of God" (John 3:3). "For all have sinned, and come short of the glory of God" (Rom. 3:23). "There is not a righteous man on earth who does what is right and never sins" (Eccl. 7:20 NIV). "All of us have become like one who is unclean, and all our righteous acts are like filthy rags" (Isa. 64:6 NIV; cf. Jer. 17:9; Isa. 53:6).

B. *You cannot save yourself.* "Not by works of righteousness which we have done, but according to his mercy he saved us" (Titus 3:5). "By the works of the law shall no flesh be justified" (Gal. 2:16). "There is a way which seemeth right unto a man, but the end thereof are the ways of death" (Prov. 14:12). "Jesus saith unto him, I am the way, the truth, and the life: no man cometh unto the Father, but by me" (John 14:6).

C. *Jesus has already provided for your salvation.* "[Jesus] his own self bare our sins in his own body on the tree, that we, being dead to sins, should live unto righteousness" (1 Peter 2:24). "For Christ also hath once suffered for sins, the just for the unjust, that he might bring us to God" (1 Peter 3:18). "God made him who had no sin to be sin for us, so that in him we might become the righteousness of God" (2 Cor. 5:21 NIV; cf. John 3:16).

D. *Jesus will enable you to overcome temptation.* "No temptation has seized you except what is common to man. And God is faithful; he will not let you be tempted beyond what you can bear. But when you are tempted, he will also provide a way out so that you can stand up under it" (1 Cor. 10:13 NIV).

Conclusion

"Believe in the Lord Jesus, and you will be saved" (Acts 16:31 NIV). Turn from sin in true repentance. "Now [God] commands all people everywhere to repent" (17:30 NIV). "Repent, then, and turn to God, so that your sins may be wiped out" (3:19 NIV). "Repent and believe the good news!" (Mark 1:15 NIV).

Confess your sins to Jesus. "For there is one God, and one mediator between God and men, the man Christ Jesus" (1 Tim. 2:5).

Confess Jesus before people. "If you confess with your mouth, 'Jesus is Lord,' and believe in your heart that God raised him from the dead, you will be saved" (Rom. 10:9 NIV).

Do it now. "Seek the LORD while he may be found; call on him while he is near" (Isa. 55:6 NIV). "Behold, now is the day of salvation" (2 Cor. 6:2).

"Do not boast about tomorrow, for you do not know what a day may bring forth" (Prov. 27:1 NIV). "For what shall it profit a man, if he gain the whole world, and lose his own soul?" (Mark 8:36).

SUNDAY EVENING, SEPTEMBER 9

Title: The Church and Its Worship

Text: "I exhort therefore, that, first of all, supplications, prayers, intercessions, and giving of thanks, be made for all men; For kings, and for all that are in authority; that we may lead a quiet and peaceable life in all godliness and honesty. For this is good and acceptable in the sight of God our Saviour" (**1 Tim. 2:1–3**).

Scripture Reading: 1 Timothy 2:1–15

Introduction

Worship is the dynamic of the church. It is in the act of meeting God in Christian worship that the believer is empowered, encouraged, and enlightened. Because of this, Paul discusses one facet of the church's worship—prayer. Let us look closely at 1 Timothy 2 and try to follow the apostle's thought.

I. The place of prayer in worship (I Tim. 2:1–8).

A. *The importance of prayer (v. 1).*

1. This we gather by implication and command. Approximately one-sixth of this letter is devoted to instructions concerning prayer. Obviously Paul considered prayer to be important.

2. Paul practiced prayer. On the Damascus road, having met Christ face-to-face, Paul prayed. In the midnight hour, with his back bleeding and his feet and hands in chains, the apostle prayed. When he considered the lost condition of his brothers after the flesh, he prayed.

3. People have always prayed. They pray for rain in times of drought. They pray for food in times of famine. They pray for victory in times of battle. They pray for strength in times of weakness. They pray for health in times of sickness. They pray when they are baffled, bewildered, and bedeviled. They pray when they can do nothing else.

4. Now Paul is exhorting or commanding the church to make their requests known to God in prayer. "I exhort therefore that ... prayers ... be made" (v. 1).

B. *The characteristics of prayer (v. 1).* There are many who have a limited view of prayer. As an illustration of this, one writer says that prayer is not praise, nor adoration, nor meditation, nor humiliation, nor even compassion. It is always asking and nothing else. Prayer is a truck that goes straight to the warehouse, loads up, and comes home with the goods. Although this author has given us a fine book on prayer, there is something wrong with this definition. It is not complete. It is not the whole truth. Prayer *is* asking, but it is more.

In our text the apostle mentions four types of prayer that are to be used in public worship (and in private also). Notice them now.

1. "Supplications" is the first word used. This is prayer that expresses the idea of personal insufficiency. It is prayer for divine help and grace. All prayer must begin at this point.

2. "Prayer" is the second word. It is an appeal to God based on past mercies. It includes acts of adoration or confession.

3. "Intercessions" is the third word. It embraces the idea of going into the King's presence to submit a petition. It implies going to someone on behalf of a third party. The prayer of Abraham for Sodom, the prayer of Moses for Israel, and the prayer of Paul for his worldly brothers all illustrate this concept. It is what the Christian must do for his fellow Christians and for the unsaved of the world. Certainly we limit the King of the universe by failure here.

4. "Thanksgiving" is the final word. It is gratitude to God for all his benefits, such as we see so prevalent in the Psalms.

C. *The circumference of prayer (v. 2).*

1. Prayer must encompass a world. Paul says we are to pray "for *all* men." God's love is for all, "for God so loved the world." Christ died for *all*. In fact, unless we can pray *for* all, we certainly will not witness *to* all. I suppose the scope of our sincere prayers more than anything else indicates the measure of our concern.

2. Specifically Paul says we are to pray "for kings, and for all that are in authority." At this time the church was the subject of great persecution. Those "in authority" were the ones instigating this bitter persecution, yet Paul says to pray for them.

   In the Sermon on the Mount, Jesus said, "Love your enemies, bless them that curse you, do good to them that hate you, and *pray* for those that despitefully use you, and persecute you" (Matt. 5:44, emphasis added). On the cross, he practiced this, saying, "Father, forgive them; for they know not what they do" (Luke 23:34).

3. Only with this kind of prayer can we expect society to be what it ought to be. This alone can make it possible for us to "lead a quiet and peaceable life." "Quiet" indicates the idea of tranquillity from without. "Peaceable" has the idea of peace from within. This is Christian citizens showing concern and their highest desire for their country.

4. Paul believed that prayer could change things. Even the "king, and those in authority" could be changed. Most of us place limitations on the omnipotent God by thinking that there are those who cannot be changed and influenced by prayer. We mark certain ones off our list, thinking that they are beyond prayer, but Christ did not—not even his enemies who were crucifying him.

D. *The charter of prayer (vv. 3–8).* Paul now gives the reasons why we should pray.

1. It "is good and acceptable in the sight of God our Savior" (v. 3). Such prayer as we have been discussing is "good and acceptable" because it is obeying the command of God. It is in keeping with the Spirit of Christ.

2. God's desire is for all people to be saved (v. 4). Therefore, our prayer should encompass all people.

3. There is one Mediator between God and humanity (v. 5). Christ is our great High Priest who intercedes with the Father for us. We can "come boldly to the throne of grace" now because he "gave himself a ransom for all" (v. 6).

4. This charter for prayer stresses the universality of the gospel of our Lord and Savior Jesus Christ. It is for all people, and anything less than this is a mockery of Christianity. He has made possible the redemption of the entire world—young and old, rich and poor, black and white, learned and unlearned. If we do not pray in the same spirit (and witness too) we are missing the Spirit of our Christ.

5. Such prayer is in accordance with God's will (v. 4). There are many prayers that we cannot be certain are according to God's will, but there never can be any doubt about prayer for the salvation of people for whom Christ died.

E. *The conditions of prayer (v. 8).*

1. In worship, people are to pray "lifting up holy hands." This refers to the position of prayer. It does not exclude other positions (kneeling, etc.); it simply stresses this one. It is the picture of a person standing before God with arms lifted and hands open toward God.

2. Paul mentions three conditions for effective prayer. People have always felt that a wrong life or a wrong motive was a barrier to access to God. Isaiah 1:15 says, "When ye spread forth your hands, I will hide mine eyes from you: yea, when ye make many prayers, I will not hear: your hands are full of blood." To be effective in prayer, the individual must have:

a. No sin—he must have "holy hands." David said long ago, "If I regard iniquity in my heart, the LORD will not hear me" (Ps. 66:18). Isaiah 59:1–2 indicates this. "Behold, the LORD's hand is not shortened, that it cannot save; neither his ear heavy, that it cannot hear: But your iniquities have separated between you and your God, and your sins have hid his face from you, that he will not hear."

Do you remember, as a child, coming to the dinner table and hearing your father say, "Let me see your hands"? If they were soiled, you could not eat from the table until you had washed them. In like manner, God says that you cannot sit at his table of abundance until you have cleansed your hands (and heart).

b. No anger—he must be "without wrath." Jesus said that if a man came to worship and had anything against his brother, he first must be reconciled to his brother (Matt. 5:24). If we are not right with our fellow believers, our Father will not hear. In the Lord's Prayer, Jesus taught us to pray, "Forgive us our trespasses in the same manner we forgive those who trespass against us." Anger, wrath, and hatred can destroy our prayer life.

c. No doubting—he must have faith. "Without faith it is impossible to please [God]; for he that cometh to God must believe that he is, and that he is a rewarder of them that diligently seek him" (Heb. 11:6). James said, "But let him ask in faith, nothing wavering. For he that wavereth is like a wave of the sea driven with the wind and tossed. For let not that man think that he shall receive any thing of the Lord" (James 1:6).

II. The place of women in worship (1 Tim. 2:9–15).

Now Paul turns his attention to the women and their place in public worship. "In like manner" refers to the men who have been mentioned above in worship.

A. *The background of this passage is the paganism in which the early church found itself.* The immorality and indecency of women in the pagan worship of idols would mean that women should guard against every appearance of evil.

B. *Their inner beauty was to be that of the inner life and not just of outer adornment.*

C. *Their restriction was that they were not to be leaders in public worship.* Because women in Paul's day did not receive religious education, they were not to exercise authority over men in teaching.

D. *Their service and opportunity was to be in the home.* Through childbearing women would be saved (v. 15), said Paul. This referred, not to a woman's salvation from sin, but to her salvation to service. She would be saved from uselessness. Since she could not teach in public, she was provided a field of service in the home. By means of rearing and instructing and winning her children, she truly became the "hand that rocked the world."

Conclusion

Now in light of all that Paul has said, let us pray and serve as God would have us and in the place he would have us.

WEDNESDAY EVENING, SEPTEMBER 12

Title: A Call to Christian Conduct in a Secular World

Text: "Dear friends, I urge you ... to abstain from sinful desires, which war against your soul" **(1 Peter 2:11 NIV)**.

Scripture Reading: 1 Peter 2:11–12

Introduction

In the first part of Peter's letter, he discusses the privileges and responsibilities of the followers of Christ who constitute the new Israel. He now begins to insist that in all areas of life Christians are to recognize and respond to the obligations and responsibilities that are inherent in their new relationship with Jesus Christ.

Peter gives exhortations of universal application by all Christians concerning their manner of life in a pagan world.

I. Dear friends.

The apostle wrote in terms of brotherly love, addressing his readers as "aliens and strangers in the world" (1 Peter 2:11 NIV). He spoke to them as foreign settlers or dwellers in a strange place who tarry for a time in a country other than their native land.

While recognizing that a Christian's citizenship is in heaven, the apostle reminds his readers that Christians are sojourners in a pagan world. They are not to live on the level of the flesh (1 Peter 2:11; cf. 1 John 2:15–17).

As citizens of the heavenly country, they are to conduct themselves as the servants of God who have been made alive by the Spirit.

II. Abstain from sinful desires.

As travelers in a strange land, Christians are not to adopt its customs. Fleshly lusts involve all of the desires that originate in our fleshly or unredeemed nature, including those directly connected with the appetites of the body.

Christians are not to live for the mere satisfaction of their natural appetites. Living on the level of the flesh ignores and denies the spiritual level and deadens one's sensitivity to the work of God's Spirit within the heart (Col. 3:1–2).

III. Live good lives among the pagans.

The pagan world in which the early church lived was very conscious of and critical toward the conduct of the followers of Christ. They were severely and unjustly criticized. They were accused of the foulest crimes because the pagan world did not understand the meaning of their doctrines or the significance of their practices. Consequently, the early church suffered great persecution.

The pagan world today waits for a living demonstration of the benevolent compassion and the sterling character that Christ is able to reproduce in those who will trust him and obey him.

IV. The testimony of good works.

Peter encouraged the Christians of his day to conduct themselves in such a manner that their lives could bear the closest examination. By so doing, they would put to silence the false accusations of ungodly people and at the same time bring honor and glory to God.

The best way by which modern Christians can put to silence the criticisms of a pagan and wicked society is by the testimony of upright and holy lives that are dedicated to ministries of mercy in the name of Jesus Christ.

Conclusion

Have you fallen in love with the pagan world in which you live? Can the secular society about you see anything distinctive that sets you apart as a follower of the Lord Jesus Christ?

Our Lord would have us to serve as the light of the world to illuminate the way to abundant life. He would have us function as the salt of the earth that we might preserve society from complete decay.

SUNDAY MORNING, SEPTEMBER 16

Title: Needed: A Double Portion of Compassion

Text: "But when he saw the multitudes, he was moved with compassion on them, because they fainted, and were scattered abroad, as sheep having no shepherd" **(Matt. 9:36).**

Scripture Reading: Matthew 9:35–38

Hymns: "Love Divine, All Loves Excelling," Wesley

"The King of Love My Shepherd Is," Baker

"When I Survey the Wondrous Cross, Watts

Offertory Prayer: Heavenly Father, today we thank you for the abundance of your grace to us. We praise you with our lips. We love you with our hearts. We glorify you with our lives. We proclaim your salvation throughout the entire world. Accept our tithes and offerings today and bless them to the end that all the nations of the earth might hear the wonderful story of your love through Jesus Christ. Amen.

Introduction

A conference speaker said, "The present-day type of Christianity will never win the world for Christ." This statement leads us to ask, "What is wrong or lacking in present-day Christianity? Why won't our Christianity meet the test of the times?" Among several things that could be mentioned as lacking in our present-day brand of Christianity is *compassion*. Read again the life of Jesus and you will discover compassion to be the secret of the untiring ministry of our Lord. It comes from two Latin words meaning "with" and "suffer." Literally it means to suffer with another—to put yourself in another's place. Hence, it means to suffer with another because of that one's misfortune or calamities. When you have compassion on another, you feel that person's pain or misfortune.

Compassion is more than pity. Pity is feeling for someone in distress; compassion is feeling plus action. For example, in the parable of the good Samaritan, the priest and the Levite both had pity on the beaten man, but the Samaritan had compassion. *Compassion engenders action.* Jesus had compassion, and we must have compassion to bring this world to Christ. Compassion is an essential part of any revival.

I. Demonstrations of compassion from the Bible.

A. *Pharaoh's daughter had compassion on the baby Moses.* When she saw the little boy lying in the bulrush basket, we read, "Behold, the babe wept. And she had compassion on him, and said, This is one of the Hebrew's children" (Ex. 2:6). Someone has said that God sent an angel to pinch the boy to make him cry. His cry stirred the compassion of the king's daughter. Because of her compassion, she did something about the baby.

B. *God had compassion on the oppressed Israelites.* "But Hazael king of Syria oppressed Israel all the days of Jehoahaz. And the LORD was gracious unto them, and had compassion on them" (2 Kings 13:22–23). When the children of Israel experienced oppression, God had compassion on them (suffered with them).

C. *Jesus had compassion on the hungry multitude.* "Then Jesus called his disciples unto him, and said, I have compassion on the multitude, because they continue with me now three days and have nothing to eat: and I will not

276

send them away fasting, lest they faint in the way" (Matt. 15:32). Jesus suffered with the multitude and did something about it.

He also had compassion on the multitude "because they fainted, and were scattered abroad, as sheep having no shepherd" (Matt. 9:36). Again, Jesus, moved with compassion, healed the sick (14:14). In Mark 1:41 Jesus was moved with compassion toward a leper and healed him.

Leaving Jericho, two blind men cried out to Jesus to have mercy upon them. "So Jesus had compassion on them, and touched their eyes: and immediately their eyes received sight, and they followed him" (Matt. 20:34).

D. *In the story of the return of the prodigal son, the father had compassion on the prodigal son and ran to him, hugged his neck, and kissed him.* Compassion led to forgiveness and restoration (Luke 15:20).

II. Compassion is a wonderful emotion.

Of all the emotions that surge through our souls, there is none finer than compassion. It identifies you with a person in need. You get underneath his load and help him bear it.

Do you have compassion for a person in sin? Do you realize his danger? Compassion leads to action.

A. *Compassion led to the adoption of the baby Moses into the home of Pharaoh's daughter.* The career of Moses owed its existence to compassion. Who can measure the life of Moses in its good to humanity?

B. *Compassion led to the relief of the oppressed people of Israel.* God's compassion led to the relief of his chosen people.

C. *Compassion caused our Lord to feed the multitudes of men, women, and children.* His miracles grew out of his compassion.

D. *Compassion caused a despised Samaritan to perform ministries of mercy for a Jew.* Why did fellow Jews, a priest and Levite, pass by the wounded man? They were like many today who have no time to soil their hands helping others. They have no compassion.

E. *Compassion is the explanation of the father's receiving the prodigal son back into the family circle.* The kiss, the best robe, the ring, the fattened calf, the feast of rejoicing—all of this was the dividend of compassion.

III. Compassion is our supreme need.

When our hearts become compassionate, we will do what our Master has commanded. We will find time to do his work. A cold heart will never rescue a baby who needs a home. A cold heart will not render aid to wounded travelers on life's highways.

A. *When does compassion come?* Go again to the Bible references to compassion. Each time it is indicated: when Pharaoh's daughter *saw* the child; when God *saw* the oppression; when Jesus *saw* the hungry crowds; when the Samaritan *saw* the wounded man; when the father *saw* his wayward son.

277

We must somehow *see* the world's needs. We must in some way *see* the world's hungry crowds. We must *see* the people lost in sin. We must in some way have a vision of a hurt humanity. No vision—no compassion.

B. *Lack of compassion is the explanation of inactive Christians, unwilling to give aid to young people, unwilling to teach a class, to give themselves in abandon to our Lord's work.* When our hearts burn with compassion, we will win a lost world for our Lord.

C. *Compassion takes away selfishness.* It causes us to go out to "seek and to save that which was lost" with our Master. Compassion makes the phrase "until he find it" in the parable of the lost sheep (Luke 15:4–7) a reality in our own lives. It makes us "sweep diligently until we find" as the woman with the lost coin. When Jesus looked at Jerusalem, he wept because of the sins of its inhabitants and the danger they were in. Compassion drives us to our knees in repentance of our own sins and drives us out to talk and pray and plead with people not to commit eternal suicide. Compassion makes us go from inward motives and not for outward show.

Conclusion

My good friend Carl Whirley, a missionary to Africa, was asked shortly after arriving, "Why do they send you missionaries to build schools and hospitals? They haven't seen us. They do not know us. We are told thousands of women forgo things they want at Christmas time in order to give sacrificially to get the gospel to us. Why do they give?" Carl answered, "They haven't seen you, but they have seen Christ, and he gave his all for you, so they have followed his example."

SUNDAY EVENING, SEPTEMBER 16

Title: The Church and Its Leadership

Text: "I am writing you these instructions so that, if I am delayed, you will know how people ought to conduct themselves in God's household, which is the church of the living God, the pillar and foundation of the truth" (**1 Tim. 3:14–15 NIV**).

Scripture Reading: 1 Timothy 3:1–16

Introduction

Paul tells us in one revealing verse why he is writing to Timothy and the members of the church. "What I have written will show you the sort of character men of God's household ought to have" (3:15 PHILLIPS). He then mentions three types of leaders in the church and gives the qualities they ought to possess. Let us see them in order.

I. The overseer of the church (1 Tim. 3:1–7).

A. *The office of overseer is the office of the pastor.* The word is translated "bishop" in the KJV and RSV. The word means "to have the care of, to oversee, to superintend." This person has the responsibility of directing the spiritual life of a church.

In the New Testament the word *overseer* occurs only five times. In 1 Peter 2:25 it is used with "shepherd" as a title. In Acts 20:28 and Titus 1:7 it is a synonym of "elder." Actually, the titles of bishop, elder, shepherd, and pastor are all the same office. In 1 Timothy 3:2–7 and Titus 1:6–9 we see that the qualifications are the same. In Philippians 1:1 Paul sends greetings to "bishops" and "deacons." Certainly he would not omit "elders." In Acts 20:17 Paul sends for the Ephesian elders and then says that they are "bishops" to feed the church of God (v. 28). "Elder" is used to describe what they are. "Bishop" is used to describe their duties. They are to oversee the flock of God's people.

B. *The qualifications of the overseer are given.* Paul lists six different characteristics to be considered.

1. He should be "blameless," or "without reproach." There should be nothing in his life that could be used by his enemies to bring shame on the cause of Christ. As pastor he is to lead the flock, and this is done best by example. To those outside the church, "he must have a good testimony" (v. 7).

2. He must not be a "novice" or an "inexperienced convert." Without maturity he would be tempted to have an inflated sense of his importance. The temptation to pride would be present (as it is even to the mature).

3. Since the pastor's work is to "feed the church of God" (Acts 20:28), he must be "apt to teach." This does not mean only that he must be able to teach, but also that he loves to teach and is ready to do so. Of course, it is understood that he must know what to teach—the glorious gospel. Without this, "grievous wolves shall enter in … not sparing the flock" (Acts 20:29).

4. He must not be guilty of covetousness nor of loving money.

5. In regard to his home life, he must be "the husband of one wife." This does not demand that he be married. It simply rules out polygamy, more than one wife, as the pagans practiced. In addition, he must "rule his own house well." His family must respect him and be subject to him. If he cannot control his own household, he certainly cannot control his Master's household.

6. He must have himself under control. "Temperate" carries the idea of self-control. He should be "sober," having a balanced judgment. He should be "gentle," not a "striker" (pugnacious) nor "contentious" (one with a chip on his shoulder).

C. *Such a man would have the respect of the congregation as well as the hand of God on his life.* He would then do "the good work" that Paul indicates to be the nature of the office.

II. The deacons of the church (1 Tim. 3:8–13).

A. *Next the office of deacon is discussed.* Paul does not mention their duties or their origin. The word *deacon* means "servant," and this more than anything else gives the nature of the office.

    The beginning of the office is probably to be found in Acts 6. When we look at this passage, we find that these men were "Spirit filled," of a "good report," and abounding in faith. Notice how the need for deacons came about. The church had grown rapidly until the pastor could not adequately minister to all the members. Some were being "neglected." So the church was called together and was told that the pastors should not neglect their preaching and praying to settle differences among the members or to distribute food to the needy members. In other words, theirs was a spiritual ministry. They were, in effect, assistants to the pastors so that the pastors could devote their time to evangelism and preaching and fulfilling the duties of their office. These were the responsibilities of the office of deacon.

B. *The qualifications for the office of deacon are given.* Paul says, "Deacons, likewise, are to be..." (NIV). "Likewise" indicates that, like pastors, deacons must possess the qualities given above. The office of deacon is a spiritual office and must have spiritual men, just as the office of pastor must have.

1. Deacons should be men who are "proved"; that is, their lives must show their readiness for the office. Men should not be selected hoping that the office will make them better men. They must be "blameless" before their selection, or else reproach will be brought on the church. Not "double-tongued," not "greedy of filthy lucre," not "given to wine" are some of the indications of being "blameless" and "proved."

2. Their own households, like the pastor's, must be considered. A deacon must be the "husband of one wife"—not more than one. Again it does not mean deacons "must" be married, though in most cases it would be best. They also must manage their own households well.

3. The wife of a deacon must be considered in selecting a man for the office. Verse 11 says, "Even so must their wives be grave, not slanderers, sober, faithful in all things."

    As far as the Greek construction is concerned, this could refer to the wives of deacons or to women who are engaged in the same type of service. Such an office would be a "deaconess." Romans 16:1 refers to Phoebe, the "deaconess" of the church. In all probability, the early church had such an office to care for the poor and needy, particularly the sick and needy women and children. This could well be what Paul is speaking of here.

    In either case, these women are to be of the highest moral character, for they will be in the eye of the congregation at all times and will represent the church before the world. They must, therefore, be reverent in their conduct, not flippant or careless. They must be able to control their tongues and be reverent and discreet in all conversation. In addition, they must be "faithful in all things."

4. They must be sound in doctrine — "holding the mystery of the faith in a pure conscience" (v. 9). They must know the "faith" and be faithful to the faith.

III. The importance of the church (1 Tim. 3:14–16).

Paul says to Timothy, "I hope to come to you shortly, but if for some reason I am delayed, I want you to know how you ought to conduct yourself in the house of God" (vv. 14–15, my paraphrase).

A. *Paul calls the church "the house of God, which is the church of the living God."* If any man ever magnified the church and stressed its importance, it was Paul. In writing to the church at Ephesus, he said, "You are ... members of God's household, built on the foundation of the apostles and prophets, with Christ Jesus himself as the chief cornerstone. In him the whole building is joined together and rises to become a holy temple in the Lord. And in him you too are being built together to become a dwelling in which God lives by his Spirit" (Eph. 2:19–22 NIV).

The concept here is that the church is a family. The members are brothers and sisters in Christ Jesus. Love is the central characteristic.

B. *Paul says the church is the "pillar and ground of the truth."* There are two possible meanings here. One is that this refers to the pillar of fire that illuminated Israel's camp and led them through the wilderness. The church then would be a shining light that guides the Christian in his pilgrimage to the Promised Land.

However, in Galatians 2:9, Paul refers to James, John, and Peter as "pillars." The "pillar" in this sense would mean a column that supports and strengthens a building. This would be a familiar sight to the Ephesians, who saw daily the temple of Diana and its one hundred plus pillars supporting the building and displaying a statue on the crown of each one. The church then has as its responsibility to support and display the truth of God for the world to see.

C. *This truth to be displayed is given in verse 16.* "And without controversy great is the mystery of godliness: God was manifest in the flesh, justified in the Spirit, seen of angels, preached unto the Gentiles, believed on in the world, received up into glory."

This truth, which was hidden in time past, is now revealed (meaning of "mystery") by God for all.

Conclusion

As members of the church of our Christ, let us see that we are truly the family of God, embodying his love for one another and for the world.

WEDNESDAY EVENING, SEPTEMBER 19

Title: A Call to Christian Conduct in Civic Affairs

Text: "Submit yourselves to every ordinance of man for the Lord's sake" (**1 Peter 2:13**).

Scripture Reading: 1 Peter 2:13–18

Introduction

Peter would have been first to proclaim that mere regular attendance at the place of prayer and worship did not constitute the full responsibility of the child of God. In the words of our Scripture reading, he directs the attention of his readers to the government under which they were living. Perhaps Peter remembered that our Lord had met his citizenship responsibilities by making provisions for the tribute or tax that was due from all citizens (Matt. 17:24–27).

Because the Christian faith was suspect by the pagan society, Peter insisted that Christians were under a special obligation to conduct themselves as good citizens.

I. Government is of God (I Peter 2:13–14; cf. Rom. 13:1–4).

Peter was encouraging the believers to conform, as far as they possibly could, to the demands and laws of the country in which they were journeying as pilgrims and strangers. Peter would have agreed with the message of Paul that it is the Christian's duty to render "tribute to whom tribute is due; custom to whom custom; fear to whom fear; honour to whom honour" (Rom. 13:7). By so doing, the followers of Christ would be able to disarm the prejudice of their enemies and prove that they were law-abiding people.

Paul encouraged Timothy and others to be in prayer for everyone who was in a position of authority over the country or community (1 Tim. 2:1–3).

II. The motive for Christian citizenship: "For the Lord's sake."

A. *The motive behind the Christian's practice of good citizenship is his desire to bring glory to his Lord.*

B. *To be a poor citizen is to discredit the Savior and his church.*

III. "The praise of them that do well."

Peter was eager that each believer and the church as a whole be held in high esteem by both the citizens and the government officials in the pagan world in which they lived. Christians have to earn the respect of their contemporaries if they are to share their faith effectively.

Conclusion

When Christians practice good citizenship, our homes are safer and society is more secure. Economic conditions improve. Political life is on a much firmer basis. Cultural life is enriched, and spiritual life is more likely to flourish.

We need to be faithful to our church. Our relationship with God must express itself in our relationships with those who live in the world about us.

SUNDAY MORNING, SEPTEMBER 23

Title: The Man Who Broke His Vow—Samson

Text: "With such nagging she prodded him day after day until he was tired to death. So he told her everything. 'No razor has ever been used on my head,' he said, 'because I have been a Nazirite set apart to God since birth. If my head were shaved, my strength would leave me, and I would become as weak as any other man'" **(Judg. 16:16–17 NIV)**.

Scripture Reading: Judges 16:15–21

Hymns: "Holy, Holy, Holy," Heber

"O Master, Let Me Walk with Thee," Gladden

"Footsteps of Jesus," Slade

Offertory Prayer: Our gracious and loving Father, help us to recognize the evidences of your continuing concern for us. Help us to see that every good and perfect gift comes from you. Today we thank you for our daily bread and for all of the material blessings of life. Today we pray your blessings upon these tithes and offerings that they might provide spiritual bread for the hungry people of our needy world. For the advancement of your kingdom, we bring these tithes and offerings as an act of worship and love. In Jesus' name. Amen.

Introduction

Samson was a judge in Israel for twenty years in the days of the Philistines. He had given them so much trouble that they became anxious to get him out of the way. We read that Samson "attacked them viciously and slaughtered many of them" (Judg. 15:8 NIV). He also put to death a thousand Philistines with a jawbone of an donkey and brought other trouble on them. Then Samson fell in love with a vicious woman in the valley of Sorek whose name was Delilah; and the lords of the Philistines entered into a plot with her to trap Samson. She agreed with them on the proposition that each of them give her one thousand pieces of silver, and she began at once to find the secret of Samson's strength.

I. Samson told Delilah to:

A. *Bind him with seven fresh thongs.* She didn't give up.

B. *Tie him with new ropes.* The one way for Samson to escape would have been to renounce Delilah immediately and leave her. The way to defeat Satan and sin is to quit listening to him.

C. *Weave his hair.* "He replied, 'If you weave the seven braids of my head into the fabric on the loom and tighten it with the pin, I'll become as weak as any other man'" (Judg. 16:13 NIV). He then went to sleep. The devil does not sleep. He works while we sleep. Here is an evidence of how foolish Samson was. He could sleep even in the grasp of a terrible temptation.

D. *Shave his hair.* "With such nagging she prodded him day after day until he was tired to death. So he told her everything. 'No razor has ever been used on my head,' he said, 'because I have been a Nazirite set apart to God since birth. If my head were shaved, my strength would leave me, and I would become as weak as any other man'" (Judg. 16:16–17 NIV).

Notice that Samson's strength was in his Nazirite vow, not in his hair. (See Numbers 6:2–5 for the Nazirite vow.) Samson had broken his vow; therefore, he had broken fellowship with God, and his strength had left him. So it is with us when we break fellowship with God. Our strength is in the Lord. We cannot resist temptations without God's help. Our will power, no matter how strong, has a breaking point if it does not have deeper roots than human strength.

So here was Samson, strength gone, vow broken, an easy victim of the Philistines. Sadly we read, "She ... began to subdue him. And his strength left him" (Judg. 16:19), and "He did not know that the Lord had left him" (v. 20 NIV). The whole foundation was crumbled before he knew it. The Philistines took him prisoner, burned his eyes out, bound him with fetters of brass, and made him grind at the mill.

II. Let us ask Samson how it came about.

A. *Samson gave ear to the wrong kind of good time.* The devil is not through with that razor. He is still using it. He is after your locks of moral strength and is just as persistent as Delilah. He will not be satisfied until he has the last lock of your moral strength and sends you forth blind and helpless. Many people today are paying the price for listening to the wrong kind of talk about what constitutes a good time. Many are grinding at the mills of Satan with eyes burned out and are helpless.

B. *Samson associated with the wrong crowd.* This is often the excuse parents give after their son or daughter has gotten in trouble. Why doesn't the parent realize that ahead of disaster?

1. A person through association gets used to almost anything. Do you remember the first time you heard profanity on television? You have gotten used to it now and never think much about it, do you?

2. We become more and more like our association.

3. Samson was a strong man, but his associates were not good, and if our associates are not good, it is inevitable that there must come a yielding, a moral decay, then blindness.

4. God help those who have become used to vile association. Lord, help that person who is so blind that he cannot see the harm in abusing alcohol or drugs in front of his children.

5. Corruption may come from the filthy magazines one reads or television shows one watches. This is an age when so much stress is put on sex that our youth get the idea that if they abstain from fornication they are missing life itself.

C. *Learn the truth of the Scripture, "For he that soweth to his flesh shall of the flesh reap corruption" (Gal. 6:8).* Samson did not have his downfall in one hour. For years he had been a sensuous man. He did not give morality much thought. He had been on the borderline of breaking his vow for years. He finally reached his downfall with Delilah.

Conclusion

Come to Christ early and live close to him. Let the things of God have first place in your life.

SUNDAY EVENING, SEPTEMBER 23

Title: The Church and Its Pastoral Ministry

Text: "Meditate upon these things; give thyself wholly to them; that thy profiting may appear to all. Take heed unto thyself, and unto the doctrine; continue in them: for in doing this thou shalt both save thyself, and them that hear thee" **(1 Tim. 4:15–16).**

Scripture Reading: 1 Timothy 4–5

Introduction

Paul has given instructions to Timothy concerning the various offices of the church. Now he gives him instructions concerning the pastor and his pastoral ministry. In the first place, he discusses:

I. The personal life and duties of the pastor (chap. 4).

Paul's concern was that Timothy and others like him be the best "ambassadors for Christ" possible. He wanted them to fulfill every facet of their ministry. In this chapter, he mentions three areas of responsibility. They are responsible for:

A. *Exposition of false doctrine (4:1–5).*

1. The seriousness of doctrinal deviation is seen in verse 1. Paul warns that "the Spirit" has said that there will be false teachers leading some to fall away from the truth. This truth is stated in the last verses of chapter 3.

Jesus warned of this in Matthew 24:11: "And many false prophets shall rise, and shall deceive many." We must expect it, recognize it, and combat it with the truth.

This will take place "in the latter times." All time before the coming of Christ is called "former times," and the period after his first coming until his second coming is the "latter times." In other words, Paul says that it is now happening.

2. Paul notes the character of these false teachers (v. 2). They are guilty of "speaking lies in hypocrisy." They pretended to be devout Christians, but their fruit indicated them to be "play actors" and deceivers. Their consciences had become seared or hardened so that they were unable to distinguish between right and wrong, truth and error.

3. The nature of the false teaching is seen in verses 3–5. It bore the characteristics of Gnosticism. The false teachers prohibited marriage and promoted abstinence from certain foods, both of which are contrary to gospel truth.

There are basically three attitudes toward the material world in which we live. Some say that everything is evil, and we must withdraw completely from the world. This is what the monks and the hermits did. Others say that this material world is neither moral nor immoral and therefore has nothing to do with one's spiritual or religious life. One, therefore, should indulge himself. "Eat, drink and be merry" is the word. The Christian's view, however, is between these two. God created this world, and therefore it is good. Genesis 1 states this, and Peter discovered it in his rooftop vision. The Christian accepts his world as a steward and gives thanks for it. He neither abstains from the world nor abandons himself to the world.

B. *Exhortation to a personal example (4:6–10).*
1. Paul says that Timothy will be a "good minister of Jesus Christ" if he constantly reminds and rebukes concerning false doctrine. To do this, he must be "nourished up in the words of faith and of good doctrine." The tense of the verb "nourished" suggests that it is not by one outstanding banquet, nor by an occasional feast, but by a regular diet of everyday feeding on good solid fare that one is able to do this. At the same time, he not only is to be nourished by good food, but he must reject the fanciful diet of "old wives' fables."

2. Paul tells Timothy that "godliness is profitable unto all things," and so it is. It is profitable to a nation, a business, a home, a church, and an individual.
   a. Godliness is profitable today—"the life that now is" (v. 8). Christianity (morality) is not pie in the sky by and by when you die. It brings joy, happiness, peace, serenity, usefulness, and satisfaction for this hour. The life that is good and does good is a Christlike life.
   b. Godliness is profitable tomorrow—"that which is to come" (v. 8). Jesus pointed to the tomorrow of the godly, saying, "Let not your heart be troubled: ye believe in God, believe also in me. In my Father's house are many mansions: if it were not so, I would have told you. I go to prepare a place for you" (John 14:1–2). Paul said, "If in this life only we have hope in Christ, we are of all men most miser-

able" (1 Cor. 15:19). Godliness is profitable in regard to an eternal home and in regard to the degree of rewards there.

C. *Encouragement to faithful service (4:10–16).*

1. Paul reminds Timothy that Christianity is not easy (v. 10). We "labour," that is, we "toil to the point of exhaustion." We also "suffer." This is a Greek athletic term picturing a Grecian putting forth his very best, straining, agonizing in order to win the contest. The servant of Christ then must be prepared to give his best in service to Christ, even to the point of suffering and exhaustion. The motive for such a life is the love and trust we have in Christ, who is the Savior.

2. Next Paul tells Timothy to do all that his ministry requires. He mentions two sides of it. (1) These things command (v. 11). He is called of God; therefore he should not hesitate to speak forth for God with authority. (2) He is to teach these things (v. 11). He is to instruct in all truth so error will find no fertile soil for its seed.

   Timothy is to minister in spite of his youth (v. 12). Actually, he was no youngster. He was probably in his late thirties. Perhaps Paul is saying, "Don't act like a child so others will look down on you." Instead, Paul encourages Timothy to be an example by word, manner of life, faithfulness, and purity (v. 12).

3. In addition, Paul says that Timothy must continue in a life of meditation and service and study of doctrine. But most of all, Timothy was to "take heed unto [himself]" (v. 16). The Old Testament writer said, "They made me the keeper of the vineyards; but mine own vineyards have I not kept" (Song 1:6). Paul is warning Timothy not to let this happen to him. If Timothy heeds this warning, he will save both himself and those who hear him (v. 16).

II. The personal relationships of the pastor (chap. 5).

Paul begins with the assumption that the church is a family; love toward every member of the family is expected. Verses 1 and 2 speak of father, mother, brothers, and sisters. This is in keeping with what he taught elsewhere. In Galatians 6:10 he speaks of the "household of faith," as in Ephesians 2:19. In Romans 8:14–15 he calls Christians "the sons of God" and says that they have been adopted into the family of God. In the context of a family, Paul tells the pastor how to conduct himself.

A. *His relation to widows is seen in verses 3–16.* There seems to have been three types of widows in the church.

1. Widows in need (vv. 3–8). The church is to care for these if the widows have no relatives to do so. To fail to do so is to be worse than the pagans, for they cared for their widows.

2. Widows as church workers (vv. 9–15). The older widows, at least sixty years of age, who met the qualifications, were to be used in the church. There seems to have been a special office in the church for these. The younger widows, however, were not to be used as servants of the church,

for they faced too many temptations. Experience showed some of these younger ones to have failed (v. 15).

   3. Widowed dependents of believers (v. 16). If a member of the church had the responsibility of a widow, he must care for her and not expect the church to do so.

B. *His relation to elders is seen in verses 17–25.*

   1. Pastors must be honored as called of God (vv. 17–21).

      a. Their work must be compensated (vv. 17–18). The term "double honor" actually means "double pay." The context shows this to be the case.

      b. Their reputation must be protected (vv. 19–20). It is easy to criticize, but Paul says it is also dangerous. Men of God can be ruined by careless talk; therefore, they must be guarded from unscrupulous men (and women).

      c. Their office must be impartial (v. 21). Favoritism has no place in the pastor's ministry. Nothing does more harm than when some people are treated as if they can do no wrong and others are treated as if they can do no right.

   2. Pastors must be selected with care (vv. 22–25). Paul gives some good advice for selecting pastors. It is easy to get the wrong man in the ministry, but it is difficult to get him out. Therefore, a man's life should be carefully evaluated before the "laying on of hands" takes place. Pulpit committees should note carefully this exhortation of Paul.

Conclusion

The office of pastor is demanding, and rightly so. No pastor would have it otherwise. At the same time it is richly rewarding when one is called of God. No greater honor could come to a person than to be an "ambassador for Christ."

God calls people today just as he did Paul, just as he did Timothy, just as he did Peter, James, and John. He, perhaps, is calling some young person today, right here in this congregation. Heed God's call! Yield your life! It will be the greatest day of your Christian life.

WEDNESDAY EVENING, SEPTEMBER 26

Title: A Call to Christian Conduct in the Home

Text: "Wives ... be submissive to your husbands so that, if any of them do not believe the word, they may be won over without words by the behavior of their wives, when they see the purity and reverence of your lives.... Husbands, in the same way be considerate as you live with your wives, and treat them with respect" **(1 Peter 3:1, 7 NIV).**

Scripture Reading: 1 Peter 3:1–7

Introduction

The home is the basic institution in our society. The home came before the state, the school, and the church. The quality of home life determines the quality of life in every other area. It is not surprising at all that the apostle Paul focused the attention of his readers on Christian relationships in the home.

In dealing with relationships between husband and wife, Peter emphasizes their responsibilities toward each other rather than their rights. He emphasizes that a wife is responsible to God for the manner in which she conducts herself in the home. In the strongest language possible, he insists that the husband is responsible to God for the manner in which he relates to his wife.

I. Instructions to Christian wives (1 Peter 3:6).

The apostle Peter gives instructions to wives who become converts before their husbands are converted. The Christian wife of an unsaved husband has problems in the modern world, but the problems that a Christian wife faced in the ancient world were more complex and dangerous. This was the case whether she lived under Jewish law, Roman law, or Greek law. In each of these areas, women had no basic human rights. They were treated as property.

It is interesting to note Peter's counsel under these circumstances.

A. *He did not suggest that the Christian wife was to leave her non-Christian husband.* Instead, he suggested that she seek to be the best wife possible even in the most difficult of circumstances.

B. *He counseled Christian submissiveness (3:1).*

C. *He counseled a life of purity (3:2–4).*

D. *He counseled reverence and respect (3:5–6).*

Confessing faith in Jesus Christ under these circumstances required unusual faith and bravery. Consequently, Peter suggested that the wife resort to the silent preaching of a reverent life. By revealing to her husband that faith in Christ makes her a better wife and mother, a woman has more hope of winning a husband to faith in Jesus Christ.

II. Instructions to Christian husbands.

Peter emphasized the Christian husband's responsibility for the welfare of his wife. Reciprocal duties are emphasized. This concept was new in the ancient world. Until Christianity taught men differently, women had no basic human rights at all.

Christian husbands are to be understanding and considerate toward the feelings and the needs of their wives.

Perfect courtesy is to characterize the husband-wife relationship at all times.

The husband is specifically instructed to recognize that the wife has equal spiritual rights with himself. They are fellow heirs of the grace of life.

Conclusion

Specifically, Peter is saying to husbands that they must treat their wives in a responsible and Christian manner if they are to enjoy the favor of God's fellowship and approval. They cannot expect to enjoy fellowship with God in prayer if at the same time they are mistreating their wives.

That which is true concerning husbands also applies to wives. Both husbands and wives are responsible to God for the quality of home life they are able to achieve together.

SUNDAY MORNING, SEPTEMBER 30

Title: Troubled Hearts

Text: " 'Do not let your hearts be troubled. Trust in God; trust also in me' " **(John 14:1)**.

Scripture Reading: John 14:1–6

Hymns: "When Morning Gilds the Skies," Caswall

        "Majestic Sweetness Sits Enthroned," Stennett

        "Let Jesus Come into Your Heart," Morris

Offertory Prayer: Holy Father, today we thank you for your servants through whom you communicated the message of your love to our hearts. Today we offer ourselves as your servants to communicate the wonderful story of your love for a needy world. Accept these gifts from our hearts and our hands. Bless them in telling the story of your love and rendering ministries of mercy. Through Jesus Christ our Lord we pray. Amen.

Introduction

When you rush up a flight of stairs or run a few yards, do you notice a shortness of breath? When you exert yourself, does your face become flushed? When you suddenly change your position from lying down to standing up, do you feel dizzy? If so, then something may be wrong with your heart. Heart trouble, as we term it, affects our bodies in many different ways. A few of the more common heart diseases are angina, coronary thrombosis, coronary occlusion, and aortic insufficiency, commonly known as "leakage of the heart." Any form of heart trouble is serious. You had better take a doctor's advice if you have heart trouble.

A long time ago the psalmist was troubled about his heart. He voiced this prayer in Psalm 119:80, "May my heart be blameless toward your decrees, that I may not be put to shame" (NIV).

We want to think about a matter that is of vital interest to every one of us. Considered both physically and spiritually, the heart is important.

I. The physical heart.

A. *How much do you know about your physical self?* Humans have 500 muscles, a billion cells, 200 different bones, 4 gallons of blood, several hundred feet of arteries and veins, over 25 feet of intestines, and millions of pores. The heart is a small part of the body and weighs from 8 to 12 ounces. It is an intricate, vital, and delicate organ. Its normal size is around 5 x 3½ inches. It is a hollow muscular organ and pumps 15 gallons of blood per hour. In 24 hours it pumps 360 gallons. It beats 72 times a minute. In a person who is 68 years of age, it will have been working for 25,000 days, which is 600,000 hours. If a person worked as hard as his heart, imagine what he could get done.

B. *But we, with all our muscles and bones and blood, are lost unless the precious blood of Jesus has cleansed our souls.* God was wise in creating humankind; God is loving in saving us; God is powerful in keeping us. May God grant eternal life to every person who sees the Christ whose muscles were torn and whose blood was shed.

II. The spiritual heart.

The spiritual heart is no less important than the physical. By heart, in this connection, I do not mean the fleshly lobe that beats away in our breasts. I use "heart" in the same way the Bible does. The Bible refers to the heart about eighty-six times. It means, in most of the places, the seat and center of the human soul or spiritual being.

A. *The Bible speaks of heartfelt religion.* Look at some of the verses: In Genesis 6:5 the heart is the center of our thinking. In Genesis 8:21 God speaks from his heart. In Exodus 23:9 the heart is used to describe a state or condition of existence: "Also thou shalt not oppress a stranger: for ye know the heart of a stranger, seeing ye were strangers in the land of Egypt." In Judges 5:16 the heart is searched for the answer to a problem. The heart rejoices in 1 Samuel 2:1. Paul said in Romans 10:10, "For with the heart man believeth unto righteousness." The Lord himself stressed the importance of the heart in our spiritual relationship to God when he said in Matthew 18:35, "So likewise shall my heavenly Father do also unto you, if ye from your hearts forgive not every one his brother their trespasses." Then Paul again stressed the importance of the heart in religion when he spoke in Ephesians 6:6 of "the servants of Christ, doing the will of God from the heart."

B. *Unless a person's heart is in that spiritual transaction we call regeneration, and unless a person's heart is in the life of service that he gives to Christ, his religion will not amount to very much.* The trouble with many churches today is that many members are halfhearted in the work. They join the church just as they would join a club. With many there is no definite and emphatic change of heart. One doesn't get much out of it nor put much into it unless his heart is in the work.

C. *The condition of your heart will affect your whole life—physically and spiritually.* The trouble with the unsaved is a diseased heart. This disease can be cured by no earthly doctor or medicine. It has to come from above.

D. *What people are at heart reveals itself in their lives, for out of the "heart are the issues of life."* People steal because they are thieves at heart. They tell untruths because they are liars at heart. People live impure lives because they are unclean in their hearts. The only way they can change their lives is to change their hearts.

III. Do you have heart trouble?

You who have named the Lord as your Savior and feel that you are saved, is your heart fully surrendered to him? We as Christians need constantly to let our prayer be that which was voiced by the psalmist when he said in Psalm 139:23, "Search me, O God, and know my heart: try me, and know my thoughts."

A. *We must not have a double, or divided, heart.* First Chronicles 12:33 gives a description of a group of God's soldiers who were equipped to go forth in battle: "They were not of double heart."

B. *If our hearts are not in our work, we will fail.* A person who goes at the business of being a Christian in a halfhearted way will never render the Lord much service. In fact, these are often a hindrance to the cause. This kind God will spew out of his mouth.

Conclusion

Christians need to keep their hearts right. We ought to be just as eager to keep our spiritual heart in good condition as the physical one. Sinner, the one thing wrong with you is a bad heart. Sin will eat up the heart of a person and thereby affect the entire individual. To remove sin means a changed life.

SUNDAY EVENING, SEPTEMBER 30

Title: The Church and Its Special Problems

Text: "But you, man of God, flee from all this, and pursue righteousness, godliness, faith, love, endurance and gentleness. Fight the good fight of faith. Take hold of the eternal life to which you were called when you made your good confession in the presence of many witnesses" **(1 Tim. 6:11–12 NIV)**.

Scripture Reading: 1 Timothy 6:1–21

Introduction

The church in Ephesus, like the church where you worship, had its problems. As long as we are in this body and as long as the devil seeks the destruction of people, we will have problems. Paul did not for a moment minimize these; but instead, he faced them squarely and sought an answer to them from God.

In this concluding chapter to Paul's letter to Timothy, Paul deals with some of the special problems faced by this pastor and congregation. He deals with the issues of slavery, living godly lives, and wealth. In doing so, he gives advice to us for our problems.

I. The problem of slaves (I Tim. 6:1–2).

Slavery was an integral part of the society in which the early church lived. As one would expect, when people of all classes and races began to call God "Father" and fellow believers "brothers," some problems were created. Paul does not deal with the morality of slavery as an institution but deals with the problems of interpersonal relationships. If a slave became a Christian, how was he to treat his master? If a master became a Christian, how was he to treat his slaves? If both were Christians, what was to be their relationship? Although the circumstances are not the same, the principles involved can give guidance to Christian labor and Christian management in today's society.

A. *Slaves of unbelieving masters (v. 1).* Paul says that a Christian slave should be obedient and faithful to his master, even if the master was cruel. To do otherwise would be to cause the unbelieving master to blaspheme God. On the other hand, if the slave could show by his attitude and action that being a Christian made a difference in every phase of his life, the master could possibly be led to know Christ.

The principle for today's society is that the Christian worker should give a full day's work for a day's pay. In fact, he should do more, since he is a personal representative of Christ Jesus. I cannot imagine that our Christ ever turned out a shoddy piece of workmanship from his carpenter's shop. Neither should we.

B. *Slaves of believing masters (v. 2).* If a Christian slave had a Christian master, there probably would be a tendency on the part of the slave to expect special favors and special treatment from the master. If it did not actually work out this way, he might despise the master. Paul urged slaves to continue to give their best service. They should give their masters even better service, since they were "brothers."

In like manner, a Christian master, because he is a Christian, should show every kindness and consideration to his slaves.

The modern application would be that Christian management must see that an adequate wage and the best working conditions are provided for his workers. On the other hand, no Christian worker should expect special treatment in the shop or factory simply because he and the manager are members of the same church.

II. The problem of living a godly life (I Tim. 6:3–16).

The goal of every Christian is to lead a godly life. There are many dangers and pitfalls, however, that cause the believer to fall. Paul discusses this.

A. *Note the dangers involved (vv. 3–10).*
1. The danger of false teachers. These teachers confront Christians and, if possible, lead them astray. Paul says that these men can be recognized by their lives. Jesus warned of false teachers and said, "By their fruits ye shall know them." Paul lists their fruits. They teach a different doctrine. They refuse sound words. They are proud. The consequence of this is strife, envy, slander, and so on. Paul says to turn away, to withdraw, from such people.
2. The danger of seeking to profit from religion. Phillips translates this to mean that some people hope to make some profit out of the Christian religion (v. 5). Their disciples are still with us today. They select a church for business or social reasons, hoping to profit thereby.

   Paul counters this improper conduct by saying that there is gain, but it is "godliness with contentment" (v. 6). What a beautiful concept! Paul said, "Not that I speak in respect of want: for I have learned, in whatsoever state I am, therewith to be content" (Phil. 4:11). Circumstances could not disturb Paul's contentment, and persecution could not destroy it. Contrast Paul with the Philippian jailer in Acts 16.

B. *Notice the action required (vv. 11–16).* Paul tells Timothy that if he is to live a godly life, he must:
1. Flee (v. 11). Paul exhorts Timothy to run away, to escape from these false teachings, false ideals, and false aims about him. There are times in every Christian's life when he should turn away and escape from his circumstances. If David had fled from Bathsheba, he would have had contentment. If Samson had fled from Delilah, his strength and consecration would have remained. If Peter had fled from the enemies' campfire, he would not have denied his Lord.
2. Follow (v. 11). The Christian must forget the things that are behind "and reach for the things which are before" (Phil. 3:13). Paul says that his goal must be "righteousness, godliness, faith, love, patience, and meekness."
3. Fight (v. 12). This is one of Paul's favorite terms. In Ephesians 6:10 he gives us the full armor of God. "Be strong in the Lord and in the power of his might." Our fight is against evil—against Satan—and without Christ as our companion defeat is certain.

   With Paul we can then say, "I have fought a good fight, I have finished my course, I have kept the faith: Henceforth there is laid up for me a crown of righteousness, which the Lord, the righteous judge, shall give me at that day: and not to me only, but unto all them also that love his appearing" (2 Tim. 4:4, 8).

III. The problem of wealth (I Tim. 6:17–19).

Paul says that wealth and the pursuit of it is a major problem.

A. *Earlier, in verses 7–10, the apostle stressed that "the love of money is the root of all evil."* Money itself is neither good nor evil. This is determined by the manner in which it is acquired and the use to which it is put. But the "love of money," the greedy, grasping desire for it, leads people into all types of evil and sinful practices that result in sorrow and heartache.

B. *Wealth is a problem, for it leads people to "trust in uncertain riches" rather than "in the living God" (v. 17).* And how uncertain wealth is! There will come a time in most people's lives when money's real value will be seen.

There was a moment on Corregidor during World War II when money didn't matter. Time was running out, and everyone knew the siege was almost over. The people had started to kill the horses, for there was nothing to eat; the meat was tough but better than nothing. It wouldn't be long now; the end was in sight for all of them. Out of the fortress vaults the finance officers brought $100,000 in currency—useless paper it would soon be. It could not be taken off the island, and it could not be left for the enemy. The only thing to do was to burn it. So the soldiers watched the fortune go up in smoke. Money didn't matter when time was running out.

Paul warns, "We brought nothing into this world, and it is certain we can carry nothing out" (v. 7). Money is valuable only as long as time lasts. You can't take it with you.

C. *True wealth, says Paul, consists of good works.* Jesus warned us, "Lay not up for yourselves treasures upon earth, where moth and rust doth corrupt, and where thieves break through and steal: But lay up for yourselves treasures in heaven, where neither moth nor rust doth corrupt, and where thieves do not break through nor steal: For where your treasure is, there will your heart be also" (Matt. 6:19–21).

Conclusion

Paul mentions only a few of the problems that a church or an individual may have. He could have mentioned dozens of others. Perhaps he did not discuss your need or problem. But there is one who stands ready to help you with it. That one is Christ Jesus. Hear him as he says, "Come to me, all your who are weary and burdened, and I will give you rest" (Matt. 11:28 NIV).

SUGGESTED PREACHING PROGRAM FOR

OCTOBER

■ **Sunday Mornings**

The messages suggested for Sunday mornings this month are devotional and evangelistic in nature. The theme for the messages is "Courageous Faith in a Chaotic World."

■ **Sunday Evenings**

Each of the evening sermons is based on a famous psalm. "The Gospel That Puts a Song in the Heart" is the theme.

■ **Wednesday Evenings**

Continue the series of expository messages based on Peter's first epistle, using the theme "Encouragement and Counsel for Difficult Times from a Seasoned Veteran of the Cross."

WEDNESDAY EVENING, OCTOBER 3

Title: Guidelines for Christian Conduct

Text: "He must turn from evil and do good" **(1 Peter 3:11 NIV)**.

Scripture Reading: 1 Peter 3:8–12

Introduction

Genuine Christian conduct will proclaim the genuineness of the gospel claims concerning Jesus Christ. Consistent Christian behavior will bring joy to the heart of each one who seeks diligently to follow the wishes of the Savior. This was true in the first century of the Christian era, and it is the great need of modern-day Christianity.

Following Peter's appeal for his readers to respond to their obligations and responsibilities as the followers of Christ in a number of different areas of life, Peter suggests some guidelines for achieving Christian conduct. He sets forth some of the great and distinctive qualities of the Christian life without which they cannot possibly hope to make a spiritual impact on those about them.

I. Christian unity is important: "Live in harmony with one another" (I Peter I:8 NIV).

Christians are to promote a spirit of unity among themselves. A critical and divisive spirit is never conducive to spiritual growth. An attitude that expresses itself in murmuring, complaining, and faultfinding never promotes the fellowship of a church or harmony within the home. Such an attitude never attracts the unbelieving world to the gospel we are trying to preach.

Paul made repeated appeals for a unity of mind and spirit (cf. Eph. 4:2–7; Phil. 2:1–3). He urged the leaders of the church at Philippi to do what they could to restore a spirit of unity between two outstanding women leaders in the church (Phil. 4:1–3).

A spirit of unity is possible among Christians because of many things we have in common.

A. *We have a common faith in Jesus Christ.*
B. *We have a common experience with the Holy Spirit.*
C. *We have a common enemy in the devil.*
D. *We have a common task that includes us all at the point of evangelizing the world.*

II. Christian sympathy is needed: "be sympathetic" (I Peter 1:8 NIV).

Christian sympathy is encouraged as a duty among those who are the followers of Christ.

A. *Sympathy causes selfishness to disappear.*
B. *Sympathy enables one to suffer with others when they suffer.*
C. *Sympathy causes one to provide help when it is needed.*

III. Christian love toward our spiritual brothers: "love as brothers" (I Peter 1:8).

Genuine unselfish love is the badge of Christian discipleship (John 13:34–35). Christian love is to be understood as a persistent, unbreakable spirit of goodwill toward others. This kind of love is the supreme gift of the Spirit to believers.

IV. Christian compassion is essential: "be compassionate" (I Peter 1:8 NIV).

To have compassion means "to suffer with." It means to be tenderhearted and concerned about others. When our Lord saw the multitudes in distress, he had compassion on them (Matt. 9:36). If we would be true followers of Christ, we must let his compassion toward the unfortunate invade and overflow the heart.

V. Christian courtesy is always appropriate: "be ... humble" (I Peter 1:8 NIV).

Many of us have never thought of courtesy as a Christian duty. However, it is easy to recognize that we never attract anyone to our Savior or convince them of the genuineness of our Christianity by being discourteous.

Christians truly can be humble when they become aware of their limitations and when they recognize the provisions of God for them. An attitude of courtesy can grow out of this humble spirit as we recognize how dependent we are on God and how eager God is that we relate ourselves to others in a proper manner so as to win them to our Savior.

VI. Forgiveness must be practiced: "Do not repay evil with evil or insult with insult, but with blessing."

Repeatedly our Lord sought to teach his apostles that, if they would be his true followers, they must not resort to revenge and retaliation (cf. Matt. 5:43–48).

On one occasion the Lord had counseled Peter to forgive until seventy times seven (Matt. 18:21–22). Our Lord counseled unlimited forgiveness because the harboring of hate creates a poison within our soul. One must forgive if he wants to know happiness. This truth took root in the apostle's heart, and he encouraged other Christians to refuse to harbor a grudge against those who mistreated them.

VII. The control of the tongue.

The apostle quotes from Psalm 34. If a Christian is to live life at the fullest, he must observe certain great negatives and positives in his life. He must control his tongue and never resort to deception. He must abhor evil and give himself to that which is good. To experience and enjoy peace, he must be peaceable in his relationships with others.

Conclusion

The doorway into the Christian life is through a simple and sincere commitment to Jesus Christ as Lord and Savior. Salvation comes as the gift of God's grace. Success in the Christian life is an achievement as the believer works with the Holy Spirit and other believers in the fellowship of the church.

Each of us needs to give careful attention to these spiritual guidelines for Christian conduct given by the apostle Peter. We will be blessed as each of us achieves success in living by these guidelines.

SUNDAY MORNING, OCTOBER 7

Title: Launch Out into the Deep

Text: "Now when he had left speaking, he said unto Simon, Launch out into the deep, and let down your nets for a draught" **(Luke 5:4)**.

Scripture Reading: Luke 5:1–11

Hymns: "Serve the Lord with Gladness," McKinney

   "Our Best," Kirk

   "Must Jesus Bear the Cross Alone?" Shepherd

Offertory Prayer: Our Father, we thank you for your love and grace to us. Your forgiveness and patience call us to devotion and commitment. We are grateful for the privilege to gather with our friends to worship you. Please accept our tithes and gifts. Use them according to your will in the redemption of humankind. For Jesus' sake. Amen.

Introduction

Every fisherman has a fish story. This is one of the most unusual fish stories ever told. It begins with the fish that did not get away. It ends with a group of fishermen getting caught.

Jesus was preaching near the little lake of Galilee. The crowd was pushing him backward toward the water. Jesus saw Peter's boat close by, stepped into it, and asked him to push out a little way from shore. Jesus used the boat for a pulpit. When he had finished his sermon, he surprised his friends by saying, "Let's go fishing. Put out to the deep water and let down your nets."

I. Exhausted resources.

The disciples had toiled all night. These expert fishermen had done all they could do, but their training and experience were not enough. They were trying to do the job they had done many times, but now they had only failure. Without Christ they were killing time. All they had to show for their night's toil were tired bodies and empty nets.

How many times do we work and toil, only to feel that all has been in vain? We try with all our might to be good neighbors, good fathers, good mothers, good Christians, only to end up with tired bodies and empty nets. This is always the outcome when we operate without Jesus Christ. Peter, as well as all the other disciples, was ever having to learn that life without Jesus is always fragmentary.

There is only one way to do the work of the Lord—Jesus' way. There is only one power that can enable us to live the Christian life and to bear our responsibilities. Peter was still learning this lesson in Gethsemane when he tried to defend Jesus from Judas and the arresting soldiers, endeavoring to keep his promise never to forsake Jesus. Surely it was love for Jesus that motivated Peter to swing the sword, ready to single-handedly do battle with a small army. But what he did was wrong, for it was not Jesus' way.

It took Peter a long time to learn what Jesus was trying to teach him in the fishing boat. But months later we hear Peter telling a beggar, "Silver and gold have I none; but such as I have, give I thee" (Acts 3:6). Peter said in essence, "I cannot give you what you ask. But I can do better. I'll give you what you need. I'll share with you the greatest discovery of my life. In the name of Jesus Christ of Nazareth, arise and walk."

Peter finally found out he did not have all the answers. He made the great discovery that life is more than physical prowess, human wisdom, and financial security. He discovered that life came to those who believed in Christ, heart and soul, and gave themselves unreservedly to God. That is what he meant when he said to the crippled man, "Such as I have give I thee." Oh, that we might make this discovery.

II. A peculiar command.

"Launch out into the deep." Fish were caught near the shore, not in the deep. They were caught at night, not in the daytime. Yet Jesus told the men to get out to the deep waters and let down their nets. Here the carpenter, a landlubber, was telling these experienced fishermen how and where to catch fish. The disciples had reason to doubt. Peter said, "Master, we are old hands at this business, and we have been here all night when and where the fish are supposed to be caught, and we have caught nothing. Are you going to try to tell *us* how to fish?" In spite of this, Peter knew that Jesus was the Captain of his boat and therefore said, "Nevertheless, at thy word I will let down the net."

III. Reluctant obedience.

"Let down your nets." Perhaps not one of us is a professional fisherman, but we all have nets that need to be let down at the Lord's command. As a fisherman, the nets were a part of Peter. They were what he had in his hand. He did with them what Jesus commanded him. Our nets are our talents, abilities, personalities, intelligence, experience, and training. Our nets are whatever we have in our hands. Ours is to do with them as Jesus commands. We may be as experienced at living as Peter was at fishing. We may know all the ins and outs financially, intellectually, and socially. But if we do not have Jesus, we will toil through all the nights of life and come up at the end with nothing but empty nets.

There will come the time when our nets no longer will be usable. The passing years will bring weakness and decay. Our nets for the last time will be let down into the sea of life. When that time comes, what will be our catch? If we will only trust him enough to follow his command and let down our net into the sea of life, we will pull on board more treasures and blessings than our little boats can carry. We will have to look around for someone else's boat to share the overflow.

The psalmist David had launched out in the deep of faith. He said, "The LORD is my Shepherd.... My cup runneth over." He had to find someone else's empty cup to catch the overflow.

IV. A humble prayer.

"Depart from me for I am a sinful man." Peter had doubted the Lord. This confession was in order. He sensed his sinfulness in the presence of Jesus. The nearer to the Lord we walk, the keener we will be aware of our sin. Thoughts, action, and attitudes that have never occurred to us as being wrong will rise up as ugly monsters in our lives.

Peter's sin previous to this confession was that of attitude. Peter felt that he knew better than the Lord. Now he was asking that the Lord might depart from him.

Imagine this scene: This is a time of breathtaking excitement even for experienced fishermen. They have come upon a school of fish such as they have never seen. Every man is shouting in excitement. The men strain every muscle pulling the nets. The fish are sliding and flopping into the boats by the dozens. The fishermen are sopping wet and knee-deep in fish. One shouts, "Look out, the nets are splitting. Don't let that big one get away." Another cries, "The boat is about to sink. We're taking on water." In all of this excitement, Peter decides to pray. He falls to his knees among the squirming fish and pours his heart out to the Lord.

It is wonderful to have a worshipful environment and a lovely building dedicated to prayer, but if someone really wants to find God, he can pray anywhere. He can confess his sins no matter what the environment. Every Christian ought to be faithful in church, but thank God, we can draw near to God wherever we are.

Again, Peter thought he knew just how things ought to be. He thought that since he was such a sinner, Jesus ought to leave him. Though Peter understood something of his sin, he did not understand Jesus. Surely Jesus would not grant his request. As long as Peter was confessing his sin, Jesus was bound to stay, though Peter's sin was as scarlet. That Peter was a sinner was all the more reason Jesus needed to be there. Jesus was later to tell the Pharisees that he did not come to the people who thought they were so righteous that they needed no repentance, but to the sinners. The only way one can become what he ought to be is in the presence of Christ.

Peter's attitude was wrong when he doubted Jesus could find any fish. His request was wrong as he prayed, but his attitude was right. Far better to pray wrong and have the right attitude than to have the wrong attitude and pray right. "Lord, I am a sinner, and I don't deserve to be here in the same boat with you. I've played the fool. I'm nothing but a sinner." This is the attitude in which the Lord wants us to pray. As a matter of fact, this is the only attitude that can secure God's forgiveness. Thank God, Jesus understood the sinner Peter. Jesus did not leave Peter all alone with his sins; Jesus stayed right with his friend.

When we feel as if we should not be in the presence of Jesus because of our sin, we can be certain that this same Christ will not leave us alone, hopeless in sin. If we, like Peter, sense that we are sinners and will so confess to God, Christ always stays around to clean up the mud of our dirty lives and pick up the broken pieces and put them back together again.

Conclusion

Christ calls you today to "launch out into the deep" of God's faith, grace, and love.

Do you respond like Peter, "But, Lord, all night long I have tried, and I really have not gotten anywhere"? "Mostly, Lord, I just made a mess. My nets are empty. I am just afraid to try anymore. Nevertheless, Lord, I know you are the Captain and Master of my life. I will do as you say. I will try again."

Like Peter, bend before God and confess that you are a sinner and hear Jesus say, "Don't be afraid. From now on I am going to make you a fisher of men. As I have blessed you, you will become a blessing to others."

SUNDAY EVENING, OCTOBER 7

Title: The Song of Salvation

Text: O magnify the LORD with me, and let us exalt his name together" (**Ps. 34:3**).

Scripture Reading: Psalm 34

Introduction

There are twenty-two verses in this psalm, and they correspond to the twenty-two letters of the Hebrew alphabet so as to form an acrostic. Charles Spurgeon suggested that the first ten verses could be likened to the song service of public worship and the remaining twelve might well be defined as the sermon. Perhaps this is so. But the entire majestic passage may well be considered as a sermon in song with each flowing and blending harmoniously with the other. The continuing theme is salvation.

I. A Savior is presented (Ps. 34:6).

"This poor man cried, and the LORD heard him, and saved him out of all his troubles." Sharing the gospel with the poor needs to be more of a priority in our day.

A. *Jesus did not overlook the prophecy that he came to preach the gospel to the poor.* The fact that the poor had the gospel preached to them was an established credential of our Lord.

> He went to Nazareth, where he had been brought up, and on the Sabbath day he went into the synagogue, as was his custom. And he stood up to read. The scroll of the prophet Isaiah was handed to him. Unrolling it, he found the place where it is written:
> "The Spirit of the Lord is on me,
>   because he has anointed me
>   to preach good news to the poor.
> He has sent me to proclaim freedom for the prisoners
>   and recovery of sight for the blind,
> to release the oppressed,
>   to proclaim the year of the Lord's favor." (Luke 4:16–19 NIV)
>   The reference is to Isaiah 61:1.

B. *Jesus is identified with the poor.* "For you know the grace of our Lord Jesus Christ, that though he was rich, yet for your sakes he became poor, so that you through his poverty might become rich" (2 Cor. 8:9 NIV).

C. *Jesus lived the life of those who were materially poor.* "Jesus replied, 'Foxes have holes and birds of the air have nests, but the Son of Man has no place to lay his head'" (Matt. 8:20 NIV).

II. A salvation is presented (Ps. 34:18).

A. *Real salvation is centered in the Lord.* "The LORD is nigh unto them that are of a broken heart; and saveth such as be of a contrite spirit."

B. *Real salvation meets three tests.*

1. The test of faith and experience (v. 8). "O taste and see that the LORD is good: blessed is the man that trusteth in him." The test is finally personal. We taste and see individually. The test is validly functional. Does it work?

It does, as is the testimony of all who have had the personal encounter with Christ in a saving experience.

2. The test of supply and demand (v. 10). "The young lions do lack, and suffer hunger: but they that seek the LORD shall not want any good thing." The young lion usually got what it wanted because it had the strength to get it. But even the young lion could not always satisfy its desires. In contrast, the Lord gives that which even the young lion cannot obtain for itself—the satisfaction of hunger. The promise is not far from that spoken by our Lord himself, "Blessed are they which do hunger and thirst after righteousness: for they shall be filled" (Matt. 5:6).

3. The test of availability and function (Ps. 34:12–17). The "eyes of the LORD" are toward them that seek him. His "ears are open unto their cry." "The LORD heareth." He delivers them out of their troubles. His face is set defensively against the enemies of his own (v. 16). Salvation's fullest demands are more than met in Christ.

A man of eighty-two years was presented the simple story of Christ. He was a wealthy man, had never married, and was an eccentric inventor. He was not the excitable type. When the claims of Jesus were presented to him, he answered, "I am sure that the millions of people who have taken the step and have found that it works couldn't be wrong. So I am ready to settle it. I accept him now as my Savior too." Of course, it worked with him also. The one unanswerable argument for salvation in Jesus is that it works. It does not submit to human explanation. It does yield to test tube analysis. It does not square with human reason. But it works!

III. A sacrifice is prophesied (Ps. 34:20).

"He keepeth all his bones: not one of them is broken."

A. *Here is prophecy fulfilled.* "In one house shall it be eaten; thou shalt not carry forth aught of the flesh abroad out of the house; neither shall ye break a bone thereof" (Ex. 12:46). These were the words of instruction concerning the Passover lamb. Divine revelation and divine inspiration do not invalidate the intelligence or knowledge of those who wrote by Holy Spirit inspiration.

B. *Here is prophecy continued.* The psalmist, guided by the Spirit, looked back to Jesus and his crucifixion. When Jesus was on the cross, his bones were not broken. Let John testify. He was there at the cross.

The soldiers therefore came and broke the legs of the first man who had been crucified with Jesus, and then those of the other. But when they came to Jesus and found that he was already dead, they did not break his legs. Instead, one of the soldiers pierced Jesus' side with a spear, bringing a sudden flow of blood and water. The man who saw it has given testimony, and his testimony is true. He knows that he tells the truth, and he testifies so that you also may believe. These things happened so that the scripture would be fulfilled: "Not one of his bones will be broken." (John 19:32–36 NIV)

C. *Here is prophecy vindicated.* However shy and sophisticated the modern mind is concerning Bible types, one thing is sure: the lambs of the Old Testament pointed to the Lamb of the New Testament. Hear Paul say, "For even Christ our passover is sacrificed for us" (1 Cor. 5:7).

Why were the bones of those crucified broken? It was a signal that the victim was dead and it was time to remove the body so it would not be taken down from the cross in desecration of the Jewish Sabbath.

Why were the bones of Jesus not broken? The bones of the Passover lambs were not broken. The bone was power. But the power of life itself was not in the bone but in the blood. It is not in broken bone but in spilled blood that we have complete salvation.

Because it is a psalm of the cross, this psalm is a song of redemption. Is it not wonderful that a thousand years before Jesus died on Calvary, the psalmist sang about it with such accuracy and ecstasy?

Conclusion

Christ is the theme of the Old Testament as well as the New Testament. The divine Scriptures can look forward with greater accuracy than human history can look backward. Now, as then, Christ is the adequate and complete Savior, and he is available. Let those who do not have him, receive him. Let those who do possess him proclaim in glad triumph that Jesus saves.

WEDNESDAY EVENING, OCTOBER 10

Title: Have You Suffered Because You Are a Christian?

Text: "But even if you should suffer for what is right, you are blessed" (**1 Peter 3:14 NIV**).

Scripture Reading: 1 Peter 3:13–4:2

Introduction

There are many people in various nations today who have suffered greatly for no other reason than that they are followers of the Lord Jesus Christ. This could be true where you live this year. How will you react if you find yourself in a position where you are going to have to suffer in order to be true to Jesus Christ?

The apostle Peter was qualified by personal experience to write words of encouragement to Christians who were experiencing persecution. He himself had known persecution at the hands of the high priest and the Sadducees (Acts 5:17–42). Peter had been in great danger during the persecution that was promoted by Saul of Tarsus (Acts 8). He had been unjustly imprisoned by Herod the king, who evidently intended to execute him, as he had done with James (Acts 12:1–4).

Although Peter had experienced some undeserved suffering, he had also experienced some remarkable spiritual triumphs and wonderful deliverances by the Lord (Acts 5:18–20; 12:5–11).

In this epistle, Peter sought to encourage his readers to be faithful even unto the point of death, in view of the assurance of eternal glory beyond death.

I. The possibility of undeserved suffering (1 Peter 3:13–14).

There are two words used in the New Testament that refer to suffering. These two words occur fifty-three times in the entire New Testament, and they are found sixteen times in the five chapters of 1 Peter. The suffering of God's people is one of the major themes with which the book deals. The writer sought to give to them, on the basis of his experience of the Lord's faithfulness, the courage that would be necessary if they were to suffer meaningfully and triumphantly.

A. *"If ye be followers of that which is good."* If the believer will lead an upright and benevolent life, no actual harm will come to him from proper constituted legal authorities. Normally people are punished only for wicked deeds, not for righteous deeds.

B. *"If ye suffer for righteousness' sake."* The apostle recognized that in a pagan world of wicked people there was a strong possibility that the innocent might suffer unjustly. Jesus had pointed out in the Beatitudes that Christian character would provoke opposition and persecution on the part of those who were willfully and maliciously evil (Matt. 5:10–12). The righteousness for which the Christian may be persecuted is not the righteousness of Christ that comes through faith and gives the believer the right standing before God. Rather, it is the righteousness that is practiced in daily life. This type of life is a constant reminder of and a rebuke to the unrighteousness in the lives of the wicked.

When believers face suffering and persecution because of Christian conduct, they are to recognize the blessedness of their condition. This type of suffering places them in the noble tradition of the great prophets and saints of the past.

The followers of Christ are to conduct themselves so as never to find themselves suffering the just results of evil deeds (1 Peter 4:15–16).

C. *"Be not afraid of their terror."* The Christians of Peter's day were encouraged not to be filled with terror because of anything their persecutors could do to them. They were to recognize that God was their protector. God is never confined to the present. He can cause his people to triumph, even if that triumph comes on the other side of the suffering of death. In the meantime they are to meet peril with calmness and courage based on their knowledge of the character and purpose of God.

II. Spiritual preparation for unmerited suffering (1 Peter 3:15–17).

A. *"Sanctify the Lord God in your hearts."* Here the NIV has "In your hearts set apart Christ as Lord." Christians are to enthrone Christ on the pedestal that belongs to him and then bow down before him in reverence and submission. Trust in and dedication to the lordship of Christ is to be their central emotion and their controlling purpose. This kind of holy regard for the Lord will help lift the believer above the fear of others.

B. *"Be ready always to give an answer to every man."* The word translated "answer" means "to defend oneself, to speak so as to absolve oneself of a charge, to make defense" (cf. its use in Acts 24:10; 16:1–2). Perhaps Peter remembered a time when, because of fear, he had not been ready to give a proper answer in the time of danger (Mark 14:66–72).

The Christian is to have a good explanation for the foundation of the hope on which he has based his life in the present and for the future. Because the Christians of Peter's day had an intelligent grasp of the truth as taught by Christ and because of the constant evidence of that truth in their lives, there were many inquirers who desired to discover the secret behind their manner of life.

C. *"Having a good conscience."* It is essential that Christians be able to witness to their faith without being hindered by a conscience that accuses them of having done wrong. They will have to suffer enough without having to endure the pains of a guilty conscience.

D. *"If the will of God be so."* Peter definitely implied that at times suffering would accompany the doing of God's will. There are some things to be learned and demonstrated in Christian suffering that cannot be revealed in any other manner. Suffering for Christ and righteousness' sake is redemptive both for the sufferer and for others.

This is a lesson that many modern-day believers have never had an opportunity to learn in actual experience.

III. Example of undeserved suffering (1 Peter 3:18–21).

A. *The example of Christ (3:18).* Peter's purpose in referring to the sufferings of Christ was not to discuss the Atonement, but rather to remind the believers that Christ had suffered greatly as an innocent person and not as an evildoer. By the example of the Savior, Peter sought to comfort and encourage the Christians of his day in the midst of their unmerited sufferings. Christ had suffered as the innocent for the guilty and as the just for the unjust. He had suffered for a purpose even though it seemed that he had failed. Instead of escape or deliverance from suffering, he was put to death in the flesh.

Peter was suggesting that the sufferings of Christ's followers can be a part of the divine purpose that will make it possible for others eventually to hear the message of God's salvation. As Christ was patient in his sufferings, even so his people should persevere in their time of trial.

B. *Noah's patience in sufferings (3:19–21).* This difficult passage must be interpreted in its context. Dr. Albert Barnes placed this passage solidly in the context of a message to those who were suffering and stated that the example of the patience and suffering of Noah should challenge and comfort those to whom Peter was writing. As Christ was saved from death by the resurrection, so Noah and his family were saved from the flood that threatened them after suffering the ridicule of a pagan world. Dr. Barnes believes it was through Noah that the Christ had preached to the "spirits in prison" while Noah was preparing the ark. They were alive then and could have responded to the "preacher of righteousness" (2 Peter 2:5) had they chosen to do so. Instead, they, like the contemporaries of those to whom Peter wrote, added to his burdens and his difficulties. Noah was used as an illustration of God's ability to deliver those who are obedient and faithful in the face of what appears to be insurmountable obstacles. For 120 years, Noah had endured their ridicule while being obedient to the command of the Lord to build an ark.

Conclusion

Peter set before those who were suffering unjustly the example of the Savior (1 Peter 2:19–24) and referred to the exaltation and glory of the Christ following his resurrection. He encouraged Christians to believe that through patience, obedience, and suffering in the present, they likewise will share in the "inheritance incorruptible, and undefiled ... that fadeth not away," which is reserved in heaven for them. In the meantime, they are to trust in the Lord who was triumphant over suffering and lived a life of obedience.

It is only natural that we should want to escape suffering. Let us pray that it never will be necessary for us to suffer to the point of shedding our blood. Let us pray that, if such a time should come, we will have a faith to match the hour.

SUNDAY MORNING, OCTOBER 14

Title: Wisdom for Real Living

Text: "If any of you lack wisdom, let him ask of God, that giveth to all men liberally, and upbraideth not; and it shall be given him" (**James 1:5**).

Scripture Reading: James 1:2–8; 2:17–21

Hymns: "Living for Jesus," Chisholm

"I Am Thine, O Lord," Crosby

"Speak to My Heart," McKinney

Offertory Prayer: Our Father, we praise your name because you have lifted us from the miry clay, put our feet on the rock, and established our lives. You have forgiven our sin and made us new creatures through your Son. We thank you also for giving us countless material blessings. We know that every possession is an expression of your grace. We worship you this morning with our hearts, hands, and our gifts. Please receive that which we have to give as an expression of our love and devotion. Use our tithes and offerings to help others to know your wonderful blessings we so freely enjoy through Jesus Christ our Lord. Amen.

Introduction

The solutions to the problems of our world are found in a source of wisdom that is not human. When we consider the wars, the explosiveness of the Middle East, the constant problems of violence, crime, pornography, immorality, hatred, racism, and so on, we are bewildered to the point of despair. In addition, we must face our personal frustrations, disappointments, and failures in the complexities of life. We find ourselves miserably inadequate to deal with our troubles.

Nations, homes, churches, and individuals stand in frantic need of divine wisdom. Without the wisdom of God, we are hopeless in our efforts to cope with the responsibilities of living. James asserts that the answers to the trials and problems of life are found in the wisdom of God. God has assured us that he will supply divine directive to all who ask him, believing he will keep his promise. He is sufficient for abundant and everlasting life.

I. The necessity for wisdom.

When James refers to the wisdom of God in a person's life, he is speaking of God's will being performed in that life. Without the wisdom of God in a person's life, there is utter emptiness. Humans are totally insufficient for living with all of its trials, problems, and decisions. There is no way to overstate the poverty of a person trying to live without the wisdom of God.

No one ever found God's wisdom and presence without knowing he needed them. When blind Bartimaeus cried out, "Jesus, thou Son of David, have mercy upon me," he had a need that needed to be met. He yearned for the touch of Jesus upon his eyes that he might see. When we feel the necessity for God's wisdom, we then seek his presence and counsel. Without him we are like a ship without a sail—empty, vacant, and inadequate for life. James says that in the time of decision or heartbreak, if we will ask God for direction, he will give it. Jesus has told us that if we seek, we will find; if we hunger and thirst, we will be filled.

The book of James indicates that trials become the occasion in which one learns in a new way his utter dependence on God. His faith is tried in order that patience may have its perfect work. God allows difficulties to come to us, not to defeat us, but to allow our faith to grow, to develop our character, to strengthen our faith, and to know the presence of the living God. The testing time comes in order that we understand our need of divine leadership, comfort, compassion, guidance, and wisdom.

Furthermore, we are to rejoice in troubled times, for then it is that God is able to do something to us, for us, in us, and with us that was impossible before the coming of the trials. James is not calling us to asceticism. However, because of our potential spiritual growth, we should rejoice in our trials. The Lord told the apostle Paul that he would not remove the thorn in Paul's flesh but that his divine power would be made perfect in Paul's weakness. To paraphrase, Paul declared, "I'm glad about my weakness, for herein is the strength of God made perfect in me. I'm happy that my weakness has become the occasion of the demonstration of God's power" (2 Cor. 12:9–10).

II. The source of wisdom.

James says, "If any of you lack wisdom, let him ask of God" (James 1:5). God is our source of wisdom.

I will never forget watching a drunk man years ago in a crowded little hamburger stand putting nickels into a pay telephone on the wall beside him, expecting the juke box behind him to play a record. He kept feeding the telephone nickels and cursing the juke box because it refused to play.

Often when we are stone sober we make a similar mistake, trying to find vitality for living and wisdom for life in the wrong places. We may try money, pleasure, position, intellect, and comforts before we will try the Lord God. James is telling us that only God is the fountainhead for wisdom. Jesus Christ is a spring that never runs dry.

A troubled world waits to hear the promise of divine comfort falling from the lips of Jesus (John 14:1–2). Here is the assurance that the Son of God himself prepares heaven for distressed and sinful people. People in the loneliness of spiritual darkness need to hear Paul when he proclaims his confidence in the inseparable, unconquerable, and unexplainable love of God expressed in Jesus Christ (Rom. 8:35–39). King David found himself in so much trouble that he felt that hell itself had grabbed hold of him. In anguish he cried out to God. Then he experienced the God of heaven bending down in his life to lift him out of his affliction and sorrow (Ps. 116:1–5). No wonder David declared the Lord as his Fortress, his Refuge, his Trust, the one and only God (Ps. 91:1–2).

The Creator of the universe, the heavenly Father who sent his Son to die on Calvary's cross, is the only source of wisdom for life. He who died for people's sins and arose from the grave to provide heaven for them is sufficient to guide them through life in this world.

III. Requirements for wisdom.

James says that we are to "ask in faith, nothing wavering. For he that wavereth is like a wave of the sea driven with the wind and tossed. For let not that man think that he shall receive any thing of the Lord" (vv. 6–7). The requirement for wisdom is faith. We must believe that God is completely able and absolutely willing to give us wisdom. Without this faith, we render ourselves incapable of receiving his promise. The firm answers of God come to those who exercise a personal trust in him.

We must realize that God never expects perfect faith. He responds to us however feeble our faith as long as it accompanies surrender, dedication, and obedience. This is what salvation is all about. The only way we can know the wisdom of God in our lives is to bring imperfect faith to a loving God and allow him to do for us what we cannot do for ourselves. It is the placing of our confidence in him who does not fail in this life or in eternity.

Conclusion

As we understand our desperate need for wisdom in life, we must know that the only source is the living God. When we earnestly desire this wisdom and trust the Lord to keep his promise, we may be assured of receiving the solid answers for life's great difficulties. Such realization and faith bring salvation to the soul, cleansing of the heart and divine counsel for godly living. The free gift of God is available to all who will receive it by personal faith in him who promises to keep his Word.

SUNDAY EVENING, OCTOBER 14

Title: The Recital of Redemption

Text: "Blessed is that man that maketh the LORD his trust, and respecteth not the proud, nor such as turn aside to lies" **(Ps. 40:4)**.

Scripture Reading: Psalm 40

Introduction

It is easier to see through the windshield than it is through the back window or to look behind through the rearview mirror. In a comparable way, it was easy for the psalmist to look forward to Jesus.

We look backward in terms of chronology. The Old Testament prophets looked forward. Just as God sees in every direction, so faith is not limited by time or place.

In our beautiful psalm, the singer gives a recital of redemption. Three themes are recited.

I. Helplessness without God (Ps. 40:2).

A. *The fall.* The condition of the lost man is described as that of being in a horrible pit. In those days pits were used for the storage of grain and other materials. Sometimes the cisternlike pit would be empty and unused for years. Although the cover might still be over the mouth of the pit, weeds obscured it and weather wore it away. Perhaps the pit was partly filled with water and mire. Then a lone person would come to the open pit or step on the rotted cover and fall in. It was literally "the fall of man."

This is a picture of the fall of humankind in the garden of Eden. When Adam ate of the forbidden tree of the garden, he fell, and through him all humankind fell. Paul talked about the fall. He said, "In Adam all die" (1 Cor. 15:22), and "By one man sin entered into the world, and death by sin; and so death passed upon all men, for that all have sinned" (Rom. 5:12).

We are helpless in our fallen state. We are lost without God.

B. *The wall.* Frequently pits were made with inverted walls. The opening at the top was small; the floor was large. This increased the volume of the pit while holding the size of the opening to a minimum. When a person fell into an abandoned pit, it was next to impossible for him to get out by himself. He could not climb such walls. He was imprisoned.

    The lost man finds himself imprisoned. He cannot climb the walls to effect his own escape.

C. *The call.* The lost man in the pit was almost always sought. The rescue party would rely on calling him and hoping for an answer. The pit was difficult to see, so the voice was used. When the calling benefactors combed the area, they would call repeatedly and listen for any answer from the pit.

    The psalmist says this is what God did for him. He was a victim of the fall. He was imprisoned by the wall, but he heard God's call and answered him.

II. Help from God (Ps. 40:1–3).

There are five things the singer recites that God has done for him.

A. *He leaned over me (v. 1).* God "inclined unto me." Eager to hear the cry of the lost and compassionate to save, God stooped down to hear the cry from the pit. Let us be encouraged that his ears are still listening for the cry of distress.

B. *He listened to me (v. 1).* "He heard my cry." When the cry came to loving and listening ears, the recital of joy began.

C. *He lifted me (v. 2).* "He brought me up also out of an horrible pit" (v. 2). It is not enough for God just to listen to him. The rescue party might listen ever so much to the pleading of the fallen victim, but it was in the lifting that the rescue from the pit was made a reality.

    This is what God does in our redemption. At Calvary God reached down to us, and in the resurrection God lifted us. He is not above dirtying his hands with us. When we cannot climb from the pit or rescue ourselves, God reaches down through the small opening of our own possibility, takes our hands, and lifts us from the miry clay.

D. *He located me (v. 2).* "He set my feet on a rock." God does not just rescue us and dump us. He puts us on sure footing. When a man whose feet have been in the mire is planted on the rock, he has cause for rejoicing.

E. *He led me (v. 2).* "He established my goings." God did not just park him; he set him in action. God saves to energize and activate. He brings us out of the pits to put us into performance. It may well be that the practical heresy of our day is that of the inactivity of God's people.

    We are not rescued to rot, not lifted to loaf, not saved to sit. There are "goings" for the Christian, and no one can go in the place of another. God not only puts us in grace; he puts us in gear!

III. Happiness in God (Ps. 40:3).

The psalmist bursts forth in joy. This joy is spontaneous; there is nothing forced about it. This happiness in God expresses itself in three ways:

A. *A song.* "He hath put a new song in my mouth" (v. 3). When God puts a song in a person's mouth, it has to come out. This makes a person sing when he is not even a singer. To have salvation is to have a song. To have Jesus in the heart is to have joy in the personality.

B. *A salvation.* "... many shall see it, and fear, and shall trust in the LORD" (v. 3). A song is not an end in itself. The salvation of others is always the focal concern of those who have been saved.

The world is afflicted with the selfish craving for happiness for happiness' sake. There are few people as miserable as those whose sole aim is to make themselves happy. The radiant confidence of the singer is that others will see his salvation and hear his song and find the redemption that has changed his life.

C. *A sharing.* "Blessed is that man that maketh the LORD his trust, and respecteth not the proud, nor such as turn aside to lies" (v. 4). When many see what God has done for them, they will follow in the blessed experience of salvation. There is no such thing as a selfish salvation.

Conclusion

Let us recall our helplessness without God. We cannot scale the wall of escape in our own strength. If you do not know the Lord, he will save you. He will do for you what you cannot do for yourself. He can do what no other can do for you. God will hear your cry; he will lift you, and relocate you, and lead you in the right paths. God's great salvation is one of joy. Our greatest joy is his salvation.

Abraham Lincoln said that men are like children playing on a nursery floor, trying to spell peace with the wrong blocks. Could it be that we are like children on a nursery floor trying to spell happiness with the wrong blocks?

It takes only five—J-E-S-U-S!

WEDNESDAY EVENING, OCTOBER 17

Title: Living on the Edge of Eternity

Text: But the end of all things is at hand: be ye therefore sober, and watch unto prayer" (**1 Peter 4:7**).

Scripture Reading: 1 Peter 4:7–11

Introduction

The early Christians lived in constant hope of the return of the Lord Jesus Christ to earth. The Lord had repeatedly promised to return to his own (Matt. 24:36–44). Following his ascension, the angels promised that he would return (Acts 1:11). Nearly all of the Epistles refer to his victorious return.

Peter followed the example of both the Lord and the apostle Paul in emphasizing the truth that Christ was going to return, that judgment was going to fall on the wicked, and that Christians should concern themselves with being ready for that day. In the interim, they were encouraged to be genuine disciples in every area of their lives.

I. Practical expressions of genuine discipleship (1 Peter 4:7–8).

Peter challenged his readers to be genuinely Christian in every area of their lives, even though such might involve them in dangerous risks. They were to live each day as in the shadow of eternity.

    A. *"The end of all things is at hand."* The word that Peter used means "to draw near." The emphasis is on being ready rather than giving a specific date. Peter was concerned primarily that Christians of his day be ready for whatever life might bring. The Lord might return at any moment. Terrible persecution might fall on them. In fact, very shortly (in AD 70) Jerusalem was doomed to be destroyed following the conquest of Titus, the Roman general. It was a fearful time in which to be alive.

    B. *"Be ye therefore sober."* *Sober* means to be "in one's right mind, or in control of oneself." Christians are counseled to be in full possession of their highest mental faculties, to see things in their proper proportions, and to exercise self-control.

    C. *"Watch unto prayer."* Peter's counsel to others was similar to that which he had received from the Lord earlier in his life (Luke 22:40, 46).

Christians are not to allow their minds to become dazed by drink, drowsiness, or indifference. They must earnestly give themselves to prayer if they are to have the inward spiritual resources that will make it possible for them to live triumphantly.

II. The priority of Christian love (1 Peter 4:8–9).

    A. *The practice of Christian love.* Above all other things, believers are to practice genuine Christian love among themselves. This love is to be understood as a persistent, unbreakable spirit of goodwill. It is to manifest itself particularly in a generous and charitable attitude. Genuine Christian love will not look for the flaws and failures in the lives of others.

    B. *Ungrudging hospitality.* Peter's epistle was directed initially to those who faced the danger of persecution. At any time they could be driven from their homes and left out in the merciless, cold world. There were no AAA motels in those days. Christians were to practice warmhearted hospitality for the casual traveler, particularly toward members of their own fellowship who were suffering mistreatment at the hands of others. This hospitality was to be provided graciously. By the practice of hospitality, Christians were given the opportunity to voice their witness to travelers. Fervent Christian love would enable strangers to feel secure. By such hospitality, mission work was made possible as Christian missionaries went from place to place.

313

III. The responsible use of God's gifts (1 Peter 4:10).

Every believer has received from God spiritual gifts to be used for the benefit of the whole church.

A. *"As every man hath received the gift."* Each one is responsible to God for the way in which he uses the gift or gifts that have been bestowed upon him by the Holy Spirit. These gifts are described as variegated, or many-colored, in nature (1 Cor. 12:4–5). The gifts have their source in the grace of God and not in human achievements. Consequently, there was no place for either selfishness or boasting. On each member of the church, God has bestowed a trust or talent that can prove to be a great blessing to the work of the Lord if used properly.

B. *Peter speaks of two distinct types of ministry.*

1. The ministry of words: "If any man speak, let him speak as the oracles of God."
2. The ministry of works: "If any man minister, let him do it as of the ability which God giveth."

He who ministers as a teacher, prophet, or evangelist is to recognize that the source of his message is the grace of God. He who ministers in deeds of mercy or acts of helpfulness is to do so with the awareness that God is the giver of that which one has to bestow on others.

Christians are to be good stewards of that which God has placed in their care.

IV. The Christian's master motive (1 Peter 4:11).

When individuals or a congregation respond in a worthy manner to God's gifts, they will experience the crowning satisfaction of bringing glory to God. God's holy character will be revealed, his wonderful grace will be experienced, and his enabling power will be discovered. Lives will be enriched and transformed when believers act as good stewards of the manifold grace of God.

Conclusion

The apostle Peter gave suggestions to believers of the first century that are relevant for Christians in the twenty-first century. We likewise live in critical times. There is a great need for us to live each day with the values and the issues of eternity in mind. To do so will enable us to be a rich blessing to others and to bring glory to our Lord.

SUNDAY MORNING, OCTOBER 21

Title: Give Me This Mountain

Text: " 'Now give me this hill country that the LORD promised me in that day. You yourself heard then that the Anakites were there and their cities were large and fortified, but, the LORD helping me, I will drive them out just as he said' " (**Josh. 14:12**).

Scripture Reading: Joshua 14:9–13

Hymns: "'Tis So Sweet to Trust in Jesus," Stead

"Trusting Jesus," Stites

"Have Faith in God," McKinney

Offertory Prayer: Dear Lord, life's troubles help us to exercise a greater faith in you. Thank you for proving your reality and love during our time of need. We bless your name for your nearness. As we bring our offerings to you, we trust that they are worthy expressions of our gratitude and love. Help us to be good trustees of all the material and spiritual blessings you have so freely given. In Jesus' name. Amen.

Introduction

In many ways life can be compared to climbing mountains. There are challenges, problems, and difficulties to be overcome. Faith in Christ and dedication to him provide the source of strength by which we conquer the mountains of life.

Caleb scored a major victory over a mighty mountain. It was made possible by his unspoiled faith, his unrelenting determination, and his undivided companionship. In this spirit he came to Joshua and said, "Give me this mountain."

I. Unspoiled faith.

The Scripture finds Caleb reminding Joshua that forty-five years previous to this occasion Moses had sent Caleb and Joshua and ten other men to spy out the land that God had promised the children of Israel. They had forgotten the promises of God. They were faithless. Caleb and Joshua insisted that they could do it because God had promised that victory would be theirs. Because of this, Moses made a promise, which was the promise of God, that the mountain where the Anakim lived was to be Caleb's inheritance as a reward for his faith.

Caleb's faith was not spoiled by the faithlessness of others. Because of the faithlessness of the people, God allowed them to wander in the wilderness for forty years. Caleb and Joshua, who were faithful to God, had to wander in the wilderness along with the unfaithful. The innocent suffered along with the guilty. This, however, did not disturb Caleb's faith. He believed God would keep his promises.

Sometimes we become discouraged in our faith because a church leader makes some mistake. We are heavily disappointed and hurt. Unkind words and careless actions expressed by other Christians leave our faith greatly weakened.

All of us become disappointed in other people. This is the reason we must have our faith in the living Lord Jesus Christ. He will not cause our faith to spoil. Paul, writing with a broken heart, told of how one of his faithful friends had forsaken him to follow the world. However, Paul did not cease preaching the gospel because Demas did. It is a shame that the faithlessness of some has caused others to refuse to claim the great victories that God has promised all those who will believe.

Waiting on God did not spoil Caleb's faith. Caleb was to learn the great lesson of patience. He not only had to wander in the wilderness because the majority of the people would not believe in the Lord, but he also waited forty-five years before he was to realize the fulfillment of God's promise. James says that the "trying of your faith worketh patience. But let patience have her perfect work, that ye may be perfect and entire, wanting nothing" (1:3–4). Faith, then, is put to the test. People must believe the promises of God, regardless of the outward circumstances.

II. Unrelenting determination.

In spite of Caleb's old age, he had unrelenting determination. Though he was eighty-five, he was not satisfied with talking of the victories of the past. He had been faithful to God, and now he knows that God is going to be faithful to keep his promise.

Many Christians go naked and hungry spiritually because they do not claim the promises of God through prayer, the Bible, the church, and sharing his love.

Caleb had unrelenting determination in spite of great difficulty. He knew that the mountain that he had requested was the hardest mountain to overcome. He knew that the enemies there were stronger than any other place in the whole land. Caleb did not ask for an easy job.

Many people are turned aside in life because they feel that certain things are too difficult. The rich young ruler came to Jesus desiring eternal life. Jesus told him that he must make the Lord God first in his life and his possessions secondary. But for the rich young ruler, this was too hard, so he turned aside, refusing eternal life in Christ.

It is difficult to win people to Christ, to discipline ourselves, to be big when others are little, to love the unlovely, and to become more Christlike. Paul says in 2 Timothy 2:3, "Thou therefore endure hardness, as a good soldier of Jesus Christ." In 1 Timothy 6:12 he says, "Fight the good fight of the faith." The Christian life and the Christian ministry always will find the going tough. It is always a battle to be won, a mountain to be conquered.

III. Undivided companionship.

The companionship of a close friend is vital. Whenever Caleb went to Joshua to claim the promise, Joshua blessed him. We cannot do without our close friends to share our ambitions, our faith, our anxieties, and our call to claim God's promise and to climb his mountain.

The companionship of fellow workers is necessary. Caleb knew that his soldiers would be loyal in battle and would fight the battle of victory. God's people must labor together, pray together, work together, love, weep, and climb the mountains together.

The companionship of the Lord is all-sufficient. Caleb knew what it was to walk with the Lord when he went the first time to spy out the land. He knew God's presence in the forty years of wandering. He would experience that same divine reality as he claimed the promised mountain.

Conclusion

If we are to climb the mountains of life, we will do so by having an unspoiled faith, an unrelenting determination, and an undivided companionship.

SUNDAY EVENING, OCTOBER 21

Title: The Scandal of a Singer

Text: "Create in me a clean heart, O God; and renew a right spirit within me" **(Ps. 51:10).**

Scripture Reading: Psalm 51

Introduction

For about three thousand years, this psalm has been a pattern of penitence. Scarcely will one find a poem that throbs with such heartbeat. Across the centuries, men who have been guilty of David's sin have found in his confession a pattern of prayer. Others whose sins have been different have found equal verbalization of their contrite and broken hearts. The psalm is autobiographical. At least four areas of the message challenge us.

I. A perversion.

A. *Committed.* In 2 Samuel 11 and 12 we read the story of David's sin. David's men were at war. One night he arose from his bed and went to the roof garden of his palace. From there he saw Bathsheba, the wife of Uriah the Hittite, bathing herself. He sent for her. She came. After they spent the night together, she returned to her own home. Later she notified David that she was to have a baby as a result of that unholy visit. The king sent Uriah into battle with instructions to Joab that Uriah should be put in the place of greatest danger. This Joab did, and Uriah was killed in battle. This was exactly what David desired. Following a period of mourning by the widow, David sent for her and brought her to his house. She became his wife and bore the child that was conceived on that shameful night.

Nathan confronted David with the story of the rich man who took the poor man's lamb and killed it, rather than one of his own, to entertain a guest. Upon the recitation of the story, David was indignant at the rich man's conduct. Then Nathan uttered to him these well-known words: "Thou art the man" (2 Sam. 12:7). The child born to Bathsheba and David died, and his death compounded the grief of the king confronting his own sin.

B. *Confessed.* "Against thee, thee only, have I sinned" (Ps. 51:4). The Bible offers no victorious solution to the problem of sin apart from confession. There is no passing of the buck. There is no plea of innocence. There is no blaming the sin on Bathsheba. There is no psychiatric rationale, no

317

situation ethics, no self-justification. David assumes full responsibility for his conduct. He has come to see the whole black chapter through the eyes of God and is sick in heart and convicted in soul.

C. *Cleansing.* The sinner asks for cleansing, and there is every reason to believe that he receives it. In the sin battle, cleansing always follows confession. "If we confess our sins, he is faithful and just to forgive us our sins, and to cleanse us from all unrighteousness" (1 John 1:9). Here, then, is our hope and our optimism: not that we sin, but that there is always a remedy for sin. There is a way out, and it is always up.

II. A prayer.

A. *David asks for mercy (Ps. 51:1).* This is always the beginning place for the guilty sinner.

B. *David asks for forgiveness (Ps. 51:1).* To blot out means to erase so completely that the pencil marks do not even show.

C. *David asks for cleansing (Ps. 51:2).* Not only must the mercy from above be called to deal with the sins of the past, but the pollution of the present demands the detergent of a divine visitation.

D. *David asks for a clean heart (Ps. 51:10).* Forgiveness is not just the neutralizing of history. It is the purging of the present. The heart is the beginning place for today and tomorrow.

E. *David asks for a right spirit (Ps. 51:10).* Steps never will be what they ought to be unless there is the right spirit within. In verse 10 David pleads for the right spirit, and in verse 11 he pleads for the Holy Spirit. It is not stretching the Scriptures to assert that the only right spirit is that born of and accompanied by the Holy Spirit.

F. *David asks for the restoration of joy (Ps. 51:12).* It is possible to lose the joy of a possession without losing the possession itself. David does not ask for a replacement of salvation but for the restoration of the joy of that salvation.

G. *David asks for support (Ps. 51:12).* The old saint voiced a familiar yearning of us all when he prayed, "O Lord, prop me up on the leaning side."

H. *David asks for deliverance (Ps. 51:14).* From the blood-guiltiness of the past sin, from the bludgeoning of the present conscience, and from the perils of tomorrow's temptations, the penitent sinner cries. And his cries are heard! The most important liberation movement is the movement of the Spirit of God in the hearts of people. More serious and obvious than any generation gap is the regeneration gap. High on the courthouse in Cleveland, Ohio, are these prominently carved words, "Obedience to Law is Liberty." Fifty years ago Dr. George Truett stood on the steps of the Capitol in Washington, D.C., and said, "Liberty without law is anarchy. Liberty against law is rebellion. Liberty within the law is the formula of civilization."

People are free, not in immunity from law or in rebellion against law, but in obedience to law.

Paul voiced it well, "For the law of the Spirit of life in Christ Jesus hath made me free from the law of sin and death" (Rom. 8:2).

III. A promise.

The promise is in three parts:

A. *I will teach.* "I will teach transgressors thy ways" (Ps. 51:13). If God will but cleanse David and make him right, he promises to spend his days in teaching others the ways and wonders of God. Our theology is expressed in our sociology. Genuine gratitude to God always is manifested in our attitude toward others.

B. *I will win.* "Sinners shall be converted unto thee" (Ps. 51:13). It is not enough to recite platitudes that we may call teaching. We must fervently win others to Christ in fruitful evangelism.

C. *I will sing.* "My tongue shall sing aloud of thy righteousness" (Ps. 51:14). To teach, to win, to sing—what greater response could come from a grateful heart!

IV. A principle.

"The sacrifices of God are a broken spirit; a broken and a contrite heart, O God, thou wilt not despise" (Ps. 51:17).

Here is a principle that operates in natural life. Flowers grow because the ground is broken for their planting. Bread is the product of broken grain. The pavements we enjoy are possible because rocks have been broken. The meat of the nut is available only when the shell is broken. The egg is broken before it becomes edible. The garments we wear are possible because bolts of fabric were broken into pattern pieces. And the sweetest perfume is the product of crushed flowers.

It is so with the spirit. Jesus was a carpenter with souls as well as with wood. And one of the works of a carpenter is to fix broken things. Christ takes the broken heart and makes it new! He has a way with broken dreams, broken homes, and broken lives. He can fix them if we let him.

Conclusion

There is basically nothing new in sinning in 2012. And God specializes in forgiving and delivering us from sin. Sin confessed, forsaken, and forgiven is still the only way to victory over sin.

WEDNESDAY EVENING, OCTOBER 24

Title: Counsel for Spiritual Leaders

Text: "Feed the flock of God which is among you, taking the oversight thereof" (**1 Peter 5:2**).

Scripture Reading: 1 Peter 5:1–5

Introduction

The two epistles of Peter appear to be a sincere effort on his part to carry out the commission of his Lord to "strengthen your brothers" (Luke 22:31–32 NIV). Specifically, Peter wrote to strengthen his brothers as they struggled to do God's will in the presence of great danger and difficulty.

I. Counsel to mature spiritual leaders (I Peter 5:1–4).

A. *"Who am also an elder."* The title "elders" can also be translated "presbyters." Peter addressed the mature leaders of the church with a word of encouragement and instruction. He did not approach them on the basis of his apostolic authority, but rather identified with them as a fellow elder, recognizing them as equals within the fellowship of believers.

Peter described himself as a witness of the sufferings of Jesus Christ. His deep awareness of how Christ had suffered equipped the apostle for the endurance of personal sufferings for Christ in order to encourage his fellow workers to be patient and faithful in the midst of great difficulties.

B. *"Feed the flock of God."* Peter gave to these spiritual leaders the same command that had been given to him by the risen Lord (John 21:15–17). The word translated "feed" contains within it the totality of the shepherd's task in providing for and protecting the flock. Church leaders are reminded that the flock belongs to God. They are only undershepherds of him who is the Good and Great Shepherd.

C. *"Being ensamples to the flock."* Peter gave some specific instructions concerning the motives and methods that were to be used by elders in their ministry to the flock. He declared that God has given them the responsibility of "oversight." This word describes the function of an elder, bishop, or pastor. These terms refer not to a position of authority, but to a function or responsibility for feeding and caring for the flock of God.

There follow (vv. 2–3) three adverbial phrases in which Peter spoke specifically concerning the spirit and motives that should control the elder or pastor as he seeks to fulfill his spiritual responsibility toward his congregation.

1. He is to serve "not by constraint, but willingly." The inner, divine constraint to be God's minister is not forbidden. However, external constraints are declared to be improper for one who would serve as an elder. He is to accept his duty cheerfully and as a work of love; he is to serve as a free man rather than like a slave facing an arduous task.

2. The second suggestion is that the elder must serve, not out of a desire for monetary profit, but with eagerness to be a servant of God to needy people. A desire for dishonorable gain would disqualify a man for worthy spiritual service.

3. The third guideline forbids an attitude of authoritarian rulership and insists that the elder must consider himself as a servant who would lead the flock by the example of his own spirit and conduct.

D. *A sure reward.* Peter directed the attention of the elders to the second coming of the Lord Jesus Christ, at which time each would receive a reward according to the service he had rendered. The reward would be "a crown of glory that fadeth not away" (cf. 1 Cor. 9:25). The crown to which Peter referred was comparable to the garland that was the reward for victory in the great athletic games. The elder who faithfully fulfills his office as a shepherd will receive his prize when the Chief Shepherd comes in glory.

II. Counsel to younger spiritual leaders (I Peter 5:5).

A. *"Submit yourselves unto the elder."* Peter strongly counseled that the younger members of the church should be careful to give due respect to the more mature members of the fellowship. Evidently, even in his day there was friction between the different age groups—as has been the case in every period of time. Peter suggested to the younger members and leaders—who were likely to feel that they had all the answers—that it was possible for them to learn from the experience of their elders.

B. *"Be clothed with humility."* The word translated "be clothed" means "to tie on securely." It probably refers to the action of a slave who wrapped an apron around himself as an indication of his station in life. Peter had a vivid memory of his Lord, who had girded himself with a towel and assumed the role of a servant and washed his disciples' feet (John 13:1–15). The apostle was urging Christians to be willing to accept any position and to perform any service, however humble, in order to be a benefit to others. They were to guard against an attitude that sought dignity and authority for self.

Conclusion

The Lord depends on spiritual leaders in the church both to witness to the unsaved and to minister to and instruct the new converts. The privilege of being a spiritual leader is not to be taken lightly. The responsibility is weighty and awesome. The reward for compassionate, faithful service will be worth all the effort and struggle involved in rendering a ministry that would be pleasing to the Great Shepherd of the sheep.

SUNDAY MORNING, OCTOBER 28

Title: Conquest in Calamity

Text: "And he said unto me, My grace is sufficient for thee: for my strength is made perfect in weakness. Most gladly therefore will I rather glory in my infirmities, that the power of Christ may rest upon me" (**2 Cor. 12:9**).

Scripture Reading: 2 Corinthians 12:7–10

Hymns: "I Must Tell Jesus," Hoffman

"Near to the Heart of God," McAfee

"Take the Name of Jesus with You," Baxter

Offertory Prayer: Our Father, we come into your presence to give back to you a portion of that which you have given to us. We know that all we have belongs to you. Please accept our tithes and offerings as an expression of our love. We also give you our time, talents, minds, and bodies. Yielded to you, we ask that you will mold us and make us according to your will. We worship you with praise and gratitude through Jesus Christ our Savior. Amen.

Introduction

Today we will consider a strange paradox in God's Word. A paradox may be defined as "an assertion seemingly contradictory, or opposed to common sense, but that yet may be true in fact." Jesus used paradoxes in many of his teachings: the first will be last, the servant will be made ruler, he who dies to self will live, and others. The paradox that we will focus on today is God's strength made perfect in weakness, or conquest in calamity.

Our text finds a great man of God in deep trouble. Hardship and disappointment all but overwhelmed him. For a while, even his prayers seemed to bring him only frustration. But through prayer and self-surrender, he came to the place where he was glad to suffer if that meant that the power of Christ would rest on him in a unique way.

I. Conquest in calamity occurs when a suffering person experiences God's all-sufficient grace.

A suffering person experiences God's grace to be sufficient for his sins. For someone to know God's grace, he must understand that he is totally unworthy. There is nothing he can do to make himself deserving. His sinful nature disqualifies him from earning his way to a right relationship with God. As a sinner, a person loves darkness rather than light. One is drawn into sin by his own lust. There is none that is good without God's grace. People are self-righteous, prejudiced, irritable, cutting, unkind, dishonest, greedy, hateful, selfish, and lustful. Paul had long since known that this was the kind of man he was without God's grace. Paul came to know that only God's grace was sufficient to lift him out of his weaknesses and sin.

A suffering person experiences God's grace to be sufficient for his troubles. Paul found himself to be a victim of Satan. We do not know for certain what the "thorn in the flesh" was, but we do know that it was a malady that was humiliating, agonizing, incurable, and so terrible that he describes it as devilish. In anguish Paul sought the Lord on three different occasions, earnestly begging that the disease be taken from him.

When God's answer came, it did not come in the form of deliverance from suffering, but in a promise of sustaining grace and a statement of divine purpose. Paul was assured that divine power is made manifest in the time of human need. The reply came in such a way that Paul knew that his pain would always be with him. God said to him, "My grace is sufficient for thee: for my strength is made perfect in weakness." Paul experienced God's grace to be sufficient for his troubles.

322

II. Conquest in calamity occurs when a suffering person allows God's strength to be made perfect in him.

God's strength is made perfect through continuing prayer. Paul continued in prayer regarding the "thorn in the flesh." He earnestly prayed that God would remove the terrible malady. The first and second sessions of prayer brought no answer. He was persistent at the throne of grace. He did not stop until he received the desire of God. When Paul's answer came, he stopped asking.

If we are to find God's strength made perfect in our lives, we must continue in prayer. The Scriptures indicate that those who seek, find; to those who ask, it will be given; and to those who knock, it will be opened. Jesus indicates that those who hunger and thirst after righteousness will be filled. In the Old Testament, Jacob gave us an example by wrestling with God's messenger until the blessings came.

God's strength is made perfect through accepting his answer. God's answer may be revealed positively and immediately. When Peter was walking on the water to meet the Savior, he fell into a desperate calamity. Upon hearing Peter's cry of distress, Jesus stretched forth his hand and immediately saved Peter (Matt. 14:22–36). Often God responds to our prayers immediately. In his wisdom, he sees no necessity for our waiting. There are times when he replies in the positive and he gives us the request of our heart. Before our eyes his miracles of answered prayer become realities in our lives.

But sometimes God's answer is revealed negatively or slowly. Paul's answer from God did not come until he had made his entreaty three times. There will be times when God, in his wisdom, will see that it is best for us to come to him many times with the same prayer request. He has asked us to keep coming to the throne of grace until he gives the answer. When the answer comes, he expects us to be satisfied with his wisdom.

The answer Paul received was clearly negative. God promised that the pain and suffering would never be removed. However, God assured Paul that divine power would be magnified in the occasion of human suffering.

God's strength is made perfect through gladly accepting one's weaknesses. When Paul realized that God's power shows up best in human weakness, he triumphantly cried, "I will boast all the more gladly about my weaknesses, so that Christ's power may rest on me. That is why, for Christ's sake, I delight in weaknesses, in insults, in hardships, in persecutions, in difficulties. For when I am weak, then I am strong" (2 Cor. 12:9–10 NIV).

This extreme commitment of Paul was no pretense. He verified it with his life. After he and Silas had been cruelly beaten, thrown into the Philippian jail, and locked in stocks, they began singing praises to God for his counting them worthy to suffer for his sake. They gloried in their suffering for Jesus' sake. It is not surprising that following their praise to God, the prison doors were miraculously opened. Not only were they set free, but an entire family received Christ as Lord and Savior.

While in prison in Rome, Paul wrote to the Philippian church: "Rejoice in the Lord always. I will say it again: Rejoice!... Do not be anxious about anything, but in everything, by prayer and petition, with thanksgiving, present your requests to God. And the peace of God, which transcends all understanding, will guard your hearts and your minds in Christ Jesus." (Phil. 4:4, 6–7 NIV).

Paul's life was a demonstration of how God's strength is made perfect in human weakness and suffering. It was from a prison that he wrote: "I have learned to be content whatever the circumstances. I know what it is to be in need, and I know what it is to have plenty. I have learned the secret of being content in any and every situation, whether well fed or hungry, whether living in plenty or in want. I can do everything through him who gives me strength" (Phil. 4:11–13 NIV).

God's own Son knew the disappointment of desertion, the heartbreak of betrayal, the blasphemy of unlawful trials, the wounds of a biting whip, the mockery of a crown of thorns, the curses of ridiculing tongues, the shame of a naked death, the agony of being nailed to a cross, and the punishment of humankind's horrible sin. He anticipated all of this in the garden of Gethsemane. He cried, "O my Father, if it be possible, let this cup pass from me: nevertheless not as I will, but as thou wilt" (Matt. 26:39).

Conclusion

In our pain, sorrow, agony, heartache, disappointment, poverty, trouble, and incapabilities, we must come to pray, "Your will be done."

Occasionally in life we meet a person who has an incurable disease or a twisted body causing profound suffering, yet paradoxically seen within that person is a consistently radiant and selfless life through faith in Jesus Christ. This is conquest in calamity.

SUNDAY EVENING, OCTOBER 28

Title: The Hills Are Alive

Text: "I will lift up mine eyes unto the hills, from whence cometh my help" (**Ps. 121:1**).

Scripture Reading: Psalm 121

Introduction

Most of us have hummed or sung the words from *The Sound of Music* that declare, "The hills are alive with the sound of music." The psalmist, too, declares that the hills are alive.

It is interesting that hills and mountains are associated with so many men of the Bible—Moses and Sinai, Noah and Ararat, Elijah and Carmel, Gideon and Gilead. The mention of our Lord brings to mind Calvary and Olivet. The Bible is filled with illustrations that the hills are alive.

In 1840 David Livingstone turned his back on a lucrative career and went to Africa where he was to expend his life as a great Christian missionary. His sister tells about his leaving home. It was on November 17 of that year, and his family rose at five in the morning. David read this psalm then prayed. From his home, he walked with his father to Glasgow where David took a steamer to Liverpool and on to Africa. We are told that when his body was found, his face was toward his open Bible and his index finger pointed to the text, "I will lift up mine eyes." In this magnificent psalm, we have two major treasures.

I. An evening hymn for the pilgrim and the soldier.

A. *For the pilgrim.* At the close of the day, the weary pilgrim needed refreshment for his body, but he also needed refreshment for his soul. When the camp was made and the party was ready for the close of the day, this psalm was either read or sung by the group. It beats with consolation for those who have borne the burdens and the heat of the day.

Observe the words that have to do with traveling. "Thy foot to be moved" and "thy going out and thy coming in" spell out action for the pilgrim. And for the tired traveler at the close of the day, there is a song of consolation for the day's journey and an anthem of hope and assurance for tomorrow's path.

B. *For the soldier.* It is a far cry from modern warfare that the people of ancient times usually fought during the day and camped at night. The surprise night attack was an unusual strategy, though it came to be used more and more. So when the day's fighting was done and the weapons were laid aside temporarily, the psalm was read or sung. It inspired the spirit and built morale.

Notice the war words: God "keepeth Israel." He who guides in their warfare during the day will "neither slumber nor sleep" while they rest. He will keep watch through the night. He will "preserve [them] from all evil." So the fighting men came to be reassured by this song at the close of the day. God was alive and concerned about them!

In the fierce days of World War II, someone asked the preacher George Truett why God did not stop the terrible conflict. His crisp reply was that God did not start it. He does not start wars. James tells us where wars come from: "What causes fights and quarrels among you? Don't they come from your desires that battle within you?" (James 4:1). But when men start wars, God is never insensitive to the cause or the call of his people.

II. An assurance of the kind of God we have.

A. *He is the almighty God.* "My help cometh from the LORD, which made heaven and earth" (Ps. 121:2). This *is* our Father's world because he made it.

B. *He is an able God.* "He will not suffer thy foot to be moved" (Ps. 121:3). God will keep the feet of his people from slipping and causing them to fall.

C. *He is an alert God.* "He that keepeth thee will not slumber" (Ps. 121:3). God's eyes are never closed to the needs of his people. He does not go to sleep at the switch. He is ever awake and alert to the cries of his children.

D. *He is equal to all conditions and circumstances.* "The sun shall not smite thee by day, nor the moon by night" (Ps. 121:6). God can handle the heat of the day, and he can handle the curtains of the night. He is able to preserve from "all" evil. Sunstroke was a dreaded experience in that ancient land and day. But the natural forces are not beyond God's domain. Whether the problem of God's people is the dangerous mountain path, the military enemy, or the forces of nature, he is equal to them all.

E. *He takes care of the main thing.* "The LORD shall ... preserve thy soul" (Ps. 121:7). The soul is the mainspring of life. In the strict sense, a person does not have a soul; a person *is* a soul. "And the LORD God formed man of the dust of the ground, and breathed into his nostrils the breath of life; and man became a living soul" (Gen. 2:7). When God preserves the soul, he takes care of what a person really is, not merely something a person has.

F. *He is a God of the thresholds.* "The LORD shall preserve thy going out and thy coming in from this time forth, and even for evermore" (Ps. 121:8). The triumphant life is punctuated with triumphant thresholds—the thresholds of birth, of the first day of school, of graduation, of marriage, of the first job, of retirement, and of death itself. The doors of destiny never swing open without God being present with his people for the crossing of thresholds. Whether the thresholds be daily at morning and evening or whether they be the big ones, God is with us!

I have saved for the last the commonly accepted translation of the text, which puts the second part of it in the form of a question: "From whence cometh my help?" Whether it is a statement or a question is of no real consequence. The matter for us is both "Where do we look for help?" and "My help cometh from the Lord."

Personal, powerful, and present is God's help for you. Will you let him help you—in his own way?

Conclusion

People need help. They look everywhere for it, but they will never find adequate help apart from God. The hills are alive because God is alive!

WEDNESDAY EVENING, OCTOBER 31

Title: Guidelines for Victorious Christian Living

Text: "Humble yourselves therefore under the mighty hand of God, that he may exalt you in due time" (**1 Peter 5:6**).

Scripture Reading: 1 Peter 5:6–11

Introduction

In the final words of his first epistle, the apostle Peter voiced some general spiritual guidelines that must be observed carefully by every Christian if victorious living is to be a reality.

I. "Humble yourself therefore under the mighty hand of God."

The word "therefore" refers to the sentence immediately preceding. The child of God must yield himself completely to the loving but mighty hand of God. Peter warned against our natural tendency to self-exaltation. Peter remembered the humble submissiveness of Jesus Christ who laid aside the form of God and clothed himself in the form of a servant, being "obedient unto death, even the death of the cross" (Phil. 2:6–8). Peter could testify from personal experience concerning the tragic results of self-sufficient pride.

Peter himself had once been proud and egotistic. He had been self-assertive. By many bitter experiences of disappointment with himself, he learned the lesson of humility.

II. "Casting all your care upon him."

The word translated "care" implies anything that distracts, divides, or creates fear.

Peter called for an attitude of trust in the compassionate care of the loving Father. He would encourage each believer to take all of his anxieties and troubles into the presence of God for help. Peter had listened to the Master and had come to believe that the goodness of God could be depended on for the basic necessities of life (Matt. 6:25–34).

III. "Be sober, be vigilant."

Peter had learned that every believer must be constantly on guard against the subtle approach and the deceptive, destructive purposes of the devil. Peter had no doubt at all concerning the reality and the power of the evil one. He issued a warning to his contemporaries and to modern believers concerning the same devil about whom he himself had been warned by Jesus (Luke 22:31).

The devil is ever on the move, seeking whom he may destroy. He uses many disguises and is most dangerous when his approach is friendly and accommodating. The devil is the enemy of God, of the church, and of your home. He is your enemy. He not only wants to destroy you but also those dearest to you. Our only hope of escape from the power of the evil one is by following our Lord closely.

IV. "Whom resist steadfast in the faith."

Peter declared that the devil must be resisted with all earnestness. The evil one had attempted to thwart the plan of God and to destroy the Messiah (Matt. 4:1–11). On one occasion, Satan had used Peter himself to try to mislead the Savior (Matt. 16:21–23). If the devil could use Peter, he can use others today.

As a fellow elder and as a shepherd who was seeking to protect the flock, Peter warned all Christians against their most dangerous and determined enemy. He stated that with firm steadfastness "in the faith" they must resist Satan's every move to infiltrate their minds or to misdirect their energies and efforts. By declaring that the devil was the common enemy of all the brothers, Peter sought to comfort them and bind them close to one another. They needed to help one another in order to be victorious over the devil.

Conclusion

Peter concluded his epistle with a doxology of praise to the God of grace who calls us out of the darkness of spiritual death into the light of "his eternal glory by Jesus Christ." The word translated "perfect" means "to restore." It is used of setting a fracture. It is used also of mending nets. Peter declared that God will supply Christians with that which is missing in their character and that they will not suffer the lack of any good thing. He assured them that God was at work within them and in the midst of their trials and troubles. He encouraged them to believe that by an attitude of humble submission and continuing trust, they could experience blessings from God in the midst of their sufferings. Peter also encouraged them to remain faithful and obedient in a time of great suffering. He affirmed that to do so would bring firmness of character and strength of purpose that would make life complete and wonderful.

SUGGESTED PREACHING PROGRAM FOR

NOVEMBER

■ Sunday Mornings

Finish the series "Courageous Faith in a Chaotic World" on the first Sunday morning in November, and begin the series "Good Stewards of the Grace of God" the following week. This is a series that will help listeners reject the lure of materialism and encourage them to live for eternal values.

■ Sunday Evenings

Complete the series "The Gospel That Puts a Song in the Heart" on the first Sunday evening. On the following Sunday, begin the series "Old Testament Biographies," sermons based on Old Testament characters. These messages will help listeners to become better acquainted with both the failures and successes that are pictured in the Bible. We can profit from both the warnings and the encouragements that these provide.

■ Wednesday Evenings

Psalm 23 provides the scriptural basis for five devotional messages in a series entitled "The Pearl of the Psalms." Interrupt the series on the Wednesday before Thanksgiving to do a Thanksgiving litany.

SUNDAY MORNING, NOVEMBER 4

Title: Full Barns and Empty Souls

Text: "Thou fool, this night thy soul shall be required of thee" **(Luke 12:20).**

Scripture Reading: Luke 12:13–21

Hymns: "For the Beauty of the Earth," Pierpoint

"Great Is Thy Faithfulness," Chisholm

"Beneath the Cross of Jesus," Clephane

Offertory Prayer: Our Father, as we bring our gifts to you, we acknowledge gratefully that we secured our material blessings first of all from your gracious bounty. You have given us abundantly above all that we ask or think. Help us in the use of what remains in our hands, and use this which we dedicate to you to proclaim your glorious gospel around our world. In Jesus' name. Amen.

Introduction

No one enjoys being interrupted when speaking. Most of us show our impatience, especially if the subject on which we are speaking is urgent. Jesus was on his way to Jerusalem to die. His words were among his last on earth. And a man interrupted him.

Did the man ask him how he could attain eternal life? Did he ask him to tell him about God, about death, about temptation? No, he interrupted the burning message of Jesus to ask him to be the referee of a disputed will. He asked him to be the arbitrator of a family feud and to decide in his favor in advance.

But Jesus maintained his poise. He pointed the man to something bigger than his covetousness. He used the occasion to give him (and us) one of the most graphic and impressive of his parables.

Jesus tells of a farmer who had a bumper crop. It was one of those years when he prepared the ground just right, the seed was planted at exactly the right time, the sunshine and the rainfall were perfect, and the crop was the greatest ever. He had worked hard. He had planned wisely. And it had paid off.

We see the farmer one evening as he looked out over his fields. Already the harvest had begun, and his modest barns were not big enough to hold the grain. He began to make his plans. He took counsel, not with God, but with himself. *I'll tear down my barns and build greater barns*, he thought.

The farmer turned toward his house and entered for the evening. His pantry also was full and running over. He sat down to a table laden with the choicest of food. Attentive servants were at his side, alert to his every need and desire. He was enjoying the fruits of his industry and his prudence. He fancied himself living to a ripe old age. He had it made. He would eat, drink, and be merry.

The farmer retired to his bedchamber and lay down to sleep. He dreamed of barns and banquets and yet more abundant harvests. Suddenly a sharp cry issued from his room, and the servants rushed to him. They were startled to find him writhing in great pain. Before they could help him, he stiffened and collapsed in death. That night his soul was required of him.

The next morning the sun arose as it always had. The cattle stirred and went out to graze in the pasture. The corn swayed in the breeze. The servants tiptoed about the house, preparing for an elaborate funeral. The rabbi was notified to prepare a glowing eulogy.

It was God's turn to say something. The farmer had been doing all of the talking for a long time. But God always has the last word. God was not impressed with the farmer's success or his plans. While people praised the farmer's memory, God called him a fool. He was a fool not because he died that night while his wealth was still unspent. He was a fool because he let something die inside him.

I. The farmer failed to look beyond himself.

He gave God no acknowledgment in his attainment of success. It was as if the farmer were responsible for life within the seed, for the fertility of the soil, and for the sunshine and the rain. Read his soliloquy and notice the first personal pronouns "I," "me," "my," and "mine."

The farmer failed to acknowledge God in his future plans. When we ignore the part God plays in our success and prosperity, we also will ignore the part God should play in our future plans. The farmer planned to spend his possessions selfishly on himself. He would eat, drink, and be merry in his intoxication. He cut God out of his plans.

Jesus did not condemn the farmer for his plans to tear down his barns and build greater buildings. Our God is a God of progress. He condemned the farmer because his purpose for building greater barns was to store his goods so he could spend them lavishly and selfishly on himself.

II. The farmer failed to look beyond the present world.

He ignored the fact that there is more to life than this present world. He evaded the prospect that he would die. It never occurred to him that he might not live to enjoy his prosperity.

If you had asked the farmer if he believed there was a God, he would have answered, "Of course I believe there is a God. A farmer cannot prepare the soil and plant the seed without believing in a God of life." His problem was that of so many today. With his mind and his lips, he acknowledged the reality of God, but in his practical plans, he purposed to live as if there were no God, as if there were no death, and as if there were no judgment. "Soul, eat, drink, and be merry," he said to himself, although beggars lay hungry at his gate. "Eat, drink, and be merry," many say today, although the church and the kingdom desperately need their concern and support.

Conclusion

J. B. Phillips tells us of a little field mouse who was born and grew up in a grain field. He raised his family in the protection and abundance of the field. There was food in every direction. The mouse somehow felt that this was his world and his harvest and that it would go on and on without end. Then came the farmer's harvest, and the stalks were chopped and the grain hauled away. The terror and disorder of the harvest were followed by the barrenness of the ground left behind. The beautiful world of the field mouse collapsed around him.

We can understand this philosophy in a field mouse, but we should know better. There will be a day of reckoning, and those who ignore this issue God calls fools.

SUNDAY EVENING, NOVEMBER 4

Title: Deserted Harps

Text: "We hanged our harps upon the willows in the midst thereof" (**Ps. 137:2**).

Scripture Reading: Psalm 137

Introduction

As we come to the beautiful but somewhat sad Psalm 137, we are reminded of the words of G. Campbell Morgan: "A text without the context is a pretext."

The setting of our Scripture is unusually important. It is a psalm of the exile. In it the entire octave of human emotions is run. It finds us and describes us and encourages us. Let us look further then and consider:

I. The context.

God's people were allowed to come into the Promised Land and possess it triumphantly. This occupation was the culmination of history, the climax of their national dream. It was the fulfillment of divine prophecy, the apex of personal joy. After decades of slavery and oppression, of wandering and fighting, the Israelites had at last entered the land that flowed with milk and honey. They had "arrived."

But then something happened. Prosperity dulled their sense of acute dependence on God. They became preoccupied with things, and their holy fervor cooled. They relaxed their spiritual standards.

So God permitted his people to be carried into Babylonian exile. There they were to be tried and refined and made ready to return as a remnant to establish a new nation. Once the people were victors; now they were victims. Once they were their own masters; now they were slaves. Once they had homes; now they were homeless in a foreign country. Once they were happy; now they were sad. Once they were busy making music for God, but now their harps were hanging idly in the willow trees as they sat on the muddy riverbanks and wept over their plight. They were taunted by their captors, broken by their environment, and demoralized by their troubles. So up into the willow trees went the harps. "How shall we sing the Lord's song in a strange land?" (v. 4) they asked.

II. The contemporaries.

There are among us today people of God who have hung their harps in willows. Once in the glow of conversion they came into the promised land of God's provision. Then something happened. Perhaps the going got tough. Perhaps someone got in the way. So they quit.

Now they will not sing or play the harps. They prefer to remain inactive. They desire status without work. They want membership without service. They want identification without participation.

III. The causes.

Why did the Israelites desert their harps?

A. *They lived in the past.* "*We wept, when we remembered Zion*" (v. 1). They looked into the past instead of into the future. And we, too, put our harps into the willows when we live in the past. We can draw an analogy from a poem someone wrote about the lightning bug:

> The lightning bug's a curious bug, .
> And of a special kind;
> For he stumbles through the darkness
> With his headlights on behind.

"Headlights on behind!" God's people didn't have life as easy as they used to have it, so they quit. So do many people today. We remember the good old days (which may not have been as good as we assess them), and because things have changed, we quit.

B. *The Israelites had moved.* "By the rivers of Babylon, there we sat down" (v. 1). They now had a new address. They were away from home, away from the moral and religious climate of their former spiritual environment.

Need we be reminded that ours is a mobile society—that the airways, waterways, and highways are choked with people on the move? It is not easy to be Christian away from home. Many people who are decent at home go wild when they attend a convention. They slip into the city, leaving their Christianity behind and hoping nobody will know what kind of sins they are up to.

C. *The Israelites could not have their own way.* "They that carried us away captive required of us a song; and they that wasted us required of us mirth, saying, Sing us one of the songs of Zion" (v. 3). It was not their idea to be there. They would prefer to perform in the temple at Jerusalem, not on a riverbank. They did not get their way, so they quit.

D. *The Israelites were mastered by worldliness.* Voluntarily or not, they served Babylon, and Babylon was a synonym of worldliness.

In almost every congregation there are those who are now idle. They have put their harps of Christian service into the willow trees. And the same people who are victimized by worldliness are the last to recognize it and the first to blame someone else for their own inactivity.

A wise man said it is all right as long as the ship is in the ocean, but woe unto the ship when the ocean gets into it. So it is with the Christian. It is good to be in the world, but woe if the world gets into us.

E. *The Israelites took the easy way out.* It is not hard to play in the temple when the temperature is just right, but it is hard to string a harp in Babylon. It is a great deal harder to sing in Babylon than it is in Jerusalem.

So when the going got hard, the captives quit. But the quitter never wins and the winner never quits. The easiest way out is to drop out, and this was the reason for their idleness. Could it be so for many of us?

It is hard to be a Christian because it is so easy to be a Christian. It is hard to be a real one because we have made it so easy to become a nominal one. We have lowered the standards to raise the statistics.

IV. The cure.

What does one do with a deserted harp?

A. *Get it in hand.* You have one. God gave it to you. Take it down from whatever willow you have parked it in, and get it in hand.

B. *Get it in tune.* Get it in tune, catching the pitch from God's tuning fork. Get it in tune by a thorough cleaning. Get it in tune by letting the Master tighten the strings and tune it for you.

C. *Get it in service.* Unused instruments get out of tune. Unused talents deteriorate. Great musical instruments are never really worn out by use but by abuse. Use what you have!

Conclusion

Know you have a harp if you are a Christian. Get it in hand, get it in tune, and get it in service.

WEDNESDAY EVENING, NOVEMBER 7

Title: The Lord Is My Shepherd

Text: "The LORD is my shepherd; I shall not want. He maketh me to lie down in green pastures: he leadeth me beside the still waters" **(Ps. 23:1–2).**

Scripture Reading: Psalm 23

Introduction

Psalm 23 is retrospective in that King David recalls familiar scenes from his younger days when he was a shepherd on the Judean hills. He remembered awakening at dawn, arising, opening the door of the sheepfold, giving the call to which his sheep responded promptly, and leading them forth to a place where ample vegetation was available for their morning meal. In choosing the locations to which he led his sheep, their welfare was uppermost in his mind. He recalled how he had taken his place on the hill above his flock but never far from them and had watched intently lest something endanger his sheep. Day after day he had stood between his sheep and prowling beasts and robbers lurking in the dark ravines. He carefully watched his flock and was ready to risk his life in defense of his sheep.

During the early hours of the morning, David's sheep enjoyed a bountiful repast. Then as midday approached with its attendant scorching sun, the sheep were panting with heat and thirst, so David led them to still waters that their thirst might be quenched. After the sheep had slaked their thirst and while it was still too hot for them to be exposed on the sun-smitten hills, David sought out a shady place so they could rest until the noontide heat had passed.

As the sun was sinking in the west, the sheep enjoyed another meal before David conducted them to the safety of the fold for the night. After he had gathered the contented sheep into the fold, he stretched out before the opening to bar the entrance and protect them from any danger.

This intimate relationship between the shepherd and his sheep was beautiful and meaningful. Constantly with his flock, he learned the unique traits and varied habits of the sheep, as well as the ailments with which they were troubled from time to time.

I. The Lord is my shepherd.

From the name Jehovah, which is here translated "LORD" and is the most revealing of God's grace toward his people, we learn three things: his self-sufficiency, his sovereignty, and his immutability. He meets every need of humans. He will be the same tomorrow and the day after as he is today, as strong and helpful then as he is now.

The sentence "The LORD is my shepherd" is a declaration of both God's deity and humanity. The former declares that he is above us, and the latter indicates that he is with us. He is both Creator and Companion. He never loses one of his own in the crowd either by day or by night but is concerned about and watches over us individually.

Retaining the shepherd heart after becoming king, David thought of himself as the "shepherd" of his people. As David meditated he realized that all he had been to his sheep and all that he sought to be to his people, the Lord was to him, and far more. Just as David cared for his sheep, anticipating their needs, watching over them with kindly concern, and protecting them from harm, the Lord was with him and would continue to be with him, leading, providing for, and protecting him. David rejoiced greatly that the Lord would never forget, never fail, and never forsake him. He had the blessed assurance that his Shepherd would supply his physical, intellectual, and spiritual needs because his riches were unsearchable, his love unchanging, his faithfulness unfailing.

How wonderful that the Great Shepherd who watches over us and provides for our well-being will supply all of our spiritual needs! Happy is the Christian who accepts the glorious truth that the Lord will take care of him and do what is best for him. Time will prove that his wondrous grace is marvelously sufficient and satisfying.

Applying the figure, the psalmist indicated that as the shepherd was to each sheep of his flock so was Jehovah to him. Jehovah knew him personally, loved him devotedly, supplied his needs bountifully, guided him daily, and protected him constantly. He found great satisfaction in the fact that the Lord was his personal Shepherd.

A striking word in this text is "my." The Lord is "my" Shepherd because he purchased me at a great price, leads me by his Spirit, feeds me with his Word, and keeps me by his power. He is my Provider, Preserver, and Protector. Since he has never forgotten, failed, or forsaken one of his own, every need of mine will be supplied.

To know that Jehovah, the eternal I AM, who made heaven and earth and who holds the universe in his hand, is one's Shepherd is altogether satisfying in its deepest implications. Because the Lord was his Shepherd, David declared that he was not afraid of lacking anything. He was thoroughly convinced that the Lord did not have less concern about and care for him than a shepherd has for the sheep that are committed to his custody. He firmly believed the Lord would not withhold anything that might contribute to his living happily under his care.

II. I shall not want.

In the Bible we find these promises concerning the Great Shepherd's care for his sheep: "They shall not be ashamed in the evil time: and in the days of famine they shall be satisfied" (Ps. 37:19); "The LORD will give grace and glory: no good thing will he withhold from them that walk uprightly" (84:11); and "My God shall supply all your need according to his riches in glory by Christ Jesus" (Phil. 4:19). We are overwhelmed with the assurance of our consummate well-being in the efficient, purposeful, and loving care, leadership, and protection of the Great Shepherd. To declare "I shall not lack" anything that is good in itself or that would be good for me, either now or in the future, is the final and consummate expression of trust. The blessed assurance that the Lord will supply the needs of his own according to his riches gives peace and poise to any Christian, whether the words be interpreted as applying to the material or the spiritual.

III. He makes me lie down.

After the shepherd leads his sheep into pastures of tender, green grass and they eat until their hunger is satisfied, they lie down and rest in peaceful repose and perfect security. In a similar manner, after God's children have sought satisfaction and security from the sources where they cannot be found, the Great Shepherd turns them away from the empty fascinations of the world and makes them lie down in places of his own choosing where they may find relaxation, rest, refreshment, and revitalization. In these blessed places he speaks to our hearts and teaches us the most important lessons. Deeper knowledge of him is a wonderful compensation for being made to lie down.

Conclusion

Has the Shepherd made you lie down? If so, you know that his purpose in doing so was to make you a better person and to prepare you to render better and more effective service for him. In this prostrate position, you will be helped greatly by prayerful waiting and submissive obedience to his blessed will. If the Shepherd tells you to lie down, do not hesitate to do so, because it will be in a place of his choosing and for your benefit. His goodness in leading you beside the waters of quietness, refreshment, and reinvigoration is sufficient cause for genuine gratitude on your part. How thankful we should be for the reassuring words "He leadeth me"!

SUNDAY MORNING, NOVEMBER 11

Title: Laboring for Food That Endures

Text: "Labour not for the meat which perisheth, but for that meat which endureth unto everlasting life, which the Son of man shall give unto you: for him hath God the Father sealed" (**John 6:27**).

Scripture Reading: John 6:24–29; Matt. 25:34–40

Hymns: "A Child of the King," Buell
  "Trust, Try, and Prove Me," Leech
  "Take My Life, and Let It Be," Havergal

Offertory Prayer: Our heavenly Father, help us to see how richly you have bestowed your blessings on us. Help us to recognize the grace of your loving purpose in all of the events and gifts that you have brought into our lives. Today we bring the fruits of our labors and place them on the altar as an act of worship and praise for your grace. Accept our tithes and offerings and bless them to the salvation of the unsaved in this community and to the uttermost parts of the earth, through Jesus Christ our Lord. Amen.

Introduction

The words and works of our Lord were always designed to meet specific human needs. Both his deeds and his words reveal great truths about God and about life as God has planned it for us.

Our text is translated by the New International Version as follows: "Do not work for food that spoils, but for food that endures to eternal life" (John 6:27).

What do the words of the text reveal about God? What deep human need does the text deal with?

We are inclined to labor for food that perishes when God intended that we should labor for food that endures to eternal life.

The devil approached our Lord while in the wilderness with the suggestion that he should have a primary concern for the food his body needed (Matt. 4:3). Jesus rejected this suggestion and resisted the temptation to live for food that perishes. On another occasion, the devil came to the Lord, using the person of the apostle Peter, and tried to thwart him from his redemptive purpose. Again he was suggesting that our Lord live for the present alone rather than live with the values of eternity in mind (Matt. 16:22–23).

We face the peril of living for an unworthy goal in life. If our goal is unworthy, life will be frustrated and unsatisfying even if we exceed our goal.

The tragedy is that one can fall into a rut of laboring for the perishable without fully realizing it.

The devil will confront each of us with a promise of prosperity and plenty if this is the lure that is needed to keep us from doing the will of God (Luke 4:5–7). There are some who labor under the erroneous impression that prosperity is always a sign of God's approval. In reality it may be the gift of the devil. He seeks to tempt us with the promise of either profit or pleasure. He has the capacity to produce these for us at least for a time.

I. Lot labored for the food that perished (Gen. 13:10–13).

A. *Material values were the determining factor in the great choices of Lot.*

B. *Lot achieved success in the city (Gen. 19:1).*

C. *Lot experienced catastrophic failure in his home (Gen. 19:14).*

D. *Lot saw his possessions go up in smoke and down in ashes (Gen. 19:28).*

E. *Lot came to the end in shame and disgrace because he had labored for food that perished (Gen. 19:29).*

II. Jonah refused to work for the food that does not perish.

A. *The command of God came to Jonah concerning his mission and ministry (Jonah 1:1–2).*

B. *Jonah chose to follow a road that led contrary to the will of his God (Jonah 1:3).*

C. *Jonah probably had a multitude of excuses that were perfectly acceptable to him.*

1. He probably hated the Assyrians because they were the enemies of his country.
2. Perhaps he was plagued with spiritual snobbery because the Assyrians were sinners with whom he did not want to associate.
3. There was an absence of love in Jonah's heart. He just did not love the people in Nineveh.
4. Jonah rejected the all-inclusiveness of the love of God. He did not believe that the love of God included the Assyrians along with the Israelites. For these and perhaps other reasons, he refused to do God's will.

Have you been guilty of rejecting an opportunity to be a Sunday school teacher or director in the church training program? Have you declined an opportunity to be a blessing to children and youth? Have you refrained from giving your Christian witness to someone who needs to know Jesus Christ as Lord and Savior?

Are you laboring for food that perishes or for food that endures to eternal life?

III. The rich farmer worked for food that perishes (Luke 12:15–21).

A. *The rich farmer, whom God called a fool, has a multitude of twin brothers.* These twin brothers live for the material values of life. They ignore the needs of those about them. They seek to feed their soul upon things; they ignore God; they live as if there will be no reckoning day.

B. *Modern-day fools.* God called the rich farmer a fool. "So is he that layeth up treasure for himself, and is not rich toward God" (Luke 12:21).

What is your cash worth at the bank? What is your spiritual worth in the bank of heaven? Do you have any treasures in heaven? Have you been laboring for that which you must leave behind when the death angel comes and stands at your front door?

IV. The rich young man was a prisoner of perishables (Matt. 19:16–22).

A. *The hunger of the heart cannot be satisfied with morality alone (v. 20).*

B. *Riches are a poor substitute for food that never perishes (v. 21).*

C. *Food that perishes caused the rich young man to reject food that does not perish (v. 22).*

Before we criticize the young man too much, let us examine our own lives. Are we living for that which is perishable or for that which is permanent?

Conclusion

The wise man said, "He that winneth souls is wise" (Prov. 11:30). The verdict of eternity is, "They that be wise shall shine as the brightness of the firmament; and they that turn many to righteousness as the stars for ever and ever" (Dan. 12:3).

The devil offers to you the kingdoms of this world if you are willing to follow him. But instead of living for the perishable, each of us should decide to live for that which endures for eternity. We can determine with the help of the Holy Spirit to be the vehicle of God's love and demonstrate Christian love in service to those about us. God would have us to be the voice that communicates his offer of forgiveness for sin and the gift of eternal life. With the help of the Holy Spirit, we can provide a demonstration of what God's grace can accomplish in the hearts and lives of those who trust and follow Jesus Christ. "Do not work for food that spoils, but for food that endures to eternal life" (John 6:27 NIV).

SUNDAY EVENING, NOVEMBER 11

Title: The Meaning of *Moriah*

Text: "Some time later God tested Abraham. He said to him, 'Abraham!' 'Here I am,' he replied. Then God said, 'Take your son, your only son, Isaac, whom you love, and go to the region of Moriah. Sacrifice him there as a burnt offering on one of the mountains I will you about' " **(Gen. 22:1–2 NIV).**

Scripture Reading: Genesis 22:1–14

Introduction

One of the most important characters to appear in human history before the birth of our Lord was Abraham, the father of the faithful and the friend of God. If we measure him by the world's standards, this would not be true. He ruled no nation. He conquered no territory. He wrote no books. He enacted no laws. The sphere of his influence was only in the religious field. Christians, Jews, and Muslims all claim him as father of their faith. It was he who gave us the blessed heritage of a belief in one God, Jehovah.

The pilgrimage of Abraham began when his father, Terah, was commanded to leave Ur of the Chaldees to go to a land preserved for him by God. There a nation was to grow that trusted in the true God. In Ur the family was surrounded by those who believed in many gods. "Come out from among them and be ye separate," God was saying. It is God's will that his people be a separate people.

The pilgrimage of Terah ended about halfway to Canaan. "And Terah died in Haran." A patient and long-suffering God began again with Terah's son, Abram (later changed by God to Abraham). "Get thee out of thy country, and from thy kindred, and from thy father's house, unto the land that I will shew thee," he told Abram (Gen. 12:1). Abram obeyed, and the adventure began. He traveled by faith, and God led him into the Promised Land.

Abraham prospered as people count prosperity. He enjoyed a vital relationship with God. He had entered a covenant agreement with God. He was heir of the promises of God. But there was one blight in his life. He had no son to bear his name and to perpetuate his life through his descendants.

Then a miracle took place in Abraham and Sarah's old age. Sarah gave birth to a son. This son, Isaac, was special to Abraham because he was the son of his old age promised by God. In him a potential nation resided. God had promised Abraham that his seed would be as "the stars of the sky in multitude, and as the sand which is by the sea shore innumerable" (Heb. 11:12). That promise rested in Isaac.

Perhaps Abraham looked up at the stars, remembering the promise of God concerning his own descendants. I can see him late one evening, sitting by his tent, waiting for the stars to come out so he might worship and exult in God. I can imagine that he noticed a wisp of smoke rising from a distant mountain. It was a heathen tribe offering a human sacrifice. I can hear him saying, "Poor benighted people! Offering up a son to a god who cannot hear, who cannot answer, who cannot respond."

Quick as a flash, the thought comes to Abraham, "Would you, worshiping the true God, be willing to offer up Isaac to him?" He brushed it away, but it kept coming back. That night as he slept, he heard the clear voice of God, "Take now thy son, thine only son Isaac, whom thou lovest, and get thee into the land of Moriah; and offer him there for a burnt offering." And as he heard the command, it seemed as if all the stars in the sky toppled to his feet.

The next day Abraham promptly obeyed. He did not rationalize. He did not argue. He offered no excuses. You know the rest of the story—the climb up Mount Moriah, the binding of Isaac, the staying of the hand of the father, the substitute ram caught in the thicket, the worship of father and son, and finally the descent of father and son arm in arm.

What is the meaning to us today of this dramatic but distant event in biblical history? I would suggest several applications.

I. The name given to the place where the scene took place—"Jehovah-jireh," "the LORD will see to it," "the LORD will provide."

Abraham learned that in God's own way, in God's own time, he would provide a sacrifice. In our day, God's will must be done God's way and by God's timetable. We must wait on him, knowing that he will provide what we need.

II. Moriah is the place where we give back our dead to God.

Our Jewish neighbors often name their cemeteries "Mount Moriah." This is where they, like Abraham, solemnly offer back their beloved dead to God. This time comes to us. Climbing Mount Moriah means to face this experience with faith, submission, and obedience. We must be good stewards of our sorrow. We must show those who are not Christians that we have an inner grace that is sufficient even for this trial.

III. Moriah means a willingness to give up that which is most precious in our lives if God commands.

It may be our child. It may be our companion. It may be a secret sin. It may be a sweetheart or a friend, one who is not best for us. God may call our child to be a missionary. It may be our business or unethical business practices. It may be our appetite, our lust, or our pride. Whatever we cling to, whatever we love more than God, we must relinquish when he commands.

IV. God does not ask of us what he was unwilling to do himself.

Just as Isaac climbed Mount Moriah with the wood of his altar on his back, so did God's Son stagger toward Mount Calvary with the wood of his altar, in the form of a cross, on his back. When they came to the top of the hill, this time there was no substitute, and God's Son died as an atonement for our sins. Fulfilled again were the words of Abraham, "God will provide himself a lamb." This time it was the "Lamb of God, which taketh away the sin of the world" (John 1:29).

Conclusion

Can't you see Isaac in the long ago as he watched that ram die? Can't you hear him saying to himself, "He's dying instead of me. But for him, I'd be up there"? As you look now at the cross, you find yourself saying, "He's dying instead of me. But for him, I'd be up there. The wages of sin is death, and I deserve to be the one dying for my sins." This is the meaning of Moriah.

WEDNESDAY EVENING, NOVEMBER 14

Title: Restored Souls and Righteous Paths

Text: "He restoreth my soul: he leadeth me in the paths of righteousness for his name's sake" **(Ps. 23:3)**.

Scripture Reading: Psalm 23

Introduction

Daily the shepherd leads his flock from the fold into green pastures and to still waters so that they may eat and drink. Aware of their proneness to go astray and their inability to care for themselves, the shepherd watches the sheep constantly, but in spite of all his painstaking care, some of them wander away. Frequently when the shepherd sees a sheep beginning to drift away from the flock, he puts a pebble in his sling and throws it in front of his sheep in an attempt to get it to turn back. He knows that sheep are so stupid that when they wander away they are helpless to find their way back. One can take a dog or cat away from home, and it will find its way back. Chickens come home to roost. A bee finds its way back to its hive. But a sheep is so helpless that when it wanders away, it lacks the ability to return to the flock. It does not return unless or until the shepherd goes after it and brings it back.

When a sheep goes astray, the shepherd leaves the flock with a keeper and goes after it himself and brings it back to the flock. Why does the shepherd leave the rest of the flock and take the trouble to go after one straying sheep? It is not only because of his personal interest in the wandering sheep, but also because his reputation is at stake. It is considered a disgrace if a shepherd permits a stray sheep to perish without going in search of it. On the other hand, if the shepherd goes in search of the straying sheep and rescues it, he is praised as a good shepherd.

A good shepherd cares for a sick sheep and restores it to health. He searches for and finds an injured sheep and then anoints and dresses its wounds. He sets its broken bones and binds them. He restores the weak and weary sheep to health.

I. We go astray.

Sheep are noted for going astray. Obstinacy is another characteristic of sheep. Because they are so headstrong, it takes the shepherd's constant attention to keep the sheep within bounds. They are determined to go where they ought not to go and to do what they ought not to do. People have the same tendencies: "All we like sheep have gone astray" (Isa. 53:6). That is a frank acknowledgment of having followed the sad example of Adam in departing from God and of our willfulness in pursuing our own sinful ways.

All have gone astray in their thoughts. Many have forgotten their Creator. They have forgotten their dependence on him and their consequent obligation to love and obey him. They have gone astray from God in their affections. Moreover, they have gone astray in their conduct, as is demonstrated by their pride, self-will, deceitfulness, covetousness, and disobedience. Scripture says, "For there is not a just man upon earth, that doeth good, and sinneth not" (Eccl. 7:20) and "For all have sinned, and come short of the glory of God" (Rom. 3:23). All have withheld from God that which was due to him and have reserved for themselves what was not theirs to keep.

Each of us has gone astray by personal choice. Each of us knew what God wanted us to be, but consciously and resolutely we wanted to be something else. Each found it easier to do wrong than to do the things that were right and pleasing to God.

Here the psalmist passes from the realm of the physical to the spiritual, from the temporal to eternal. In doing so, he refers to the most precious thing in God's creation, namely, the human soul: "He restoreth my soul." The word "restoreth" is meaningful in the Hebrew language. It means to turn back. God brings his wandering children back into intimate fellowship with him by warning, by exhortation, and by chastening.

David remembered his personal straying from the way in which God required him to live. He committed the terrible sins of wrecking the home and taking the life of a faithful and loyal soldier, Uriah. And these sins injured David greatly and grieved him deeply. Miserable because he could not erase them from his memory, David finally acknowledged his transgressions—adultery, treachery, and murder—which were deliberate and willful violations of the expressed will of God. He had an intense desire to be cleansed entirely; he wanted his sinful record erased.

II. He restores our souls.

Longing for God to give back to him the joy that had been his before he had sinned so grievously, David prayed to the Father, saying, "Restore unto me the joy of thy salvation" (Ps. 51:12). Joy may be restored to a wayward child of God when the cause of the loss of that joy has been forgiven and removed.

It is sad that Christians should ever stray from the paths of duty, but inasmuch as they do and therefore need restoring, it is truly wonderful that through God's marvelous grace restoration is possible. The manner in which God restores souls to fellowship and service is revealed in 1 John 1:9: "If we confess our sins, he is faithful and just to forgive us our sins, and to cleanse us from all unrighteousness."

God's restoration of our souls is for a definite purpose: to lead us in paths of righteousness. "He leadeth me" implies that there is special guidance for every child of God.

III. He leads us in the paths of righteousness.

"He leadeth me in the paths of righteousness" carries with it the thought that we cannot rightly order our own steps. It is not easy to follow the right course and to walk in the paths of righteousness. In fact, this is one of the most difficult things we are called upon to do. Clear vision, earnest devotion, strong determination, patient endurance, and heroic sacrifices are needed if we are to walk in the paths of righteousness. The Lord will lead us in right paths if we are willing to be led and if we are willing to place our lives in his hands.

Whereas the future is unknown to us, God knows what tomorrow and every other day holds in store for us and so is able to lead us aright. At times the Great Shepherd may lead us in ways that we do not understand, but remember that he always knows and does what is best for us. We are not to stray from the paths of righteousness or to murmur at or rebel against the leadership of the Great Shepherd, but we must surrender our lives to him. If we will only follow him, he will lead us in paths of righteousness, there will not be any limit to the blessings we will enjoy or the good we can do, and we will bring tremendous honor and glory to his name.

Conclusion

Our text reminds us that the Great Shepherd leads us in paths of righteousness that his name may be glorified. As you strive to follow his leadership, ever bear in mind that the secret of the victorious and righteous life is in looking to and following the Great Shepherd whose desire it is to "make you perfect in every good work to do his will, working in you that which is well-pleasing in his sight" (Heb. 13:21).

SUNDAY MORNING, NOVEMBER 18

Title: "The Lord He Is God"

Text: "Know ye that the LORD he is God: it is he that hath made us, and not we ourselves; we are his people, and the sheep of his pasture" **(Ps. 100:3).**

Scripture Reading: Psalm 100

Hymns: "We Praise Thee, O God, Our Redeemer," Cory

"Great Redeemer, We Adore Thee," Harris

"I Would Be True," Walter

Offertory Prayer: Holy Father, we rejoice in the privilege of being the sheep of your pasture. We rejoice in and praise you for your leadership. We rejoice in the ample provisions that you have made for our physical well-being and for our spiritual nurture and growth. We rejoice in the glad consciousness of forgiveness from sin. We praise you for the privilege of being children within your family. Today we come bringing tokens of our love and gratitude. Accept these tithes and offerings. Bless them in the growth of your kingdom and your ministries of mercy to those who are in need spiritually and physically. In Jesus' name we pray. Amen.

Introduction

Psalm 100 is a psalm of praise. It contains seven great imperatives to the heart of the devout worshiper. Let us note these imperatives.

1. "Make a joyful noise unto the LORD."
2. "Serve the LORD with gladness."
3. "Come before his presence with singing."
4. "Know ye that the LORD he is God."
5. "Enter into his gates with thanksgiving."
6. "Enter . . . into his courts with praise."
7. "Be thankful unto him, and bless his name."

Let us concentrate our attention on the fourth imperative (v. 3). This great imperative contains two challenges: first, we are warned against a great peril; second, we are invited to make a response to God that will be most beneficial to us and to others also.

I. We are warned of the peril of forgetting that the Lord is God.

The apostle John warned the followers of the Lord to beware of the danger of forgetting God and yielding the allegiance of their hearts to substitute gods (1 John 5:21). Our nature is such that we have need again and again to be instructed that the Lord is God.

A. *Idolatry is the failure to let God be God.* Moses warned the children of Israel against the peril of forgetting that God is God. "Be careful that you do not forget the LORD your God, failing to observe his commands, his laws and his decrees that I am giving you this day" (Deut. 8:11 NIV). Moses further insisted that the Israelites should properly utilize their memory at all times: "But remember the LORD your God, for it is he who gives you the ability to produce wealth, and so confirms his covenant which he swore to your forefathers, as it is today" (Deut. 8:18 NIV). The psalmist spoke to his own soul and charged himself with the responsibility of not being forgetful of the Lord as the source of all of the blessings of life (Ps. 103:2).

Each of us faces the peril of forgetting that God really is God and that he is alive and available and at work. It is reported that on one occasion the wife of Martin Luther came into his presence dressed in mourning and with a sad look on her face. When Luther inquired concerning her dress and manner, she replied that evidently God must be dead and that she was mourning his decease. Luther was shocked by this strange behavior of his wife, and then she revealed that she had dressed in this manner to shock him out of a mood of discouragement and to encourage him to put his trust in the living God.

B. *The Egyptians refused to believe that the God of Moses was the true God until a plague had taken the firstborn of all who lived in Egypt on whose doorpost the blood of the Passover lamb was not found.* The plagues were not mere exhibitions of power. Each of them was a contest between the God of Moses and the gods of the Egyptians. In each contest, the God of Moses proved to be superior in power to the gods of the Egyptians (cf. Ex. 9:13–27; 11:4–7).

C. *During the days of Elijah the prophet, the children of Israel neglected to regard the Lord truly as their God.* They drifted into idolatry and gave themselves to the worship of false gods. The contest on the top of Mount Carmel between Elijah the prophet of God and the false prophets of Baal was intended to reveal in an unmistakable manner that "the LORD he is God." Elijah concluded his prayer with this plea: "Answer me, O LORD, answer me, so these people will know that you, O LORD, are God, and that you are turning their hearts back again" (1 Kings 18:37 NIV). The Scripture tells us, "Then the fire of the LORD fell and burned up the sacrifice, the wood, the stones and the soil, and also licked up all the water in the trench. When all the people saw this, they fell prostrate and cried, 'The LORD — he is God. The LORD — he is God!'" (18:38–39 NIV). The people were called back to a recognition that the Lord is God.

II. We are invited to recognize and respond to God as our Lord.

A. *The Lord is our Creator.* "It is he that hath made us, and not we ourselves." We forget the Creator and act as if we were self-made people. The story is told of a multimillionaire who visited in the home of one of his employees. He arrived before the family had finished their evening meal. A small son finished his meal early and went into the living room where the guest was. The guest noticed that the little boy was giving him a rather studied look. Finally, the little fellow said, "Why did you make yourself that way?" The guest replied, "What do you mean, son?" The lad replied, "Mother said that you were a self-made man." The Lord is our Creator (Ps. 94:9).

B. *The Lord is our rightful owner.* We are his people and the sheep of his pasture. Are you resentful of the fact that the earth is the Lord's and the fullness thereof, the world and they that dwell therein? Have you repudiated the Lord's ownership of you? The Creator cares for his creation and provides for his creatures. He loves us. He is the Good Shepherd who provides for his sheep. We can trust him.

The Corinthian Christians were either forgetful or uninformed of the fact that they belonged to the Lord, that he was their owner, that they did not belong to themselves (1 Cor. 6:19–20).

C. *The Lord is our bountiful Benefactor.* The psalmist encourages us to be thankful to him and to give voice to praises that are his due.

D. *The Lord, our Creator, is good.* The mercy of the Lord is from everlasting to everlasting. He is faithful throughout all generations. He can be depended on. There is no fluctuation or change in his character and in his benevolent purpose.

Conclusion

It is not enough merely to recognize that the Lord is God. We must have a proper response to him. Isaiah saw the Lord high and lifted up in the temple. He responded with humility and confession. He experienced cleansing and forgiveness and received a commission to serve.

Thomas was granted the privilege of an experience with the resurrected and living Christ. He responded to this recognition with the declaration, "My Lord and my God" (John 20:28).

The rich young ruler saw Christ and recognized him as a good Master who could give guidance concerning the way to eternal life. He responded negatively and went away sorrowful, unwilling to meet the conditions for discipleship.

The conversion experience is something more than just a recognition of Jesus Christ as Lord and Savior. For it to be genuine, there must be a response to Jesus Christ as Lord, Teacher, Friend, and Guide in home life, social activities, and economic enterprises.

SUNDAY EVENING, NOVEMBER 18

Title: Isaac — the Link between the Old and the New

Text: "Isaac reopened the wells that had been dug in the time of his father Abraham, which the Philistines had stopped up after Abraham died, and he gave them the same names his father had given them" (**Gen. 26:18 NIV**).

Scripture Reading: Genesis 26:12–25

Introduction

In the biblical history of Israel, sandwiched between Abraham and Jacob, is Isaac, the son of Abraham and the father of Jacob. Of the three, Isaac is the least distinguished. Even in his old age, Abraham towered high above his son. In Isaac's home, his life was dominated by his aggressive wife, Rebekah. In his old age, his wife and his son Jacob conspired to deceive him and to cheat him from carrying out his deepest purpose in his life.

Two events stand out in the life of Isaac. One was the experience on Mount Moriah when Abraham attempted to offer him as a sacrifice. Let it be said to the credit of Isaac that he voluntarily agreed to be sacrificed. Abraham felt that he had to offer Isaac, but he could not carry through with his purpose without the cooperation of his son. Abraham was old and feeble. Isaac was young and vigorous. Let us suppose that it had been the wild son, Ishmael, who was to be offered. He likely would have pushed the old man to the ground and run madly down the mountain. Isaac climbed up on the altar and crossed his hands so that Abraham could bind his wrists. Isaac lay inert as Abraham raised his knife. Just as Jesus voluntarily offered his life as a sacrifice, so Isaac was willing to offer his life if God so commanded.

The second event was the deception of Jacob and his scheming mother as they robbed Jacob's twin brother, Esau, of a blessing of God from the hands of his father, Isaac. As a result of this deed, Jacob fled. Esau became so embittered that his life and usefulness were permanently impaired.

Abraham left to his son Isaac not only a spiritual heritage and a covenant promise from God, but also a vast estate of land and herds and flocks and servants. One of the forms of wealth was a set of wells that he had dug. He made it easier for his son. He dug, not just for his own day, but for those who would follow him. We take for granted so many things that have been done by those before us. We take for granted our freedom, bought at a great price by others. We enjoy fruit and shade and beauty from trees planted by an earlier generation. We travel highways and cross bridges built by others. We attend colleges founded and supported by others. We worship in churches perpetuated by the blood of martyrs and in buildings erected by those before us. Our cities were carved from a wilderness conquered by pioneers.

As is so often true in life, the wells of Abraham became choked by the neglect and vandalism of a new generation. Isaac decided to redig those wells. He did not say, "My father didn't know what he was doing when he dug those wells. I will seek out new places and ignore his old and tested sites." Instead, he hunted up and redug the wells of his father. He gave the wells the old names. He found in them pure and refreshing water for his family and his flocks.

There are new things that may glitter and fascinate. But the old and tested must not be forsaken. Some old and tested wells from which we drink are:

I. The Bible.

The inspired Word of God is timeless in its message and is relevant in its application in our day. An accommodating so-called new morality must not replace the authoritative moral righteousness of the Bible. A zeal to unite with other Christians must not be at the cost of the compromise of our convictions. Let us drink deeply of the well of biblical inspiration and instruction.

II. The well of prayer.

Only humans have the ability and privilege to worship God. We should exercise this privilege in the prayer closet. We also should forsake not the assembling of ourselves in public worship. Hard work never will take the place of prayer. In fact, prayer will make our service easier, more enjoyable, and more effective. Let us drink deeply of the practice of prayer.

III. The Christian home.

Today the Christian home is fighting for its life. The Christian home has always been God's plan for people. It is the oldest institution founded by God. Wherever Abraham went, he built an altar. How we need a return to this vital practice.

IV. The well of the church.

We live in a day when many have abandoned the church. Many churches are choked by worldliness, doubt, compromise, pride, provincialism, and indifference. The church is Christ's bride. We cannot be loyal to Christ and disloyal to his church at the same time. If a Christian could be as good a Christian outside the church, Christ would not have founded his church. The church needs renewal and even reform, but it does not deserve abandonment.

The new generation is striving to build new wells. This is not bad. Progress comes through daring adventure. Isaac the peacemaker also dug new wells. But we must leave unchoked the wells that have refreshed the pilgrims through the centuries.

Conclusion

One of the great wells of history was located just outside the village of Sychar. Jesus sat one day on the edge of that well and presented to a woman the claims of God and the grace of God in the form of the Water of Life. Her life was choked by sin and rebellion and despair. "Drink of this well," our Lord said, "and you will never thirst again." When she drank of that well, she became so excited that she left her water pots and hastened into town to tell others the good news. That same water can refresh and renew your choked life and give you exuberant joy and blessed peace. Drink deeply of God's love, forgiveness, and grace.

WEDNESDAY EVENING, NOVEMBER 21

Title: Thanksgiving Litany*

*Scriptures used are from the Revised Standard Version.

This litany can be used with small groups or with the entire congregation; adapt it to your own needs.

Each of the seven sections of the litany has four parts:

1. A call to thanksgiving for a specific kind of blessing by the worship leader.
2. An exposition or illustration of this blessing from the Scripture by a reader, choir, or other selected group. This should be given from a balcony or from some point other than the podium.
3. A scriptural response of praise by the entire group or congregation.
4. Prayers of thanks in keeping with the subject. These can be either spontaneous or assigned in advance.

Additional ideas: appropriate musical numbers may be interspersed throughout, and colored slides that illustrate each section can be shown.

Section 1

Thanks for Material Provisions

Worship Leader: We are grateful, Lord, for your plentiful provisions for our material needs.

Reader:

> Thou visitest the earth and waterest it,
>> thou greatly enrichest it;
> the river of God is full of water;
>> thou providest their grain,
>> for so thou hast prepared it.
> Thou waterest its furrows abundantly,
>> setting its ridges,
> softening it with showers,
>> and blessing its growth.
> Thou crownest the year with thy bounty;
>> the tracks of thy chariot drip with fatness,
> The pastures of the wilderness drip,
>> the hills gird themselves with joy,
> the meadows clothe themselves with flocks,
>> the valleys deck themselves with grain,
>> they shout and sing together for joy.
>
>> Psalm 65:9–13

People:

> Let the peoples praise thee, O God;
>> let all the people praise thee!
> The earth has yielded its increase;
>> God, our God, has blessed us.
> God has blessed us;
>> let all the ends of the earth fear him!
>
>> Psalm 67:5–7

349

Prayer(s) of thanks for material blessings.

Section 2

Thanks for Family and Friends

Worship Leader: We are most appreciative, God, for each other—for loved ones and family and friends.

Reader: "We give thanks to God always for you all, constantly mentioning you in our prayers, remembering before our God and Father your work of faith and labor of love and steadfastness of hope in our Lord Jesus Christ" (1 Thess. 1:2–3).

Prayer(s) of thanks for family and friends.

Section 3

Thanks in Time of Trouble

Worship Leader: Help us to express thankfulness, O Lord, even in times of trouble, poverty, and opposition.

Reader: "And when they had inflicted many blows upon them, they threw them into prison, charging the jailer to keep them safely. Having received this charge, he put them into the inner prison and fastened their feet in the stocks. But about midnight Paul and Silas were praying and singing hymns to God, and the prisoners were listening to them" (Acts 16:23–25).

People:

> Though the fig trees do not blossom,
>   nor fruit be on the vines,
> the produce of the olive fail
>   and the fields yield no food,
> the flock be cut off from the fold
>   and there be no herd in the stalls,
> yet I will rejoice in the LORD,
>   I will joy in the God of my salvation.
>   Habakkuk 3:17–18

Prayer(s) for thankfulness in times of trouble.

Section 4

Thanks for Times of Gladness

Worship Leader: We are most appreciative, O God, for the return of sunshine after the storm; for pleasure, joy, and gladness.

Reader:

> Sing praises to the LORD, O you his saints,
>   and give thanks to his holy name.
> For his anger is but for a moment,
>   and his favor is for a lifetime.
> Weeping may tarry for the night,
>   but joy comes with the morning.
>   Psalm 30:4–5

People:
> Thou hast turned for me my mourning into dancing;
>> thou hast loosed my sackcloth
>> and girded me with gladness,
> that my soul may praise thee and not be silent.
>> O Lᴏʀᴅ my God, I will give thanks to thee for ever.
>
> Psalm 30:11–12

> O magnify the Lᴏʀᴅ with me,
>> and let us exalt his name together!
> I sought the Lᴏʀᴅ, and he answered me,
>> and delivered me from all my fears.
>
> Psalm 34:3–4

Prayer(s) of thanksgiving for times of gladness.

Section 5
Thanks for Jesus Christ

Worship Leader: We thank you, Father, for our Lord and Brother Jesus Christ, who was sent to live for us, to die for us, and to rise for us from the dead.

Reader: "And they went with haste, and found Mary and Joseph, and the babe lying in a manger.... And the shepherds returned glorifying and praising God for all they had heard and seen, as it had been told them" (Luke 2:16, 20).

People: "Thanks be to God for his inexpressible gift!" (2 Cor. 9:15).

Reader: "As he was now drawing near, at the descent of the Mount of Olives, the whole multitude of disciples began to rejoice and praise God with a loud voice for all the mighty works that they had seen, saying,

People: "Blessed is the King who comes in the name of the Lord! Peace in heaven and glory in the highest!" (Luke 19:37–38).

Reader: "Then he said to Thomas, 'Put your finger here, and see my hands; and put out your hand, and place it in my side; do not be faithless, but believing.' Thomas answered him,

People: 'My Lord and my God'" (John 20:27–28).

Prayer(s) of thanks for Jesus Christ.

Section 6
Thanks for Salvation

Worship Leader: We are thankful, loving God, for cleansing from sin and for the promise of life eternal.

Reader: "May you be strengthened with all power ... giving thanks to the Father, who has qualified us to share in the inheritance of the saints in light. He has delivered us from the dominion of darkness and transferred us to the kingdom of his beloved Son, in whom we have redemption, the forgiveness of sins" (Col. 1:11–14).

People:

O come, let us sing to the LORD;
let us make a joyful noise to the rock of our salvation!

Psalm 95:1

Reader: "Then I heard what seemed to be the voice of a great multitude, like the sound of many waters and like the sound of mighty thunder peals, crying,

People: " 'Hallelujah! For the Lord our God the Almighty reigns. Let us rejoice and exult and give him the glory, for the marriage of the Lamb has come, and his Bride has made herself ready' " (Rev. 19:6–7).

Prayer(s) of thanks for salvation.

Section 7

Thanks for the Opportunity to Serve

Worship Leader: We thank you, Lord, both for a place of service in your kingdom and for the privilege of sharing.

All: "I thank him who has given me strength for this, Christ Jesus our Lord, because he judged me faithful by appointing me to his service, though I formerly blasphemed and persecuted and insulted him" (1 Tim. 1:12–13).

Prayer(s) of thanks for the opportunity to serve.

SUNDAY MORNING, NOVEMBER 25

Title: Heaven's Welcoming Committee

Text: " 'I tell you, use worldly wealth to gain friends for yourselves, so that when it is gone, you will be welcomed into eternal dwellings' " (**Luke 16:9 NIV**).

Scripture Reading: Luke 16:1–9

Hymns: "To God Be the Glory," Crosby

"Bring Them In," Thomas

"Must I Go, and Empty-Handed," Luther

Offertory Prayer: Our Father, hear us as we pray the prayer your Son and our Savior taught us to pray, "Lead us not into temptation but deliver us from evil." Help us to resist the temptation to be poor stewards of our material possessions. Make us good stewards of your trust. We bring back to you today a portion of your gracious provisions for our lives, as a part of ourselves and as a symbol of our recognition of your total ownership of us and ours. Bless us as we offer our gifts and ourselves. In Jesus' name we pray. Amen.

Introduction

It is interesting to note how our text is translated in other versions of the New Testament. Phillips translates the verse, "Now my advice to you is to use 'money,' tainted as it is, to make yourselves friends, so that when it comes to an end, they may welcome you into eternal habitations." The New English Bible translates it: "So I say to you, use your worldly wealth to win friends for yourselves, so that when money is a thing of the past you may be received into an eternal home."

The text is the application of the two parables it connects—the parable of the shrewd but dishonest steward and the parable of Lazarus and the rich man. The parables of Jesus are God's picture book; they present to us a picture that contains a significant and profitable truth.

The parable of the shrewd but dishonest steward has presented a problem for many. A superficial consideration might cause one to think that the Lord himself was commending a crook for his crookedness. In reality, it was the rich man who commended the dishonest steward rather than our Lord. Our Lord uses the story of a cunning crook to illustrate a great spiritual truth. A parable is a short earthly story with a heavenly meaning. It usually has one great central point.

In our parable, the rich man corresponds to God. The steward corresponds to us. The children of this world are those who live a secular life of dedication to earthly ends. In the parable, the shrewd crook did that which was profitable within the sphere of his life. The children of light are those who have the hope and the assurance of an eternal home.

Let us pray our way into the meaning of this parable. Let us discover what the living Lord would say to us through it. In the statement of the rich man to his steward, "Give account of thy stewardship," there is a challenge to each of us.

I. A challenge to self-examination

It would be wise for each of us to face the facts and to recognize and respond to reality.

A. *God is the owner of everything.* The earth is the Lord's. Those who live in the world are his by right of creation and preservation. From the beginning of time, humanity has sought to defraud and to deny to God his ownership rights. We have even attempted to steal that which belongs to God.

B. *We are trustees, stewards, and managers, and we are to use everything that comes into our possession or under our management for the glory of God.*

1. We are trustees of our time. It is the gift of God to us for responsible use.

2. We are trustees of our talents. We were not endowed with talents for selfish indulgence. We were endowed with gifts from God that we might use them responsibly.

3. We are trustees of the treasures of the world that come into our custody. In the sphere of human activity we may be owners. In the final analysis, we are only the trustees or stewards of that which God has permitted us to acquire and to control for a time.

If, upon examining ourselves, we discover that we are guilty of embezzlement, theft, and mismanagement, let us have grace enough to acknowledge this and confess such to our Lord. He loves us in spite of our sins. He will forgive us and grant to us the opportunity for significant service if we will let him.

II. A challenge to honest comparison.

A. *Who are the children of this age?* Was Jesus not referring to those men and women who live in the world as if they are creatures of time alone? Was he not talking about those who live as if they are creatures of one world only? He was talking about the secular person who lives for the satisfaction of earthly appetites and ambitions. Consider the following characteristics of the children of this age.

1. They place no limits on their earthly ambitions.
2. They do not ration their energy.
3. They surrender and dedicate their time to the securing of their earthly goals.
4. They spare no expense that is considered necessary. Often they are speculative and will take great risks.
5. They are always ready to seize the opportunity or circumstance that seems to promise a profitable return.
6. They are always striving for success in their chosen endeavor.

B. *Who are the children of light?* Was not our Lord referring to those who have put their faith in God and are trusting in the Lord Jesus Christ for light for the road of life? Was he not referring to those who believe that they are creatures of eternity and that they should live in time with the issues of eternity in mind? Consider some disturbing questions.

1. Do we place limits on our spiritual ambitions at the point of winning people to faith in Jesus Christ?
2. Do we seek to conserve our energy and put forth the least possible effort in this matter of serving God and evangelizing the world?
3. Do we place great restrictions on the use of our time for spiritual ends? How much time have you spent in prayer and Bible study in the past week? What will be your reaction if the sermon goes two minutes beyond the regular hour today?
4. Are we stingy with our money as far as providing adequate support for the Lord's work? Do we try to get by with the poorest equipment and with the least personnel and with inadequate facilities?
5. Do we seize every opportunity to speak a good word for Jesus Christ or to render a ministry of mercy in his name to those who are in need?

    It was a sad observation that our Lord made that the children of this age work with more cunning, more diligence, more dedication, and more sacrifice than do the children of light.

III. A challenge to decisive action.

Specifically our Lord was suggesting and commanding his disciples that they invest and use their financial resources in such a manner as to guarantee that converts would spend eternity in heaven because of their actions and investments.

A. *The children of light have title to eternal habitations in contrast to the temporary quarters of this age.* It follows that the children of light should be far more interested in their eternal habitation than the children of this age are in their temporary quarters.

B. *The children of light may increase their joy and rewards by the right use of money, talent, or opportunity.*

Our Lord is giving some sound financial advice. Have you considered him as an investment counselor? He is suggesting that it is possible for us to invest tithes and offerings above the tithe in such a manner as to be responsible for the unsaved hearing the gospel of salvation. He is suggesting that some people may enter heaven because of your proper use of money.

C. *The children of light may exchange the currency of this world into a form they can transfer to the eternal habitations.*

When one travels from one country to another country, he has to exchange the currency of his native land for that which he is visiting. If you go to England, you exchange dollars for pounds. If you go to France, you exchange dollars for francs, and if you go to Japan, you exchange dollars for yen. When you leave this world, the only way that you can take dollars to heaven is to have those dollars invested in such a way that there will be converts in heaven because of those dollars.

D. *The children of light will have social needs in the eternal habitation.* Jesus speaks of being received into eternal habitations by friends who have become such through the right use of money. Heaven will be a place of friendship and fellowship. Some will rejoice throughout eternity because they exchanged the coin of earth for the currency of heaven.

Will anyone there at the Beautiful Gate be watching and waiting for you?

Conclusion

The parable that follows our text is the parable of the rich man and Lazarus. Will you be like the rich man throughout eternity? Are you forgetting God? Are you forgetting others? Are you living as if eternity does not exist? Are you majoring on meeting the needs of your body while neglecting that which can enrich your soul? Have you forgotten that Christ died for you in order that you might live for him and win others to him?

This is your day of decision concerning whether you will work for the Lord with the same energy, ingenuity, and dedication as the children of this age labor to achieve success in activities that will be worthless once they enter their eternal habitation. There will come a day when our value system will be turned upside down. Money will be neither needed nor spent.

Our Lord would suggest to each of us that we dedicate ourselves to spiritual values and to redemptive activity with the same energy and dedication that the children of this age use for achieving fame and fortune.

SUNDAY EVENING, NOVEMBER 25

Title: Jacob—Back to Bethel

Text: "Then God said to Jacob, 'Go up to Bethel and settle there, and build an altar there to God, who appeared to you when you were fleeing from your brother Esau'" **(Gen. 35:1 NIV)**.

Scripture Reading: Genesis 32:22–28

Introduction

One of the crisis times in a family is when a grown child leaves home. Parents are tortured with questions, "Is it time?" "Is he ready?" "Have we prepared him?" "Will he stay true?" If we have failed our child, it is too late to start over. We must leave him in the hands of the God who gave him to us as a baby.

It was a trying day for a loving father when the prodigal son left home. It is God's plan that our children come to the time when they ask to be free to leave home and we must be willing to let them go. The sadness of the occasion for Jacob was that sin thrust him out from his home. It was sin that caused the prodigal son to leave home. It was sin that thrust Adam out of the garden of Eden. It was sin that sent the murderer Cain out into a hostile world. The writer John tells us that Judas, after he received the sop, went out, "and it was night." What a tragedy when sin sends one out into the darkness.

Jacob was not the great person his grandfather Abraham had been. He was shrewd and calculating. He was crafty and scheming. He was a cunning trickster. He chose to live by his wits. His name Jacob means "supplanter," and he lived down to his name.

The first night away from home is one never to be forgotten. That first night for Jacob was in the barren wilderness where he was frightened and alone. He fearfully listened for the approaching footsteps of his avenging brother, Esau. With a rock for a pillow and the stars as a covering, he fell asleep. As he slept he had a dream. God transformed that bleak scene into a "house of God, the gate to heaven."

The next day Jacob erected an altar as a monument, vowed a solemn vow to God, and named that blessed place Bethel. Then he proceeded on his journey to the house of Laban where love, prosperity, and success awaited him. Then God commanded him to go back to Bethel to renew his vows and claim his birthright.

I. Sin makes a coward of us.

Jacob trembled as he approached a confrontation with his brother Esau. Always before he had outmaneuvered him. He had cheated him out of everything he wanted. Now he realized that payday had come. To add to his terror, it was reported to him that Esau had four hundred armed men with him. Sin has a way of making cowards of us. Once we have compromised, we find it harder to live up to our convictions. The writer of Proverbs wisely wrote, "Fear of man will prove to be a snare" (29:25 NIV).

II. Sin endangers our loved ones.

Jacob had left home without a wife, without children, without land, and without money. Somehow he had felt that his sin, at the most, would only endanger himself. Now he looked out and saw the tents in the moonlight where his wives, children, and devoted servants slept, and he knew they were in danger also. Sin and its results are very personal, but they are also social. Those innocent people whom we love the dearest often suffer the most for our sins.

III. Sin can be conquered, and renewal is possible.

That night witnessed a strange struggle. Jacob struggled with a mysterious wrestler. All his sins came before him. In the land of Laban, although he was blessed by God, he had relaxed his convictions. He was no longer as devout as in the past. His enthusiasm for God was dulled. He had grown worldly, and money was his god. In his struggles to outwit the covetous Laban, he had himself become covetous.

God had said to him, "Destroy your idols. Put away the sin in your life. Make things right with your brother. Take your rightful place as husband, father, and religious leader in your home."

As the morning broke, Jacob arose limp but radiant.

A. *Jacob had a new name.* No longer was he a trickster, but Israel, a "prince of God."

B. *Jacob had a new outlook.* He was right with God. He was right with his brother. No longer did he trust in his cleverness, his shrewdness, his riches, or his own righteousness. He left it up to God, in whom he trusted.

C. *Jacob had a new life.* Old things had passed away. Behold, all things had become new. His family saw the difference. No longer was he a fugitive from God and from his brother. He who had been dead was alive again. He who had been lost was found.

Conclusion

Jacob named that hallowed place Peniel, which meant "I have met God face-to-face." As you have heard this message, have you been saying, "That describes me. I have drifted away. I have grown cold and indifferent and worldly. I have neglected my vows"?

What was your "Bethel" in the past? Was it your conversion experience, as your heart first glowed with the joy and peace of God's forgiveness? Was it some great revival or some camp experience? Was it some great joy or sorrow? Was it your wedding, your firstborn child, or that little child who died? God is calling you to come back to the warmth and thrill of a fresh experience with him, in which you renew your vows and open your heart fully to his Spirit.

WEDNESDAY EVENING, NOVEMBER 28

Title: Thou Art with Me

Text: "Yea, though I walk through the valley of the shadow of death, I will fear no evil: for thou art with me; thy rod and thy staff they comfort me" **(Ps. 23:4)**.

Scripture Reading: Psalm 23

Introduction

Through the centuries the shepherds in Palestine have found it necessary to lead their flocks through dark ravines and narrow valleys. In these rocky gorges the sheep are exposed to the attacks of their enemies, but they are not afraid because their shepherd is with them. With a keen eye, a brave heart, a strong arm, and a good rod, the shepherd stands ready to spring to the defense of his helpless animals in the event they are about to be attacked or stolen. As long as the sheep remain close to the shepherd, there is no reason for them to be frightened.

Doubtless, on many occasions while serving as a shepherd, David had risked his life while beating back a wild animal that was attempting to spring on one of his sheep or while fighting off a thief who was trying to steal one or more of them. Such experiences would have been fearful had it not been for the Lord's presence with him.

I. We all walk through valleys.

No life is immune to dark and painful experiences. Some good thing is withheld from or some sad thing is added to every life. All of us live through hours that are dark and mysterious, and some of them are fraught with danger and sorrow. Most of us will have experiences in which we will be tested thoroughly.

A weak body or a chronic ailment brings many of God's children into the shadows. Sleepless nights and weary days of tossing on a bed of sickness tend to take the sunshine out of life. Many of those who go down into the valley of sickness lose heart and become despondent. Yet even in the valley of physical affliction, the Great Shepherd walks and talks with his own and says what he said to Paul: "My grace is sufficient for thee: for my strength is made perfect in weakness" (2 Cor. 12:9).

One wonders if any verse of Scripture has brought more encouragement and comfort to Christian hearts than "My grace is sufficient for thee." This promise, which the Lord made to Paul and is applicable to all believers, is not that of a bare adequacy, just covering the need with no overlapping margin. He promised grace in proportion to the real needs of believers. That rolling river of grace has been flowing for thousands of years, but it does not show any sign of depletion.

Many of God's children enter the valley of disappointment. Some cherished possession is taken from you, or some object on which you had set your heart is snatched out of your reach, or some friend whom you had trusted implicitly suddenly proves unfaithful, and you experience the bitterness of disappointment.

Many have gone into the valley of bereavement, and the rest of us will do likewise. The shadows are dark when we have to say good-bye to father or mother, brother or sister, husband or wife, son or daughter, as his or her eyes are closed in death. The shadows are so dark, and yet those of us who have gone into the valley of bereavement know that in this experience Christ is nearer and dearer than at any other time in life. In experiences like these, he gives a peace that passes all understanding.

Another valley into which people go is the one our text calls "the shadow of death." Death is a word that brings terror to many, but the effect is softened considerably by the phrase "the shadow of death." Certainly the shadow cannot be the same as the substance. There must be a substance before there can be a shadow, but God's children will never know the substance of death. In its substance death means separation from God, and Christ experienced that in order that it might not be necessary for us to do so. Christians go through the valley of the shadow of death, but they will neither know the sting of death nor experience the substance of it. By his death and resurrection, Christ took away the substance of death and left us only the mere shadow of it with which to reckon. Therefore, there is no justification for our being fearful.

Upon entering the valley of the shadow of death, one must say good-bye to all the living who are near and dear to him. Loved ones can neither keep one from entering the valley nor accompany him through it. Only the Good Shepherd can accompany the sheep or children of God as they go through the valley of the shadow of death. With the assurance of his presence and companionship, there is no reason for complaint or fear. Nothing else matters when he is with us. The fact that "Thou [God] art with me" is a positive guarantee that all will be well.

Those who have traveled over a railroad have been shocked slightly when the train suddenly plunged from the sunlight into the darkness of a tunnel, but they were not afraid, because they knew there was a way out on the other side of the hill or mountain. Even so, those who "walk through the valley of the shadow of death" are not afraid because they know that the Shepherd who has cared for them throughout their lives, and who has never failed nor forsaken them, and who is walking beside them through the valley will bring them safely to the exit and into the Father's house and the presence of the dear ones who have preceded them. What a comfort!

II. God is with us in our valleys.

"Thy rod and thy staff they comfort me." A rod, which was approximately three feet in length, was a weapon the shepherd used to defend his sheep in times of danger. It was used primarily to beat off the enemies of the sheep when they attempted to ravage his flock. A staff, which was some six or seven feet in length, was used primarily by the shepherd in guiding the sheep over right paths, in drawing aside the brush, and in indicating to them the path they should take. It was also used in rescuing the weak, weary, fallen, or injured ones. The rod and the staff were symbols of the shepherd's presence and constant care. One was a weapon of protection, and the other was an instrument for guidance, direction, and restoration.

Conclusion

Those who have the Lord as their Shepherd enjoy the sweetest and most cheering companionship that can be found. From him we receive guidance, protection, comfort, and assurance. Aren't you glad to know that you can do what you should because the Good Shepherd is your Companion, Protector, and Enabler?

SUGGESTED PREACHING PROGRAM FOR

DECEMBER

■ **Sunday Mornings**

The theme for Sunday mornings this month is "The Meaning of Christmas." A new year's message is provided for the last Sunday morning of the year.

■ **Sunday Evenings**

Complete the series "Old Testament Biographies" on the first Sunday evening. The theme for the remaining Sunday evenings this month is "Communicating the Significance of the Coming of Jesus Christ." Missionary activity should not be considered as something that our Lord attached to the conclusion of his ministry. Missionary activity is not just for specialists. Every worshiper of Jesus Christ is to be a missionary.

■ **Wednesday Evenings**

Complete the series "The Pearl of the Psalms" on the first two Sundays of the month. The last Wednesday evening messages for the year focus on Christmas and the new year.

SUNDAY MORNING, DECEMBER 2

Title: God's Greatest Gift

Text: "For unto us a child is born, unto us a son is given" **(Isa. 9:6)**.

Hymns: "Jesus Shall Reign Where'er the Sun," Watts

"Angels from the Realms of Glory," Montgomery

"Glory to His Name," Hoffman

Offertory Prayer: Our Father and our God, you who are the author and giver of every good and precious gift, to you we give thanks for your unspeakable gift to us, Jesus Christ, your Son and our Savior. Today we give ourselves and our substance in grateful worship to you. Bless these gifts to the honor and glory of your name. Amen.

Introduction

God's greatest gift to people is often overlooked at Christmastime. We concentrate our attention on the gifts that the good and gracious heavenly Father sends our way. The prophet foretold the giving of God's greatest gift—his only begotten Son (Isa. 9:6).

It is a tragedy of tragedies that so few have properly related themselves to the Christ who was born in Bethlehem and laid in a manger. The wise men came asking, "Where is the one who has been born king of the Jews?" (Matt. 2:2 NIV). We should be asking, "Who is he? What do you think of Christ?"

Is Jesus Christ merely a mythical or legendary figure? Is Christ simply the most notable figure on the pages of history? His birthday gave the world a new era dividing the past from the future at a focal point. His spirit has given the world its most immortal paintings. His love has inspired the world's masterpieces of art, sculpture, and music. His influence has inspired earth's greatest philanthropies. More books have been written about him than have been written about all of the kings who have ruled from earthly thrones.

Who is this Son whom God has given?

I. God has given to us a supernatural Son.

A. *Jesus was supernaturally conceived and born of the Virgin Mary.*

B. *Christianity is built and based on a supernatural Christ.* You can have Buddhism without Buddha, Confucianism without Confucius, and Islam without Muhammad, but you can't have Christianity without Christ. Christianity is more than a creed or code. It is fellowship with a risen and living Christ.

Those who would reject the virgin birth, explain away Christ's miracles, and deny his resurrection have only a pale, powerless, poor anemic human Christ who has no power with which to save a sinful race.

II. God has given unto us a sinless Son. Christ was "in all points tempted like as we are, yet without sin" (Heb. 4:15).

A. *Christ refrained from all willful transgression.*

B. *He was the very essence of personal purity.*

C. *The verdict of Pilate, the Roman governor, was, "I have examined him in your presence and have found no basis for your charges against him" (Luke 23:14 NIV).*

At the time of Jesus' baptism, there was a voice of testimony from heaven expressing the complete divine approval of Christ (Matt. 3:17). There was a second expression of divine approval at the time of the transfiguration (Matt. 17:5). The resurrection of this Christ was a public demonstration of the divine acceptance of his substitutionary death on the cross.

III. God has given us a Son who suffered as our substitute.

A. *The prophet Isaiah foretold the substitutionary death of the suffering servant of God (Isa. 53:5–6).*

B. *The angel told Joseph that the unborn child of Mary was divine and that he would be the Savior of his people (Matt. 1:21).*

C. *When John the Baptist introduced Jesus to his disciples, he called him the one who would bear the sin of the world (John 1:29).*

D. *Jesus defined his objective for coming into the world in terms of giving his life as a ransom for many (Mark 10:45).*

E. *Jesus described himself as the Good Shepherd who lays down his life voluntarily for his sheep (John 10:11).*

F. *Paul declared that while we were still rebel sinners against God, God loved us and Christ died for us (Rom. 5:6).*

G. *The Sinless One, by a divine decree, was made to be sin for us that he might suffer in our place that we might be saved from the penalty of sin (2 Cor. 5:21).*

H. *He who was rich beyond imagination became a pauper that we, through his poverty, might be made indescribably rich (2 Cor. 8:9).*

I. *God's greatest gift, his sinless Son, suffered for us sinners that he might return us to God (1 Peter 3:18).*

IV. God has given us a Son who is an all-sufficient Savior.

A. *He takes care of the past by the pardon of every sin and the forgiveness of every transgression.*

B. *He takes care of the present by his abiding presence.*

1. He is the mind of God speaking out to people.
2. He is the voice of God calling out to people.
3. He is the heart of God throbbing for people.
4. He is the hand of God reaching out to people.
5. He is the Savior who can meet the deepest needs of the human soul.

C. *He takes care of the future by providing a home at the end of the road.*

Conclusion

Have you received the royal Guest into your heart? It is time to let him in. Do not ignore him or shut him out. Accept God's greatest gift by receiving his Son as the Lord of your heart and life.

SUNDAY EVENING, DECEMBER 2

Title: Joseph — The Man Who Said No
Text: "But he refused" **(Gen. 39:8).**
Scripture Reading: Genesis 39:4–9

Introduction

Not every boy grows up to be a man. Some men remain boys in immaturity and childishness. Of those who grow up, no two boys mature on the same schedule. The ideal process of maturing is to grow gradually, naturally. But the time comes in the lives of some youths when they must become men with dramatic suddenness. A crisis arises. A father dies. Economic reverses are experienced. A great responsibility is thrust on him. An overwhelming temptation assails him.

Joseph, the favored son of Jacob, had to mature quickly. He was the object of favoritism by his father. He had never had it so good. Nevertheless, he was the victim of envy and resentment by ten brothers.

Joseph left home early in his youth, but not by his choosing nor with his father's counsel and help. His brothers sold him into slavery in a foreign land. Joseph had helped to bring about his own plight by being arrogant and overbearing around his brothers. He flaunted his self-styled superiority over them.

As a result, he found himself a slave in the household of Potiphar in Egypt. His master was impressed with his intelligence, his talent, and his industry. Joseph was personable and dependable. Potiphar became genuinely fond of him and promoted him rapidly.

Then came the great crisis of temptation. Potiphar's wife, a scheming and sensuous woman, set her evil eye on Joseph and vowed to seduce him into a relationship that would deny all that he believed and had been taught. As he resisted her advances and broke her clutches, he became the innocent victim of her accusations and the object of the jealousy and wrath of her husband. Although Joseph was faithful to his God and to his higher self, he landed in a lonely cell in an ancient prison.

Joseph's temptation is a true story with all the intrigue and suspense of a modern production. Potiphar's wife was a woman of rank, beauty, and fashion. She was brazen and persistent. Joseph was young, handsome, and ambitious, probably in his late teens or early twenties. But he was a slave and was looked upon, not as a person, but as chattel property. He could well have lost his sense of dignity and self-respect, vital factors in resisting the temptation of baser sins. As a slave, he was expected to do as he was told, and this was his master's wife who commanded him.

Joseph was a long way from home. Satan could whisper in his ear, "No one will know. No one will get hurt. Everyone else in Egypt indulges in these sins when opportunity arises." How easy it would have been to rationalize himself into saying yes to this temptation.

Joseph's response to Potiphar's wife reveals a remarkable understanding of sin.

I. The faith of Joseph's master.

"My master trusts me," Joseph was saying. "Think of my master ... he has entrusted me with all that he has" (Gen. 39:8 NEB). He knew that this sin would mean the betrayal of a trust. We, too, have a trust. Our loved ones trust us. Our friends trust us. When a young man takes a young woman on a date, her family trusts him. What a responsibility we have toward those who love us and those who trust us.

II. The faith of his God.

"God trusts me," Joseph added in his conversation with the temptress. "How can I do anything so wicked and sin against God?" He was aware that, although he was a long way from home and those back home might never know, God would know. Although his family back home could not see him, God had his eye upon him. All sin is against God.

When is a child old enough to become a Christian? Someone has answered, "When he is old enough to know the difference between right and wrong and to know that wrong is against God and must be made right with God." Whenever we sin, we sin against God. Whenever we hurt someone, we hurt God even more. When we disappoint God, he is deeply hurt, for he is our Father, and he loves us.

King David, in his penitential psalm, cries out, "Against thee, thee only, have I sinned, O God" (Ps. 51:4). Actually, David knew that he had sinned greatly against Bathsheba in seducing her, against Uriah in having him killed in battle, against his family, against his kingdom, and against himself. But he seems to be saying, "My sin against God is so much greater than my sin even against these that it is as if against God and him only have I sinned." Sin is against God and must be confessed by the sinner and forgiven by God.

This account of Joseph has a storybook ending. The Scripture says that "the LORD was with him ... and made everything he did to prosper" (Gen. 39:23). We are glad we have the story of Joseph to punctuate the principle "It pays to do right." But what if the story had not ended happily? What if Joseph had rotted in the jail? This still would have been a marvelous story of refusing to yield to temptation. The remarkable thing about Daniel and the lion's den is not that he came out alive the next day, but that he was willing to be thrown to the lions rather than to compromise his convictions. Had he been eaten by the lions, this still would have been an inspiring story.

Conclusion

Do you want victory over temptation? Do you want to do right? Then the way to say no to temptation is to say yes to Christ. Commit your heart and life to him, and the Lord will be with you and give you the grace and strength to fulfill his will.

WEDNESDAY EVENING, DECEMBER 5

Title: The Guest of God

Text: "Thou preparest a table before me in the presence of mine enemies: thou anointest my head with oil; my cup runneth over" **(Ps. 23:5).**

Scripture Reading: Psalm 23

Introduction

In the first four verses of this psalm, the writer pictured the Lord as the Shepherd, his children as the sheep, and the pasture as the scene of action. In verse 5 the psalmist pictured the Lord as the Host, his friends as the guests, and his table as the center around which his guests are gathered for a banquet without the possibility of any interference from others. While it is good to be the sheep of his pasture, it is certainly much better to be a guest at his table.

David's statement "Thou preparest a table before me in the presence of mine enemies" is a reminder that he had many enemies. Like all others, the psalmist experienced the pull of something within or without to get him to cease being what he ought to be or to fail to do what he knew he should do. Finding it easier to do wrong than to do right, David yielded to temptation and broke five of the Ten Commandments. He placed the god of lust before the God of heaven, coveted the wife of his neighbor, stole her from her husband, committed adultery with her, and then had her husband murdered. For these terrible sins he suffered the pangs of an accusing conscience.

I. Sin brings enemies into our lives.

Burdened greatly with the consciousness of his own sinfulness, David refused to offer any excuses for his sins or to attempt to justify himself in any way. Whereas others usually try to justify their sinful deeds by blaming the tendencies they have inherited, the training they have or have not received, the circumstances under which they have been placed, or the temptations by which they have been assailed, David readily admitted that the guilt of his sins was his alone. He said, "I acknowledge my transgressions: and my sin is ever before me" (Ps. 51:3). His transgressions—idolatry, covetousness, treachery, theft, adultery, and murder—were deliberate and willful violations of the expressed will of God.

Abhorring himself and the terrible sins that he had committed, and earnestly desiring to be forgiven and cleansed, in deep penitence David confessed his sins and sobbed out his prayer to God for forgiveness and restoration. Out of the depths of his degradation and remorse he acknowledged the full measure of his wrongdoing and cried: "Have mercy upon me, O God, according to thy lovingkindness: according unto the multitude of thy tender mercies blot out my transgressions. Wash me thoroughly from mine iniquity and cleanse me from my sin" (Ps. 51:1–2), whereupon he was forgiven immediately and thoroughly cleansed. Later when he looked back across the yesterdays to his unforgettable experiences, he realized that God had prepared for him a table of grace and mercy in the presence of his enemies. Thereafter when David was pressed by his enemies, God supplied his needs and enabled him to overcome them. It is encouraging to note that God continued to supply the needs of David and his devoted followers.

II. Children of God have enemies.

Can it be that all of the children of God have enemies? Certainly. When the Lord Jesus Christ was on earth, he had enemies, and "the disciple is not above his master" (Luke 6:40). If Christians do not have enemies, they are not like Christ, for he said, "If the world hates you, keep in mind that it hated me first" (John 15:18 NIV). If you are without enemies, you should ask yourself, "Am I a friend of God and a follower of Christ?"

Among our enemies are the world, the flesh, and Satan. Not one of them vanished from us when we were saved. The world will war against us as long as we remain on earth, the flesh will tug against us as long as we are in it, and Satan and his cohorts will oppose us as long as they are free and we remain alive. Whether the enticements to do wrong come to us from the realm of the appetites of adventure or of ambition, on the table of plenteous grace which the Lord has prepared for us in the midst of his and our enemies, he has placed sufficient strength to enable us to triumph over the world, the flesh, and Satan.

III. God prepares a table for us in the midst of our enemies.

When the Lord our Shepherd prepares a table for his own in the presence of their malicious enemies, he always places on it exactly what they need at that particular time or what he knows will prove to be beneficial or invaluable in preparing them for the trying experiences awaiting them. Whether their needs are material or spiritual, his resources are always plentiful and satisfying. Due to his protecting grace, they enjoy in perfect security the sumptuous feast he has provided, even though they are partaking thereof under the scrutiny of their frustrated enemies.

IV. He anoints our heads with oil.

"Thou anointest my head with oil." This striking statement calls to our remembrance the scene of an Middle-Eastern shepherd at eventide standing at the entrance to a sheepfold carefully scrutinizing each sheep that is about to enter the fold. If a sheep appears to be weak, weary, or worn, the shepherd promptly bathes the face and head of the faltering or exhausted animal with oil before permitting it to enter. If a sheep has bruised itself or torn its flesh during the day, the shepherd applies the healing oil before allowing it to enter the fold. The faithful shepherd examines each sheep so carefully that no wound escapes his notice.

V. Our cup runs over.

Neither does any wound of the flesh or of the spirit ever escape the all-seeing eyes of the Lord, our Shepherd. And his constant, watchful care over us extends to the minutest details of our lives. To us he gives "the oil of gladness for the spirit of heaviness," and that is an incalculable blessing, as many can testify. Through his marvelous grace, we have received protection and healing for which we will ever be grateful. The anointing of the head with oil is a symbol of the anointing of the Holy Spirit, empowering us to render effective, God-pleasing, and Christ-honoring service. For this wonderful gift, we should express our thanks with our lips and through our lives.

Conclusion

Having learned from observation and experience that God's resources and blessings always exceeded the physical, mental, material, and spiritual needs of his children, and being filled with joyous satisfaction and genuine gratitude for the exceedingly gracious and generous manner in which the Father had dealt with him personally, the psalmist magnified God's abounding grace and mercy by saying, "My cup runneth over." Through the centuries the cups of millions have been filled to overflowing with God's grace and blessings. Today the cups of true and obedient Christians are overflowing with joy and appreciation because God has been supplying all of their needs "according to his riches in glory by Christ Jesus." The assurance that our cups will continue to overflow with his grace, mercy, and blessings as we keep on living for him affords us great and joyous satisfaction and should inspire us to introduce others to Christ in order that their cups may be filled to overflowing also.

SUNDAY MORNING, DECEMBER 9

Title: What Is Christmas?

Text: "Glory to God in the highest, and on earth peace among men in whom he is well pleased" **(Luke 2:14 RSV)**.

Scripture Reading: Luke 2:1–20

Hymns: "O Come, All Ye Faithful," Anonymous

"Angels from the Realms of Glory," Montgomery

"Brightest and Best of the Sons of the Morning," Heber

"I Can Hear My Savior Calling," Blandly

Offertory Prayer: Dear Lord and Father of humankind, we thank you for showering your great love on us. Your presence and your watchful care are so evident day by day if we but have spiritual eyes with which to see. We pause today to offer up to you our love and devotion along with a plea for forgiveness. In return for your bountiful love to us, we now bring a representative portion of our income into your storehouse. Accept, we pray, our tithes and offerings in the spirit in which we present them, through Jesus Christ our Lord. Amen.

Introduction

Some things we accept by tradition and never question. The happy Christmas season we accept with never a question as to what it really is all about. "Well, it is a time of happiness and family fun," we say. Yes, it is a time for Christmas trees, the wide-eyed looks of children as they contemplate the visit of Santa Claus, the pleasant aroma of spicy cookies wafting its way from the kitchen, the great stack of glittering Christmas cards that fills the mailbox, the beautiful sound of Christmas carols—it is all of this. But let us hasten to remember that Christmas is so much more than this. At the beginning of this season, there is a great need for each one of us to pause and reflect on the significance of this great festival of Christendom. What is Christmas all about anyway? Let us ask ourselves the following three questions.

I. What do unbelievers say about Christmas?

A. *Unbelieving historians may wish to banish Palestine and the story of Bethlehem's stable from their plan of world history, teaching our pleasure-loving generation that nothing really began then as relates to spiritual life.* Yet these self-same historians cannot satisfactorily explain the power of Jesus' life. Jesus was born in lowly circumstances, lived among the low-income bracket citizenry, never attended a school of higher learning, never ran for an office, and never distinguished himself on the field of combat. He was a transient lay preacher who never had a pulpit of his own. He had an uncanny knack for rubbing the leaders in contemporary society the wrong way, of incurring their wrath. He died after three short years of ministry as a result of a mock trial based on trumped-up charges. He died the death of a common criminal on a cross between two thieves. And yet the world has never been the same since that occasion in Bethlehem's stable.

"An artist once drew a picture of a winter twilight—the trees heavily laden with snow, and a dreary, dark house, lonely and desolate in the midst of the storm. It was a sad picture. Then, with a quick stroke of yellow crayon, he put a light in one window. The effect was magical. The entire scene was transformed into a vision of comfort and cheer. The birth of Christ was just such a light in the dark world" (*Nuggets of Life*, compiled and distributed by Leo Bennett, Denton, Tex., no. 33, November 1956).

B. *The average unbelieving man, if stopped in his frantic search for a suitable last-minute Christmas gift for his wife and questioned as to the meaning of Christmas, would likely remark in the words of Scrooge, "Bah, humbug!"* The chances are that he would see only the commercialization of the season and would probably deny the truth of the Christmas story, declaring it to be nothing more than the figment of the imagination of the biblical writers. Or he might simply be a "practicing atheist" with a poorly defined faith. The average unbeliever of our modern, sophisticated day seemingly takes pride in denying the miracle of Bethlehem's stable, but his denial has yet to change the glorious truth of these twenty centuries of revelation.

II. What does the Bible say?

The Bible, which each believer rightly accepts as the revealed word of God, speaks plainly about the true significance of Christmas. It tells us that:

A. *Christmas is the expression of God's love.* "God so loved the world that he gave" (John 3:16). God set the example of giving for those who did not deserve his gift nor who had the ability to reciprocate, and thus Christians desire to give gifts to those in need who may not deserve such gifts and who cannot reciprocate.

B. *Christmas is the celebration of what God did—gave his only begotten Son to come down to earth to reveal that God is a God of love and not simply a God of righteous indignation.* There are people who say that Jesus is a historical figure, a good man, but not any more the Son of God than you or I are sons of God. This only indicates that they have never had a personal experience with Christ. When a person has had a personal experience with Christ, he knows what Christ's power has done for him and is therefore able to recognize Jesus as the Son of the living God and to recognize that Jesus is very God and also very man—both divine and human. Thus, he recognizes that God identified with the great needs of humankind in this way.

C. *Christmas is God's purpose in redemption: "That whosoever believeth in him should not perish, but have everlasting life."* Christmas is the fulfillment of God's plan of the ages to step into the pages of human history and intervene on behalf of his sinful condition. Through the birth of Jesus in Bethlehem's stable, God set into motion his plan for saving sinful people who were totally unable to save themselves. God identified himself with human misery, causing himself to be available to be "tempted like as we are" (Heb. 4:15). The glorious completion of that plan would be found in the scene of the cross of Calvary.

D. *The hosts of heaven announced Christ's birth.* God's ministering heavenly hosts, his angels, blessed earth briefly with their visible and audible presence, singing the sweetest carols ever sung, setting the example for all Christendom to follow at this season as we sing the carols about the birth of our Lord.

III. What do you say?

Most pertinent to the issue is this last question, which should strike home to the heart of each of us. It is easy to pick at flaws in the theology of others, but it is hard to look inward and be so objective. What do you say about the significance of that event in Bethlehem's stable nearly two thousand years ago:

A. *In your heart?* Is Christmas a time of solemn review in your heart of what the coming of the babe in Bethlehem's stable means to you, of how your faith in him has given you a new perspective of the meaning of life and the hope of eternity? I feel sorry for those acquaintances of mine who spend their life's energies in denying that Jesus Christ is the Son of the living God. They have no hope of eternal life. Do you have a deep and abiding faith in your heart in the babe of Bethlehem's stable? Has he been born in your heart?

B. *By your life?* Has the truth of Christmas changed your way of life? Have you placed your faith in him to the extent that he has changed your way of life? Even on beds of affliction we are able to reveal that the babe of Bethlehem has been born not only into the world but also into our hearts by the way our attitude toward our infirmity exhibits itself. A friend whom I visited in the hospital told me, "If I can serve my Lord through my sickness and by the way I face up to it, then that is well with me. I have already learned that my attitude toward my sickness has been an example to someone else in this hospital to bear his sickness as a Christian soldier should."

Still more recently I heard of a lovely couple who were separated suddenly by death. On the night following his death, the new widow gathered her children together around the table at the evening meal and led them in singing the Doxology, which begins, "Praise God from whom all blessings flow," thus letting her faith shine through. By your life are you revealing that the truth of Bethlehem's stable resides in your heart?

Conclusion

In the beginning of this season, let us so conduct ourselves that all may see revealed in our hearts and lives the glorious truth that the true significance of Christmas is that it is the commemoration of the birth of Christ, who was truly God coming down to earth to seek and to save those who were lost.

SUNDAY EVENING, DECEMBER 9

Title: God's Eternal Plan of Missions

Text: "For he shall save his people from their sins" (**Matt. 1:21**).

Scripture Reading: Matthew 1:18–22

Introduction

In Matthew 1:21 we have a thrilling pronouncement by the angel of the Lord concerning the mission of the Messiah. He said that the purpose of the coming child to be born of the Virgin Mary is that "he shall save his people from their sins."

This wonderful statement is made in the midst of a conversation between the angel of the Lord, and Joseph who was engaged to be married to Mary. This talk between Joseph and the angel reveals the love of Joseph for Mary in refusing to have her stoned to death as a public example. It also reveals the miraculous power of the Holy Spirit in bringing conception to the Virgin Mary. However, one of the most outstanding meanings in this passage is the revelation of God's eternal plan of missions. The angel said about Jesus, "He shall save his people from their sins." This statement of the angel was the culmination of God's eternal purpose and plan of missions for human redemption.

I. God's plan of missions was originally revealed to Abraham.

In Genesis 12:2 God said to Abraham, "I will make of thee a great nation, and I will bless thee, and make thy name great; and thou shalt be a blessing." As we look back to the first eleven chapters of Genesis, the book of beginnings, we read the story of God's creation. In the selection of Abraham, we get an interesting insight into God's willingness to use unqualified and imperfect people in bringing his redeeming grace to a lost world. However, Abraham was willing to follow God and be taught by him. He was a willing instrument in God's hands.

In Abraham we see a great principle emerging in God's selection of imperfect people to proclaim his redeeming message to sinners. God said to Abraham, "Be thou a blessing." We often are prone to overlook this statement. We like to think of God blessing Abraham, making his name great, and making of him a great nation, but we do not magnify the fact that Abraham was to be a blessing to others.

So it is with most of us today. We want God to bless us—to make our name great—to exalt us in the world, but we often are not willing to be a blessing to others. We are not willing to witness and be a missionary for our Lord. We are not willing to help heal humanity's hurt. We are not willing to be an instrument in God's hand—to help do what the angel said Jesus would do "to save his people from their sins."

II. God's plan of missions was stated repeatedly.

A. *It was repeated to Abraham.* God's missionary plan of sharing his redemptive grace with all humankind is not limited to one isolated verse of Scripture. From time to time, at every great crisis in Abraham's life, God restated his missionary purpose for the world through Abraham.

1. The missionary purpose was repeated when Sodom was to be destroyed (Gen. 18:17–18). The specific thing we note in this passage is that God is saying that all nations of the earth will be blessed in Abraham. This missionary promise came to its full fruition when Jesus was born in Bethlehem. When the angel announced to Joseph, "He shall save his people from their sins," it was the beginning of the final fulfillment of God's purpose in Abraham that "all the nations of the earth shall be blessed in him."

2. God's missionary purpose was repeated at the interrupted sacrifice of Isaac (Gen. 22:15–18). In this episode in the life of Abraham, he became convinced that God wanted him to offer his promised son, Isaac, as a sacrifice. After Abraham had made all the necessary preparations and had stretched forth his hand to take Isaac's life, God spoke through his angel and stopped the sacrifice. He provided a ram caught by his horns in the thicket instead of Isaac for the sacrifice. Then God spoke through his angel to Abraham and said in Genesis 22:17–18, "In blessing I will bless thee, and in multiplying I will multiply thy seed as the stars of the heaven, and as the sand which is upon the sea shore; and thy seed shall possess the gate of his enemies; and in thy seed shall all the nations of the earth be blessed; because thou hast obeyed my voice."

   Abraham and all humankind should have learned two great lessons about God in this traumatic crisis experience: first, that God requires and rewards absolute and unquestioning obedience; second, that God does not require, nor does he want, human sacrifice. As important as these two lessons are, there is still a third and more important lesson in this passage. It was that Isaac is the beginning of the fulfillment of God's promise to Abraham. Perhaps neither Abraham nor Isaac ever caught the full significance of what it meant to be a blessing to all nations. Like most of the Christian world today, they wanted God's blessings without the responsibility of the missionary proclamation of the redeeming grace of God.

B. *God's missionary purpose was repeated to others.* God did not stop with Abraham in giving his missionary purpose, but continued to give it to generation after generation of Abraham's descendants.

1. In Genesis 26:4, during a great famine when God sent Isaac to Egypt that he might have food, God repeated his missionary purpose when he said, "In thy seed shall all the nations of the earth be blessed."

2. In Genesis 28:14 God repeated his missionary purpose to Jacob, the son of Isaac. Jacob was selfish and crafty and had little natural religious interest. After he had conned his brother out of his birthright and slyly deceived his father, thereby stealing his brother's blessing, he was forced to flee for his life from the presence of his brother. At night when Jacob was asleep, the angel of God appeared to Jacob in a dream and said, "In thee and in thy seed shall all the families of the earth be blessed."

On and on this goes throughout the Old Testament—God giving his missionary purpose to leader after leader. To Moses, God said in Exodus 19:6, "Ye shall be unto me a kingdom of priests." In 1 Kings 8:41–43 King Solomon led a prayer of dedication for the first temple in Jerusalem, and under the inspiration of God, Solomon noted that the temple was not for those of Hebrew blood alone, but for all humankind. In praying that God would heed the petitions of foreigners, he gave the very purpose for which the Jews had been chosen—"That all people of the earth may know thy name, to fear thee, as doth thy people Israel" (v. 43).

In the Psalms and in both the Major and Minor Prophets, we see the growing revelation of God's missionary purpose for all humankind.

Conclusion

We note the tremendous importance of the statement made by the angel of the Lord to Joseph when he said about Jesus, to be born of the Virgin Mary, "He shall save his people from their sins." Jesus came to forgive people's sins—to reconcile people to God—to seek and save that which is lost. He was God incarnate in human flesh, loving people in their sin, though hating the sin. When persons are spiritually reborn into the kingdom of God, their primary function as Christians is to be missionaries in their whole lives, seeking to reconcile sinful people to a loving Savior.

WEDNESDAY EVENING, DECEMBER 12

Title: In the House of the Lord

Text: "Surely goodness and mercy shall follow me all the days of my life: and I will dwell in the house of the LORD for ever" **(Ps. 23:6).**

Scripture Reading: Psalm 23

Introduction

The words "goodness and mercy" are fascinating because they are attributes of God. "Goodness" has to do with the nature and character of God, in whom there is no darkness at all. Of all God's attributes, none is more beautiful than mercy, which is simply love in action. His goodness to his people through the centuries has been expressed in his wonderful acts of mercy in his dealings with them. Goodness has ever been the root of which mercy has been the fruit. The former has been the cause; the latter, the effect. Mercy flows out of goodness. According to Romans 2:4, goodness leads to repentance: "The goodness of God leadeth thee to repentance." According to Titus 3:5, mercy brings about regeneration: "He saved us, not because of righteous things we had done, but because of his mercy. He saved us through the washing of rebirth and renewal by the Holy Spirit" (NIV).

I. Goodness and mercy will follow our lives.

The psalmist was looking at his yesterdays at the time our text was penned. As he did so, his entire past opened before him in marvelous clarity. As he gazed intently at the panorama of his past life and recounted the numerous blessings God had bestowed upon him, he saw a rear guard of goodness and mercy for which he was deeply grateful. Whether the former days had brought to him showers or sunshine, sickness or health, adversity or prosperity, sadness or gladness, the psalmist was thoroughly convinced that he had been the recipient of various expressions of God's goodness and mercy through all the days. The Lord's presence with him had sweetened every bitter cup, and his power had enabled him to triumph over his enemies on numerous occasions. As he thought of his experiences during the years and meditated on the many expressions of God's goodness and mercy, he came to realize more fully that the divine mercies had been new every morning and fresh every evening, as evidenced by the sustenance of his physical, mental, and spiritual life.

The psalmist had tested God in many difficult and trying experiences and had found him equal to every emergency. On various occasions, David had failed God, but God had not failed David in a single instance. He knew beyond a doubt that God was absolutely trustworthy. Many of us can also give this testimony. Without any hesitation, we gladly acknowledge that it has been through God's goodness, grace, and mercy that we have been enabled to live in accordance with his will; to yield ourselves to him for the accomplishment of his purpose in, for, and through us; to render the service that he has required; and to complete the assignments with which he has entrusted us.

In our text, we note the writer turning from retrospect to prospect or from meditation on the past to a contemplation of the future. Without a doubt, the Lord had been with David, bestowing numerous favors upon him, some of which were delightful surprises to him, making his life truly worthwhile so that he had every reason to believe that God would be favorable toward him in the future.

Remembering with genuine gratitude the goodness and mercy of which he had been the recipient, David firmly resolved that he would trust the Lord fully and implicitly to do as much for him during all the days that were yet to come. On the basis of his experience, David firmly believed that he would enjoy the presence, preservation, protection, and provision of God. Therefore, David did not face the future with gloomy anticipation but with great confidence, faith, courage, and optimism.

As we face the future with our eyes fixed on the Lord, we may rest assured that we will see additional expressions of his goodness and grace every morning. Though we do not know what our future needs may be, we have no right to think that they will not be met adequately, because the divine supply is certain to be in excess of our needs.

"Only goodness and mercy shall follow me all the days of my life." This remarkable statement is confirmed in Romans 8:28: "All things work together for good to them that love God, to them who are the called according to his purpose." Everything that happens to God's children is not good, but through everything that does happen to his trusting, loving, and obedient children, he works in such a manner as to make it possible for something good to emerge. In the trying and puzzling experiences of life, it is encouraging and comforting to know that God can use every circumstance as the raw material for the shaping of a new and unexpected good. Often we do not see it when it happens, but afterward, when we look back and reflect, we can trace the hand of God working for our ultimate good. This is both a glorious certainty and a great comfort.

What did the psalmist see when he looked toward the future? He could see goodness and mercy following him through the remainder of his life on earth and God being favorable toward him in eternity. David could not have spoken more positively or with greater certitude than when he declared: "And I will dwell in the house of the LORD for ever."

II. We will dwell in the house of the Lord forever.

While we continue our sojourn on earth, there is not much likelihood that we will always remain in the houses in which we are now dwelling. Most likely we will live in more than one additional house before coming to the end of life's journey, as our people are noted for changing residences quite frequently. Whether we change earthly houses or not, as time passes our family circles will be broken by death. At the time determined by God, each of us will take his or her departure from an earthly house for the last time.

Since those of us whom the Lord has saved will be going to the Father's house when we leave here, as many of our relatives and friends have done already, our thoughts should dwell lovingly and longingly on our eternal home, the habitation of God and the eternal dwelling place of all his children. This place, which Christ called heaven, is spacious enough for all who will become prepared to enter it from the beginning to the end of time. It is a place of inconceivable and indescribable beauty, spotless purity, complete knowledge, perfect happiness, and sweet rest. The things that mar our lives on earth, such as sin, sickness, suffering, separation, and sorrow, will never appear "in the house of the LORD."

Conclusion

It is a joyous privilege to be a sheep of God's pasture and a guest at his table, but it will be far more wonderful to be in his home for eternity. I do not know anything that can comfort and cheer like the blessed assurance of being with Christ and all of the saved "in the house of the LORD for ever."

SUNDAY MORNING, DECEMBER 16

Title: Putting Christ into Christmas

Text: "And the angel said unto them, Fear not: for, behold, I bring you good tidings of great joy, which shall be to all people. For unto you is born this day in the city of David a Savior, which is Christ the Lord" **(Luke 2:10–11)**.

Scripture Reading: Luke 2:8–12

Hymns: "The Heavens Declare Thy Glory, Lord," Watts

"Hark! the Herald Angels Sing," Charles Wesley

"Angels, from the Realms of Glory," Montgomery

Offertory Prayer: Our heavenly Father, we come before you with thanksgiving in our hearts. Your patience and forbearance have been evident this week as we have failed you through our sins of omission and of commission. At this season of the year, we turn our thoughts toward Bethlehem's stable where you touched the earth with your sacred presence, giving to people the revelation of yourself as you are. We now return to you a tangible token of our love for you through our tithes and offerings. In Jesus' name. Amen.

Introduction

If we were to place a citizen of a third world country in one of our busy shopping malls during the Christmas season and he were to see the hustle and bustle of the crowds, what would be his impression of the meaning of the Christmas festivities? By the sight and sound of our Christmas preparations, would he be able to discern the true meaning of Christmas? Could we explain to him the real meaning? Would he believe us? The glitter, tinsel, buying and selling, drunken parties, and so on—do these speak more loudly to such people than do the testimonies of our churches and of our individual Christian lives?

Our own children are rapidly losing sight of the true meaning of Christmas, for Christ has been taken out of Christmas, his place having been usurped by our own selfish pleasure in its outward celebration. At this beginning of the Christmas season, let us gather our families together and remind them through the reading of the Christmas story of the real meaning of this great Christian celebration. Let us attempt to cause them to see for themselves that there is a great depth to the richness of the glorious message of Christmas. Let us teach them that the Christmas season is a time:

I. For adoration and praise of our Lord.

This is a truism that is so obvious that it has been overlooked by many in our generation. At this season of the year, we ought to give full expression to our great love for the Lord through unashamed praise.

A. *A baby has been born to bless the world in a unique way.* When any baby is born into a home, we rejoice over such a blessed addition to the family. The birth of the Christ child, when viewed from the full scope of the centuries, should cause such rejoicing as our hearts cannot contain. As the wise men of the East came to give adoration to him, so ought we to give adoration to him. They only knew by partial revelation that he was to grow up to be a very special person. We know by the testimony of the centuries what a special person was born in Bethlehem's stable. We know through his life, teachings, miracles, sacrificial death, and glorious resurrection from the dead that he truly is the Son of the living God, that God came down to earth that night so long ago in Bethlehem's stable.

B. *This babe came as a fulfillment of the promise that the one called "Wonderful, Counselor, Mighty God, Everlasting Father, Prince of Peace" (Isa. 9:6 NIV)* would be born of a virgin (Isa. 7:14). Hundreds of years prior to this great event in Bethlehem's stable a prophecy in rather minute detail was given concerning the circumstances of his birth and of his character and ministry. For such a glorious promise to find such complete fulfillment for human good is indeed cause for our adoration and praise. The Son of God stepped into the pages of history as complete fulfillment of God's promises to humankind and for the purpose of reconciling people with God. At this season of the year, this great truth ought to cause us to sing our great Redeemer's praise!

C. *The shepherds watching their sheep in the valley below the mountain of Bethlehem were startled out of their drowsiness on that night by the most beautiful music they had ever heard, the carol being sung to them by a heavenly choir.* That music lingered in their hearts and minds throughout their days, causing them to set in motion songs of praise to the Christ child. Let there be depth of meaning to the words we sing; let these carols be expressive of our real feeling toward the Christ of Christmas.

II. Of realization of the meaning of his coming.

What does the coming of Christ into the world really mean to our hearts today? What was his purpose in coming into the midst of humankind?

A. *He came to bring peace among people of goodwill by giving them the gift of peace in their hearts through the redemption of their souls.* This world today, even as in every preceding age, is crying out for peace. Nation is set against nation, race against race, philosophy against philosophy. We claim we want peace, but until we are willing to have peace on God's terms, we can never find it. We have the promise of Micah the prophet, "And he will be their peace" (Mic. 5:5 NIV). Jesus said, "These things I have spoken unto you, that in me ye might have peace. In the world ye shall have tribulation: but be of good cheer; I have overcome the world" (John 16:33).

B. *He came to bring hope — hope for this present life and hope for eternity.* Isaiah the prophet had predicted centuries earlier, "The people that walked in darkness have seen a great light: they that dwell in the land of the shadow of death, upon them hath the light shined" (Isa. 9:2). God's people at the time of Christ's birth were in a hopeless situation. They were a people dominated by a foreign empire, Rome. They saw no prospect of a happy future, actually no prospect of a future of any sort. They knew little of life beyond the grave. Humankind in that day viewed life beyond the grave much as modern-day atheists view it — eternity without hope.

C. *He came to teach people how to love the Lord their God with all their hearts and to give expression to that love by loving their neighbors as themselves.* How beautifully Jesus told the story of a Samaritan who kindly treated a Jewish man who had fallen among thieves on the winding road through the hot desert area between Jerusalem and Jericho. He told this so realistically that it causes one to wonder if by chance he was the person to whom it had happened. This was a new concept to those living under the law, for they had a philosophy of "live and let live," not of "live and help to live." And Jesus said, "Thou shalt love thy neighbour as thyself" (Matt. 22:39). The babe of Bethlehem's stable was born as a result of God's great love for lost and bewildered humanity; this babe so loved lost humanity that he later laid down his life that we might have eternal life. Such an example of love ought to inspire us to have true love for God and for our fellow humans.

III. For giving to others with no hope of receiving.

The commercialization of Christmas is something that true Christians deplore. The idea of giving ought to be based on love, of giving to others in the spirit of Christ.

A. *Let us give to those in need instead of simply "exchanging" gifts.* Look about you this year and find some child who may not have any Christmas gifts because his parents have hit hard times. Assist those parents on behalf of the child's Christmas toys. Help an older couple living on limited means. Help the down and out person. Give to those from whom you could not possibly expect a gift in return. The wise men came bearing rich gifts for a baby born of poor parents. They gave with no expectation of a gift in return. Let us give to others in the name of Christ and surprise ourselves with the greatest return gift of all—that nice, warm feeling of joy in our hearts!

B. *Let us give the greatest of all gifts at this season of the year, the gift of the Christ child himself to someone who does not know Christ personally.* Take the message of Christ to a person who is not a Christ follower. Introduce that person to Christ. Endeavor to lead that person to a saving knowledge of Christ. Give Christ at Christmas.

Conclusion

This year let us really put Christ into Christmas by making him the focal point around which all of our celebration takes place. Let us give him our praise and adoration. Let us remember why Christ emptied himself of heaven's glory in order to come down among sinful people and later die for them. Let us return to the joy of real gift giving at Christmas, giving the greatest of all gifts, Christ Jesus himself!

SUNDAY EVENING, DECEMBER 16

Title: God's Preparations for World Missions

Text: "This was done, that it might be fulfilled which was spoken of the Lord by the prophet" **(Matt. 1:22)**.

Scripture Reading: Matthew 1:22–25

Introduction

The coming of Jesus Christ into the world did not constitute a change in God's plans for bringing his redeeming grace to sinners. Instead, it demonstrated his love, concern, and willingness to sacrifice, and it revealed his eternal missionary purpose to provide a personal Savior for all nations of the earth.

Our text reads, "All this was done, that it might be fulfilled which was spoken of the Lord by the prophet." "All this" refers to all the wonderful events that occurred during the time immediately before and at the birth of Jesus Christ.

We remember the visit of the angel Gabriel to the Virgin Mary when he said, "Greetings, you who are highly favored! The Lord is with you.... Do not be afraid, Mary, you have found favor with God. You will be with child and give birth to a son, and you are to give him the name Jesus" (Luke 1:28, 30–31 NIV).

We also remember the visit of the angel to Joseph while he was in a quandary as to what to do with Mary when he learned that she was with child before they had come together in marriage. The angel appeared to Joseph in a dream, saying, "Joseph, son of David, do not be afraid to take Mary home as your wife, because what is conceived in her is from the Holy Spirit. She will give birth to a son, and you are to give him the name Jesus, because he will save his people from their sins" (Matt. 1:20–21 NIV).

We think of the events of the coming of the wise men from the East and of King Herod inquiring about when the King of the Jews was to be born. We recall the journey of Joseph and Mary from Nazareth to Bethlehem and the story of "no room in the inn." We think of the angel of the Lord bringing good tidings to the shepherds and of the shepherds' journey to Bethlehem, where they "found Mary and Joseph, and the babe lying in a manger." These, and others like them, are wonderful events that occurred at the birth of Jesus Christ; but the coming of Jesus Christ and the beginning of the Christian era in no way brought an abrupt change in God's plans and missionary purpose for the world. God did not begin to love the world at the coming of Christ. He has loved the whole world and all its people from the beginning.

The coming of Jesus Christ did not bring a radical change in God's method of dealing with people. "Abraham believed God, and it was accounted to him for righteousness" (Gal. 3:6). Even so we today must come to God in faith, believing that he is a rewarder of them who diligently seek him.

I. Jesus was a prophet proclaiming God's missionary message.

We know that Jesus was more than a prophet, but he was a prophet. In Luke 4:16–32 we have the story of Jesus entering into the synagogue on the Sabbath in Nazareth, and he stood up and read from the prophet Isaiah (61:1–2), "The spirit of the Lord is on me, because he has anointed me to preach good news to the poor. He has sent me to proclaim freedom for the prisoners and recovery of sight for the blind, to release the oppressed, to proclaim the year of the Lord's favor." When he had finished, he said, "Today this scripture is fulfilled in your hearing" (vv. 18–19, 21 NIV). He went on to tell them many wonderful things and to interpret the Scriptures, but they rejected him and dragged him out of the city and were about to throw him over a cliff when he slipped away. In the midst of this experience, Jesus said in Luke 4:24, "No prophet is accepted in his hometown" (NIV). Thus, Jesus himself affirms that he is a prophet.

Jesus understood that he stood at the end of a long line of prophets. As any other prophet, he had at least two messages. One was to speak forth God's message for people of his day; and the other was to speak about coming events in God's eternal plans. For Israel, in his day, Jesus was a messenger of divine judgment on God's people because of their sins and failure to share God's redeeming grace with all people of all nations.

Again and again the relationship between God and Israel was strained in the historical books of the Old Testament. An example can be seen in Judges: "The Israelites did evil in the eyes of the LORD; they forgot the LORD their God and served the Baals and the Asherahs. The angel of the LORD burned against

Israel so that he sold them into the hands of Cushan-Rishathaim king of Aram Naharaim.... But when they cried out to the LORD, he raised up for them a deliverer ... who saved them" (Judg. 3:7–9 NIV).

This passage is the sad story of Israel often repeated throughout their long history. Israel was obviously the chosen people of Jehovah. As a chosen people, Israel was expected to serve the Lord God and to share, through world missions, their faith in God with all other nations. Instead, Israel committed two blunders that rendered the nation useless as a spiritual instrument in the hand of God. The first blunder was that Israel as a nation generally forsook the Lord their God and followed the evil practices of the heathen nations around them. Israel's second mistake was that they refused to be missionary in spirit toward other nations. Israel welcomed proselytes into their religious faith but with severe restrictions. Generally the nation of Israel was selfish and jealous of their worship of Jehovah and sought to keep the worship of the true God only to themselves. They never, through a missionary spirit, tried to share their God with other nations.

However, the Scriptures show repeatedly that there was always a righteous, God-fearing, remnant in Israel. Again and again God raised up prophets in Israel who sought to lead the nation both to follow God in righteousness and to share the worship of Jehovah with other nations. It was from this remnant of believers that the Lord God brought forth his Son Jesus the Christ as the Savior of all peoples.

II. Christ's prophetic strategy was twofold.

A. *He sought the Jewish nation.* From the beginning of his public ministry, Jesus preached especially to the Jewish people. In Matthew 4:23, 25 we read, "And Jesus went about all Galilee, teaching in their synagogues, and preaching the gospel of the kingdom, and healing all manner of sickness and all manner of disease among the people.... And there followed him great multitudes of people from Galilee, and from Decapolis, and from Jerusalem, and from Judea, and from beyond Jordan."

In the beginning of Jesus' ministry, he sought literally to proclaim the message of God in every Jewish village, town, and province. He even enlisted the aid of disciples to help him with this task. We read in Luke, "The Lord appointed seventy-two others and sent them two by two ahead of him to every town and place where he was about to go." He said, "Go! I am sending you out like lambs among wolves" (10:1–3 NIV). They were to carry neither purse, nor bag, nor sandals. If the people of a home would not hear the disciple sent forth, then that disciple was to shake the dust of that house off his feet.

B. *He sought all nations.* While Jesus was concerned about Israel, he was and is a Savior for all races and nations of people on the earth. In Acts 1:8 Jesus said to his disciples just before his ascension into heaven, "You will be my witnesses in Jerusalem, and in all Judea and Samaria, and to the ends of the earth" (NIV).

Conclusion

God provided and revealed his final plan of salvation for all nations in Jesus.

WEDNESDAY EVENING, DECEMBER 19

Title: The Promised Messiah

Text: "For to us a child is born, to us a son is given, and the government will be on his shoulders. And he will be called Wonderful Counselor, Mighty God, Everlasting Father, Prince of Peace" **(Isa. 9:6 NIV)**.

Introduction

Isaiah looked forward by inspired faith to the coming of the ideal ruler who would bring salvation and peace to his people. The prophet had spoken previously of the birth of a child that would indicate the presence of God with his people (Isa. 7:14; 8:8–10).

Isaiah, speaking as he was moved by the Holy Spirit, prophesied of a coming Messiah. This prophecy was beyond the prophet's capacity to fully understand at the time. He visualized an ideal and royal ruler as having a unique relationship with God. The word *government* here is a bit unusual and probably refers to some symbol of majesty or authority that was to be worn on the shoulder of the promised Ruler.

It was a common custom in Isaiah's day for persons of royal position to receive honorary titles that were indicative of their personality, position, power, or significant achievements. The messianic titles bestowed on the coming ruler by the prophet Isaiah were promises concerning his capacity as a ruler and the character of his rule. He would be wise and powerful and at the same time paternal and peaceful. These titles reflect rays of heavenly truth that should inspire faith in and love for the Messiah.

I. The Messiah is called Wonderful Counselor.

Literally he is called "A wonder of a Counselor." The Messiah was to be the Wonderful Counselor because his counsel would come from God. He would be constantly with his people. The consequences of his counsel would be wonderful. His counsel is wonderful today because of who he is, what he has done, and what he can do in the lives of those who trust him.

II. The Messiah is called the Mighty God.

Literally he is called "God of a hero." This title has been translated "divine warrior." It refers to the courageous, heroic nature of the life and ministry of the Messiah. He was to be a brave conqueror who would overcome Satan and the world by a sinless life. He was to overcome sin on the cross. He was to conquer death and the grave by his resurrection. Consequently, he was to be exalted to the right hand of God in sovereign majesty.

III. The Messiah is called the Everlasting Father.

Literally he is called "Father of eternity." In the Middle East men often were given a name or title that signified some quality or characteristic for which they were famous. One could be a father of wisdom or a father of folly. The promised Messiah is said to be "the Father of perpetuity, or the Father of eternity, or the Father of the forever." This is an emphatic assertion of the Messiah's deity. Only God is eternal. As the everlasting Father, the Messiah will occupy his throne forever.

IV. The Messiah is called the Prince of Peace.

The hunger of the people of Isaiah's day, like that of today, was for peace.

As the Prince of Peace, the Messiah was to do something infinitely more than bring about a cessation of hostilities. Through him the people were to experience the rich, harmonious, and joyous creative life of God's redeemed people.

Christ becomes the Prince of Peace in an individual's heart when he is known and trusted as the Wonderful Counselor, the Mighty God, and the Everlasting Father.

Conclusion

The traditional Jewish view of this prophecy finds its fulfillment in Hezekiah, the son of Ahaz. Likely Isaiah wished that Hezekiah would be the kind of king described by this beautiful prophecy. However, the hopes and dreams of the prophet were not fully realized until Jesus Christ was born of the Virgin Mary to be the King of the Jews and Savior of the world.

During this Christmas season, let us worship in sincerity and truth him whom God has appointed to be our King and Savior.

SUNDAY MORNING, DECEMBER 23

Title: A Wise Man's Gift

Text: "And when they were come into the house, they saw the young child with Mary his mother, and fell down, and worshipped him: and when they had opened their treasures, they presented unto him gifts; gold, and frankincense, and myrrh" (**Matt. 2:11**).

Scripture Reading: Matthew 2:1–12

Hymns: "Holy, Holy, Holy," Heber

"Thou Didst Leave Thy Throne," Elliott

"It Came upon the Midnight Clear," Sears

"Jesus Paid It All," Hall

Offertory Prayer: This morning, Father, we bow ourselves before your throne of grace in a spirit of submission. We see ourselves as creatures of your creation, creatures who are too often bent on self-destruction because we are bent on having our own selfish ways. We see ourselves as sheep who wander away from the Good Shepherd. We see you as the Good Shepherd, who, in your loving-kindness, has been merciful in your providential love, blessing us far beyond measure, causing us to receive from your bountiful care far more than we can ever deserve. We come now to bring into your storehouse our tithes and offerings as representative tokens of our sense of stewardship and gratitude to you. Accept these tokens of our love and gratitude through our Lord Jesus Christ. Amen.

Introduction

What is Christmas giving? It is giving something you probably like but which the receiver could care less about. It is the December 26 grand fruit basket turnover as people rush back to the stores to exchange their gifts for something they really want.

One Christmas season our family decided that instead of gift items we would just send money in order that the recipients might choose something of practical value to them, something they really wanted instead of our usual "gift mistakes."

The precedent for Christmas gift-giving was set by the wise men when they brought gifts to the Christ child. Let us look at them for a moment. These "wise men" were from the Far East, possibly from the Babylonia area. The Greek word from which "wise men" is translated is *magoi*, transliterated *magi*. The word denotes astrologers and magicians generally. The magi seem originally to have been a Median tribe of priests; later the word refers to the Zoroastrian priestly caste. History tells us that in AD 66 an embassy of Parthian magi paid homage to Nero at Naples and returned home by another route. It is probable that Matthew in his gospel account is thinking of Babylonian astrologers. The Bible does not say how many wise men there were. Traditionally we refer to three wise men because the Bible mentions the three gifts they brought. So the number three pertaining to the wise men is from tradition and not from biblical fact.

I. The wise men saw the star when busy at their own task.

A. *Often the revelation of God can be found as we are busy with our workaday world.* We can see our God's look of hurt when we hear a fellow workman take God's name in vain. We can hear Jesus say, "Inasmuch as ye have done it unto one of the least of these my brethren, ye have done it unto me" (Matt. 25:40) as we minister to our needy brothers. We should look at our brothers in the ghetto sections of our cities who often stand listlessly in line before the employment agency hoping to be hired for a day's wages with which to buy some food to feed their hungry children. Yes, we should look at them and visualize the Master standing longingly there. The cursing man of the street we should see as a mission field for the teaching of a Christ who can cleanse such a person.

B. *The handiwork of God should point us to the hope in Christ. Thomas Hardy, despite his skepticism, found a thrush's song such an ecstatic sound that he guessed there trembled through it "some blessed Hope, whereof he knew and I was unaware."*

C. *Daily fidelity to the task at hand gives us, for some reason, a quicker awareness of the truth.* Sticking to their scientific task of astrology day by day trained the magi to be alert and aware of revealed truth. If you and I had been there, would we have noticed the presence of the special star? Would we have noted the unusual? The reason that the unusual star did not attract the attention of Herod may not have been the distance or the contour of the earth but rather that he just never noticed.

II. It took "outsiders" to point out a great fact.

It takes an outsider to notice and to point out a truth sometimes. We who live with a certain condition day in and day out may never notice the slight changes that occur each day. An outsider who appears on the scene only occasionally may readily notice the change each time he does appear.

A. *The magi pointed out by their coming to Bethlehem that this young King was to be King over all the world.* This was a foreign thought to the Jews of that day. In South America at the crest of the Andes Mountains, which separate two formerly warring nations, Argentina and Chile, there stands the statue of the Christ of the Andes. It silently points out to the two feuding nations that Christ is King of both and peacemaker between the two.

B. *These magi acted with complete abandon, leaving their daily toil, saddling their camels, and heading westward, knowing not where.* They were obsessed with the fact that they must pay homage to the newborn King. Many years ago, Robert Morrison began our knowledge of ancient China, which was housed in by the Great Wall, by throwing caution to the wind and foolishly going into this mysterious and forbidding land. Later he was honored as a wise and gracious man, speaking to scholars and societies on his original research in the Chinese language. He did not go for the acceptable and solid reasons of establishing trade with China or of doing language study. He went for the foolish (in the eyes of the skeptical world) purpose of taking the gospel of Jesus Christ to the people of China. Let us examine our hearts and lives and see if we react as most Christians should.

III. The wise men gave their gifts in an act of worship.

A. *Gifts of charity often do more harm than good.*

1. Too often we give with a "down-the-nose, better-than-thou" attitude.

2. Those receiving such gifts do not feel their hearts warmed by the act even though their bodies may be. Some years ago a man of God spoke to a great group of dedicated missions-minded women. He pointed out to them that the kind of ministry that is not done out of love, but is simply done from a sense of decency or in aesthetic response to the ugliness of life, is totally inadequate. He stressed that commitment to service means to love. Love means that the giver must identify with the person who is in need.

B. *They gave to the newborn King with love and in an act of reverent submission.* Our gift of means when presented to Christ must be accompanied with the gift of self in submission to him. We must yield, as it were, the nerve center of consent to our God. Commitment means to make all the manifold expressions of one's personality a voice through which Christ can speak. In a church service, the minister spoke on giving oneself to the Christ child at Christmas. When the offering plate was passed at the close of the service, a little lad whispered, "Hold the plate lower." Finally, the ushers discerned that he was trying to get into the plate. The lad's explanation was, "I want to give myself." Isn't that what Christ really wants of us at Christmas?

Conclusion

The hymn "We Three Kings of Orient Are," tells of Caspar, who came bearing a gift of gold, denoting one's livelihood and substance given to the Christ child; of Melchior, who came bearing frankincense, an item easily symbolizing our inner treasure of thought and influence; of Balthazzar, who brought myrrh, an item used often in that day for embalming, appropriately symbolic of our sorrow and suffering that can be used as a gift to glorify Christ. Will you at this Christmas season give a wise man's gift?

SUNDAY EVENING, DECEMBER 23

Title: Missions Is Giving

Text: "God so loved the world, that he gave ..." (**John 3:16**).

Scripture Reading: Luke 1:26–35

Introduction

As we approach the Christmas season and once again read the story of Jesus' birth as recorded in the gospels of Matthew and Luke, we cannot help being impressed with the many gifts involved in the Christmas story.

We are aware immediately of the fact that God is giving his Son. The wise men of the East gave Jesus gifts of gold, frankincense, and myrrh. The angel gave messages to both Joseph and Mary. When Mary went to visit her cousin Elizabeth, Elizabeth was filled with the Holy Spirit and said to Mary, "Blessed art thou among women, and blessed is the fruit of thy womb." When Jesus was eight days old, his parents offered a sacrificial gift according to the law of the Lord, "a pair of turtledoves, or two young pigeons." Although we may not understand all these gifts, we do know that "every good gift and every perfect gift is from above, and cometh down from the Father of lights" (James 1:17).

Giving and missions are interrelated and inseparable. Jesus' mission of coming into the world was to give God's eternal salvation to all the world. "God so loved the world that he gave his only begotten Son ..." (John 3:16).

I. Missions requires giving yourself in Christian living.

A. *Living the teachings of Christ.* Whether a Christian lives and serves on a foreign mission field or in his own local community, the thing that sets him apart, that makes him a dynamic Christian witness, is his moral conduct based on the teachings of Jesus. In Matthew 5:16 Jesus said, "Let your light so shine before men, that they may see your good works, and glorify your Father which is in heaven." Some of the strongest teachings Jesus gave on a high moral standard of Christian living were given in the midst of the Sermon on the Mount.

B. *Live the teachings of Christ in a sinful society.* We live in a world of hate, dishonesty, lying, cheating, and sexual laxity. The spiritual good within people has more often than not surrendered to the evil desires of the flesh. Christians live in this kind of a society. What a refreshing sweet breath of heaven it would be if Christians would rededicate themselves to Christlike living in this sinful society. We could become preserving salt in a world of immorality. We could become the leaven that leavens the whole loaf. We could become a missionary force that would change society. This is exactly what happened in the early Christian era.

C. *The early church lived the Christ-filled life.* They let the Holy Spirit of God come into their minds, souls, and bodies and literally fill their lives. It was no accident that three thousand souls were added to the church on the day of Pentecost. It happened because God's people were filled with God's Holy Spirit.

II. Missions is giving a personal witness.

A. *In your family.* A Christian family that prays together, studies God's Word together, goes to church together, and lives Christian principles in its community becomes a great missionary force for winning others to faith in Christ. When parents become prayerfully concerned about the spiritual welfare of their children, they can be an instrument in God's hand in bringing them to know Christ as Savior.

B. *To casual acquaintances.* Every day millions of Christians rub shoulders with factory employees, doctors, lawyers, merchants, and the casual bystander on the street. We work and play with our friends and casual acquaintances. Many of these, and in some cases most of them, have no personal faith in Christ as Savior. The question often arises as to who has the greatest influence—the Christian or the non-Christian. If all Christians would live out the teachings of Christ and show personal concern for a spiritual rebirth of their casual friends, this could be a most effective way of witnessing.

A pastor passing a department store one day followed a sudden impression to speak to the owner. He said, "Sir, I have talked carpets, beds, and furniture with you, but I have never talked with you about my business. Will you give me a few minutes of your time?" The owner led the pastor into his private office where the pastor took out his New Testament and directed the owner's attention to passage after passage and urged him to become a Christian. Finally, the tears began to roll down his cheeks, and he said, "I'm seventy years of age. I was born in this city, and more than a hundred pastors and hundreds of church officers have known me in a business way. You are the only man who ever spoke to me about my soul." This illustration could be multiplied a thousand times, but it should not be so. Christians need to feel the missionary pull of the gospel and begin to witness to their casual acquaintances.

III. Missions may require giving your life.

A. *In daily living.* When a Christian openly lives his faith in modern society, it often brings criticism and reproach, and he may be ostracized from friends. Because of this, Christians often follow the crowds into sinful practices rather than the example of Christ in open witnessing.

B. *Missions may require giving your life in special service.* Jesus said in Mark 16:15, "Go ye into all the world, and preach the gospel to every creature." Often, as we give our lives in daily surrender to the Master's call, we feel a spiritual tug at our hearts to do more than witness in our immediate community. God calls to a larger service. This call can be a foreign country or a special home missions field. In such a call, God is actually asking you to lay your life on the altar of missionary service. You may have to leave loved ones and friends. You may need to sacrifice a good job or a lovely home. The pay you receive and the equipment with which you work may be inadequate. When you answer such a call, however, you probably will find more happiness, genuine peace of mind, and spiritual strength than you ever knew was possible.

C. *Many have given their lives in missionary witnessing.* God gave his Son to die for the sins of the world. Stephen, the first deacon, was stoned to death while giving his witness for Christ. Most of the early Christians endured great sacrifices in order to give a missionary testimony for the gospel.

Conclusion

Being a Christian missionary in the world today can cost you your life. History is full of stories of Christian missionaries who literally gave their lives to give a witness for Christ.

Missions is giving.

WEDNESDAY EVENING, DECEMBER 26

Title: Looking Backward and Forward

Text: "Grace and peace be multiplied unto you through the knowledge of God, and of Jesus our Lord" (**2 Peter 1:2**).

Scripture Reading: 2 Peter 1:1–11

Introduction

As we come to the end of one year and approach the beginning of a new year, it would be profitable to take a look backward and count our blessings and then take a look forward and make our plans to cooperate with the Lord.

The first few verses of Peter's second epistle provide us with an opportunity to look at some of the blessings God has bestowed on us in the past. It also provides us with some words of instruction and encouragement to live a life in which we are growing spiritually and serving significantly.

Peter addressed his message "to them that have obtained like precious faith with us through the righteousness of God and our Savior Jesus Christ." He wrote from the perspective of an aged pastor who was living on the edge of eternity. He spoke of his body as a tabernacle, or tent, from which he would soon depart. He referred to his approaching death as his exodus, or departure—the word used for the departure of the children of Israel from Egypt.

I. The blessings of the past (2 Peter 1:3–4).

The apostle called to the attention of his readers the exceeding great and precious gifts from God to them through Jesus Christ. These two verses are a spiritual treasure chest that reveal the blessings that God has bestowed on believers through Jesus Christ. The generosity of God's provisions for his children is magnified and emphasized.

- A. *"All things that pertain unto life and godliness."* In Christ Jesus, believers have received everything necessary for experiencing the abundant life. It is unnecessary for them to turn to any other teacher or discipline in order to be all God would have them to be.
- B. *"Through the knowledge of him that hath called us to glory and virtue."* Through the beauty and the glory of the life and character of Jesus Christ, God calls all people to himself. The initiative belongs with God. Salvation is of the Lord. The human response to the gospel is a voluntary commitment of faith that makes possible the bestowal of these divine gifts.
- C. *"The exceeding great and precious promises."* The Bible is a record of God's promises to his people. The Old Testament contains a continuing series of promises concerning the Messiah who was to come. Peter had witnessed the fulfillment of these exceeding great and precious promises in the person and life of Jesus Christ.

  Jesus made many promises to his disciples. We will greatly enrich our spiritual life and deepen our faith if we will discover these promises, claim them for our own, and move forward depending on the Lord to keep his promises as people of faith have done in the past.
- D. *"That by these ye might be partakers of the divine nature."* Faith in the promises of God makes possible the new birth. The new birth does not produce a divinity in people, but it does mean that the divine character, the divine nature, has been imparted in embryonic form. This new nature provides

389

the believer with the possibility of experiencing and demonstrating the holiness, the tenderness, the gentleness, and the power of God.

By every means at our command, we should cooperate with the Holy Spirit as he seeks to develop the new nature that came to us in the miracle of the new birth.

E. *"Having escaped the corruption that is in the world through lust."* Through their experience with Jesus Christ, believers receive the potential for complete deliverance from the powerful evil forces that work in the world. Christ has granted forgiveness from sin. He provides spiritual power to overcome the contaminating presence of evil in the world. Through faith in him and through obedience to him, we can be victorious over the assaults of the devil.

II. The opportunity of the future (2 Peter 1:5–7).

The gift of new life has been given to those who had put faith in the promises of God. This new life is like a divine seed that needs to be developed by earnest care. Spiritual growth will not take place automatically or accidentally. Peter encouraged his readers to hasten with all diligence to cooperate with the Spirit of God in developing the beautiful graces that are associated with spiritual maturity.

As we enter a new year, we should give careful consideration to these words of encouragement from the apostle Peter.

A. *"Giving all diligence, add to your faith."* Faith is the human response to God's grace that makes possible the gift of new life. Faith is the basic foundation for all spiritual growth and service.

Peter challenged his readers to supplement their faith with the Christian graces that are needed for fruitful Christian living. Seemingly, each of the graces mentioned grows out of the preceding grace. The word translated "add" probably would be more correctly translated by the word "supply." This word was used by the Greeks to describe the actions of those who provided financial resources for the production of the great plays and dramas. It was also used for the action of furnishing the provisions and supplies for an army. Peter declared that Christians are to supplement their faith with these virtues, which are actually the pieces of equipment needed for the living of a genuine Christian life.

The apostle gives us a blueprint for spiritual progress.

B. *In your faith supply virtue.* Faith makes possible the power by which virtue is to be developed. The word *virtue* means courage, moral excellence, noble character. It is not tame and passive; it is active, aggressive, and on the march.

C. *To virtue supply knowledge.* In the practice of virtue an effort is put forth to gain knowledge, which is practical skill in choosing the right and refusing the wrong. To secure this knowledge, one must make a diligent study of God's Word.

D. *To knowledge supply temperance or self-control.* Self-restraint enables one to curb his evil impulses and resist the lures of sin in the world that surrounds him. Each person must be in command of his own moods and impulses, or his life will end in ruin.

E. *To temperance supply patience.* The grace needed is endurance, steadfastness, fortitude, perseverance. Patience is that attitude of determination that enables one to stay under the load until the victory is won.

F. *And to patience add godliness.* Godliness is that trait that characterizes the life of one who lives continually "as seeing him who is invisible." Perhaps this grace refers to the growth of the divine nature received in the new birth.

G. *To godliness supply brotherly kindness.* The life of reverence for God is issued in brotherly kindness. The genuine worship of God will affect one's attitude toward fellow human beings (1 John 4:20).

H. *To brotherly kindness supply love.* The crown of Christian graces is love. Paul affirmed that love is the chief gift of the Holy Spirit (1 Cor. 13:13). It was concerning Peter's love that the Lord had inquired (John 21:15–17). Peter recognized and commended the believer's love for Christ (1 Peter 1:8) and encouraged love within the Christian brotherhood (1 Peter 1:22).

Conclusion

The apostle Peter was concerned that his readers experience the benefits that flow from spiritual maturity. He was eager that they escape the tragic results of persistent immaturity (1 Peter 2:8–9).

By adding, or supplying, Christian graces, believers will be assured that they can avoid both idleness and unfruitfulness in their experience of salvation through Christ. Peter declared that he who does not put forth a sincere effort to grow toward Christlikeness is blind. This term most likely refers to a state of mind that is alienated from spiritual reality. The phrase "cannot see afar off" refers to a condition of shortsightedness. The picture is that of a man who is squinting his eyes because of the light. Consequently, he is greatly limited in forming a true perspective concerning the things that really matter. In contrast to these conditions, it is inferred that the believer who strives for growth will experience meaningful activity, fruitful productivity, and spiritual insight into the meaning of life.

We are approaching the end of another year in the journey of life. The past is gone. Nothing can be done concerning the past except to admit and to confess past failures. The future is before us. With God's help, let each of us respond to the apostle's challenge for the future.

SUNDAY MORNING, DECEMBER 30

Title: A Call to Christian Consecration for the New Year

Text: "But you were washed, you were sanctified, you were justified in the name of the Lord Jesus Christ and by the Spirit of our God" (**1 Cor. 6:11 NIV**).

Scripture Reading: 1 Corinthians 6:11–18

Hymns: "Joyful, Joyful, We Adore Thee," Van Dyke

"How Sweet the Name of Jesus Sounds," Newton

"Onward, Christian Soldiers," Gould

Offertory Prayer: Our Father, as the old year is passing and the new year is dawning, we pause before your throne of grace to thank you for all your mercies showered upon us during the past year. You have been gracious to us, giving us health and strength for life's living. We thank you for these and all other blessings that are too numerous to name. At the same time, Father, we ask your guidance for the coming year. We know that there will be trials and temptations along the way, and we will need the power of your Spirit to give direction to our footsteps. Now we come before you with our tithes and offerings, laying them at your feet in an act of personal dedication to your great kingdom cause. Accept our tithes and offerings and use them in your kingdom's service. We offer this prayer in the name of Christ our Savior. Amen.

Introduction

Suppose you were to go to the ticket window of your local airport and say, "I want a ticket." The clerk would ask, "To where, sir?" And you would say, "Well, anywhere; for what places do you have tickets?" The ticket salesperson would say immediately, "How stupid! You'll never get anywhere, because you don't know where you want to go." Too often we approach the new year in just that fashion — without goals and without sound resolutions. Before us spread in panoramic view, yet with a deep veil separating us, is a whole new year of adventuresome living. Spiritually, we should and can see a great breakthrough into many hearts that are steeped in the blackness of sin as they come to know Christ as Savior and Lord and thus come into the sunshine of his saving grace.

For us as individuals it can be the greatest year yet if:

I. We resolve to make this the most wonderful year yet.

It should be a wonderful year because:

A. *You have a wonderful relationship with the Lord of all life, Jesus Christ.*

1. We must know him as Savior by a personal encounter without which there is no knowledge of him. "Except a man be born again, he cannot see the kingdom of God" (John 3:3).

2. We must know him intimately through day-to-day fellowship with him. A dear saint once said to her pastor, "Pastor, I could not get through a

day without an active fellowship with my Master. I am constantly in an attitude of prayer."

    3. We must know him as Lord of our daily lives. We should make no decisions without first consulting our Master; we should wait for his instructions and leadership each day of our lives.

B. *You have a thrilling anticipation of what lies ahead.* We ought to be spiritually excited about the new year and what can be accomplished for the Lord.

C. *You have a system to harness your enthusiasm for the coming year.* Here are three ways you can harness your enthusiasm and cause it to produce for you during the coming year:

    1. Write down the things that you want to accomplish during the coming year, numbering them "1, 2, 3," and so on, thus having down in black and white something definite toward which to work.

    2. Study your job, its requirements, its possibilities, and its potential for at least one hour each day for five days a week. If you will do this honestly, you probably will be looked on as an expert in your field within five or six years.

    3. Spend at least thirty minutes per day in deep meditation concerning ideas for the improvement of your job, jotting down at least a half dozen or so of these ideas. Perhaps at the end of the week, you will discover that out of the many ideas jotted down there will be at least one great idea that will carry you forward in your work.

Most of these ideas just enumerated have concerned themselves with secular life. As Christians we could well afford to carry out these ideas for self-improvement. The Christian faith is in a time of great competition with ideologies that grab the imagination of the youth of our land. We need to know our weaknesses, our strengths, and the best methods of communicating our faith.

II. We resolve that we will live positively this year.

A. *Endeavor to control life and not to let it control you.* In the face of calamities, endeavor to turn catastrophes into blessings.

B. *Do not wait for your wishes and dreams to come true.* Go out and face life head-on, and help those dreams and visions to come true. Young William Carey, a shoe cobbler of England, wanted to do more for missions in India. He heard a harsh rebuke: "Sit down young man; when the Lord gets ready to save the heathen, he will do it without your help." William Carey thought otherwise and packed up and went to India to tell the unsaved about Jesus Christ's saving power.

C. *Venture out, dare, live thrillingly as Christians.* Desiring to see the lost people of our community come to know Christ personally, let us dare to believe that they can be won if we are willing to be Christ's missionaries carrying the good news of his love for the lost.

We would like to see our church be able to meet all of its obligations in the support of the great mission undertaking and in its local areas of need. Let us determine to bring into the Lord's storehouse a tithe of our income.

III. We resolve that we are going to be better people than we were last year.

A. *As a nation, we seem to be facing anarchy.* There is on every hand a breakdown in law and order, a breakdown in morality, psychological confusion, and spiritual ignorance and indifference. We need new life in our nation. The only way to obtain this is for individuals in our nation to find new life in Christ Jesus.

B. *As individuals, we can expect to have a better year only by being better people.* We can be better people only if we will surrender to the saving power of Christ Jesus. If we are already Christians, we can be better people only if we let Christ truly be Lord of our lives.

Conclusion

At the end of the old year and at the beginning of the new year, let us make spiritual resolutions that will be meaningful to our lives and to the lives of those around us. Let us look toward the upcoming year with a high degree of spiritual expectancy, seeing the next twelve months as a challenge. You will have opportunities for witnessing for Christ such as you have never had before. Let our motto during the coming year be, "For me to live is Christ" (Phil. 1:21).

SUNDAY EVENING, DECEMBER 30

Title: Missionary Adversaries

Text: "For Herod will seek the young child to destroy him" **(Matt. 2:13)**.

Scripture Reading: Matthew 2:7–15

Introduction

While there was great rejoicing in many hearts when Jesus was born in Bethlehem, King Herod sought to destroy him. Herod feared that Jesus would be a threat to his ruling authority. Therefore, while pretending to the wise men that he wanted to worship Jesus, in reality he wanted to learn where Jesus was so he could have him killed.

This attitude of Herod's is often the attitude the unbelieving world today shows toward Jesus. Somehow ungodly people seem to feel that the teachings of Jesus are a threat to their happiness and success in life. This attitude often leads people who otherwise are good citizens to oppose any missionary effort.

I. Christ's adversaries.

During the public ministry of Christ on earth, he was confronted on many occasions by adversaries who sought to stop or change his ministry.

A. *The religious leaders were one group that sought to stop his teaching and preaching.* In Mark 2:1–12 we are told of the miracle of Jesus healing a man sick with palsy. When the sick man had been let down through the roof, Jesus said to him, "Son, thy sins be forgiven thee" (v. 5). Then the scribes showed their opposition by asking, "Why doth this man thus speak blasphemies? who can forgive sins but God only?" They, like the unbelieving world today, refused to believe that Jesus was God incarnate and could therefore forgive sins.

B. *The civil authorities also opposed Jesus.* Our text tells us that at the birth of Jesus, "Herod [would] seek the young child to destroy him."

When Jesus was on trial before Pilate, he was accused by the chief priests and elders. Matthew 27:18 says that during the trial of Jesus, Pilate knew that for envy they had delivered Jesus, and when Pilate could find no fault in Jesus, he washed his hands before the multitude saying, "I am innocent of the blood of this just person." Even though Pilate could find no fault with Jesus, he turned Jesus over to be crucified. His opposition to Jesus was not because he found wrong in him but because his teachings and mighty works had created disorder in his kingdom. Rather than do the right thing, Pilate decided to let Jesus be crucified.

II. Persecutors have sought to stop missionary advance.

From the beginning of the Christian movement, various individuals, groups, and even nations have allied themselves together to stem the missionary spread of the gospel of Christ.

A. *Religious leaders sought to stop the missionary work of Christians.* When the power of the Holy Spirit fell on the assembled Christians on the day of Pentecost and the Christians began to speak in foreign languages, Acts 2:12–13 tells us, "They were all amazed, and were in doubt, saying one to another, What meaneth this? Others mocking said, These men are full of new wine." Peter then preached a great sermon and three thousand souls were converted.

A few days later, Peter and John healed a crippled beggar who was laid daily at the gate of the temple that is called Beautiful. After the miracle, Peter again preached to the people who came together in amazement at the miracle. Then in Acts 4 we see that the priests, the captain of the temple, and the Sadducees were upset that they preached the missionary gospel of Christ, so they put them in jail until the next day. Their crime was preaching the missionary gospel of Christ. Many other religious leaders did the same.

B. *Political rulers also tried to stop the missionary spread of the gospel.* Saul, with letters from the ruling authorities, went to Damascus to hunt down Christian men and women and bring them bound to Jerusalem. The Lord himself intervened in this and converted Saul to Christ while he journeyed to Damascus.

In Acts 12:1–4 we read where Herod killed James the apostle. When he saw it pleased the Jews, he took Peter also and threw him in jail and kept him there, intending to bring him out for public trial after the Passover. This means that he probably meant to kill Peter. Again God miraculously intervened in answer to the prayers of his people and delivered Peter from prison with an angel's help.

There were ten major persecutions of the early church beginning in AD 67 under the reign of Emperor Nero and continuing intermittently until the last one began in AD 303.

III. Christian failures have hindered missionary work.

While outside forces have made strong attacks on the missionary efforts of the church, perhaps failures within the church have been the biggest adversary of Christian missions.

A. *The lack of dynamic personal witnessing on the part of every Christian has been a constant adversary to the missionary spread of the gospel.*

B. *Worldly living by Christians or failure to live the Christ-controlled life has caused Christians to lack zeal in missions.*

C. *Disunity among Christians has been a big adversary to world missions.* One of the greatest spiritual revivals of all time occurred in the beginning of the early church. The people had prayed together in one accord and then the Holy Spirit came and filled all of them, and all began to witness as missionary fires burned brightly. Thousands were converted to Christ. Throughout history it has been true that anytime a church or a denomination gets together, prays together, and begins to witness together, God's Holy Spirit comes in great power and the missionary witnessing of God's people brings thousands to know Christ as personal Savior.

Conclusion

World missions will always have adversaries, but God will always give an increase, and missions will grow when God's people are willing to live the Christ-controlled life.

MISCELLANEOUS HELPS

MESSAGES ON THE LORD'S SUPPER

Title: The Bread of Heaven

Text: "Jesus declared, 'I am the bread of life. He who comes to me will never go hungry, and he who believes in me will never be thirsty'" (**John 6:35 NIV**).

Scripture Reading: 1 Corinthians 11:20–29

Introduction

Our text is taken from the great "Bread" chapter in the gospel of John. The words that Jesus spoke concerning his flesh and his blood were treated as offensive by his Jewish listeners (John 6:52). Jesus affirmed, "Unless you eat the flesh of the Son of Man and drink his blood, you have no life in you. Whoever eats my flesh and drinks my blood has eternal life, and I will raise him up at the last day. For my flesh is real food and my blood is real drink" (John 6:53–55 NIV).

Jesus' words have been taken literally by Roman Catholics. They believe that in the Mass the elements literally become the flesh and blood of the Savior. Evangelical Christians believe that Christ is speaking significantly but in symbolic terms. This belief is based on John 6:63: "The Spirit gives life; the flesh counts for nothing. The words I have spoken to you are spirit and they are life" (NIV).

I. The flesh of Jesus' humanity (John 1:1).

The Christ was affirming his humanity. He was expressing the necessity for a proper recognition with both the mind and the heart of what God was doing in the incarnation. He was trying to communicate to his listeners the great truth that the eternal God had clothed himself in human flesh and was dwelling on earth among people.

II. The blood of Jesus' sacrificial death.

Our Lord was making reference to the fact that he had come on a mission to give his life as a sacrifice for the sins of a guilty world. In instituting the Lord's Supper, our Lord did not encourage us to remember his birth, his boyhood, his baptism, or the beauty of his life. Instead, he focused the minds of his followers on his sacrificial and atoning death on the cross. We enter into a right relationship with God, not through following his noble example, but through a trust in his substitutionary and atoning death on the cross and a commitment to his living presence as he reveals himself as the Victor over death and the grave.

III. The meaning of eating Jesus' flesh and drinking his blood.

Our Lord was not referring to a literal consumption of his body. Instead, he was affirming the necessity of his disciples completely assimilating into their being both his humanity and his sacrificial death for their sins. As we eat physical food for the nourishment of our physical body, even so we assimilate into our minds and hearts the great truths of his coming, his dying on the cross, and his living again. In this manner, we do indeed "eat the flesh of the Son of Man and drink his blood."

IV. It is the Spirit that gives life.

Simply to consume the elements of the Lord's Supper brings no blessing at all to the participant in this sacred ceremony of worship. There is nothing magic or supernatural about the bread and the fruit of the vine. They are but symbols of the humanity of God in the person of Jesus Christ and his suffering and death on the cross for us.

Conclusion

As we partake of the Lord's Supper, let us remember that Christ himself is the Host and we are the guests. We sit at his table by his invitation. As we focus on Calvary, we can assimilate into our being the significance of what took place there. By so doing, we can nourish our spiritual life, deepen our devotion to our Lord, and increase our sense of obligation to him. We should rededicate our lives to his purposes for us. Let us pray that such might be the case with each participant as we now partake of the elements of the Lord's Supper.

Title: The Love of God

Text: "But God commendeth his love toward us, in that, while we were yet sinners, Christ died for us" (**Rom. 5:8**).

Scripture Reading: Romans 5

Introduction

Today we approach the observance of the Lord's Supper with reverence and with a prayer that we might be filled with holy awe as we partake of the elements that symbolize the humanity of our Savior and his sacrificial death on the cross for our sins.

Our Lord instituted this rite at the Passover feast, a commemoration of the deliverance of the Israelites from the bondage and slavery of Egypt. Jesus gave the elements of this feast new significance. The Lord's Supper was to be a celebration of and a memorial to his sacrificial death on the cross for our deliverance from the slavery and penalty of sin.

With imagination inspired by the Holy Spirit, let us journey to Calvary. At Calvary we see our sin revealed in its awful ugliness, because it was our sin that required that Jesus die that we might be forgiven and delivered. Here we see the tremendous sacrifice that was made that we might receive forgiveness. At the cross, we see the supreme revelation of the love of God spoken of in our text. Let us focus on the cross as we observe the Lord's Supper.

I. The fact of God's love is demonstrated.

While evidences of God's plan and design and power are revealed in nature, it is only in Jesus Christ that we come to a recognition of God's great love for a rebellious race. God gave his Son for our salvation.

II. The nature of God's love is discovered.

God's love is a love that suffers and sacrifices in order to save. God's love gives and forgives and keeps on giving. God's love gave the highest and best for us when we did not deserve it.

III. The purpose of God's love is disclosed (John 3:16).

Christ died for our sins. Christ gave up his life for the spiritually dead that we might receive the gift of eternal life through faith in what he did on the cross on our behalf.

IV. The time of God's love is declared.

The apostle Paul affirms that "God commendeth his love toward us, in that while we were yet sinners, Christ died for us." The death of Jesus Christ on the cross did not secure for us the love of God. He loved us prior to the crucifixion. His love is eternal. It was his love for us while we were yet rebellious sinners that caused him to give his Son Jesus Christ to die on the cross for us.

God did not wait until we were lovely before demonstrating his love. In indescribable love, God took the initiative. By the gift of his Son and by the sufferings of his Son, the heavenly Father would woo his way into the hearts of people that he might deliver them from a bondage far worse than that which the Israelites experienced as slaves in Egypt.

Conclusion

Let us concentrate our mind and our affections on Jesus Christ, remembering how he suffered and died for us. Let us fill our deepest being with an awareness of the value that God has placed on us and rejoice in his love. Let us decide now to live in grateful service because of the greatness of his love for us and because that love extends to others.

MESSAGES FOR CHILDREN AND YOUNG PEOPLE

Title: Winning the Crown

Text: "Do you not know that in a race all the runners run, but only one gets the prize? Run in such a way as to get the prize" (**1 Cor. 9:24 NIV**).

Scripture Reading: 1 Corinthians 9:24–10:12

Introduction

To excel in any area, one must discipline himself against spending his strength on other things. This is true in the world of Christian discipleship as well as in the world of sports. Revelation pictures the end of time in terms of people casting their crowns before the Lord. This means that they were able to lay before Christ their lives crowned with victory and faithfulness. Paul tells us how one wins such a crown.

I. Desire it fervently (1 Cor. 9:24–25).

A. *Desire it because it is incorruptible.* In Greek athletic games, the winners received a garland of ivy that soon faded and lost its beauty, finally falling apart. The crown of which Paul speaks is an everlasting crown that never decays.

B. *Desire it because it is handed out by God.* In the Greek athletic games, only one person won the prize, but in the Christian life every person can win the prize if he or she desires it fervently enough. In Revelation 2:10 we read, "Be faithful, even to the point of death, and I will give you the crown of life" (NIV).

II. Prepare earnestly for the race of life (1 Cor. 9:25).

A. *Prepare in all aspects of life.* In the Isthmian games held every two years in Greece, each man had to show proof that he had trained ten months and that he had attended the gymnasium daily for the past thirty days. After a victor was crowned, his native city usually tore a breach in the town walls through which he entered upon his return in an effort to say that such a city needed no protection with a citizen like him residing in it.

B. *Prepare consistently because of the prize.* Many people don't care enough about a fully crowned life to prepare for it. Yet it is life's most valuable prize. It can be yours only by accepting daily responsibility and performing that daily responsibility faithfully. In Matthew 11:28 Jesus challenges us to take his yoke upon ourselves, to make him our Teacher, and to follow his way of life and thereby prepare for the prize.

III. Run for the prize (1 Cor. 9:26–27).

A. *Run with all you have.* Paul challenges us to take life seriously. He explains that his struggle in life is not to be construed as some type of shadow boxing. Life's battle is real for him (1 Cor. 9:26–27). He brings every area of his life under strict discipline lest he should be considered a castaway (lest he forfeit his place of service in God's vineyard).

B. *Run with no presumption.* Paul continues the same thought in 1 Corinthians 10, where he discusses the presumptuous sins of the children of Israel. They disqualified themselves because they failed to discipline themselves. In speaking of the Israelites, Paul explains that although the whole multitude had the same experiences and the same opportunities, they were not all well-pleasing to God. We must learn from their failures lest we make the same mistakes (1 Cor. 10:6). Once the Israelites had disqualified themselves, God had to wait for a whole new generation before he could continue his work through them. The rest were doomed to live out their lives wandering in the wilderness.

Conclusion

Paul won the prize in his personal battle of life. We hear him say to Timothy toward the end of his life: "Henceforth there is laid up for me a crown of righteousness." Paul, who won the crown, tells us that we too may have it if we desire it fervently, prepare earnestly, and run life's race with all our strength.

Title: Facing the Facts of Life

Text: " 'Enter through the narrow gate. For wide is the gate and broad is the road that leads to destruction, and many enter through it. But small is the gate and narrow the road that leads to life, and only a few find it' " (**Matt. 7:13–14 NIV**).

Scripture Reading: Matthew 7:13–24

Introduction

There is a great deal of talk about when young people should be told the facts of life. As important as this may be, there is a set of spiritual facts of life that is much more urgent.

When any issue is at stake, you can take one of two approaches: you can pretend there is no issue, or you can take an honest look at it, realizing that such a look may see you in a bad light, may find you in great need, and may indeed demand a great deal from you.

At this point in the Sermon on the Mount, Jesus begins his conclusion and in effect says, "I have explained my kingdom; now what are you going to do about it?" He challenges us with a certain summary of the basic facts of life.

I. There are two ways of life (Matt. 7:13–14; see also Deut. 30:19; Jer. 21:8).

    A. *The broad way.* This often is thought to be the way of freedom. Today more than ever before, humankind has thrown off all bonds of religious awe, and now people are not happy with their newfound freedom but have discovered it rather to be a curse.

        It was the broad way that allured the prodigal son to the unhappiest experiences of his life. For a description of the broad way, one has but to read the newspapers. Their daily copy reveals those things for which people are prepared to risk their eternal souls.

    B. *The narrow way.* This is the way marked off by Christ. To walk the narrow way is to live the Christian life. This is the way set out in the Sermon on the Mount. This is a way that provides a real legacy for one's children.

The Beatitudes set out this way by describing the life of the happy person, the one who has found fullness and meaning in life.

II. There are two final destinies.

Often during political campaigns, voters are heard to say that they feel a frustration because there seems to be no real choice they can make. This is not true with regard to spiritual matters that determine final destinies. Only a fool would spend a lifetime on the road of life and never stop to ask where he was going.

A. *There is a heaven.* The Bible pictures heaven in terms of a place of unhampered life where the fullness that God intended will be experienced. It is a place where there are no fleshly limitations and no destructiveness of sin (Rev. 21:1–4).

B. *There is a hell.* This is described in the Scripture as a place of outer darkness where there is eternal sorrow and regret. The greatest earthly similarity that Jesus could use to describe hell was that of a city dump where the maggots never died and the fires never stopped burning.

III. The crowd cannot be trusted (Matt. 7:13–14).

The broad way is filled with the multitudes, but it is the way of destruction. The narrow way to life is not crowded. Often one must travel alone on the narrow way.

The crowd becomes a Judas goat that leads the unthinking multitudes to the slaughter just as the stockyards use a Judas goat to lead animals to their death by calming them with the innocent ringing of the bell about the goat's neck.

In the German war camps, hundreds of Jews were led to death under the guise of going to take a shower. Once inside the building, they learned too late that the shower outlets spewed forth poisonous gas. Likewise, Satan uses the allurement of the world to disguise his deadly game of death.

IV. You must decide for yourself.

A. *You already are in the broad way.* You do not have to do anything to be unemployed. It comes quite naturally by growing up without ever taking a job. Neither do you have to do anything to travel the broad way. It is where you will automatically find yourself. Life becomes a great conveyor belt that moves you along through life by the tide of the multitudes on the broad way. Once an age of accountability is reached so that you recognize your plight, indecision becomes fatal (Rom. 3:10, 19, 23).

B. *Getting off the broad way takes action.* To be saved a person must step from the broad way through faith in Jesus Christ. To trust in Christ is a solitary and lonely decision whereby mental assent gives way to positive commitment (Rom. 10:8–10; Josh. 24:15).

V. Some day it will be too late.

At any moment, the angels may well raise the trumpets to their lips and sound the clarion call that marks the end of time. If this does not happen within our lifetime, then the quiet footsteps of death mark our last opportunity. Either way, time is brief and opportunity is fleeting.

In Luke 13:24–25 Jesus warns that there will come a time when the master of the house will shut the door, forever precluding the entrance of anyone else. Life's only real option is to walk the narrow way through faith in Christ.

Conclusion

The longer you wait, the further apart become the broad and narrow ways. Sins have a way of stacking up and entangling their victims more securely day by day. Recognize now the abyss that lies on either side and at the end of the broad way. To step from the broad way to Jesus Christ is to step from death to life.

Title: What Is Life?

Text: "What is your life? You are a mist that appears for a little while and then vanishes" **(James 4:14 NIV)**.

Scripture Reading: James 4:13–17

Introduction

A number of years ago there was a very popular television program called *This Is Your Life.* The program portrayed the highlights of some important person's life. The Bible suggests that we take such a look at our life ahead of time rather than after it is over.

I. The content of the question.

Life has many aspects. It is composed of happiness and tragedy, of feasting and fasting. Even the breath of life is itself a great mystery.

Life is viewed differently by different age groups. To the aged patriarch whose life is well spent, his life has a different hue than to a young child on his mother's lap. The rich and powerful see life from a different vantage point than do those who have been doomed to poverty and drudgery all their lives.

Life is conflicted with many temptations. Everyone has his own secret temptations and his own peculiar weaknesses that he must fight. He has his own anxieties and fears. He is forever tempted to make nothing more of life than having plenty to eat and a place to sleep.

In spite of life's many facets, there is one ingredient necessary if life is to have meaning—the spiritual ingredient, God's will for your life.

II. The context of the question.

The context of the question is a misplaced confidence (James 4:13, 15). We are forever placing too much confidence in our own planning. We think that it is our carefully laid plans that make the world go round. If we are not careful, our plans will become the center of all of our thoughts and efforts. Such a misplaced confidence causes us to make many foolish decisions. It opens to us the danger of so totally planning our own lives that we actually let life pass us by without ever knowing it. We all are related to the rich farmer described in the gospel of Luke who forgot that death could separate him from all the tomorrows and from all of his full barns.

III. The corrective to the question (James 4:15).

There is only one answer to a misplaced confidence: "You ought to say, 'If it is the Lord's will, we will live and do this or that'" (NIV). Instead of placing confidence in ourselves, we need to learn to place our confidence in God, seeking his will as we make our plans.

The secret to life is learning to live it dependently, placing trust in God. This means we turn our future plans over to God and learn the joy of living day by day in his will. Since tomorrow belongs to God, we do well to seek the place in life he wants us to fill tomorrow.

Our lives tomorrow will be the sum of all our yesterdays. The drug addict and the alcoholic are but shadows of what God intended them to be. They did not arrive at that condition instantaneously. They got there as a result of a long line of yesterdays.

Imagine the confusion that would result if the architect of a house had one plan and the contractor had another. The whole procedure would be a line of conflicts. Walls would be built in the wrong places and would have to be torn down. Thus, we see the need of God being the architect who supplies the plans for our lives.

IV. The conclusion of the question.

The only way in which all the aspects of life can be fitted together is through a faith commitment to Jesus Christ.

Human beings are made in the image of God, are responsible to God, and are never content until they experience fellowship with God.

Conclusion

Life is what you allow God to make it. If you choose to hold your life apart from God, it not only will be as brief as the morning mist but also as useless. Along with the gift of life comes the message of the gospel wherein Jesus reminds us that if we seek to save our lives we will lose them. Life is meaningful only as we lose our lives in service to him.

FUNERAL MEDITATIONS

Title: The Doctrine of Death

Text: "Brothers, we do not want you to be ignorant about those who fall asleep, or to grieve like the rest of men, who have no hope" (**1 Thess. 4:13 NIV**).

Scripture Reading: 1 Corinthians 15

Introduction

Dr. Elton Trueblood suggested that in the Christian life it is not possible to have fruits unless we have roots. The fragrant flowers of Christian comfort do not grow without the roots of truth. There are many doctrinal roots in the Bible. We speak of the doctrines of God, of salvation, of faith, of works, of baptism, and so on. There is also a doctrine of death. The discovery and acceptance of this doctrine of death provides a root system for stability and productiveness in the storms. One can find the doctrine of death throughout the Bible but especially in 1 Corinthians 15, the resurrection chapter.

I. Death is inevitable.

"For this corruptible must put on incorruption, and this mortal must put on immortality" (1 Cor. 15:53). It is not morbid to accept the fact that all die. It is honest. Someone has suggested that the death rate is the same the world over — one death per person. "It is appointed unto men once to die" (Heb. 9:27), and there is no breaking of the appointment.

II. Death is inexplicable.

"Listen, I tell you a mystery" (1 Cor. 15:51 NIV). Here "mystery" refers to that which can be known only by those who have been initiated. When we are initiated into Christ, a new dimension is added to our knowledge. But when all the books have been written and the songs have been sung and the sermons have been preached, death is still a mystery. There are some things we do not understand about it and therefore cannot explain. To accept this fact is to be on our way to comfort.

III. Death is intermediate.

"We shall not all sleep, but we shall all be changed" (1 Cor. 15:51). The Bible teaches that there is more after this earthly life. Death is not the end; it is the entrance. It is not a destiny; it is a door. Job asked, "If a man die, shall he live again?" (Job 14:14). A thousand voices answer in the affirmative.

IV. Death can be tragic.

"If only for this life we have hope in Christ, we are to be pitied more than all men" (1 Cor. 15:19 NIV). We live in a world whose daily diary is punctuated by tragedy. It screams to us through the news media. But the supreme tragedy is to live and die and go into eternity without God. A tragic death really is not determined by the manner of one's going but by his spiritual unpreparedness at his going.

V. Death can be triumphant.

"Thanks be to God! He gives us the victory through our Lord Jesus Christ" (1 Cor. 15:57 NIV). It is here that all the lights of Christ's own resurrection are turned on for us. He arose victoriously, and we will follow in his course. It is not easy to distinguish the picture of a sunset from a picture of a sunrise. To the unbeliever, death is a sunset; but to the Christian, it is a sunrise.

Conclusion

Our victory over death, with all its appalling haunts, fear, and heartaches, is in Christ Jesus our Lord.

Title: My Departure

Text: "For I am now ready to be offered, and the time of my departure is at hand" (**2 Tim. 4:6**).

Scripture Reading: 2 Timothy 4

Introduction

In the Bible death is pictured in many figures of speech. It is the breaking of a bowl, the breaking of the pitcher at the cistern, the loosing of the silver cord, and the withering of a flower.

Here in our text there is another meaningful figure to describe the death of a Christian. Paul came to the end of the way and thus described his own passing from this world. He used the word *departure*. We understand that in Paul's world the word was used in at least four ways.

I. It described the release of an animal from its burden.

The ox was hitched to pull a cart or plow. The donkey bore a burden on its back. When the day was over or the task was completed, the animal had the load disconnected or the burdens removed. Paul said that death is like that. The burdens of this life are heavy, and the journey is often long and exacting. The worker gets tired, and the traveler grows weary.

Then the Master comes and lifts the burden and takes away the load. We love to think that our friend in whose memory this worship service is held has been blessed by the visitation of the Master and the release from the tasks well done.

II. It described the shedding of bonds and fetters by a prisoner.

Prisoners often were kept in chains or stocks for long periods of time. Their wrists and ankles were rubbed raw by these crude restraining devices.

But then would come a day of release. The chains and shackles would be removed and the prisoner would go free. Paul used the idea to describe a Christian's death. This life always has its restraints. The flesh is a house, and sometimes it becomes a prison house. To a Christian, death is not only an entrance into the "house not made with hands," but it is the exit from this physical house, the frailties and restraints of which are very real to us. Death is the release, the opening of the jail doors, the removal of all restraints, so that the real person may be free.

III. It described the untying of the ropes of a tent when it was taken down for removal to another site.

Paul was a tentmaker and knew how the word was used. He spoke of life, not as a permanent structure, but as a tent. "Now we know that if the earthly tent we live in is destroyed, we have a building from God, an eternal house in heaven, not built by human hands" (2 Cor. 5:1 NIV).

There comes a day when the tent has served its purpose in its present location. It must move on. It is taken down and made ready for the new location. To Paul, this was death. For those who die in the Lord, death is not annihilation; it is moving to a new home.

IV. It described the untying of the ropes that held a ship in port.

When a ship came into port, it was secured with ropes and remained tied until it was unloaded and then reloaded with new cargo. When departure time came, the ropes that secured the ship were untied so that the ship could move out of the harbor to its new destination.

Paul knew the language of the sea. To him his own death was but a time when the ship of his life was loosed so that he might move out and make his way to the final port. This is what death is to the Christian. The idea is put beautifully by an unknown author in the following:

> I stand upon the sea shore. A ship at my side spreads her white sails to the morning breeze and moves softly out to the blue ocean. She is an object of beauty and strength. I stand and look at her until at length she hangs like a speck of white cloud just where the sea and sky come down to mingle with one another.
>
> Then someone at my side exclaims, "Look, she's gone!"
>
> Gone where? Gone from my sight, that is all. She is just as large in mast and hull as she ever was. Her diminished size lies in me, not her. And at the very moment when someone at my side exclaims, "Look, she's gone," there are other eyes eagerly watching her approach, and other voices ready to take up the glad shout, "Look, she's coming home!"
>
> And that is death.

WEDDINGS

Title: Three Things That Will Last Forever

Holy and happy is the sacred hour when two devoted hearts are bound by the enchanting ties of matrimony. Marriage is an institution of divine appointment and is commended as honorable among all. Marriage is God's first institution for the welfare of the race. In the quiet bowers of Eden, before the forbidden tree had yielded its fateful fruit or the tempter had touched the world, God saw that it was not good for the man to be alone. He made a helpmate suitable for him and established the rite of marriage while heavenly hosts witnessed the wonderful scene in reverence.

The contract of marriage was sanctioned and honored by the presence and power of Jesus at the marriage in Cana of Galilee and marked the beginning of his wondrous works. It is declared by the apostle Paul to be honorable among all. So it is ordained that a man shall leave his father and mother and cleave unto his wife, and the two shall be one flesh, united in hopes and aims and sentiments until death alone shall part them.

(The minister should now ask, "Who gives this woman in marriage?")

Faith, hope, and love form the foundation for a happy and successful marriage. To be abundantly happy, you will need something in addition to romantic attraction for each other. Happy indeed will be your marriage if you will determine to let it be characterized by those great qualities that will last forever. Let us read Paul's description of the kind of love that you need in marriage to help you walk through the higher halls of human happiness throughout the balance of your life together. (At this point read 1 Corinthians 13:1–13, preferably from a modern translation.)

If ye, then, _____ (Groom), and _____ (Bride), after careful consideration and in the fear of God, have deliberately chosen each other as partners in this holy estate and know of no just cause why you should not be so united, in token thereof you will please join your right hands.

Groom's Vow

_____ , wilt thou have this woman to be thy wedded wife, to live together after God's ordinance in the holy estate of matrimony? Wilt thou love her, comfort her, honor and keep her in sickness and in health, and forsaking all others keep thee only unto her as long as ye both shall live?

Answer: I will.

Bride's Vow

_____ , wilt thou have this man to be thy wedded husband, to live together after God's ordinance in the holy estate of matrimony? Wilt thou love him, honor him, and keep him in sickness and in health, and forsaking all others keep thee only unto him as long as ye both shall live?

Answer: I will.

Vows to Each Other

I, _____ (Groom), take thee, _____ (Bride), to be my wedded wife, to have and to hold from this day forward, in prosperity or adversity, in sickness or in health, in advances or reverses, to love and to cherish till death do us part, according to God's holy ordinance, and thereto I pledge thee my faith.

I, _____ (Bride), take thee, _____ (Groom), to be my wedded husband, to have and to hold from this day forward, in prosperity or adversity, in sickness or in health, in advances or reverses, to love and to cherish till death do us part, according to God's holy ordinance, and thereto I pledge thee my faith.

Then are ye each given to the other for richer or poorer, for better or worse, in sickness and in health, till death alone shall part you.

From time immemorial the ring has been used to seal important covenants. The golden circlet, most prized of jewels, has come to its loftiest prestige in the symbolic significance it vouches at the marriage altar. Its untarnishable material is of the purest gold. Even so may your love for each other be pure and may it grow brighter and brighter as time goes by. The ring is a circle, thus having no end. Even so may there be no end to the happiness and success that come to you as you unite your lives together.

Do you, _____ (Groom), give this ring to your wedded wife as a token of your unending love for her?

Will you, _____ (Bride), receive this ring as a token of your wedded husband's love for you, and will you wear it as a token of your love for him?

Do you, _____ (Bride), give this ring to your wedded husband as a token of your unending love for him?

Will you, _____ (Groom), receive this ring as a token of your wedded wife's love for you, and will you wear it as a token of your love for her?

Having pledged your faith in and love to each other in the sight of God and these assembled witnesses, and having sealed your solemn marriage vows by giving and receiving the rings, acting in the authority vested in me as a minister of the gospel by this state, and looking to God for divine sanction, I pronounce you husband and wife.

Therefore, what God hath joined together, let no one put asunder.

(Close with prayer.)

Title: A Permanent Union

The institution of marriage is as ancient as humanity. Our Creator himself is its author. Marriage is subject to the directions and sanctions of God's laws. Back in the garden of Eden, God saw that it was not good for the man to be alone, so he formed and gave to man woman for his companionship in a union so intimate and tender that they are regarded as "one flesh."

This union, like that of the body and the spirit, is to be broken only by the hand of death. It is a relationship, therefore, not to be lightly or hastily entered. A similarity of mental viewpoint, of mutual esteem, and of genuine affection that transcends every earthly love are indispensable to the happiness that the relation is designed to impart.

The Holy Scriptures, which are designed to be a lamp for our path in every relationship of life, will provide you with directions that you need for this relationship.

The beauty and the nature of this blessed relationship is expressed most graphically in the words of Ruth to Naomi: "Where you go I will go, and where you stay I will stay. Your people will be my people and your God my God. Where you die I will die, and there I will be buried. May the LORD deal with me, be it ever so severely, if anything but death separates you and me" (Ruth 1:16–17 NIV). Although these words were not spoken by a wife to her husband, they give beautiful expression to the relationship that should exist between them. Marriage was intended to be a continuing fellowship of trust, love, and mutual help. While marriage is a separation from parents to form a new family, it also is a union of two traditions and two families into a new family. For marriage to be its highest and best, it should be a spiritual union. Each should be able to say to the other, "Your God is my God." May our Lord bless you with this kind of a union of your two lives.

With a consciousness of the eternal purpose and of the abiding presence of our Lord, we now will proceed to hear your solemn sacred marriage vows to each other.

(The minister will now ask, "Who gives this woman to this man in marriage?")

You will please take each other by the right hand.

Do you, _____ (Groom), take the woman whose right hand you hold, to be your lawful wedded wife? Will you promise in the presence of God and these witnesses that you will keep her in health and in sickness; in prosperity and adversity; that you will be to her a kind, affectionate, and faithful husband; and that, forsaking all others, you will keep yourself to her and to her only till death shall separate you?

Do you, _____ (Bride), take the man whose right hand you hold, to be your lawful wedded husband? Will you promise in the presence of God and these witnesses that you will continue with him in health and in sickness; in prosperity and adversity; that you will be to him a kind, affectionate, and faithful wife; and that, forsaking all others, you will keep yourself to him and to him only till death shall separate you?

I do, then, by virtue of the authority vested in me as a minister of the gospel, by the laws of this state, and looking to God for divine approval and benediction, pronounce you husband and wife. Henceforth may you be one in interest and destiny and in affection until death alone shall part you.

(Pastor should close with a prayer of thanksgiving and intercession for the couple.)

Sentence Sermonettes

Jesus comes, not to put people into heaven, but heaven into people.

The Holy Spirit is God with us today.

You will not find joy where you are going unless you take the ingredients with you.

A person is known by what he emphasizes.

Most sins are habit-forming.

Be a peacemaker, not a peacebreaker.

The Holy Spirit remains with us. There is no record of his return to heaven.

Let us never fear for the future or despair for the present, since the Holy Spirit of God remains with us.

Trying to do the work of the Spirit with the arm of the flesh is one of life's supreme follies.

A Spirit-filled Christian should be the rule, not the exception.

Great faith in the wrong things spells emptiness and ashes.

Little faith in the right things spells tragedy.

Christianity is not meant to be merely a fire escape from a world of woe.

The Christian's resource with God and others is prayer.

If we are to do God's work, we must have God's equipment.

All commands to pray are linked with a promise.

Prayer is the greatest sin killer in the world.

The best way to find happiness is to make others happy.

Take thought of time before time is ended.

When people sin they set in motion a train of consequences that has no end.

Do not let the world destroy your visions or rob you of your dreams.

Our God is able to meet our deepest needs.

Faith in Jesus makes the difference between despair and hope.

The Christian does not experience sorrow without hope.

Enthusiasm is God in you.

The only real limitations we encounter are those we place on ourselves.

After all is said and done, there is more said than done.

The devil is ever on the move, seeking whom he may destroy.

Little is much when God is in it.

If you do not know where you are going, you are already there.

Tomorrow is in the womb of time; yesterday is in the tomb of time; today is all we have.

Nothing worthwhile is easy, and he who is taking it easy is doing nothing worthwhile.

Consecrated lives are the building stones of the kingdom.

We cannot all live on easy street, but we can all live on the square.

Delayed obedience is always costly.

An extraordinary person is an ordinary person plus an extraordinary will.

Subject Index

Index of Scripture Texts